CONSUMERS UNION REVIEWS
CLASSICAL RECORDINGS

CONSUMERS UNION REVIEWS
CLASSICAL RECORDINGS

MARTIN BOOKSPAN
Music Consultant to Consumers Union

A CONSUMER REPORTS BOOK

1978

CONSUMERS UNION, MOUNT VERNON, NEW YORK

NOTE ABOUT THE COVER: *The designs used on the cover are the product of an invention by Edward Lias, physicist in sound. The designs, called Cosmographs, are visual records of patterns produced by interfering sound waves and represent musical chords.*

Consumers Union Reviews Classical Recordings is a Consumer Reports Book published by Consumers Union, the nonprofit organization that publishes CONSUMER REPORTS, the monthly magazine of test reports, product Ratings, and buying guidance. Established in 1936, Consumers Union is chartered under the Not-For-Profit Corporation Law of the State of New York.

The purposes of Consumers Union, as stated in its charter, are to provide consumers with information and counsel on consumer goods and services, to give information and assistance on all matters relating to the expenditure of the family income, and to initiate and to cooperate with individual and group efforts seeking to create and maintain decent living standards.

Consumers Union derives its income solely from the sale of CONSUMER REPORTS and other publications. Consumers Union accepts no advertising or product samples and is not beholden in any way to any commercial interest. Its Ratings and reports are solely for the information and use of the readers of its publications.

Neither the Ratings nor the reports nor any other Consumers Union publications, including this book, may be used in advertising or for any commercial purpose of any nature. Consumers Union will take all steps open to it to prevent or to prosecute any such uses of its material, its name, or the name of CONSUMER REPORTS.

INTRODUCTION

The record reviews in this book originally appeared in CONSUMER REPORTS magazine. They have been gleaned from the feature "Record Reviews," which is published five or six times a year, and have been reevaluated by Consumers Union's music consultant, Martin Bookspan—a critic and author. Bookspan has been our music consultant since 1968. He is the second authority to hold this position since "Record Reviews" started in 1959.

We obviously are not presenting traditional CONSUMER REPORTS product information when we publish a single critic's views. Rather, we offer music lovers helpful guidance to a variety of interesting works and performances. In *selecting* records for review in the magazine, Bookspan attempts to meet a wide range of tastes in classical music. In *evaluating* records, he has found that sometimes the artists are of paramount importance; sometimes the compositions are; and sometimes, happily, both are blended into an outstanding recording.

New recordings of familiar works by different artists continue to appear and individual preferences are therefore subject to change. Accordingly, Bookspan has used his "Comment" section, following an original review, to express new thoughts within the larger context of the current repertoire of recordings.

Reviews of records no longer readily available have not been included in this book. The criterion for market availability is a listing in the last issue before press time of the *Schwann Record & Tape Guide,* a widely accepted directory of recordings. In the first edition of *Consumers Union Reviews Classical Recordings* (1972) it was the April issue of *Schwann,* and 379 records survived for publication. For this edition—with a total of 444 records—we have used the August 1978 *Schwann.* (We suggest that readers check the most recent *Schwann,* available at most record stores and counters, when contemplating the purchase of a recording listed here. Even though a record may have been discontinued after August 1978, it may be worthwhile asking for it since some stores may still have it in stock.)

This book, like the first edition, is compiled alphabetically by composer and then by composition. Where more than one composer is represented in

(continued)

an album, it is listed by the composer of the primary composition; an index of the other composers appears at the back of the book. Indexes of conductors, orchestras and groups, and performers are also provided. A special collection of an artist's work will be found listed in a section headed "Collections" at the end of the main body of reviews.

The month and year of the issue of CONSUMER REPORTS in which the original review was first published appears immediately above each entry. Where an eight-track cartridge tape or a cassette tape of the same performance is available, it is noted by the symbol ▲ or ●, respectively.

When more than one performance of the same work was reviewed in CONSUMER REPORTS, the reviews are presented here in the order of their appearance in the magazine, with Bookspan's comments following the last review in the group.

The only substantive changes made in the original reviews have been to update the names of record publishers that have taken on new label identities (e.g., RCA Victor is now RCA, Capitol is now Angel or Seraphim, Epic is now Philips), and to delete references to specific records that are no longer available or to a mono record when a superior stereo version exists.

During the past decade, the recording industry has been phasing out the production of monophonic discs. For the most part, the recommended performances in this book exist in stereo-only releases. But whether stereo or mono, the choices have been made with the performances—rather than the quality of recorded sound—given the greater weight. Care has been taken to avoid any record that is tonally inadequate for comfortable listening.

There has been some fluctuation in the price of discs, but a $7.98 list price for classical recordings has become the industry standard. Now some labels are moving up to an $8.98 price. However, discounts are generally available, although they may vary widely. It is also encouraging to note that there has been a dramatic growth in the repertoire of certain budget-price labels— witness Nonesuch, RCA Victrola, Seraphim, Odyssey, Turnabout, and Quintessence.

A special feature of this book is the basic discography prepared by

Bookspan. The discography lists more than five hundred compositions that legitimately can be called masterpieces, with one, or occasionally two, recommended recordings for each. This edition of the discography is the result of a whole new look at the repertoire and of new evaluations of available discs and tapes. It is, of course, not exhaustive; no discography can be. But this listing can serve as a basis for a beginner's record collection and can aid the experienced listener in a wider investigation of the repertoire.

THE EDITORS OF CONSUMER REPORTS BOOKS

**ALKAN: Funeral March for a Pappagallo; and Other Grotes-
queries.** Raymond Lewenthal, piano. Columbia M30234, $5.98.

Charles-Henri Alkan was one of the most fascinating figures of nineteenth-
century romanticism. An almost exact contemporary of Liszt, Alkan was also
an extraordinary pianist—but he seldom played in public. Instead, he lived
much of his life as a recluse in Paris, composing music and devoting most of
the rest of his time to the study of the Hebrew law, the Talmud. Indeed, it
was his Talmudic scholarship that brought about his freakish death: The
heavy volumes toppled over and crushed him.

Until just a few years ago, Alkan was only a name in the music history
books. Then his cause was taken up by the American pianist, Raymond
Lewenthal, who researched Alkan's music, incorporated some of it into his
concert repertoire, and then played Alkan recitals in New York's Town Hall
and Carnegie Hall in 1964 and 1965. Shortly thereafter, Lewenthal made the
first recording ever of any of Alkan's music (RCA LSC2815) and the stam-
pede was on. Other pianists have turned their attention to Alkan's output
since then, and the last several years have seen a genuine Alkan rediscovery.

Lewenthal's disc of half-a-dozen years ago is devoted to some of Alkan's
large-scale works for solo piano, including a symphony. The present disc
contains mainly short, almost epigrammatic selections, many of which reveal
Alkan's obsession with the eerie and fantastic. Throughout these miniatures,
Alkan emerges as an extraordinary inventive visionary: There are anticipa-
tions of piano music composed half a century and more after Alkan died (by,
among others, Bartók, Prokofiev, and Cowell). And the compositional skill
shown in these pieces marks Alkan as one of the truly inspired creators of
Romantic piano music. Considering that he was a musical genius on a par,
perhaps, with Chopin, it is truly ironic that his music has waited a century to
be discovered and appreciated.

Two exceptions to the rule of brevity among the works on this disc are a
four-movement *Sonatine* that runs for almost 16 minutes and an 8½-minute
vocal scene scored for mixed chorus, three oboes, and bassoon titled *Funeral
March for the Death of a Pappagallo*. The latter is a phantasmagorical setting of a
dialogue between a parrot and its master. The piece is a brilliant combination
of wit, hallucinatory imagination, and eeriness.

To everything on the disc, Lewenthal brings an extraordinary technical
equipment and a musical personality that responds to Alkan's fantasies.
There is no piano part in the *Funeral March,* so Lewenthal stands up and
conducts the vocal and instrumental ensemble and contributes a basso pro-
fundo solo.

In addition to having written his own fanciful notes for the record jacket,
Lewenthal—in a small bonus record packaged in—probes the Alkan personal
and musical psyche, verbally and through piano illustration. The entire production is an amazing tour de force in honor of the hermit-genius, Charles-
Henri Alkan. Unequivocally recommended as one of the highlights of this or
any other recording year.

(continued)

Comment

Also available now is a recording of an Alkan piano trio. Though less individual and imaginative than some of the composer's music for solo piano, the *G Minor Trio for Piano, Violin, and Cello* is a valuable addition to recorded literature. The performance, a serviceable one, is included in Genesis 1058/9 and played by the Mirecourt Trio. ∎

November 1975

BACH: Brandenburg Concertos (complete). The Virtuosi of England conducted by Arthur Davison. Vanguard Everyman SRV313/14SD (2 discs), $7.96.

This latest set of recordings of Bach's *Brandenburg Concertos* takes as its text a new edition of the music prepared by the musicologist Richard Townsend. In a prefatory note, Townsend explains that the "added ornamentation, cadenzas and rhythmic alterations tries to reproduce the original style and spirit of performance in all its details but without presuming to lay the dead hand of mere authentic antiquarianism on the performers. . . ." He need have had no fears. The present performances are anything but solemnly respectful. There is a dynamism and vitality to the performing approach that, if anything, might be *too* vigorously outspoken.

Performances of the *Brandenburg Concertos* exist in recordings of all shapes and sizes, from the basically romantic, voluptuous approach of Benjamin Britten (London CSA2225) to the scaled-down, one-player-to-a-part performance under the direction of Neville Marriner (Philips 6700045). This new account under Arthur Davison is closer in philosophy to Marriner's way than to any other. Along with the vitality already mentioned, perhaps the other principal characteristic of this new set is the microscopic clarity of the sound reproduction. Indeed, there are legitimate grounds to complain that the sound is too detailed, too defined, too sharply focused, with the result that there is little bloom to the reproduction; more air around it all would have produced a more natural and more pleasant environment.

The Virtuosi of England, an ensemble previously unknown to me, lives up to its name: there are some astonishingly secure solo performances here, most notably perhaps from trumpeter Gordon Webb in the *Second Concerto* and harpsichordist Leslie Pearson in the *Fifth*.

In a field already crowded with a number of unusually stimulating integral recordings—Harnoncourt's (Telefunken S9459/60), the Collegium Aureum's (RCA Victrola VICS6023), and Ristenpart's (Nonesuch 73006), in addition to the Britten and Marriner versions already mentioned, this new set of the *Brandenburg Concertos* is certain to find admirers, particularly at the Vanguard/Everyman budget price.

Comment

Besides the many complete recordings of the *Brandenburgs*, several individual performances of some of them deserve to be singled out. The *Third Concerto* is included in Pinchas Zukerman's album of Bach's *Violin Concertos in A minor and E major* (Columbia M31072) with the English Chamber Orchestra. The *Fifth Brandenburg Concerto* receives a stunning performance in Columbia's four-disc album (M430540) devoted to Bach's complete harpsichord concertos; the harpsichordist is Igor Kipnis, with Neville Marriner conducting the Academy of St. Martin-in-the-Fields—(here called the "London Strings," for contractual reasons). ∎

January 1968

BACH: Concerti for Harpsichord Nos. 3, 5, 7 in D major, F minor, and G minor. Glenn Gould, pianist, and Columbia Symphony Orchestra conducted by Vladimir Golschmann. Columbia MS7001, $5.98.

Most listeners will immediately identify two of these works. The *D major Concerto* is Bach's adaptation for piano and orchestra (harpsichord and orchestra, in Bach's day) of the familiar *E major Violin Concerto;* and the *G minor Concerto* is a similar adaptation of the *A minor Violin Concerto.* Some scholars go on to infer that the *F minor Clavier Concerto* may be Bach's adaptation for harpsichord of a lost violin concerto. Bach often used the same music in different treatments. But whatever their origin, there is nothing at all violinistic about these three concerti. Gould plays them in his typically original manner. He employs a nonlegato type of phrasing, perhaps in an attempt to suggest the harpsichord. His articulation is impressively clear, his rhythm flexible, his tempi spirited. If harpsichord music must be played on the piano, this is the way to do it. The recorded sound is beautiful: clear, crisp, undistorted. As usual, Gould can be heard huffing, puffing, and humming in the background. He is in especially good voice during the slow movement of the *D major.*

Comment

This reviewer's ears are less willing now than a few years ago to accept these works on the piano. The timbre of harpsichord and strings, it seems to us, is so integral to the basic musical concept that even the most perceptive pianist—and Gould is assuredly perceptive—falsifies some of the most important values inherent in the scores. Several outstandingly successful issues of this music played by a solo harpsichord and strings are available. Perhaps most commendable of all is the four-disc Columbia set (M430540) for which Igor Kipnis is the harpsichord soloist (see previous Comment). In addition to all the authentic, reconstructed harpsichord concertos by Bach, the album also contains a propulsive account of Bach's *Fifth Brandenburg Concerto* (in which the harpsichord is the chief solo instrument.) ∎

January 1965

BACH: Concerti for Two, Three, and Four Harpsichords (complete). Anton Heiller, Erna Heiller, Kurt Rapf, and Christa Landon, with Solisti

(continued)

11

di Zagreb conducted by Antonio Janigro. Bach Guild 70659, 70660, 2 discs, $5.98 each.

For two harpsichords, there are a concerto in C and two in C minor. One of these C minor concerti is our old friend, Bach's *Concerto in D minor for Two Violins* in the composer's own two-harpsichord transcription. The other may be a transcription by Bach of an earlier work by him or another composer. The *Concerto for Four Harpsichords* is Bach's transcription of Vivaldi's *Concerto for Four Violins*. Scholars are in doubt about the pair of *Three-Harpsichord Concerti*, which also may be adaptations. But the transcriber was, after all, J.S. Bach, and all of the music clearly has Bach's workmanship. These new recordings rank with any previously made. As interpretations they are stylistically sound. As examples of recorded sound they are unusually faithful, with a good deal of effective separation in the stereo. Thus, at the beginning of side two of 70660, one harpsichord is in the left speaker, the other in the right, and the effect is most beautiful as they play together.

Comment

A three-disc Philips album (6747194) is now available that contains nine Bach Concertos for one, two, three, and four harpsichords. Raymond Leppard conducts the English Chamber Orchestra; the harpsichord players are Leppard himself, Andrew Davis, Philip Ledger, and Blandine Verlet. The performances are vibrant and stylish, and the recorded sound is unusually lifelike and detailed. ∎

September 1963

BACH: Concerti for Violin: No. 1 in A minor and No. 2 in E major. David Oistrakh, violin, and members of the Vienna Symphony Orchestra. **Concerto for Two Violins in D minor.** David and Igor Oistrakh, with Royal Philharmonic Orchestra conducted by Sir Eugene Goossens. Deutsche Grammophon 138820, $6.98. ▲ ●

David and Igor (King David and Prince Igor, some of the fancier columnists call them) are the great Russian father-and-son violin team. Both are representative of a Romantic tradition of violin playing, a tradition—stemming from Leopold Auer—that features tone and technique above all. And about the tone and technique of these two violinists, none will cavil. Judged purely as a violinist, David Oistrakh is one of the great instrumentalists, and his son is not far behind. But instrumental virtue alone does not necessarily make a Bach player. Most musicians of the West would regard as completely unstylistic the slides, vibrato, and tempi of the elder Oistrakh in this kind of music. As violin playing it is beautiful; as Bach playing it is considerably less satisfactory. As for the *Concerto for Two Violins*, the balance favors the first violinist (presumably David) to the point where the second fiddle is second-fiddle indeed.

Comment

Among several other discs that group these selections, special mention should be made of a disc that presents performances by Vienna's distinguished specialists in this genre, the Harnoncourts (Telefunken 641227). As in the Harnoncourt recording of the *St. Matthew Passion*, painstaking care with style produces performances that are transparent textures imbued with rhythmic vitality.

Another fine and more recent grouping of these three works also comes from specialists in this field: Eduard Melkus and the Vienna Capella Academica (Archive 2533075). Price may be a factor in choosing between the Harnoncourt and Melkus performances since each is surpassingly fine; the Harnoncourt disc lists for less than the Melkus. ∎

January 1961

BACH: Italian Concerto in F major for Harpsichord; Partitas No. 1 in B flat major and No. 2 in C minor. Glenn Gould, piano. Columbia MS6141, $5.98.

Gould is at it again. His playing gets more and more mannered. And he continues to add vocal accompaniments to his piano playing. (Those strange sounds in the background are Gould humming away.) He has a wonderful keyboard facility and his infallible fingers were made to play Bach. But his notions about tempo, ornamentation, touch, and phrasing are so unorthodox as, often, to be bizarre. Purists should keep away from this disc. Others should keep in mind that this is a highly personal Bach, with a strong suggestion that the pianist considers himself more important than the composer. The sound is clear and faithful. Tape hiss, however, may be detected.

Comment

These performances of the first two *Partitas* are the same as those included in Columbia's integral edition (M2S693) of all six of the composer's keyboard *Partitas.* Less quixotic piano performances of the *Italian Concerto*, the *Second English Suite*, the *C Minor Fantasia*, and the *Sixth French Suite* may be heard from Alicia De Larrocha (London CS6748). A fine harpsichord performance of the *Italian Concerto* by Igor Kipnis is available on Angel S36096. ∎

April 1964

BACH: Partitas for Harpsichord (6, complete). Glenn Gould, piano. Columbia M2S693, 2 discs, $11.96.

Ever since Gould broke on the recording scene some years back, with his disc of Bach's *Goldberg Variations,* he has been accepted as a Bach player par excellence. Since then he has matured as an artist, and this new album of all the six *Partitas* by Bach is a technical and musical triumph. Gould, as most
(continued)

listeners may know, is a most controversial musical figure, and there are those who cannot understand many of his musical premises. But even those in the anti-Gould camp will have to respond to, if nothing else, the sheer perfection of Gould's pianistic mechanism as reflected on these two discs. No matter how complicated the writing, Gould handles it easily. Counterpoint is clarified with uncanny ease; dynamics are so precise that they suggest harpsichord registrations; and all of the running passages are etched with delightful articulation. As for the interpretations, Gould's ideas are completely original. Most listeners without preconceived notions about how this music should be played will find Gould's approach altogether convincing. Some of his ideas are explained in the program notes, which should be carefully read. The important thing is that Gould manages to make living music out of the *Partitas*, and few will fail to find this album an absorbing experience. One drawback has to do with one of the pianist's less agreeable mannerisms. He hums and sings while playing, and those noises are terrible intrusions. There is a jacket note by Columbia that the *Partitas Nos. 5 and 6* are "electronically rechanneled for stereo." The sound, though, is monophonic. There is some surface noise and tape hiss.

Comment

Gould's idiosyncracies—and they cover the full range of the performing spectrum: rhythmic waywardness, exaggerated dynamic contrasts, capricious phrasing, and the like—pervade these performances of the Bach *Partitas*. And yet there are moments of sheer inspiration and exuberant music-making that is in short supply in these days of homogenized, antiseptic performances. No more provocative edition of the *Partitas* has ever been recorded, and this set is likely to keep that distinction for years to come. Igor Kipnis is recording the six *Partitas* in installments. As of this writing, numbers 5 and 6 had not yet been released, but the two discs containing the first four *Partitas* (Angel S36097 and 36098)—with both played, of course, on the harpsichord—are ebullient and invigorating. ∎

January 1960

BACH: The St. Matthew Passion. Teresa Stich-Randall, soprano; Hilde Rössl-Majdan, alto; Waldemar Kmentt, tenor; Walter Berry, bass; Uno Ebrelius, tenor; Hans Braun, bass; Vienna Chamber Choir; Schottenstift Boys Choir; Vienna State Opera Orchestra conducted by Mogens Wöldike. Vanguard S269/72, 4 discs, $11.92.

A mixed reaction is sure to greet this *St. Matthew*. Those used to an orthodox approach, with a big chorus and orchestra, may consider the present version thin and not rising to the big climaxes. Those who like their counterpoint clear, who like an eighteenth-century approach, will greet this version as the greatest *St. Matthew* ever put on records. This listener inclines to the latter view. It is true that a feeling of strength is lacking in the climaxes of the first and last choruses. On the other hand, the finesse of the singers, the flexibility of the chorus, and the clarity of instrumentation make this version unique. Details hitherto obscured in any previous recorded performance come through clearly. It would take thousands of words to go into the musicological (and also emotional) niceties of Wöldike's approach. This is a fascinating, well-recorded performance.

Comment

Smoother and more clearly defined performances conducted by Münchinger, with interpretations that resemble the basic Wöldike approach are now available (4-London 1431) and Richter (4DG Archive 2712001), but the considerably lower cost of the Wöldike set may be the clincher for many buyers. Also available is a unique recording by the Vienna Concentus Musicus under Nikolaus Harnoncourt (Telefunken 4635047). It uses only instruments of Bach's time, or reproductions of them, and takes the greatest pains to provide stylistically accurate phrasings and textures. There is an overall feel for the drama in the *Passion* that sets Harnoncourt's performance apart from all other recorded performances. The Harnoncourt set has been renumbered by Telefunken. It now is listed in the catalogue as 4635047, four discs. But by whatever number it is known, it is a unique and wonderful presentation of this masterpiece. ∎

January 1966

BACH: Toccata and Fugue in D minor; Fantasia and Fugue in G minor; Prelude and Fugue in D major; Trio Sonata No. 2. Karl Richter, organ. Deutsche Grammophon 138907, $6.98. ▲ ●

Richter is one of those sound, intelligent organists who never let the listener down. Unfortunately he seldom raises the listener, either. In these four Bach works (three of them very popular; the *Trio Sonata* less well known), his tempi tend to be metronomic, and he seems preoccupied with achieving a smooth delivery rather than with exploring the emotional content of the music. Walcha's series of Bach organ recordings (also on Deutsche Grammophon) are much more imaginative. The recording has very quiet surfaces, though there is some distortion at the end of side two.

Comment

Some listeners may also be drawn to the flashier presentations by Biggs, in his Bach series for Columbia, although he sometimes has problems of rhythmic unsteadiness. Leopold Stokowski's extraordinary orchestration of the *D minor Toccata* and *Fugue* is now available in a resplendent, full-bodied stereo recording played by the Czech Philharmonic Orchestra conducted by Stokowski (London SPC21096). ∎

November 1965

BARBER: Concerto for Violin and Orchestra; HINDEMITH: Concerto for Violin and Orchestra. Isaac Stern and the New York Philhar-
(continued)

monic conducted by Leonard Bernstein. Columbia MS6713, $5.98.

Stern, who plays everything and plays it well, is the most protean of living violinists. Here he turns his attention to a pair of modern concerti. The Barber is lyric, melodic, attractive, and very much in the nineteenth-century tradition. Hindemith's concerto, somewhat more acerbic, displays the composer's dexterous craftsmanship, the neobaroque style he represented so convincingly, and a big, strong sweep. Stern handles both works in an entirely controlled, musicianly manner. His is a modern instrumental violin style, in which a rather slow, evenly centered vibrato is used and in which phrases are molded with sureness and without affectation. In short, it is a style perfectly suited to this music. Bernstein's orchestral support is impeccable. There is resonant, full recorded sound, and the violin is firmly centered, without the annoying spread it so often has.

Comment

In the Barber *Concerto* the team of Stern and Bernstein dominates the field. In the Hindemith *Concerto*, however, the recording by David Oistrakh, with the composer conducting (London CS6337), gives the team strong competition. ■

September 1967

BARTÓK: Concerti No. 1 and No. 3 for Piano. Peter Serkin, piano, and Chicago Symphony Orchestra conducted by Seiji Ozawa. RCA LSC2929, $5.98.

Bartók composed three piano concerti. *No. 3* is heard quite often. It was one of the Hungarian composer's last works and also one of his more easygoing, accessible ones. But *No. 1*, seldom heard, is a wild, barbarous affair, with powerful dissonances, lunging rhythms and almost no melody in the accepted sense of the word. Nevertheless, it grows on the listener, and after a few hearings its exuberance should come through.

The two young participants collaborate to maximum effect. Serkin, the son of the famous Rudolf Serkin, is a fine artist in his own right—a powerful technician and a musician with ideas and an obviously passionate commitment to the music he plays. Ozawa is a young Japanese conductor who in ten years or so will be one of the world's great ones.

June 1970

BARTÓK: Concerti No. 1 and No. 3 for Piano. Daniel Barenboim, piano, with the New Philharmonia Orchestra conducted by Pierre Boulez. Angel S36605, $5.98.

Composed nearly twenty years apart (1926 and 1945), these two scores pretty well define the extremes of Bartók's creative gamut. The *First Concerto* is all rhythmic propulsion and headlong impetuosity, the *Third* is gentle and poetic; both are the essence of Bartók.

Barenboim and Boulez—the former in his late twenties, the latter in his early forties—are among the most accomplished performers on today's international music scene. They have previously collaborated in a recording of Berg's *Chamber Concerto* (Columbia MS7179) that is a model of personal interaction. Here, too, the two concerti of Bartók benefit from the amalgamation of Barenboim's warmth and Boulez's structural organization. Both artists convey the full measure of Bartók's coloristic effects in the scoring for piano and orchestra.

The balance has been criticized elsewhere as being exaggerated in favor of the piano, but this listener finds no such problem. Indeed, there are orchestral details that emerge more tellingly here than in any other recording of either score. All told, this is a most successful release.

Comment

The team of Barenboim and Boulez finds more poetry in both scores and is less feverish and intense than Serkin and Ozawa. The pairing of these two works by Stephen Bishop (see Comment, page 20), with Colin Davis conducting (Philips 9500043) is also noteworthy. These artists are particularly successful in the "Night Music" (slow) movement of the *Third Concerto*. ■

March 1965

BARTÓK: The Miraculous Mandarin Suite; Music for Strings, Percussion, and Celesta. London Symphony Orchestra conducted by Georg Solti. London 6399, $5.98.

The Miraculous Mandarin is a relatively early Bartók work; the *Music for Strings, Percussion, and Celesta* is a late one. Each is a masterpiece in its way. The early score is wild, turbulent, still a shocker. The late one is deep, full of Bartók's strong and very personal nationalism, yet abstract for all that. The score requires repeated hearings and deserves them, for it is one of the significant compositions of the century. Solti seems to have this music in his blood. Like Bartók, he is Hungarian, and he responds automatically to the complicated rhythms of both scores. He also has a strong feeling for color.

Clear recorded sound, rather prominent surface noise.

Comment

This disc has a new catalog number: London CS6783. The performances are still impressive; the playing and reproduction are consistently first-rate. ■

November 1965

BARTÓK: Quartets (6, complete). Juilliard Quartet. Columbia D3S717, 3 discs, $11.59.

(continued)

The Juilliard Quartet has, in a way, a monopoly on these important works. About fifteen years ago it was the Juilliard group that was responsible for the first integral recording of them. The music is a permanent part of the players' repertoire, and through the years they have achieved a kind of rapport with it that no other ensemble can duplicate. This foursome is composed of young players, and the modernity of the music strikes a responsive chord in them. These six quartets spread over Bartók's entire creative span and are accepted as monuments of twentieth-century music. Like many of Bartók's other compositions they may sound forbidding and cacophonous at first. Much of the writing is atonal and highly dissonant, especially in the last four quartets. But patience will be rewarded for those listeners who give the music a chance. A good deal of it is based on a sort of transmutation of old Hungarian melodies and snappy folk rhythms. To the strong and incisive performances of the Juilliard Quartet is added fine recording. In the opening of the first quartet, each instrument enters, one by one, in a slightly different placement, giving the illusion of a quartet in one's living room.

Comment

The Guarneri Quartet has recently entered the lists with an equally arresting account of the Bartók *Quartets* (RCA ARL32412). The recorded sound is even more finely detailed than that provided for the Juilliard players. ∎

January 1973

BAZELON: Symphony No. 5; Chamber Concerto No. 2 for Fourteen Players ("Churchill Downs"). The Indianapolis Symphony Orchestra conducted by Izler Solomon (in the Symphony); an instrumental ensemble conducted by the composer (in the Chamber Concerto). Composers Recordings Incorporated SD287, $5.95.

Irwin Bazelon, born in Chicago in 1922, may be one of America's best-known anonymous composers: he created the four-note theme that NBC News has been using for some years, and has been responsible for many film scores and commercial jingles. He has also written a substantial body of concert music, including seven symphonies at last count.

The *Fifth Symphony* is intense and passionate, containing elements of atonal technique blended with what the composer labels a "synthetic" jazz spirit. The first movement is brooding and introspective, the second and third movements have characteristics of dance, and the final movement is a stern and ultimately serene section that grows out of the third movement. This symphony is a tough and sometimes disturbing one, and it reveals Bazelon as a composer with much to say about our present condition.

The *Second Chamber Concerto* is totally different—an exercise in progressive jazz, with riffs, flourishes, embellishments and improvisations with an infectious lilt. It is about half as long as the symphony; Bazelon knows just when to end it before it begins to outwear its welcome. Bazelon has written that his "Churchill Downs" subtitle is not an attempt "to describe the sights and sounds of the racetrack . . . but rather to accent the fact that it is a 'fun' piece."

Both works are exceedingly difficult to play, with constant shifts of pulse and meter and intricate inner workings among the various instrumental choirs. Both scores are performed with maximum effect, enhanced by recorded sound that is among the very best yet produced by the valuable CRI label.

Comment

It is a shame that we have had no further recordings of Bazelon's music since the release of this disc. He is a creative and imaginative composer whose works should be heard by a wide public. ∎

August 1972

BEETHOVEN: Piano Concerto No. 1 in C, Opus 15; Piano Sonata No. 5 in C minor, Opus 10, No. 1. Stephen Bishop, piano, with the BBC Symphony Orchestra conducted by Colin Davis (in the Concerto). Philips SAL6500179, $5.98.

This performance of Beethoven's *First Concerto* is stunningly more successful than the results of an earlier Bishop and Davis collaboration on the composer's *"Emperor" Piano Concerto* (Philips 839794LY). In the majestic *"Emperor,"* Bishop and Davis were unaccountably timid; here their style produces a performance perfectly scaled to the more classical outlines of the *First Concerto.* This presentation has an easy flow and grace that brings out the score's many felicities of nuance and phrasing. All in all, this is one of the very best of the available readings of this *Concerto.*

Bishop is similarly convincing in the early *Sonata,* which he endows with a subtle innocence and spontaneity. Clearly, the young American pianist (long a resident in London) is emerging as a keen and provocative artist.

Comment

The team of Bishop and Davis is now represented in the catalogs by recordings of all five of the Beethoven piano concertos. Each performance takes the same approach: intimacy almost of chamber music proportions, with unusually clear textures both in the solo piano playing and in the orchestral support. As stated earlier, this reserved approach to the music denies the *"Emperor" Concerto* some of its heroic grandeur, although the other four concertos shine forth with a rare, individual spontaneity. The Bishop-Davis collaboration is available on single discs and also in a four-disc album (Philips 6747104). ∎

March 1973

BEETHOVEN: Piano Concerto No. 3 in C minor, Opus 37; Piano Sonata No. 8 in C minor, Opus 13, "Pathétique." Stephen Bishop,

(continued)

piano, with the BBC Symphony Orchestra conducted by Colin Davis (in the Concerto). Philips 6500315, $6.98.

The *C Minor Piano Concerto* is the third of Beethoven's five piano concertos to be recorded in an ongoing Bishop-Davis project. This latest addition is masterful, full of the ebb and flow of Beethoven's writing, sensitive to the delicate balance between the solo instrument and the orchestra, and particularly perceptive by Davis and the sound engineers to the prominent part played by the woodwinds. Bishop plays with a gratifying combination of tensile strength in the outer movements and mellow relaxation in the slow movement. This is one of the best performances of the *C minor Concerto* in the current catalogs.

Bishop is similarly successful in the *"Pathétique,"* delivering a performance of vigor and abandon. This record will be a valuable addition to any collection.

Comment

The remarks concerning the collaboration of Bishop and Davis in Beethoven's *First Piano Concerto* (Philips SAL6500179) apply here. It remains to be added that Bishop has recently decided to proclaim his Yugoslav ancestry, so you may find him listed on recordings and concert programs as Stephen Bishop-Kovacevich. ∎

February 1964

BEETHOVEN: Concerto for Piano No. 4 in G major. Van Cliburn and Chicago Symphony Orchestra conducted by Fritz Reiner. RCA LSC2680, $5.98. ▲

A good but not very interesting performance. The trouble is that Cliburn, who handles the pianistic end of the concerto very well indeed, has few ideas to go with his fingers. In the first movement he is overly slow and careful; in the other two he plays almost by rote. His tone is beautiful, however, and his technique altogether superior. Thus some may enjoy the record for the craft alone, plus Reiner's split-second accompaniment. But for a more memorable musical experience one must turn to Gilels, Rubinstein, or Novaes.

Comment

Later recordings by Ashkenazy (London CS6856) and by Pollini (DG2530791) provide performances of irresistible poetry and grace. ∎

March 1965

BEETHOVEN: Concerto for Piano No. 5 in E flat (Emperor). Artur Rubinstein and Boston Symphony Orchestra conducted by Erich Leinsdorf, RCA LSC2733, $5.98.

As Rubinstein grows older he becomes even more aristocratic. And there seems to be no deterioration in his technique. The man is a marvel, and here he gives us a beautiful performance of Beethoven's grandest concerto. His playing has life, power, finesse, and grandeur, without the least trace of vulgarity or nervosity. Needless to say this disc is highly recommended, not only for Rubinstein's magnificent performance but for the tidy, well-coordinated contribution of Leinsdorf.

The recorded sound is not all that it might be, and a noticeable pre-echo starts the recording.

October 1974

BEETHOVEN: Piano Concerto No. 5 in E flat (Emperor). Rudolf Firkusny, piano, with the New Philharmonia Orchestra conducted by Uri Segal. London SPC21097, $5.98.

Beethoven's *"Emperor" Piano Concerto* is perhaps the most popular work for piano and orchestra in the entire repertory. So it is naturally one of the most recorded of all works. In order to command attention, then, any new recording must possess qualities that set it apart from the many already available—interpretive excellence, perhaps, or extraordinary new insights, or outstanding sound reproduction.

Unfortunately, no such qualities manifest themselves here. One would like to welcome this new release wholeheartedly, for Firkusny is one of the most intelligent and sincere artists now before the public, and Segal is an admired young Israeli conductor here making his American recording debut. But there is nothing in this release to raise it above the level of routine. In a field that contains the fiery and passionate contributions of such teams as Serkin-Bernstein (Columbia M31807), Fleisher-Szell (included in Columbia M4X30052) and Ashkenazy-Solti (included in London CSA2404), the Firkusny-Segal collaboration is an also-ran.

August 1977

BEETHOVEN: Piano Concerto No. 5 in E Flat (Emperor). Alfred Brendel, piano, with the London Philharmonic Orchestra under the direction of Bernard Haitink. Philips 9500243, $7.98. ●

This is the first in a projected series of recordings by pianist Brendel and conductor Haitink of all the Beethoven piano concertos. Neither artist comes to this recorded repertory as a stranger: Brendel performed the concertos with various orchestras and conductors some 20 years ago in Austria and Germany, and Haitink conducted Claudio Arrau's recordings of the same works. But it's clearly time for Brendel, an esteemed interpreter of Beethoven, to give us his latest reading of these inexhaustible scores.

The performance of the *"Emperor"* Concerto is solid, steady, dependable, confident, and relaxed, with details carefully worked out. In its way it is a deeply satisfying performance. The orchestra's playing is first-rate and the engineering superlative. (Note, for example, the perfect balance between

(continued)

solo piano and tympani in the imaginative dialogue near the end of the *Concerto*.)

The quiet virtues of the Brendel-Haitink collaboration augur well for the Beethoven concertos still to come. If, however, you prefer the *"Emperor"* to be performed in truly heroic, heaven-storming fashion, the Serkin-Bernstein disc (Columbia M31807) may be more to your liking.

Comment

This was the first of the five Beethoven concertos that Rubinstein recorded with Leinsdorf. The combination began auspiciously—and the sound improved with subsequent recordings in succeeding seasons. Since then Rubinstein has made still another complete set of all the Beethoven piano concertos—this time with Daniel Barenboim conducting the London Philharmonic Orchestra (RCA CRL51415). The *"Emperor"* Concerto performance is available as a single disc as well (RCA ARL11420). Although there are many felicities in the playing of the nearly ninety-year old Rubinstein, there is no denying the fact that the earlier performance, with Leinsdorf conducting, is steadier and stronger.

The Rudolf Serkin-Leonard Bernstein-New York Philharmonic recording (Columbia M31807) is muscular and viscerally exciting. Many will find the Brendel-Haitink collaboration the best of all for its thoughtful insights, first-rate recorded sound, and the splendid teamwork of soloist, conductor, and orchestra. ∎

September 1959

BEETHOVEN: Concerto in D major for Violin (Op. 61). Jascha Heifetz, violin; Boston Symphony Orchestra conducted by Charles Munch. RCA LSC1992, $5.98. ▲ ●

Although the stereo version only recently has been issued, this is not a new recording. It was originally released as a monophonic disc several years ago. At that time—and again, on rehearing the performance—the playing impressed one as being extremely brilliant, ineffably efficient, and rather heartless, with a concentration on the violin rather than on the music. RCA has not done too well with the stereo version, which is harsh in sound.

May 1960

BEETHOVEN: Concerto in D major for Violin (Op. 61). Isaac Stern, violin, and New York Philharmonic conducted by Leonard Bernstein. Columbia MS6093, $5.98.

Stern and Bernstein, almost exact contemporaries, are two of the most distinguished names in American music, and any collaboration between them is sure to attract a wide audience. In this performance of the *Concerto*, Stern is rock-steady, spinning out a consistently pure tone and handling the musical problems with the utmost probity. A spectacular technician, he never abuses the gift. Bernstein, too, is a spectacular technician, but he does have a tendency to make too much of his technique. He will hold on to a note a fraction too long, or shade a phrase with too much calculation. Thus, his performances have a tendency to become mannered. There is tape hiss, and the solo violin has too much of a spread, as in the cadenza of the first movement. There the violin is centered in the middle, but it also has a tendency to take off to the right. This disc does present a most interesting conception, but those who like a more traditional kind of Beethoven should also compare Grumiaux (Philips 900222), Milstein (Angel S35783) or Oistrakh (Angel S35780).

Comment

In the intervening years RCA has rereleased the legendary Heifetz performance of 1940 in which his collaborators were Arturo Toscanini and the NBC Symphony Orchestra (included in RCA VCM7067, two discs; mono only). It is a superefficient reading with little of the ebb and flow that other violinists bring to this work. Among other efforts that "breathe" more easily, the collaboration of Zino Francescatti and Bruno Walter is particularly genial and relaxed; at its budget price—it is now available on Odyssey Y30042—it is a splendid bargain.

In the late 1970s two more performances became available, each on the highest level of accomplishment: one, a recording by Pinchas Zukerman; the other, a rerecording by Isaac Stern. In each case the conductor is Daniel Barenboim. Stern's version (Columbia M33587) has Olympian grandeur and serenity; Zukerman's (Deutsche Grammophon 2530903) has grace and spontaneity. ∎

May 1972

THE COMIC BEETHOVEN: Dances, Satiric Songs and Canons. Anneliese Rothenberger, soprano; Nicolai Gedda, tenor; Walter Berry, bass; with the Chorus of the Bavarian State Opera, the Vienna Academy Chamber Choir, the Munich Convivium Musicum, and the Consortium Musicum conducted by Xaver Mayer, Wolfgang Baumgart, Erich Keller and Fritz Lehan. Seraphim S60180, $2.98.

Though late in reaching these shores—the disc was issued in Europe to coincide with the 1970 celebrations of the bicentennial of Beethoven's birth—this is one of the most delightful releases of any year. The repertoire is a far cry from "normal" Beethoven output: In place of the heaven-storming visionary, the Beethoven of this disc is a genial, easygoing and fun-loving composer whose aim is to produce music for entertainment. Included here are five of Beethoven's *Country Dances*, six of the *German Dances* and two of the *Viennese Dances*, along with vocal settings of folk songs, poems and other texts of Beethoven's period.

The performances are all superlative: Obviously, everyone connected with the enterprise had a thoroughly good time. Among many other delights, one encounters here the choral tribute *To Mälzel*, composed in honor of Johann

(continued)

Mälzel, the inventor of the metronome (and in which Beethoven employs a theme also found in the second movement of his *Eighth Symphony*); his setting of Goethe's *Song of the Flea*; and a traveling-salesman's narrative of how he deals with an older lady who has taken an unwanted shine to him (the *Carpet-Seller's Song*). Included with the disc is a leaflet giving all the texts and translations of the songs, and the sound reproduction is first-class. A disc not to be missed!

Comment

The disc is still not to be missed. The sense of enjoyment conveyed by all the performers is contagious and irresistible, and the recorded sound holds up very well indeed. ■

January 1963

BEETHOVEN: Fidelio. Christa Ludwig, mezzo-soprano (Leonore); Walter Berry, bass (Don Pizarro); Jon Vickers, tenor (Florestan); Gottlob Frick, bass (Rocco); Ingeborg Hallstein, soprano (Marzelline). Philharmonia Orchestra and Chorus conducted by Otto Klemperer. Angel S3625, 3 discs, $17.94.

Now there are several *Fidelio* recordings available, and this is by far the best. All of the casting is good, and Klemperer brings to the music a sense of dedication, and a feeling for the humanity of the score, unsurpassed by any conductor who has approached it. Ludwig up to now has sung only mezzo roles on records, but she handles the soprano part of Leonore (which does not go above a high B) with complete assurance, both vocally and musically. Vickers employs his large voice impressively, and both of the low-voiced singers—Frick and Berry—are superb. One of the surprises of the opera is the work of Hallstein. She is not well known, but if her lovely singing here is typical of her, she will be heard much more often in the future.

Good recorded sound.

March 1965

BEETHOVEN: Fidelio. James McCracken, tenor (Florestan); Birgit Nilsson, soprano (Leonore); Tom Krause, baritone (Pizarro); Kurt Böhme, bass (Rocco); Graziella Sciutti, soprano (Marzelline). Vienna Philharmonic and State Opera Chorus conducted by Lorin Maazel. London 1259, 2 discs, $11.96.

Fidelio is not everybody's opera, but for some it provides an overwhelming emotional experience. And it is heard on this disc in a generally superior performance. Sparking the cast is Birgit Nilsson, one of the few living sopranos who can sing the role of Leonore and end up sounding fresh. Her big voice is well used here, despite a few edgy sounds. In this kind of repertoire she is unapproachable. The lusty-voiced McCracken also produces a big sound, and the other singers—artists all—have the style securely in hand. Lorin Maazel moves the opera along with plenty of vigor and even speed, but he doesn't give the impression of rushing except at one spot—the introduction to the greatest aria in the opera, the *"Abscheulicher."* All of a sudden the cellos and basses take off in a mad spurt, almost as though the turntable had suddenly speeded up.

The sound is clear and well detailed. The stereo includes one effective and rather amusing gimmick. This occurs near the beginning of side two, where Pizarro reads the letter. He is heard from the right speaker. Then he crosses the room in a rage, and one can follow him by his footsteps. He calls for the captain, and more footsteps are heard, approaching the right speaker. Shades of the early stereo demonstration records!

Comment

If one is prepared to accept the generally slow tempos favored by Klemperer, then his is indeed an imposing, noble account of Beethoven's only opera. Maazel's is the exact opposite: Where Klemperer meanders and scrutinizes, Maazel is all forward motion and impetuousness. A middle ground between these two extremes is adopted by Karl Böhm in his recording (Deutsche Grammophon 2709031). Still to come is an unreleased recording of *Fidelio* conducted by Leonard Bernstein on the Deutsche Grammophon label. ∎

March 1962

BEETHOVEN: Missa Solemnis in D. Eileen Farrell, soprano; Carol Smith, contralto; Richard Lewis, tenor; Kim Borg, bass. New York Philharmonic and Westminster Choir conducted by Leonard Bernstein. Columbia M2S619, 2 discs, $11.96.

Along with Bach's *B minor Mass* and Handel's *Messiah,* Beethoven's *Missa Solemnis* is one of the monumental works of the choral literature. It is very difficult to present properly. As in many works of Beethoven's last period, it is craggy, profound, full of technical difficulties and hard to hold together. But what a flaming masterpiece! Bernstein presents a strong performance, one in which he is obviously most attracted by the dramatic elements of the score. Occasionally he is a little too tricky for comfort, as at the beginning of the *Et Vitam Venturi Seculi,* where he slides into the music by way of a slackening of tempo. But, on the whole, his is a confident, alert, and frequently exciting conception. His soloists are excellent, especially Farrell, whose enormous voice rides over the entire ensemble. Columbia has done a good job with the recorded sound. If your machine takes the fortissimo ending of side one without distortion, rest content.

January 1967

BEETHOVEN: Missa Solemnis in D. Elisabeth Søderstrøm, soprano; Marga Höffgen, contralto; Waldemar Kmentt, tenor; Martti Talvela, bass. New Philharmonia Orchestra and Chorus conducted by Otto Klemperer. Angel S3679, 2 discs, $11.96.

(continued)

Beethoven's *Missa Solemnis,* of course, ranks with the great Bach and Handel scores as a monument of the choral literature. And in the past there have been several noteworthy recordings—those of Toscanini, Karajan, Bernstein, and Klemperer himself. The previous Klemperer, though, must be more than fifteen years old and is superseded by this new album. The great German conductor's performance is typical. Where Karajan displays a sort of super-efficiency and objectivity, where Bernstein goes in for the dramatic elements and favors extreme contrasts, Klemperer has a monolithic approach, with slow tempi, overpowering strength, and a complete lack of fussiness. Only Toscanini can match this kind of propulsion. But while the Toscanini set is historic, it is a dated recording. The new Klemperer version enjoys contemporary sound. No stereo gimmicks are used. The four good singers come through excellently, and there is a feeling of depth even though the engineers have not indulged in extreme separation. No better performance is available.

Comment

Fine as Klemperer's performance is, the Bernstein version may well convey more lasting pleasure for those who want a more propulsive account of this vibrant score. ∎

September 1970

BEETHOVEN: Quartet No. 14 in C sharp minor (Op. 131). The Yale Quartet. Vanguard Cardinal C10062, $3.98.

Here is one of the most impressive Beethoven recordings of this Beethoven anniversary year (the composer was born in 1770). Without extravagant display, the Yale Quartet (Broadus Erle and Syoko Aki, violins; David Schwartz, viola; and Aldo Parisot, cello) has been going about its business of giving occasional concerts and making recordings. This is their third recorded Beethoven quartet, and it becomes increasingly evident that these four seasoned players have forged one of the finest string quartets ever to make music together. They are fresh and flexible, yet in thorough ensemble and with great maturity of musicianship.

As in several of the Yale's previous recordings, one finds a fully responsive performance that is especially appropriate to the shifting moods of this most visionary of Beethoven's quartets. The recorded sound is splendidly alive and cleanly focused. If we eventually have the full cycle of the sixteen Beethoven quartets in recorded editions by the Yale Quartet, the world of music will owe a large debt of gratitude to Vanguard Cardinal.

Comment

Unfortunately, the Yale Quartet did not record the complete Beethoven quartet cycle for Vanguard. Those that are available, besides this disc, are the *Quartets in E Flat, Opus 127* (Vanguard C10054); *B Flat, Opus 130* (Vanguard

10096);*A Minor, Opus 132* (Vanguard C10005); and *F Major, Opus 135* (Vanguard C10097). ∎

October 1964

BEETHOVEN: Sonata for Piano No. 8 in C minor (Pathétique, Op. 13); DEBUSSY: Three Preludes, Book II ("Les Fées sont d'exquises danseuses"; "Bruyères"; "General Lavine—Eccentric"); CHOPIN: Étude in C minor (Revolutionary, Op. 10, No. 12); Étude in C sharp minor (Op. 25, No. 7); Scherzo No. 1 in B minor (Op. 20). Vladimir Horowitz, piano. Columbia MS6541, $5.98.

Horowitz's third Columbia record follows his usual pattern, being a miniature recital centered around one big work. His performance of the *Pathétique Sonata* is typical; big in line, miraculous in finger clarity, emotionally Romantic. The superpowerful sforzando attacks of Horowitz remain as exciting as ever. As if to show that he is as "classic" as the next pianist, Horowitz takes the last movement at a slow tempo. But the massive build-up here, coupled to the unearthly pianistic control, again is typically Horowitzean. It's a remarkable performance, and so is Horowitz's performance of the three Debussy preludes. He does not play much Debussy; but how many pianists could match this kind of color, clarity, and style? Here Horowitz scales down his dynamics to provide some ravishing playing. In the Chopin he is in familiar territory. He has not previously recorded the *Revolutionary Étude*, and he gives it a brilliant, textually faithful performance. In the *B minor Scherzo* he ends not with the unison scales that Chopin wrote, but with interlocked octaves. What an effect! Horowitz, with his enormous sonority, must create special problems for the engineers. Not all have been solved on this disc. Toward the end of the *B minor Scherzo* some of the chords sound splintery, and there is a general loss in tonal quality. Otherwise good sound.

Comment

The recital pattern favored by Horowitz for his first Columbia discs has been largely abandoned in his most recent recording ventures; they have tended to conform to the one-composer-per-disc format that is standard in the industry. The combination of Beethoven-Debussy-Chopin on this disc certainly affords the listener a wide gamut of listening pleasure—especially in these finely polished performances. Horowitz has now returned to the RCA label, and everything released so far comes from live concert performances, as his new contract requires. ∎

May 1963

BEETHOVEN: Sonatas for Piano No. 14 in C sharp minor (Moonlight, Op. 27, No. 2); No. 26 in E flat (Les Adieux, Op. 81a); No. 8 in
(continued)

C minor (Pathétique, Op. 13). Artur Rubinstein, piano. RCA LSC2654, $5.98.

Rubinstein has previously in his long career recorded the *Pathétique* and *Les Adieux Sonatas* but—amazingly—never the *Moonlight*. He gives it a plastic, lovely, poised performance. In the second movement he has some original ideas, using a few unorthodox accents and a somewhat slower tempo than most pianists use. The torrential last movement goes with real abandon, but with an abandon that never suggests a lack of control. The total effect of the playing is one of poetry and the kind of singing line that Rubinstein alone of contemporary pianists seems to have at his disposal. The same kind of singing line is encountered in the other two sonatas on the disc. Rubinstein is a Romantic pianist without Romantic exaggerations. His may not be the kind of Beethoven that the German pianists give us, but on its own terms it is equally convincing. There is unusually fine recorded sound here.

Comment
RCA has repackaged the Rubinstein performances of the *Moonlight* and *Pathétique Sonatas* in combination with his equally masterly *Appassionata Sonata*. The three sonatas are on LSC4001, a disc essential to any record collection. ■

September 1968

BEETHOVEN: Sonatas for Piano No. 30 in E major (Op. 109) and No. 32 in C minor (Op. 111). Bruce Hungerford, piano. Vanguard 71172, $5.98.

This disc is the first in a projected Vanguard series of all the Beethoven piano sonatas to be performed by Bruce Hungerford, an Australian-born artist who recently made a concert tour of the United States after ten very successful years in Europe. In this initial release he shows himself to be a pianist of earnest intent and thoughtful insights, and with formidable technical equipment. His monolithic approach to Beethoven is reminiscent of Klemperer, but in Hungerford's case the relentless seriousness of it all becomes progressively less rewarding. Both sonatas could stand a leavening lightness occasionally—in some of the variations in the second movement of the C *minor Sonata,* for example—and a greater degree of spontaneity. But Hungerford's interpretations are always interesting—he is a pianist with a point of view about what he is playing. Vanguard's recorded sound is full-bodied and the record surfaces are very quiet. The Dolby noise-suppressing system was used, but when the record is played on very wide-range equipment, the noise level is not appreciably lower than that on many conventional recordings.

Comment
Nearly a third of the thirty-two Beethoven sonatas are available in Vanguard

recordings by Hungerford. His are solid readings that leave largely unexplored the elements of fancy and fantasy that are to be found in the Beethoven sonatas.

Alfred Brendel offers more colorful and stimulating performances of both sonatas. They are on two separate discs: *No. 30* (with Beethoven's *Sonata No. 28)* is on Turnabout 34391, and *No. 32* (with *Sonata No. 31)* is on Turnabout 34393. Turnabout's budget price is a strong attraction too—one can have four of Beethoven's most profound works for little more than the price of two. ■

October 1964

BEETHOVEN: Sonatas for Violin and Piano (complete). Joseph Szigeti, violin, and Claudio Arrau, piano. Vanguard 1109/12, 4 discs (mono only), $11.58.

At the Library of Congress, in 1944, Szigeti and Arrau presented the ten Beethoven *Sonatas for Violin and Piano.* A recording was made at that time for the Library's archives. Now Vanguard has received permission to issue it commercially and has done so at a special low price for the four discs. This is an important release, for it marks the work of two of the finest instrumentalists of the century, who have seldom appeared together. Arrau's work is well known, for he is still performing frequently before the public. But Szigeti doesn't appear in public any more. He was a greatly admired violinist, despite certain technical limitations. He never had a particularly good tone; his bow arm was not in the supervirtuoso class, nor was his left hand. But he had a fine, probing musical mind and splendid rhythm, and he always managed to dig far deeper into the music than did most of his more polished colleagues. His playing on these discs is characteristic in its power, integrity, and musicianship. Occasionally there is a flawed note or an awkward-sounding passage—and one could not care less. Arrau, as always, is a powerhouse, and he seems inspired by Szigeti; he seldom indulges in the abnormally slow tempi that sometimes can be bothersome. The recorded sound is not bad. There are audience noises, and the piano is a trifle too forward, but the reproduction is clear and honest.

March 1962

BEETHOVEN: Sonata for Violin and Piano No. 9 in A major (Kreutzer, Op. 47). Jascha Heifetz, violin, and Brooks Smith, piano. **BACH: Concerto in D minor for Two Violins.** Jascha Heifetz and Erick Friedman, violinists; New Symphony Orchestra of London conducted by Sir Malcolm Sargent. RCA LSC2577, $5.98.

The *Kreutzer Sonata* occupies most of this record, with the Bach *Two-Violin Concerto* filling out the second side. Heifetz has recorded the *Kreutzer* several times previously, but never better—in his fashion. That is, his conception has always been incredibly violinistic, sharp and clear, with a tendency to press forward rather than dwell on detail. (Of course, being the violinist he is, Heifetz never misses out on detail, but that is different from concentrating on it.) As violin playing, this *Kreutzer* is stupendous. In the Bach *Concerto,* Heifetz works with one of his pupils, Erick Friedman, who has been making a name for himself on the international circuit. Friedman on this disc subdues himself in favor of his master, and this does not lead to the best ensemble playing. Heifetz is too dominant. But the playing of both violinists is extremely smooth and pleasant to hear.

November 1965

BEETHOVEN: Sonata for Violin and Piano No. 9 in A major (Kreutzer, Op. 47); DEBUSSY: Sonata for Violin and Piano No. 3 in G; BARTÓK: Sonata for Violin and Piano No. 2; Rhapsody No. 1 for Violin and Orchestra. Joseph Szigeti, violin, and Béla Bartók, piano. Vanguard 1130/1 (mono only), 2 discs, $9.96.

Béla Bartók, a refugee from Nazism, arrived in America on April 11, 1940. Two days later he played the piano in a recital at the Library of Congress with his Hungarian friend and colleague, the violinist Joseph Szigeti. The latter, of course, was then at his height, one of the great instrumentalists of the century. Bartók was recognized the world over as a major composer, and his great reputation as a creative figure had a tendency to make many forget what an altogether admirable pianist he was. It is fortunate for posterity that the Library of Congress recorded the entire recital, and it is our good fortune that Vanguard has received permission to bring it out. For, while there is no lack of Szigeti recordings, Bartók as a pianist is represented on miserably few discs, all of them collectors' items very difficult to find. His playing in this album is magnificent. As an instrumentalist he stemmed from the Romantic school, which means broad tempi, plenty of color, rhythmic flexibility, and subtle details of nuance. He and Szigeti had appeared together many times. Both musicians represented much the same tradition, and it is little wonder that their collaboration is near perfect. Szigeti's playing is typical—a little rough with some rasps and awkward-sounding bowings, but always immensely musical, powerful, and stylistically impeccable. Special interest attaches to the performance of the Bartók *Second Sonata* (its only available recording), for there is the final touch of authenticity when a composer who is a skilled performer is heard in his own music.

Considering its age, the recorded sound is not bad at all. This is a fine album, historically important and musically fascinating.

Comment

More than a half-dozen different integral recordings of all the Beethoven *Sonatas for Violin and Piano* are now available. None of them surpasses the Szigeti-Arrau in flaming commitment and visionary breadth.

The versions of Beethoven's *Kreutzer Sonata* by Heifetz-Smith and Szigeti-Bartók represent opposite poles in interpretation: Heifetz is technically impeccable, with a cool detachment; Szigeti has his moments of technical insecurity, but he is afire with the passion of the music. Each in his own way is masterly. Both Szigeti-Vanguard albums have been renumbered: The collection of Beethoven sonatas with Arrau is now Vanguard 300/3E (four discs) and the miscellaneous collection with Bartók at the piano is Vanguard 304/5E (two discs). ■

September 1968

BEETHOVEN: Symphony No. 3 in E flat (Eroica, Op. 55). BBC Symphony conducted by Sir John Barbirolli, Angel S36461, $5.98. ▲ ●

Some listeners may consider this the finest *Eroica* ever committed to disc; it may not appeal to everyone's taste, however. Barbirolli adopts what can only be called a massive approach to this symphony: His tempo is broad and expansive throughout, resulting in a cumulative inexorable drive that makes a stunning effect. The *Funeral March* slow movement is masterful; without sentimentalizing the music, Barbirolli builds it to an extraordinary pitch of intensity and passion. In the two final movements he relaxes the tension and allows the whimsy of Beethoven's imagination its full play. The Barbirolli-conducted BBC Symphony sounds better than it has in years, and the Angel sound is one of that company's richest orchestral productions ever.

November 1975

BEETHOVEN: Symphony No. 3 in E flat (Eroica); Coriolan Overture. The London Symphony Orchestra conducted by Leopold Stokowski. RCA ARL10600, $6.98. ▲

BEETHOVEN: Egmont Overture; Symphony No. 7 in A major. The Los Angeles Philharmonic Orchestra conducted by Zubin Mehta. London CS6870, $6.98.

BEETHOVEN: Symphony No. 9 in D minor. The New Philharmonia Orchestra and the Ambrosian Singers conducted by Seiji Ozawa; with Marita Napier, soprano; Anna Reynolds, contralto; Helge Brilioth, tenor; Karl Ridderbusch, bass. Philips 6747119 (2 discs), $15.96. ●

Although he was well into his 90's when he made this recording, his very first of Beethoven's *"Eroica" Symphony*, Stokowski delivers a rendering of the score that brims over with vitality and youthful fervor. The first movement may seem a bit too studied and careful, perhaps even finicky in spots, as Stokowski painstakingly sorts out minute details in the structure and sonic fabric of the score. But from the beginning of the slow movement until the blazing triumphant chord that concludes this symphony, this is one of the most propulsive and invigorating performances of the *"Eroica"* I have ever heard.

There are many felicities to admire: the sentiment-laden (but unsentimental) account of the Funeral March slow movement; the thrust of the third movement (the superb horn section of the London Symphony Orchestra makes the middle section of this movement pure tonal and intonational magic); the headlong attack on the start of the last movement; the account, *(continued)* full of character, of each of the variations in the last movement.

The same qualities of impetuosity and inspiration are to be found in the performance of the *Coriolan Overture,* which completes side two. Both in the *Overture* and in the *Symphony* there are momentary spots of less-than-perfect instrumental ensemble, but these matter little against the cumulative impact of Stokowski's vision of this music.

RCA's recorded sound is clear, detailed, and rich, with especially full reproduction of the low string sonorities. Few among the nearly two dozen other available *"Eroica"* recordings propel me into the world of this score in quite the way this one does.

Mehta's performance of the *Seventh Symphony* has many qualities in common with Stokowski's *"Eroica."* Here, too, one could level a charge of over-deliberate calculation against the first movement. But things become freer as the movement progresses, and from the slow movement on, Mehta brings a surge and momentum to his performance that I find irresistible. During the last few years, the Los Angeles Philharmonic Orchestra has become one of the best orchestras in the world, particularly rich in the strings. And the recorded sound captured by the engineers in UCLA's Royce Hall is among the most vivid ever accorded the orchestra.

As with Stokowski's *"Eroica"* the disc includes a Beethoven *Overture*—in this instance the *Overture* from the composer's incidental music for Goethe's play, *Egmont.* All concerned would have been far better off if the *Egmont Overture* had been omitted. The interpretation is lifeless; the playing of the orchestra is shockingly below the standards set in the *Seventh Symphony;* and even the recorded sound, so vital in the *Symphony,* is cavernous and dull.

Ozawa's performance of the *Ninth Symphony* is not yet a fully formed conception. Perhaps the principal fault is a tendency toward rhythmic slackness. That is most apparent at key points in the last movement, which lacks the bite that surely is appropriate; similarly, the repetitions of the great "Ode to Joy" theme and its buildup, culminating in the near-delirious trumpet decorations of the melody, seem curiously lacking in tension, so that an essential ingredient of this music is undervalued. Ozawa can apply plenty of tension from the outside, but the much more important and organic tension from inside the score is too often slighted.

There are, of course, things to admire: London's New Philharmonia Orchestra is at the absolute top of its form—a reassuring fact in light of the sloppiness that had intruded on the orchestra's standards in recent years. Also at the top of its form is the chorus, London's extraordinary Ambrosian Singers, who deliver singing of great sensitivity, dynamic shading, and sectional balance. The recorded sound provided by the Philips engineering team is generally superb—vivid, well-balanced, and alive. The four vocal soloists are not the best-matched team imaginable, and they are recorded in a more distant perspective from that of the chorus and orchestra.

Ozawa's pacing of the music is not materially slower than that of many other conductors who have recorded the *Ninth Symphony;* yet the performance is lavishly distributed over four full sides, an extravagance that puts a price tag on the set that is ridiculous. With Ansermet's recording available at $3.49 and those of Cluytens, Munch, and Toscanini at $3.98, this new Philips release becomes an expensive redundancy.

Comment

Recordings of the Beethoven symphonies proliferate from month to month. Barbirolli's of the *"Eroica"* is inexplicably underrated, but it remains for me a highly convincing account of the music, emphasizing its grandeur and nobility. Another very personal but highly successful recording of the *"Eroica"* is Bernstein's (Columbia M31822). For the *Seventh,* an alternative to Mehta's would be the Carlos Kleiber-Vienna Philharmonic recording (Deutsche Grammophon 2530706), which fairly crackles with electric excitement. For the *Ninth,* one could do worse than investigate the Stokowski performance (London SPC21043), an intriguingly individual account that boasts fine sonics, a superbly matched vocal quartet for the last movement, and a manic overall propulsion that sweeps up the listener. ∎

June 1975

BEETHOVEN: Symphony No. 5 in C minor, Opus 67; The Creatures of Prometheus: Overture. The London Symphony Orchestra conducted by André Previn. Angel S36927, $6.98. ▲ ●

André Previn, ex-glamor boy of Hollywood film music, has developed into one of the most perceptive and persuasive conductors around. He is rightly considered a national institution in England, where he has been principal conductor of the London Symphony Orchestra since 1968—yet suspicion persists in the United States that Previn is "over his head" as a symphony conductor. Previn's superb handling of this work, the best-known in the symphonic repertoire, proves he is no imposter. It is, quite simply, one of the best recordings ever made of Beethoven's *Fifth Symphony.*

The very deliberate tempo Previn adopts in the first two movements may not be to everyone's taste. The first movement, especially, lacks the headlong thrust other conductors have brought to it. But the expansive approach gives the movement measured dignity—and a dignity very well suited to its content. Previn's third and fourth movements have a cumulative power and intensity that are quite overwhelming. And, on the same disc, the tricky overture to Beethoven's only ballet, *The Creatures of Prometheus,* crackles with orchestral virtuosity.

The London Symphony's musicians respond to Previn's leadership with hairtrigger discipline. Their playing is on the very highest level throughout the symphony and overture. The reproduction is rich, warm, and detailed.

July 1976

BEETHOVEN: Symphony No. 5 in C minor. The Vienna Philharmonic Orchestra conducted by Carlos Kleiber. Deutsche Grammophon 2530516, $7.98. ▲ ●

Perhaps only a philistine would complain about the price per minute of a musical recording—especially of a recording that has already won deservedly good reviews on both sides of the Atlantic. But be forewarned: This disc

(continued)

lasts barely 33 minutes, even with all repeats including that of the last movement's exposition. At Deutsche Grammophon's list of $7.98, that makes the unit price of this performance very high indeed. Many competing versions of Beethoven's *Fifth* manage to get all of the symphony on one side of the record, leaving the other free for another symphonic work.

Economics aside, this is unquestionably a superlative account of the best-known symphony in the history of music. Carlos Kleiber is the son of the distinguished conductor Erich Kleiber, who also made an extraordinary recording of Beethoven's *Fifth*. The elder Kleiber's treatment was notable chiefly for directness, rhythmic vitality, and urgency. Like father, like son— except that Carlos Kleiber delivers even more passionate orchestral playing. The engineers have captured its robust, rich sound to perfection. But do consider the merits of the following recordings of the *Fifth:* the Boston Symphony Orchestra conducted by Charles Munch (RCA AGL11268), the Chicago Symphony Orchestra conducted by Fritz Reiner (RCA LSC3295), the Concertgebouw Orchestra of Amsterdam conducted by George Szell, (Philips 802769). Besides doing justice to that symphony, the Munch and Reiner discs both include Schubert's *Symphony No. 8 (Unfinished)* and Szell's has on its overside Mozart's *Symphony No. 34*.

Comment

Previn's principal activity now is as music director of the Pittsburgh Symphony Orchestra. He has a number of recordings with that orchestra to his credit on the Angel label, and more are sure to follow. Although Previn's recording of Beethoven's *Fifth Symphony* with the London Symphony Orchestra is fine indeed, Kleiber's performance with the Vienna Philharmonic is really in a class by itself. If cost is not a factor in your buying decision, then Kleiber's performance—which is full of fire—is unhesitatingly recommended. ■

February 1977

BEETHOVEN: Symphony No. 6 in F (Pastoral). The BBC Symphony Orchestra conducted by Colin Davis. Philips 6500463, $7.98. ●

This disc is the latest installment in Philip's continuing effort to record all of Beethoven's symphonies under the direction of Colin Davis; only Numbers 1, 2, 7, and 9 remain to be released. This handling of the *Pastoral* and the recently issued *Fourth Symphony* are the best of the Davis-Beethoven performances. Davis treats this lovable score affectionately but never smothers it with attention. He pulls out all the stops where necessary, and the music surges with drama, as in the fourth (Storm) movement, for example.

Throughout, the BBC Symphony sounds like one of the world's best, and the Philips-recorded sound is robust yet warm, rich yet cleanly detailed. Another plus: Davis is one of the few conductors to record the *Pastroal* with a repeat of the first movement's exposition. If you are coming to this score for the first time, or want to add a fine performance of it to your record collection, this version is likely to gratify your taste.

34

Comment

Philips has now added a *Seventh Symphony* conducted by Davis to its recordings of the Beethoven cycle (PHS9500219). It is a fine performance, although lacking something of the swagger and spontaneity Davis brought to his earlier recording of this symphony (Angel S37027). ∎

September 1967

BEETHOVEN: Symphony No. 8 in F major (Op. 93); MENDELSSOHN: Symphony No. 4 in A major (Italian). Marlboro Festival Orchestra conducted by Pablo Casals. Columbia MS6931, $5.98.

Strong and vigorous performances are offered by the venerable Casals, who was near ninety when he made this record. In both symphonies, his musical approach is unusual. Accents are sharp; tempi exceptionally broad; rhythms stamp instead of dance. But the interpretations have surprising personality, and are a lovely memento of the grand old man of music.

Along with this record comes a bonus disc—*Casals, A Living Portrait* (Columbia PC1), derived from television shows, Casals' own master classes, and other sources. Casals talks and plays. His wise, old-fashioned but fervent remarks about music and performing style should be pondered with great respect.

The symphonies were recorded at an actual performance, with coughs in the background and Casals' grunts in the foreground. Excellent sound.

Comment

The performance of Mendelssohn's *Italian Symphony* is also included in a two-disc set (Columbia MGP32) devoted to Casals-Marlboro Festival recordings of three other favorite symphonies: Haydn's *Surprise*, Mozart's *Jupiter*, and Schubert's *Unfinished*. ∎

July 1969

BEETHOVEN: Symphony No. 9 in D minor (Op. 125). New York Philharmonic and Juilliard Chorus conducted by Leonard Bernstein, with Martina Arroyo, soprano; Regina Sarfaty, mezzo-soprano; Nicholas Di Virgilio, tenor; and Norman Scott, bass. **Fantasia in C minor for Piano, Chorus and Orchestra (Op. 80).** Rudolf Serkin, piano, and the Westminster Choir, with the New York Philharmonic conducted by Leonard Bernstein. Columbia M2S794, 2 discs, $11.96.

This release of Beethoven's *Ninth Symphony* is part of a complete Bernstein cycle of all the Beethoven symphonies. The performance is puzzling. Some things about it are marvelous—the titanic rendering of the stormy first-movement development, for example, and the seraphic quality of the

(continued)

third-movement reverie. But one is also frustrated and irritated: The scherzo second movement is grim and hard-driven, and the last movement is grossly overemotional. That last movement, incidentally, is helped not at all by the two male soloists. Scott's first entrance is awkwardly phrased and poorly controlled, and Di Virgilio's clumsy straining in his martial solo is embarrassing. The two women are better, but the overall ensemble of the vocal quartet is undistinguished.

The Serkin-Bernstein performance of the *Choral Fantasy* is perceptive and ebullient. It has twice seen service—as the filler on their disc of Beethoven's *Third Piano Concerto*, and in an album of all the Beethoven piano concerti. Its appearance on side four of the present album is not inappropriate: The choral writing appears to have served Beethoven as a warming-up exercise for the last movement of the *Ninth Symphony*.

Columbia's surfaces throughout are very good, and the quality of the recorded sound is also quite good except for an occasional overload in the heaviest choral passages.

September 1973

BEETHOVEN: Symphony No. 9 in D minor. The Chicago Symphony Orchestra and Chorus conducted by Georg Solti, with Pilar Lorengar, soprano, Yvonne Minton, mezzo-soprano, Stuart Burrows, tenor, and Martti Talvela, bass. London CSP8, $11.96. ●

Solti has prepared for us a careful and loving performance of Beethoven's mighty colossus, eliciting hair-trigger discipline from the orchestra and generally satisfying work from the four vocal soloists. But somehow he has not brought to this recording the spontaneity and magic that so distinguish his recordings of the Wagner "Ring" operas. Awesome as is the *Ninth*, it should be approached with a little less austerity and reverence and a little more abandon—abandon such as Solti does indeed achieve briefly, and with exhilarating results, in the coda of the last movement.

The recorded sound is simply spectacular. And there is no doubt that its impressive richness and vibrancy have been achieved, at least in part, by the wide groove spacing that takes up four entire disc sides. But a number of beautiful recordings of the *Ninth* have been managed on three sides, and some—notably those by Stokowski and Schmidt-Isserstedt—on only two. Both of those are also on the London label, and both offer sound quality of a very high order and performances that are consistently stimulating—and, with Stokowski's sometimes electrifying.

All in all, this release falls short of its high promise, and the added expense engendered by the lavishly spaced four sides seems questionable.

May 1976

BEETHOVEN-LISZT: Symphony No. 9 in D minor; LISZT: Festival Cantata. Richard and John Contiguglia, duo-pianists. Connoisseur Society CSQ2052 (2 discs), $9.98.

Liszt transcribed for piano all of the Beethoven symphonies—the first eight for piano solo and the *Ninth* for two pianos. These Liszt transcriptions served for many generations—until symphony orchestras proliferated and the technology of recording was developed and perfected—as the only form in which the Beethoven symphonies could be widely heard.

The two-piano transcription of the *Ninth* is remarkable and surprisingly successful. Of course there is no way to communicate Schiller's "Ode to Joy" in the last movement without using the words themselves, so that this aspect of the work is lost in the transcription. But otherwise it is fascinating to savor the great symphony in this different guise. The Contiguglias' performance of the score in London in April 1972 may well have been the first ever given of the Liszt transcription in public. It is good to have it now in recorded form, particularly since the Connoisseur Society's sound and pressing are, as always, superlative.

The fourth side of this set is given over, appropriately enough, to Liszt's one-piano four-hands version of the *Festival Cantata* he composed in 1845 to honor the unveiling of a statue of Beethoven in his native Bonn. The Liszt cantata was ultimately scored for soloists, chorus, and orchestra; the piano setting was probably a preliminary draft. The work is not without its prolixities, but it is an anticipation of much that was later to become characteristic of the Liszt style, including cyclical form and theme transformation. The climax of the piece is a setting of the slow movement from Beethoven's *"Archduke" Trio*, minus some of the variations and transposed to the key of C.

Again, the Contiguglias play with a refreshing conviction and abandon. This is a most welcome release.

Comment

The principal attraction of Solti's recording is the conductor's faithful observance of the repeats marked by Beethoven in the score. Bernstein's recording has its moments, but they do not add up to a satisfying whole. Interestingly, Bernstein has embarked upon another recorded cycle of all the Beethoven symphonies—this time with the Vienna Philharmonic Orchestra for the Deutsche Grammophon label. Meantime, more satisfying versions of the *Ninth* are to be had elsewhere: Schmidt-Isserstedt's (London 1159) or Stokowski's (London 21043), for example (see Comment, page 33). The Liszt piano transcriptions of the Beethoven symphonies enjoyed a certain vogue in the early 1970s. Besides the Contiguglias' album of the *Ninth*, there was a Glenn Gould account of the *Fifth* (Columbia MS7095) and RCA in England released a Roger Woodward performance of the *"Eroica" Symphony*. That vogue now seems to have passed. ∎

September 1968

BEETHOVEN: Trio No. 3 in C minor (Op. 1); MENDELSSOHN: Trio No. 1 in D minor (Op. 49). The Istomin/Stern/Rose Trio. Columbia MS7083, $5.79.

(continued)

Virtuoso performers are not always able to blend their talents in ensemble playing, so it's pleasant to report that in these performances the total is actually greater than the sum of the parts. Isaac Stern and Leonard Rose perform as well in ensemble as one would hope, and Eugene Istomin, whose solo playing has been more uneven than that of the other two, transcends himself. The recording engineers have produced sound that is pellucid and naturally balanced.

Comment

The performance of the Beethoven trio by the team of Istomin-Stern-Rose is also included in Columbia's five-disc album (MS30065) devoted to all the Beethoven piano trios. The Mendelssohn trio, a real gem of Romantic chamber music, is given an ardent and impetuous performance by these master instrumentalists. ∎

January 1973

BEETHOVEN: Trios for Piano, Violin and Cello in D major, Opus 70, No. 1 (Ghost), and E flat major, Opus 70, No. 2. Wilhelm Kempff, piano, Henryk Szeryng, violin, and Pierre Fournier, cello. Deutsche Grammophon 2530207, $6.98.

This formidable trio of outstanding instrumentalists was brought together by Deutsche Grammophon to record all the Beethoven piano trios for release during the bicentennial celebrations of Beethoven's birth in 1970. The present disc is extracted from the resulting set of six discs (DGG2720016); presumably, other records from the collection will also be released separately.

The individual performing styles of Kempff, Szeryng and Fournier mesh together readily in ensemble. All three performers have a rather lofty and patrician musical attitude, an attitude that sets the tone for the two performances here. Other performances have been more impassioned and personal—notably those given by the team of Isaac Stern, Eugene Istomin and Leonard Rose in their traversal of the complete Beethoven trios (Columbia M30065, 5 discs)—but the Kempff-Szeryng-Fournier team presents a convincing alternative. And there are many moments of subtle and breathtaking beauty, as in the hushed mystery of the slow movement of the *D major Trio*, the movement that gives the work its "Ghost" nickname.

Comment

Two other single disc releases have resulted from the Kempff-Szeryng-Fournier collaboration: DG2530408, which combines Beethoven *Trios Opus 1* (No. 2) and *Opus 11*, and DG2530147, which offers the best-known of the Beethoven piano trios, the *"Archduke."* All are given performances very similar to those we have here, so that my preference for the more richly personal accounts by the Istomin-Stern-Rose Trio remains. ∎

BELLINI: I Puritani. Joan Sutherland, soprano (Elvira); Pierre Duval, tenor (Arturo); Renato Capecchi, baritone (Riccardo); Ezio Flagello, bass (Giorgio); Margreta Elkins, mezzo-soprano (Enrichetta). Maggio Musicale Fiorentino conducted by Richard Bonynge. London 1373, 3 discs, $17.94.

Bellini's *I Puritani* has not been a repertoire opera for many years, but thanks to the recent interest in operas of the bel-canto period it has now been taken out of mothballs. It demands an entire cast of virtuoso singers. Not only does the leading soprano have all kinds of coloratura stunts—almost everybody in the cast has to do the near-impossible. For the last act Bellini wrote a tenor aria *("Vieni fra queste braccia")* that contains three high D's (most tenors strangle on a B natural). The baritone part of Riccardo has all kinds of fearsome technical flourishes, and so does the bass role of Giorgio.

Joan Sutherland is the world's leading exponent of bel-canto roles; and her husband, Richard Bonynge, who conducts this recording, is an authority on the style of early nineteenth-century singing. Between the two they help make this *Puritani* recording an authentic-sounding experience. They have opened standard cuts, and they have even supplied an ending not normally encountered, using an early edition of the score. As a singing machine Sutherland is spectacular. She has a large, flexible voice and a thorough knowledge of the stylistic traditions of the Bellini literature. Technically she sings rings around any living coloratura. Of her supporting singers, Flagello is superb and Duval is a lusty-sounding Arturo. He has to strain for those high D's, but he does get there. Capecchi, competent as always, produces a fine sound, though he simplifies some of his part. Elkins handles her role well. Bonynge is not a conductor with much personality, but he is thoroughly sound, works well with the singers, and takes logical tempi. Recorded sound is excellent, with unusual brightness and presence.

Comment

The team of Sutherland and Bonynge has rerecorded *I Puritani* with what amounts to an all-star cast of associates: Luciano Pavarotti, Piero Cappuccilli, and Nicolai Ghiaurov (London 13111, 3 discs). Admittedly, the new Sutherland recording improves on the old one in terms of dramatic fire and conviction. However, the model for a performance remains the recording made a quarter of a century ago by the late Maria Callas (Angel 3502; mono only). Opera-lovers will have to decide between the supremacy of the Callas characterization and the fluency of the Sutherland singing. The choice is not easy. ∎

BELLINI: La Sonnambula. Joan Sutherland, soprano (Amina); Margreta Elkins, mezzo-soprano (Teresa); Nicola Monti, tenor (Elvino); Sylvia Stahlman, soprano (Lisa); Giovanni Foiani, bass (Alessio); Fernando Corena, bass (Rodolfo). Maggio Musicale Fiorentino conducted by Richard Bonynge. London 1365, 3 discs, $17.94.

(continued)

Unlike most performances in the opera house, these three records are unabbreviated and present every last note that Bellini wrote. *La Sonnambula,* composed in 1831, is a bel-canto opera: Its leading singers have to have bravura voices plus a cantabile (melodic, flowing) style. This combination of coloratura and style is rare today, and Sutherland is its leading exponent. What is exciting about her voice is its size. There are a few sopranos around who can match her in agility, but none has the agility backed up by a voice big enough to sing *spinto* roles. (A *spinto* role lies between dramatic and lyric. Tosca, for instance, is a *spinto* role.) Sutherland, if she wanted to, could handle anything up to Wagner. Yet her brilliance and alliance with the belcanto style should not blind one to her defects. She does lack temperament, she does have a tendency to sing off pitch, and her diction is often bad. To her admirers this will make little difference; and the fact remains that when she gets into the supple, sad phrases of *"Ah! non credea"* and the blazing fireworks of *"Ah! non giunge,"* there is not a singer alive who can touch her. She adds her own cadenzas, as tradition decrees. All of the other singers in the cast, Corena included, have to simplify the difficult sections of the vocal line. One example of simplification occurs in the *"Son geloso"* duet. The tenor has a florid passage, the soprano a simpler one. Temporarily reversing their roles, Monti sings the soprano part here, and Sutherland the tenor. Stahlman is a fine, sensitive singer, and Corena is, as always, resonant and authoritative. Monti, though, has a tendency to push his tones. Bonynge, Sutherland's husband, conducts with good rhythm and not much subtlety. An exciting set, thanks to Sutherland. The recorded sound is excellent.

Comment

The La Scala-derived recording that features the extraordinary Amina of Maria Callas (Seraphim IB6108, two discs, mono) is available again. As pure sound, Sutherland's voice is far more reliable, but in her characterization—in human and dramatic terms—Callas sings rings around Sutherland. The prestereo sound in the Callas set is still more than serviceable. ■

February 1969

BELLINI AND DONIZETTI HEROINES (coloratura soprano arias). BELLINI: I Capuletti ed i Montecchi and La Sonnambula; DONIZETTI: Lucia di Lammermoor, Linda di Chamounix, Roberto Devereux, and Rosmonda d'Inghilterra. Beverly Sills, soprano, with Vienna Volksoper Orchestra and Akademie Chorus conducted by Jussi Jalas. Audio Treasury Series ATS20001, $5.98. ▲ ●

Beverly Sills, the reigning prima donna of the New York City Opera Company, has given opera lovers a number of memorable, and even great, portrayals, including Cleopatra in Handel's *Julius Caesar,* the Queen of the Night in Mozart's *The Magic Flute,* and the title role in Douglas Moore's *The Ballad of Baby Doe.* She has appeared on records before, notably in the RCA *Julius Caesar,* the Heliodor *Baby Doe,* and the Vanguard-Cardinal pressing of

Mahler's *Second Symphony*. The present disc, however, is her first solo album; it serves to justify her prominence among present-day operatic singers. The Sills voice is flexible, highly expressive and, most of the time, superbly controlled. The arias in this recital have been largely within the preserve of Joan Sutherland in recent years, and Miss Sutherland's voice may well be smoother and more effortless. But Miss Sills outpoints Sutherland in the clarity of her diction and in overall communicative warmth. A special highlight of the disc is her meltingly beautiful projection of Juliet's heartbreak in *"Oh! quante volte"* from *I Capuletti ed i Montecchi*.

The chorus and orchestra are conducted by Jussi Jalas, the chief conductor of the Finnish National Opera, with a fine feeling for the music. This, plus the handful of other recordings in which Jalas has been involved, demonstrate that he is better than many of the conductors now performing. Why do the record companies not employ his talents more frequently? ATS's recorded sound matches the excellence of the performances on this disc.

Comment

"In the short time since these words first appeared in print, Miss Sills has become a reigning star of the international recording circuit, with several additional solo albums and featured billing in a number of complete opera projects undertaken solely because of her availability. If the 1960s were dominated by Sutherland, the 1970s may well be the decade of Miss Sills." These words, written for the first edition of *Consumers Union Reviews Classical Recordings*, turn out to have been prophetic indeed. It was during the 1970s that Beverly Sills became the reigning prima donna of the operatic world and a media superstar as well. With the announcement of her intention to retire in 1980, came the news that she would become co-director (with Julius Rudel) of the New York City Opera, a post that promises to add still another dimension to her already incredible accomplishments. ∎

March 1966

BERG: Wozzeck. Dietrich Fischer-Dieskau, baritone (Wozzeck); Helmut Melchert, tenor (Drum Major); Fritz Wunderlich, tenor (Andres); Gerhard Stolze, tenor (Captain); Karl Christian Kohn, bass (Doctor); Kurt Böhme, bass (First Apprentice); Robert Koffmane, bass (Second Apprentice); Evelyn Lear, soprano (Marie). Berlin German Opera conducted by Karl Böhm. Deutsche Grammophon 2707023, 2 discs, $13.96.

Wozzeck, which received its world premiere in Berlin on Dec. 14, 1925, is one of the greatest operas of the century. Strong, bitter, imaginative, full of new concepts, it was once regarded as the height of insane modernism. Performances were scarce in this country, and most Americans who knew the work knew it through the old Columbia recording made by Dimitri Mitropoulos in the early 1950s. But the postwar dissemination of all kinds of avant-garde music has made the idiom of *Wozzeck* much more familiar, and hence easier to take, than it was about thirty years ago.

(continued)

The new recording—the first since the aged Mitropoulos performance—is a brilliant job. All the power and bitterness of the music come through. *Wozzeck* is many things. It is one of the supreme examples of the wedding of word and music. It is a social document, with a libretto concerned about injustice to the little men of the world. (It is completely unsentimental, though. There was nothing of the bleeding heart about either Berg or Georg Büchner, who in 1836 wrote the play on which the libretto is based. If anything, Wozzeck is an anti-hero.) The opera is full of fresh sounds, fresh techniques, fresh ideas. In short, it is a masterpiece.

The participants in this recording—singers, orchestra, conductor—are well versed in the style demanded of them, and there is none of the awkwardness or hesitancy heard when American groups try to stage the opera. In so uniformly admirable a cast, it is hard to single out anyone for special mention (and, anyway, *Wozzeck* is not a "singing" opera in the orthodox sense of the word). It may be noted, however, that Fischer-Dieskau is a remarkable exponent of the title role and that Karl Böhm conducts with formidable precision and style. The recording is bright and clear. *Wozzeck* is not an opera that lends itself to special stereo effects, and the engineers made no attempt to gimmick the album.

Comment

A couple of years after this recording was released, CBS undertook yet another new *Wozzeck* (Columbia M230852) with Boulez conducting what is essentially the production he supervised at the Paris Opera during 1963 and thereafter. The Boulez performance, penetratingly analytical, in no way dims the luster of the vibrant, warmly human account led by Böhm. ∎

January 1963

BERLIOZ: Harold in Italy, for Viola and Orchestra. William Lincer, viola, and New York Philharmonic conducted by Leonard Bernstein. Columbia MS6358, $5.98.

It is hard to see how this disc can compete with several others, especially the Primrose-Boston Symphony version (RCA LSC2228). Bernstein's impossibly fast tempo for the "Pilgrims' March" shows his basic lack of sympathy for the music, and Lincer, while a fine musician, is nowhere near the level of Primrose.

Comment

Bernstein has now rerecorded *Harold in Italy* for Angel (S37413), with the French National Orchestra and Donald McInnes as violist. It is a fine and perceptive account of the score, aside from the recessed reproduction of the viola part. Another uncommonly penetrating recording is Barenboim's, with the Orchestre de Paris and Pinchas Zukerman as violist (Columbia M34541). ∎

BERLIOZ: Les Nuits d'été (Op. 7); Five Other Songs for Solo Voice and Orchestra. The London Symphony Orchestra conducted by Colin Davis, with Sheila Armstrong, soprano; Josephine Veasey, mezzo-soprano; Frank Patterson, tenor; John Shirley-Quirk, baritone. Philips 6500009, $5.98.

The 1969 centenary of the death of Berlioz sparked many commemorative celebrations, among the most important of which are the Berlioz recordings undertaken by the Dutch recording firm of Philips, with today's outstanding Berlioz conductor, Colin Davis, in charge. To the memorable Philips-Davis recordings of Berlioz' *Roméo et Juliette, Symphonie funèbre et triomphale,* and *Requiem* is now added this release of the *Nuits d'été* song cycle together with five other superb songs for solo voice and orchestra. What distinguishes this edition of the *Nuits d'été* from all previous recordings is that the six individual songs in the cycle are sung by four different singers. Among them, they are able to provide a variety of timbres. The light-hearted first and last songs *("Villanelle"* and *"L'ile inconnue")* are sung in innocent and naive fashion by tenor and soprano, respectively, while the four more passionate and intense interior songs evoke a more dramatic style from each of the four soloists. The scheme certainly adds variety to the performance, and Davis, for his part, finds all manner of subtleties in the score, underlining an emotion here, highlighting a poetic text there, and clarifying the orchestral texture as no other conductor has done before.

The five songs on the reverse side are also varied in texture and content, and the singers—though none of them possesses a vocal instrument of great beauty—all infuse the songs with emotional depth. The London Symphony Orchestra plays expertly throughout.

Comment

Since this is the only available recording of Berlioz' remarkable cycle to employ a variety of voices in the separate songs, the disc retains its uniqueness. In a version of *Les Nuits d'été* that adheres to the usual practice of having one singer for all six songs, Janet Baker's performance with the late Sir John Barbirolli conducting (Angel S36505) is perhaps more atmospheric. Also available: a recording conducted by Pierre Boulez (Columbia M34563) in which the songs of the cycle are divided between female (Yvonne Minton) and male (Stuart Burrows) voices. But overall the Baker-Barbirolli performance has more surge and passion. ∎

September 1960

BERLIOZ: Requiem. Léopold Simoneau, tenor; New England Conservatory Chorus; Boston Symphony Orchestra conducted by Charles Munch. RCA VICS6043, 2 discs, $5.98.

In the early days of stereo on disc, about two years ago, two companies
(continued)

rushed out versions of the Berlioz *Requiem*. Neither was a success, though the score was made for stereo. As Berlioz conceived it, the full orchestra is supplemented by four brass bands located at different points of the church (or auditorium). Talk about separation! The earlier versions were unsuccessful for a variety of reasons, musical as well as technical. Now, however, comes a reasonably good version of the mighty choral work. Munch is, of course, a specialist in French music; and in addition, he has a great orchestra to work with plus a well-trained chorus and a brilliant tenor. The results could have spelled success in advance. But what about the recorded sound? On the whole, it's satisfactory, with a few reservations. Most of these reservations have to do with a certain amount of muddiness in the registration of the chorus. Another concerns the undue amount of surface noise. A treble reduction helps. Otherwise, there is much to praise. The brass bands in the *"Dies Irae"* are extremely effective in stereo; indeed, the engineers would have been remiss had they not aimed for extreme separation here. But in other sections the sound is allowed to flow naturally.

Comment

A second Munch recording of the score has since been released by Deutsche Grammophon (2707032), a product of recording sessions held in Munich not long before Munch died. The basic conception is the same as in his earlier Boston recording, but he had a better orchestra and tenor soloist in the RCA version. The Berlioz *Requiem* field has now been taken over totally, however, by the Colin Davis recording (Philips 6700019), an evocative response to the poetry and to the passion in the music, and a superb example of reproduction that does justice to the most shattering climaxes Berlioz ever scored. ■

February 1969

BERLIOZ: Symphonie fantastique. Orchestre de Paris conducted by Charles Munch. Angel S36517, $5.79.

During his distinguished career as a conductor, Charles Munch recorded the *Symphonie fantastique* four different times, this last in November, 1967, with the Orchestre de Paris, an orchestra created especially for him by the French government. Two more Munch-conducted discs with that orchestra still await release. This recording, though, is a fitting memorial to Munch's art. The Munch interpretation is familiar—mercurial, passionate, and supercharged. At the time this recording was made, the Orchestre de Paris was not yet the completely responsive unit it proved to be under Munch when they toured here last fall. But the intensity of the playing overrides the few minor mishaps in ensemble. The sound is full and resonant.

November 1969

BERLIOZ: Symphonie fantastique. The New York Philharmonic conducted by Leonard Bernstein. Columbia MS7278, $5.98, including a seven-inch bonus record entitled *Berlioz Takes a Trip*.

The past few months have seen a whole rash of releases of this ever-fascinating score, including performances conducted by Ansermet, Munch, Prêtre, and Stokowski. This new Bernstein release is actually a recent rerecording of a performance first recorded about five years ago.

On the face of it, Bernstein and this impetuous, audacious music should be ideally matched. The kaleidoscopic nature of the music might be expected to stimulate and challenge the conductor to produce one of his most unbridled and impassioned performances. Unhappily, the expectation is only partially realized. There are some stunning moments, to be sure: the first appearance, breathless and anguished, of the obsessive theme in the first movement and the snarling tuba statement of the *"Dies Irae"* theme in the last movement. In the main, however, the performance is labored and consequently very much below the best of the other versions, including Bernstein's own earlier recording. Sonically, too, the new version is inferior to the earlier one—a result of the general inadequacy of New York's Philharmonic Hall as a recording site (the earlier performance was recorded in Manhattan Center).

The bonus record, *Berlioz Takes a Trip*, is derived from a Bernstein television program of last spring that was devoted to the Berlioz masterpiece. Like the program, the record is guilty of a tasteless and sophomoric attempt to "modernize" the score by injecting elements of bad psychedelia.

July 1978

BERLIOZ: Symphonie fantastique. The Budapest Symphony Orchestra under the direction of Charles Munch. Hungaroton SLPX11842, $7.98.

This work was a great showpiece for the late Charles Munch. He included the "Fantastic Symphony" in his first sequence of programs as guest conductor with the New York Philharmonic in early 1947, and he made four different recordings of the work: with the Paris Conservatory Orchestra in the 1940s, with the Boston Symphony Orchestra (twice) during the 1950's, and with the Orchestre de Paris in 1967, less than a year before his death.

This disc, just released, is the product of rehearsals for a broadcast by the Hungarian State Radio in 1966. According to the liner note, "there was no studio audience, but the control room was crowded to capacity to witness the effect of Charles Munch's captivating suggestive personality and music."

That effect seems to have been magnetic indeed, even though the Budapest Symphony is not one of the world's great virtuoso orchestras. One senses a ground swell of excitement that evokes Munch's dynamism in the concert hall. That dynamism, incidentally, was only intermittently present in the artist's studio recordings; here, however, it is central. The interpretation is familiar: a kaleidoscope of color, dynamics, and hair-raising effects. Though the recorded sound is somewhat cavernous, this is a very special disc.

Comment

The Munch-Budapest Symphony recording will remain special for as long as it is available. Other noteworthy recordings of this score: the second Munch-Boston Symphony disc (RCA LSC2608), and the Colin Davis-Amsterdam Con-
(continued)

certgebouw Orchestra collaboration (Philips 6500774). Among other felicities of interpretation is Davis's decision to incorporate the optional cornet parts; that may make his recorded performance the one many listeners prefer. Bernsstein had another "go" at the *Symphonie fantastique,* this one with the French National Orchestra (Angel S37414); it is generally the more successful of the two Bernstein *Fantastique* recordings, with plenty of passion but with the moments of near hysteria in his earlier account under more control. ■

September 1973

BERNSTEIN: Symphonic Dances from West Side Story; RUSSO: Three Pieces for Blues Band and Orchestra. The San Francisco Symphony Orchestra conducted by Seiji Ozawa, with the Siegel-Schwall Band (in the Russo score). Deutsche Grammophon 2530309, $6.98. ▲ ●

With this—and a disc devoted to musical settings of the Romeo and Juliet story by Tchaikovsky, Prokofiev and Berlioz—the San Francisco Symphony Orchestra once again joins the very thin ranks of American orchestras that have a recording contract. On the evidence here provided, Ozawa has built a formidable virtuoso ensemble in San Francisco during his brief tenure there.

The music itself is a mixed bag. The symphonic dances from Leonard Bernstein's *West Side Story* comprise a clever potpourri of some of the best music from the composer's extraordinary Broadway score. Ozawa conducts it with taste and affection—and somewhat less frenetically than does the composer himself (in a recording with the New York Philharmonic on Columbia MS6251). The Russo work is a hodgepodge of banal and rhetorical clichés. As a blend of rock and symphonic elements, it simply does not work.

Unlike many European-originated Deutsche Grammaphon releases, this disc was apparently recorded with the microphones close in.

Comment

After the original review of this work, Ozawa left the San Francisco Symphony Orchestra to concentrate on his duties as music director of the Boston Symphony Orchestra. This disc, and one released some years later (DG2530788, combining Gershwin's *An American in Paris* with still another of Russo's rock-cum-symphony orchestra manifestations, *Street Music*), is eloquent testimony to the orchestral polish Ozawa achieved during his years in San Francisco. ■

January 1965

BERNSTEIN: Symphony No. 3 (Kaddish). Felicia Montealegre (speaker); Jennie Tourel (mezzo-soprano); Camerata Singers, Columbus Boychoir, and New York Philharmonic conducted by Leonard Bernstein. Columbia KS6605, $6.98.

The *Kaddish* is the Hebrew prayer for the dead, and this symphony is dedicated "To the beloved memory of John F. Kennedy." But the dedication came after the work had been composed. What Bernstein has tried to do is present modern man in relation to his God—the God of the Old Testament, not of the New. The text, written by the composer-conductor, uses the Hebrew prayer itself, followed by a long poem in what one critic has described as the best Norman Corwin manner. It would appear that Bernstein needs some sort of extra-musical crutch on which to lean. Both of his previous symphonies have literary backgrounds—*No. 1, The Jeremiah* (Old Testament), and *No. 2, The Age of Anxiety* (Auden). This *Kaddish Symphony* is a brilliantly scored work in Bernstein's traditional, eclectic style. The music backs up the words very well—perhaps too well. It is illustrative music, almost "movie music." And one might question its wearing qualities. After a few hearings the score might sound pompous. Certainly the thematic material is basically second-rate, with its strong echoes of Copland and what not. One thing that cannot be faulted, though, is the quality of recorded sound. It is full and clear, with great depth and color.

Comment

Bernstein obviously felt some of our misgivings: After an initial flurry of performances, he withdrew the *Kaddish Symphony* and in recent years has made extensive revisions in it, the most obvious being the shift of the speaker's part from female to male voice. Bernstein has recorded the revised version of the *Kaddish Symphony* with the Israel Philharmonic Orchestra; the speaker is his longtime friend, Michael Wager. As of this writing, the new *Kaddish Symphony* recording had not yet been released, but it is promised on the Deutsche Grammophon label before the end of 1978. ∎

November 1969

BERWALD: Overtures to Estrella de Soria and Drottningen av Golconda; Polonaise from Estrella de Soria; Erinnerung an die norwegischen Alpen (Memories of the Norwegian Alps); Elfenspiel (Elves' Games); Bajadärfesten. Swedish Radio Orchestra conducted by Sixten Ehrling. Nonesuch 71218, $2.98.

Franz Berwald, who has been called Sweden's greatest composer, shows influence by his contemporaries, Schubert, Berlioz, and Mendelssohn. However, his work is distinctively his own. It is only in recent years—and thanks largely to recordings—that Berwald has become more than just a name to a large American audience.

This collection of overtures and tone poems adds to our knowledge of Berwald and serves to introduce to us several fanciful scores—notably *Bajadärfesten* and *Elves' Games*—that might well become staples of the light concert repertoire. The performances seem thoroughly responsive to the material. All the more regrettable, therefore, is the fact that the recording is acoustically dead and not at all up to the best we expect from Nonesuch.

(continued)

Comment

Despite the inadequacy of the reproduced sound, the disc is well worth investigating: It's highly unlikely that this repertoire will soon be rerecorded. ■

May 1960

BIZET: Carmen. Victoria de los Angeles, soprano (Carmen); Nicolai Gedda, tenor (Don José); Janine Micheau, soprano (Micaela); Ernest Blanc, baritone (Escamillo). Orchestre National de la Radiodiffusion Française and Radiodiffusion Française Chorus, Petits Chanteurs de Versailles conducted by Sir Thomas Beecham. Angel S3613, 3 discs, $17.94.

At last, after many years, a decent performance of *Carmen* on records! Victoria de los Angeles surprises by singing the gypsy girl with temperament. One would not have imagined, from her previous work on records—beautiful but placid—that she could bring this kind of excitement and understanding to one of the most difficult roles in the repertoire. Although a soprano, she sings everything in the original mezzo keys. Not once does she transpose. Gedda is a firm-voiced Don José; Blanc, a vigorous-sounding Escamillo; Micheau (the weakest of this quartet), a rather hard-sounding Micaela. Beecham is unorthodox. He gets a wonderfully transparent texture from his orchestra, but some of his choices of tempi are opposed to anything one is accustomed to hearing. Often they make sense; once in a while (as in the first-act choruses), they are inexplicable. But we must bear with the foibles of great men. On the whole, a brilliant accomplishment. The British engineers do not go in for much in the way of separation, as opposed to American engineers (see the review of Verdi's *Macbeth*). Thus, the recording is bound to be less exciting. It is generally clear, barring an occasional fuzziness in the chorus, as at the end of Act II. But there is some tape noise and even an occasional patch of distortion. At its best, however—and the recording maintains a good level—the sound has presence and life.

April 1964

BIZET: Carmen. Regina Resnik, mezzo-soprano (Carmen); Mario Del Monaco, tenor (Don José); Joan Sutherland, soprano (Micaela); Tom Krause, baritone (Escamillo). Orchestre de la Suisse Romande and Geneva Grand Theatre Chorus conducted by Thomas Schippers. London 1368, 3 discs, $17.94.

Bizet's *Carmen* is one of the most popular operas ever written, but there are surprisingly few complete recordings of it, and fewer satisfactory ones. The main reason, of course, is that our decades have not produced a singer who is hailed as a great Carmen, as Calvé used to be many years ago, as Farrar was, as (vocally) Bruna Castagna was. Regina Resnik, who started her career as a soprano and switched to mezzo roles a few years ago, makes an interesting try in the title role, but for several reasons does not achieve complete success. One of her handicaps is vocal. When she lets her voice out, especially in high notes in the upper register, it becomes shrill and tremolo-ridden. The effect is decidedly unpleasant. And carefully as she has planned the characterization, it lacks conviction. The best thing about Resnik's Carmen is its musicality. There is less of the clenched-teeth singing that so many Carmens go in for, under the impression it is sexy. Of the others in the cast of this recording, Mario Del Monaco is unsubtle and ear-splitting. This is a major bit of miscasting. Joan Sutherland provides some lovely singing but little in the way of characterization. Thus this *Carmen* recording leaves quite a bit to be desired. The best available version—and it, too, is far from ideal—is the one conducted by Beecham, with Victoria de los Angeles as Carmen.

March 1965

BIZET: Carmen. Leontyne Price, soprano (Carmen); Franco Corelli, tenor (Don José); Robert Merrill, baritone (Escamillo); Mirella Freni, soprano (Micaela); Frank Schooten, bass (Zuniga). Vienna Philharmonic Orchestra, State Opera Chorus, and Boys Choir conducted by Herbert von Karajan. RCA LSC6199, 3 discs, $17.98. ●

The chief interest here is the Carmen of Leontyne Price. She has not yet sung the role on any stage, and it is said that she does not intend to. Whatever her reasons, they are probably not vocal. Price sounds entirely comfortable; she does not have to transpose any of the arias (the role is a bit low for sopranos, and many in the past have transposed up). She has sumptuous chest tones and an intelligent musical approach. The suggestion on this record is that she may lack the temperament to be a great Carmen. She seems to be somewhat on the surface in matters of characterization. But in this album she does provide as well-sung a Carmen as is currently available on discs; and the conductor, Herbert von Karajan, provides a thrilling, if somewhat personalized, reading. Corelli, as Don José, has plenty of voice and a minimum of subtlety. That Italian sob of his is more suitable for *Pagliacci* than *Carmen*. Freni sings a lovely Micaela, and Merrill is his usual resonant self as Escamillo.

Very good recorded sound. RCA has supplied plenty of separation. A typical example occurs in the first act, at the *"Au secours"* chorus. Some of the women sing from the left, some from the right, just as they would in the opera house. When Carmen enters, she is heard from dead center, with Zuniga at the left and Don José at the right. Good, clean stereo fun; and here it is all legitimate.

July 1965

BIZET: Carmen. Maria Callas, soprano (Carmen); Nicolai Gedda, tenor (Don José); Andréa Guiot, soprano (Micaela); Robert Massard, baritone (Escamillo). Orchestre du Théâtre National de l'Opéra de Paris, Choeurs René Duclos, and Choeurs d'Enfants Jean Pesneaud conducted by Georges Prêtre. Angel S3650X, 3 discs, $18.94. ●

Many readers will have seen the ads: Callas *Is* Carmen, they trumpet. She is, in this album, because she sings the role. People do not blow hot and cold

(continued)

about this singer. They blow hot or cold. To some she is the greatest diva of the age, a few vocal discrepancies notwithstanding. To others her inferior technique and shaky, variable vocal production do not make amends for her undoubted temperament and brains.

Callas has never sung the role of Carmen on any stage. On the face of it she would appear to be a natural. Bizet conceived the role for a mezzo-soprano—it has no high notes which in recent years have been giving Callas considerable trouble. As things turn out, she does sound much more comfortable in this opera than she does in most of her recent albums. But, curiously, she sings a surprisingly careful and even restrained Carmen. Her conception is certainly not sultry. If anything, it is aristocratic. It does have its own kind of emotional consistency and is less awkward a characterization than the recent one by Leontyne Price. But one hesitates to call the Callas Carmen a great one. Good, yes; unforgettable, no.

The other singers in the cast are competent, with special praise to the full-throated singing of Gedda as Don José. And the conducting is forceful and accurate. Angel has supplied not only the French-English libretto, but also a booklet with the entire Prosper Mérimée novelette from which the libretto was taken. As for the recorded sound, it is exceptionally fine, with plenty of presence and "air." Voices are more forward than they would be in the opera house, but that is a characteristic of records. All stereo effects sound completely natural.

Comment

Another Angel, *Carmen* (S3767), under Frühbeck, with Grace Bumbry in the title role, was an innovation: The recitatives composed by Guiraud, which are normally sung, were replaced by spoken dialogue. Two other worthy challengers then followed that lead. One was Bernstein, with Marilyn Horne as Carmen (Deutsche Grammophon 2709043), and the other was Solti, with Tatiana Troyanos (London 13115). Bernstein's is an uneven performance, although inspired in its best moments, and full of drama; Solti's is surprisingly tame and reined-in. Deutsche Grammophon has scheduled a release of this work with Claudio Abbado conducting Teresa Berganza in the title role; the artists made the recording shortly after their highly acclaimed performances at the 1977 Edinburgh Festival. ■

November 1972

BIZET: Symphony in C; Jeux d'enfants; Suite from the opera, The Fair Maid of Perth. The French National Radio and Television Orchestra conducted by Jean Martinon. Deutsche Grammophon 2530186, $6.98.

Bizet wrote his only symphony when he was 17; then for 80 years it lay unknown and unplayed in a pile of the composer's manuscripts at the Paris Conservatory. In 1933 D.C. Parker, a Scottish musicologist, discovered it and took steps to bring it to public attention. Ever since its 1935 world premiere, the symphony has been a repertory staple. The present release brings to seven the number of available recordings of the score; indeed, it is the second Martinon-conducted performance to be issued in about a year.

Martinon did his first recording while he was the Chicago Symphony's music director, but it sat around in RCA's icebox for several years before it was finally released (VICS 1628). A comparison between Martinon-in-Chicago and Martinon-in-Paris yields little because the two performances are fairly consistent; in both, Martinon adopts a rather objective approach to the music, striving for clarity and clean technique. The first movement tempo in the new recording is slightly faster than in the Chicago Symphony recording, the last movement slightly slower. In general, the Chicago Symphony performance is a bit less rigid than the new one, but the sound reproduction in the new recording allows the details of the scoring to stand out in bolder relief. As a matter of fact, the DGG microphoning is a good deal closer and more precise than one usually hears on that label.

The two works on the reverse side are relatively minor, although charming. They both receive tender treatment from all concerned: conductor, musicians and engineers.

October 1974

BIZET: Symphony in C; PROKOFIEV: Symphony in D, "Classical."
The Academy of St. Martin-in-the-Fields conducted by Neville Marriner. Argo ZRG719, $6.98. ●

The pairing of these two symphonies is eminently sensible. Yet this is only the second time they have been coupled on a disc, the first being Bernstein's zestful performances (Columbia MS7159). But good as Bernstein's versions are, these are better.

The Academy of St. Martin-in-the-Fields is one of the most versatile small orchestras in the world ("academy" in the title is used in the sense of "ensemble"). And Neville Marriner is rapidly emerging as one of the most perceptive and interesting international conductors. In addition to his work with the academy, he is conductor of the Los Angeles Chamber Orchestra, and he will surely become much more active with the great symphony orchestras on both sides of the Atlantic.

The work of Marriner and the academy is distinguished by meticulous attention to detail (phrasing and dynamics particularly), rhythmic buoyancy that imparts polish and glow, and spontaneous freshness. The recorded sound here has a glow all its own, so that this is one of the most successful recent releases.

Comment

Either of Martinon's recordings of the Bizet symphony is a fine reading of the score. But there also exists a version recorded in London by Martinon's conducting teacher, Charles Munch—one that is an absolute miracle of winged inspiration and ecstatic joy. Originally made for mail-order distribution by the *Reader's Digest*, this Munch recording (Quintessence 7048) is one of the supremely great discs of our time. The sound is fully up to the best of today's standards, although the recording dates back to the early 1960s. On the other
(continued)

side of the disc we are given a Munch-conducted performance of Tchai-kovsky's symphonic fantasia, *Francesca da Rimini,* that blazes with passion and excitement.

Another recording of the Bizet symphony worthy of consideration is the one made by Leopold Stokowski in June 1977, just a few months before he died. Stokowski was ninety-five at the time, but his performance (Columbia M34567) is alive with youthful vitality.

Marriner has indeed become more active in the United States, appearing as guest conductor with the Boston Symphony, the Buffalo Philharmonic, and the New York Philharmonic, among others. It is mainly his preeminence in baroque and early classical literature that has been on display. But he knows the entire span of symphonic literature—for years he was leader of the second violins in the London Symphony Orchestra—so it's inevitable that he will take on the big works of the nineteenth and twentieth centuries. ■

July 1965

BLOCH: Concerto for Violin and Orchesta. Yehudi Menuhin and Philharmonia Orchestra conducted by Paul Kletzki. Angel S36192, $5.98.

Like the Busoni *Indianische Fantasie* the Bloch *Violin Concerto,* composed in 1938, makes use of American Indian themes. Many will find a Hebraic quality too, never far from Bloch's music. This is a strong, moving piece that deserves to be more popular. Menuhin, who has always been associated with the score, gives us some of his finest playing in recent years. He is equal to the large-scale muscular demands of the writing, and Kletzki's support is impeccable. A fine disc. Good sound—a better job than most discs in centering the violin without making it sound as if it were spread out.

Comment

The Bloch *Concerto*, one of the noblest works for violin written in the twentieth century, still languishes in neglect. This Menuhin recording is a first-class realization of the strength and character of the music. ■

August 1978

BORODIN: Prince Igor: Polovtsian Dances. RIMSKY-KORSAKOV: Russian Easter Overture; Capriccio Espagnol. MUSSORGSKY: A Night on Bald Mountain. The Chicago Symphony Orchestra under the direction of Daniel Barenboim. Deutsche Grammophon 2536379, $8.98. ●

In a sense, this disc is a Rimsky-Korsakov festival of Russian orchestral favorites: It groups the composer's dazzling *Russian Easter Overture* and *Capriccio Espagnol,* and the Borodin and Moussorgsky works, both of which Rimsky-Korsakov orchestrated. All four scores are riotous with color and teem with the excitement of a symphony orchestra in full flight. Barenboim's conducting emphasizes those elements without overdoing them.

In his meticulous preparation for a performance, Barenboim is sometimes guilty of overinterpretation, though the only work here to suggest that even faintly is the *Capriccio Espagnol*—its blending of phrases could have been a bit less obtrusive. Otherwise, these scores get forthright, exciting readings. The popular dances from Borodin's opera (reworked on Broadway these days as the musical *Timbuktu,* itself a reworking of *Kismet*) are given without chorus, in their orchestra-only form. The Chicago Symphony's musicians play superbly, as usual. The recorded sound is less "distant" than customary for Deutsche Grammophon.

Comment

The tendency is to associate Barenboim with the German-Austrian repertoire that is central to symphonic literature: Haydn, Mozart, Beethoven, and Bruckner. These days, however, as music director of L'Orchestre de Paris, Barenboim is also developing into a committed champion of the French repertoire. This disc displays him in still another kind of symphonic music—and, on the whole, he is most impressive. ∎

February 1964

BORODIN: Quartet No. 2 in D major; SHOSTAKOVICH: Quartet No. 8 (Op. 110). Borodin Quartet. London STS15046, $2.98.

The Borodin Quartet is a Russian group that has been playing in the West (this recording was made in London). Like many other Russian musicians, these have extroverted ideas. Thus they lean toward pronounced rubatos, a heavy vibrato, fancy ritards, and other expressive devices. This does not lead to subtle performances; but there is something rather likable about the group's somewhat näive approach. The Shostakovich *Quartet* is a musical game, composed in 1960. In the score are letters from Shostakovich's name (D, E flat, which is "S" in German nomenclature, C, and so on). The score is also full of quotations from earlier Shostakovich scores, including the *First Symphony,* the *Cello Concerto, Lady Macbeth of Mzensk,* and the *Piano Trio.* It is all very Shostakovichian and musically "safe," with prevailing tonality offset by a few clashes of dissonance.

Comment

Originally released in London's full-price CS series, these performances are now available in the firm's budget-price Stereo Treasury series—and truly a bargain! ∎

November 1972

BORODIN: Symphony No. 1 in E flat; RACHMANINOFF: The Rock. The Moscow Radio Symphony Orchestra conducted by Gennady Rozhdestvensky. Melodiya/Angel SR40182, $5.98.

(continued)

Borodin's *First Symphony* was the first Russian symphony to achieve fame and success in the West, and it sparked the subsequent interest in Borodin's own *Second Symphony* as well as in the symphonies of Tchaikovsky, Rachmaninoff, Prokofiev and Shostakovich. Ironically, Borodin's *First* has now largely fallen out of the active repertory; this release is only its second recording and the first in stereo.

The *First* is a well-crafted score in the traditional 19th-century symphonic format. The first movement, after a slow introduction, is vigorous and propulsive; then comes a fanciful scherzo, followed by a contemplative slow movement and an exhilarating finale.

Rachmaninoff's symphonic fantasy, *The Rock,* has also been recorded only once before—by André Previn and the London Symphony Orchestra (RCA LSC2990, along with a performance of Rachmaninoff's *Third Symphony*). *The Rock* is a very early work, composed when Rachmaninoff was 20. Unlike the solemn and severe title, the music itself is light-textured and gentle. Its inspiration derives from a Lermontov poem that begins: "The little golden cloud spent the night/On the chest of the giant crag." The piece is minor Rachmaninoff—colorful and atmospheric.

Both the Borodin symphony and the Rachmaninoff symphonic fantasy receive dedicated attention at the hands of Rozhdestvensky, his orchestra and the engineers. This disc is recommended to those in search of offbeat 19th-century Russian orchestral music.

Comment

Several recordings of the Rachmaninoff symphonic fantasy have come along since this disc, but this is the only individual recording of the Borodin symphony currently available. One would therefore have to recommend this disc to anyone interested in the development of the symphony as a form in nineteenth-century Russia. As it is, Rozhdestvensky delivers a thoroughly perceptive, idiomatic account of the score—which may be why no other conductor and record company have chosen to challenge this performance. ∎

November 1965

BOYCE: Eight Symphonies. I Solisti di Zagreb conducted by Antonio Janigro. Bach Guild 70668, $5.98.

William Boyce (1710-79) was an English composer whose only claims to fame are these symphonies. It is not that he composed no other music (some of it has even been recorded), but that nothing of his has captured the imagination as have these eight fine works. They are called "symphonies," though many listeners will find them much closer in style and treatment to the Handel concerti grossi. The music is lovely, bracing, and beautifully written—baroque at nearly its best. Some movements of the symphonies are very British in feeling, suggesting hornpipes, country dances, and even street calls. Thus there is an element of personality that is lacking in much baroque music. As in most of the Solisti di Zagreb performances, the playing is direct, musical, scholarly, and supple. This is one of the best groups of its kind. There can be nothing but praise for the realistic quality of the sound. The strings are velvety; the surfaces are quiet; there is plenty of resonance.

Comment

Time has in no way tarnished the sterling qualities of this collection. Performances and recordings are first-rate throughout all eight of the miniature symphonies. The disc now bears the Vanguard catalog number HM23. ■

May 1959

BRAHMS: Concerto No. 1 in D minor for Piano (Op. 15). Gary Graffman, piano, and Boston Symphony Orchestra conducted by Charles Munch. RCA VICS1109, $2.98.

Generally considered one of the best American pianists, Graffman always has been a rather severe musician whose playing leans more toward contour and architecture than color and flexibility. He has a big style, and this concerto was made for him. Graffman plays it with power, technical expertise, and clarity of phrasing. In years to come he will get more out of the slow movement, but this still remains one of the better performances on records. This despite the fact that RCA has not solved all the problems here. In the fast movements, the piano sounds natural enough, but in the slow movement it sometimes seems to stretch from speaker to speaker, with the treble on one side and a disembodied sort of bass on the other.

May 1965

BRAHMS: Concerto No. 1 in D minor for Piano (Op. 15). Van Cliburn, piano, and Boston Symphony Orchestra conducted by Erich Leinsdorf. RCA LSC2724, $5.98. ▲

Everybody today plays the Brahms *D minor*, and it has not lacked good performances on records: Arrau, Backhaus, Curzon, Rubinstein, and Serkin, among others. What can Van Cliburn offer? As it turns out, he does have something of his own to contribute. His approach is serious, his ideas valid, and he plays with unfailing taste and dedication. Then there is the matter of piano tone. Cliburn can produce one of the richest sounds of any pianist in action today. Technically, too, he is able to toss off the awkward Brahmsian figurations. There are those who tend to consider Cliburn nothing more than a pianistic glamor boy, but they could not be more in error.

RCA, however, has not done its best for the pianist. Sections, especially in the inner grooves, are overloaded, and some pickups may have difficulty tracking the disc without distortion or shatter.

February 1977

BRAHMS: Piano Concerto No. 1 in D Minor. Artur Rubinstein, piano, with the Israel Philharmonic Orchestra conducted by Zubin Mehta. London CS7018, $6.98. ●

(continued)

The fourth recording by Artur Rubinstein of Brahms's youthful *First Piano Concerto* is undoubtedly the last in the unique career of a cherished artist. Rubinstein, over 90 when he made this recording in Tel Aviv last April, reveals in a touching liner note: "I played with a great handicap as my eyesight was nearly gone at the time of the recording." That he could play at all is quite remarkable; that he could play with such assurance borders on the miraculous.

I would question Rubinstein's assessment of this performance as "perhaps the most intense" of his four recordings of the score. To be sure, there are many memorable moments, but they are mostly in the quieter, most introspective sections of the work—and especially in the slow movement, where Rubinstein casts a spell of hypnotic reverie. Lyrical warmth abounds, too, in the stormier movements. But the flames of passion burned brighter in his earlier recordings of this work.

The Israel Philharmonic is at the very top of its form these days, as attested by its performances during a recent tour of the United States and Canada. It is a supremely flexible orchestra, with abundant riches in every section, particularly in the strings, whose sound is both vibrant and mellow. The orchestra's playing and Mehta's conducting are all one could wish. The recorded sound is on the dry side, an accurate image of the sound as it would be in the Fredric Mann Auditorium, the Israel Philharmonic's home in Tel Aviv. On the whole this new version of a masterwork for piano and orchestra is commendable indeed.

July 1977

BRAHMS: Piano Concerto No. 1 in D Minor. Artur Rubinstein, piano, with the Chicago Symphony Orchestra under the direction of Fritz Reiner. RCA ARL12044, $7.98. ▲ ●

Recently, we reviewed the recording of Brahms' First *Piano Concerto* that Artur Rubinstein made last spring in Israel with Zubin Mehta and the Israel Philharmonic Orchestra (London CS7018). Rubinstein had recorded the same *Concerto* earlier—in the 1950's, with Fritz Reiner and the Chicago Symphony, and in the 1960's, with Erich Leinsdorf and the Boston Symphony.

The performance of the *Concerto* under Reiner has long ranked as one of the great achievements in the distinguished pianist's brilliant career. The recording sessions devoted to it in 1954, moreover, were among the earliest to experiment with stereophonic sound reproduction. RCA recently discovered the stereo master pressings in its vaults and found the discs to be of unusually high quality. And so it is that the Rubinstein-Reiner-Chicago Symphony Orchestra recording is being released for the first time in stereo—nearly a quarter-century late.

This performance has the eloquence and herculean grandeur we associate with Rubinstein at his very best. Reiner and the Chicago Symphony are also at the top of their form. The stereo sound is a tribute to the technical know-how of RCA's engineers at a time when stereo recording was in its infancy. The reproduction is clear, full-bodied, and spacious. In my judgment, this is the best of Rubinstein's four recordings of a musical masterpiece.

Comment

The Rubinstein-Mehta-Israel Philharmonic disc is apparently the last concerto recording we shall have by Rubinstein. That the Brahms *D Minor* should be his last recording of a concerto is quite fitting; after Chopin, it is perhaps Brahms for whom Rubinstein felt the closest affinity.

Some other splendid performances are those by Curzon and Szell (London CS6329), Fleisher and Szell (Odyssey Y31273), Gilels and Jochum (Deutsche Grammophon 2530258), and Serkin and Szell (Columbia MS7143). ■

March 1961

BRAHMS: Concerto No. 2 in B flat major for Piano (Op. 83). Sviatoslav Richter, piano, and Chicago Symphony Orchestra conducted by Erich Leinsdorf. RCA LSC2466, $5.98. ●

The way the public and some critics have been carrying on about Richter, all other pianists—one gets the idea—should close up shop. Well, Richter is a fine artist, but he is not *that* divine. In this recording of the Brahms *Second Piano Concerto* he reveals strengths and weaknesses in a rather unconventional interpretation. His strength is the peculiar mixture of intellect and emotion with which he approaches the music. Obviously he is a sincere and dedicated musician with original ideas. His weaknesses are a technique that has its sloppy moments (sections of the fourth movement, for instance, are inaccurate), and some notions about tempo that make the music crawl. This is a very interesting performance, but it is easily matched by Gilels, Rubinstein, and Serkin. The recorded sound leaves something to be desired.It is muffled in the bass, with some "breakup" in fortissimo passages and a prevalent shrillness in the strings. The piano sounds spread over too large an area, and the close-up miking often makes the piano blot out the orchestra.

January 1968

BRAHMS: Concerto No. 2 in B flat major for Piano (Op. 83). Rudolf Serkin, piano, and Cleveland Orchestra conducted by George Szell. Columbia MS6967. $5.98.

Many great pianists have recorded the big *B flat Concerto* by Brahms. No other has done it with Serkin's authority. This work has been one of his specialties throughout the years, and his conception has continued to grow. He has recorded it several times previously. This new disc supersedes all others, and one is tempted to say that Serkin gives the greatest performance of the concerto ever recorded. It has drive, power, and insight and exhibits remarkable technical command. As is well known, the Brahms *B flat Concerto* is one of the most difficult piano pieces ever composed. It requires stamina, power, and an ability to negotiate some of the most ungrateful stretches of piano writing in the entire literature. But as Serkin plays the work, the grateful listener never feels the strain that is almost always present when most other pianists tackle the score. Serkin is invariably on top of the notes, playing
(continued)

with elegance and poetry, and yet with all the sonority and massiveness the concerto demands. This performance is a remarkable achievement. The same can also be said for the conductor; Szell and his great orchestra are at one with the pianist. The recorded sound is nothing but brilliant.

Comment

A more recent Richter recording of this concerto, with Maazel conducting the Orchestre de Paris (Angel S36728), is even more quixotic than the 1961 Richter (now reissued as AGL 11267). Tempos are leaden and the music sounds ponderous and drained of its vitality. Clearly, the Brahms *B flat* is not Richter's piece. Be that as it may, it *is* Serkin's piece, and his recording of it with George Szell and the Cleveland Orchestra (Columbia MS6967) is a very strong contender for top honors.

The performances reviewed here cover most of the options available to the soloist and conductor in this score. The individual listener will have to decide which stylistic approach is more personally satisfying. ■

August 1970

BRAHMS: Concerto in A minor for Violin and Cello. David Oistrakh, violin; Mstislav Rostropovich, cello; with the Cleveland Orchestra conducted by George Szell. Angel S36032, $5.98. ▲ ●

This and a disc of the Brahms *Violin Concerto* played by Oistrakh with Szell and the Cleveland Orchestra (Angel S36033) represent the fruits of recording sessions held in Cleveland in May 1969. Along with two discs by Seiji Ozawa and the Chicago Symphony Orchestra, the Szell-Cleveland releases mark the debut of Angel—a British recording company—as producer of orchestral recordings made in this country.

It is an auspicious debut. This performance of Brahms' *Double Concerto* is notable for its superbly disciplined interaction among the three principals. Oistrakh and Rostropovich have each made several earlier recordings of the concerto, but with different partners; this, their first joint recording, demonstrates an uncommonly unified conception and performing style. Such a quality is particularly appropriate here, where Brahms frequently tosses themes and phrases back and forth from one instrument to the other. The Oistrakh-Rostropovich collaboration creates the impression that a single extraordinary string player is performing on a marvelous instrument that embraces a range from the lowest registers of the cello to the highest reaches of the violin. And Szell, serving as the power generator behind the whole musical enterprise, delivers a reading of warm power and passion. The reproduced sound—a product of the British technicians who were flown to Cleveland for the occasion—features such American characteristics as close microphoning, which results in some overprominent contributions from the orchestral soloists. The sound is thus more American than European.

Comment

If a more Romantic approach to the music—greater overall ease and warmth and more tempo flexibility—is to your liking, the team of Francescatti-Fournier-Walter (Columbia MS6158) will undoubtedly satisfy you. ∎

February 1964

BRAHMS: Concerto in D for Violin (Op. 77). Zino Francescatti, violin, With New York Philharmonic conducted by Leonard Bernstein. Columbia MS6471, $5.98.

This is the sixteenth current version of the Brahms *Violin Concerto* (according to the most recent Schwann guide). Every great violinist has had a crack at it: Francescatti himself, a few years back, Heifetz, Kreisler, Menuhin, Milstein, Morini, Stern, Oistrakh, Szeryng. What a company! Francescatti is well up among the leaders. By temperament a Romantic fiddler, he has always had an emotional approach to music. Some have brought more introspection to the work; others more intellectuality; but none has brought a greater violinistic sweep or equivalent ardor. The anti-Romantics may query Francescatti's extremely rapid, wide vibrato, and it is true that in the slow movement he does bear down too heavily on the fingerboard. For some the effect may be slushy. But Francescatti, after all, does represent an older school, one that is not afraid to show emotion. Technically his playing is marvelous, with all problems met head-on and conquered. Good support from Bernstein. Good recorded sound, too, with the violin dead center between the speakers. Unfortunately the slow movement has an unusually high amount of surface noise.

Comment

There are nearly a dozen different recordings available. Among the alternatives, the Oistrakh-Klemperer offers a massive and impressive account of the music (Angel S35836) and the Heifetz-Reiner (RCA LSC1903) a more nimble and fleet-fingered performance. The Perlman-Giulini version (Angel S37286) is a noble, warm, immensely-rewarding rendition of this masterpiece. ∎

September 1966

BRAHMS: Deutsche Volkslieder (Bks. 1-6). Elisabeth Schwarzkopf, soprano; Dietrich Fischer-Dieskau, baritone; Gerald Moore, piano. Angel S3675, 2 discs, $11.96.

Do not be deceived by the apparent simplicity of these songs. They are late works by Brahms. The entire collection consists of forty-nine settings of German folk songs, of which forty-two are included here. (The other seven are scored for chorus.) Schwarzkopf and Fischer-Dieskau split the assign-
(continued)

59

ment, she singing the "feminine" songs, he the "masculine," and both coming together in songs that have both elements. The idea of singing several of these songs as a duet is unconventional, and is not sanctioned by the text; but no great harm is done, and the results are quite charming. There is no continuity to the songs in this album, and it is not the kind of music that should be taken in one long gulp. Rather it is an ideal collection into which to dip, enjoying a dozen or so songs at one sitting, then later coming back for more. The music is exceedingly attractive: lyric, sentimental in the best sense of the word, full of nostalgia and charm. Needless to say, two such fine singers as Schwarzkopf and Fischer-Dieskau, helped by the expert pianism of Moore, cannot help but make the music a rewarding experience. Some hiss mars the otherwise fine stereo discs.

Comment

This album is recommended unhesitatingly to all who admire the individual and collective artistry of these three superlative musicians. ■

November 1971

BRAHMS: Hungarian Dances No. 5 and No. 6 and Waltzes (Op. 39); SCHUBERT: Marche militaire and Fantasia in F minor. Richard and John Contiguglia, duo-pianists. Connoisseur Society S2037, $5.98.

The performance of four-hand piano duets—a uniquely satisfying musical give-and-take for both professional and amateur performers—is now largely gone from American life. What a pity! For there was a time in the early years of this century when from many a Main Street living room could be heard the sounds of a Mozart or Beethoven symphony pounded out by the twenty eager fingers of two enthusiasts seated at a single keyboard. Duet piano-playing enjoyed perhaps its finest hour in nineteenth-century Vienna, and many of the great composers of the era—Schubert, Brahms, and Mendelssohn among them—wrote some of their most endearing music for four-hand piano duet. The present disc is devoted to some of that literature, in joyous performance by two young men who infuse their playing with a contagious enthusiasm.

The best-known works on the disc are the two *Hungarian Dances* by Brahms (yes, they were composed originally for piano duet) and Schubert's *Marche militaire*. All three are far better known in their orchestral transcriptions, but they sparkle unexpectedly in these original-version performances. Similarly, the sixteen waltzes of Brahms' *Opus 39* and Schubert's large-scale *F minor Fantasia* emerge as full-blown masterpieces of the genre.

This is the second disc by the twin brothers, Richard and John Contiguglia, to be released by Connoisseur Society. As in their debut release of Bartók's *Suite for Two Pianos* and fourteen selections from the composer's *Mikrokosmos* (S2033), the sound reproduction is remarkably clear and lifelike.

Comment

Since the above review appeared, it has come to CU's attention that Connoisseur Society records may not always be readily available on local dealers' shelves. They can easily be ordered directly from the Society's main office at 390 West End Avenue, New York, N.Y. 10024. ∎

September 1967

BRAHMS: Liebeslieder Waltzes (Op. 52 and Op. 65). Elsie Morison, soprano; Marjorie Thomas, contralto; Richard Lewis, tenor; Donald Bell, baritone; Vronsky and Babin, duo-pianists. Seraphim S60033, $2.98.

Originally issued in 1959, this disc now comes out in the low-price Seraphim line. It's a good buy. The music is attractive, and the performances of both sets of *Liebeslieder* are sung and played with spirit and finesse. Brahms liked waltzes and composed some fine ones in his day, but these are his very best. Texts in German, with English translation, are included with the record.

Comment

This graceful, easy chamber music is so immediately appealing that the score has several times been transcribed for different instrumental combinations—string orchestra, orchestra and chorus, etc.—to enlarge the performance possibilities. Brahms's own intimate setting for two pianos and vocal quartet is infinitely preferable to any of the other arrangements. The performances are mellow. ∎

July 1966

BRAHMS: Quartets (3) (complete); SCHUMANN: Quintet in E flat major for Piano and Strings. Budapest Quartet, with Rudolf Serkin, piano. Columbia M2S734, 2 discs, $11.96.

Brahms composed a great deal of chamber music, but only three string quartets—the *C minor* and *A minor* (*Op. 51, Nos. 1* and *2*), and the *B flat major* (*Op. 67*). Each of these is a masterpiece—rich, lyric, mature, beautifully written—with strongly defined characteristics of its own. The *C minor* is stormy; the *A minor* is reflective, a sheer outpouring of song from beginning to end; and the *B flat major* is bucolic, light, charming.

The Schumann *Piano Quintet in E flat major* (*Op. 44*) is by common consent one of the great pieces of chamber music of the nineteenth century. And yet for some weird inexplicable reason, this new Budapest-Serkin disc seems to be the only stereophonic version available, at least in the American catalogues. Fortunately this new interpretation was well worth waiting for.

(continued)

It is strong, virile, and lyric, sparked by the curiously personal style of Rudolf Serkin. Showing pronounced ideas about the music, Serkin takes many liberties in phrase and tempo, and yet manages to make his conception believable. He is also up to his old trick of humming along, and this can be distracting.

In the three Brahms *Quartets*, the Budapest has little competition. There is a Kohon Quartet Vox album (in a three-disc Vox Box, along with the three Schumann *String Quartets*), not bad but without the sweep and Romantic style of the Budapesters; and there is a Deutsche Grammophon disc played nicely by the Amadeus Quartet. Though the Budapest group may be a little rough these days and may show patches of bad intonation, it is still one of the best groups around.

This album is eminently worth having. It has good, warm, and faithful sound, with pronounced separation in the stereo.

Comment

There are now no fewer than four other recordings of the Schumann quintet available. The Serkin-Budapest collaboration is surely among the best. This set is to be treasured even more now that the Budapest Quartet no longer exists. ∎

January 1968

BRAHMS: Quintet in F minor for Piano and Strings (Op. 34). Artur Rubinstein and the Guarneri Quartet. RCA LSC2971, $5.98.

Artur Rubinstein is the oldest of the musical old masters, and the Guarneri Quartet is composed of four very young players. For several years Rubinstein had been wanting to rerecord some of the chamber works he had done in the 1930s and 1940s, and when he heard the quartet play he was sufficiently impressed to ask them to undertake the project with him. This disc is the first of a series that will include Schumann, Brahms, and Fauré.

The Marlboro Festival was responsible for the genesis of the Guarneri Quartet. The four players, who came together to study there under Serkin and Casals, decided to form the quartet. When they made their debut, about three years ago, they were enthusiastically received, with a unanimous prediction that they were on their way to greatness. This record in no way alters the prognosis. Their playing is impeccable: perfectly integrated, with a high degree of polish, and with more than enough strength for the music. Rubinstein matches his young colleagues in ardor as well as in technical finesse. He leads the four players in a joyously exuberant performance.

Comment

The combination of poetry and vitality that marks this performance by Rubinstein with the Guarneri is matchless. Among other available recordings, the Serkin-Budapest Quartet collaboration (Columbia M6631) is particularly noteworthy in that it marks one of the very few times that these sterling artists recorded together. ∎

August 1970

BRAHMS: Rinaldo (cantata); Schicksalslied (Song of Destiny). The New Philharmonia Orchestra and the Ambrosian Singers conducted by Claudio Abbado, with James King, tenor (in *Rinaldo*). London 26106, $5.98.

Rinaldo, a cantata for tenor, male chorus, and orchestra, is the closest Brahms ever came to composing an opera. Though the music is unmistakably Brahmsian, it has an unrelieved monotony that explains its obscurity in the Brahms canon. Too, Brahms exhibits a sense of strain in some places. The performance here lacks passion, but it is questionable whether even that would have succeeded in creating much interest in the score.

Far more successful is the *Song of Destiny,* set to words by the German poet Friedrich Hölderlin. The poem itself is an unrelievedly solemn rumination about man's fate. Brahms, however, introduces an optimistic major-key conclusion. Too, the *Song of Destiny* performance is more alert than that of *Rinaldo,* but it does not keep one from regretting that earlier recordings by both Bruno Walter and Sir Thomas Beecham are no longer available. For their part, the engineers have done their job well, capturing clear, spacious and well-balanced sound.

Comment

Since this is the only available *Rinaldo* recording—and it seems likely to remain so for some time—there is no choice. If you must have *Rinaldo*, this is it. As for the *Schicksalslied*, the performance by the Occidental College Concert Choir and Columbia Symphony Orchestra under Bruno Walter (Columbia MS6488) is at once more pliant and subtle than Abbado's performance. This was Walter's second recorded performance of the score, made not long before his death; Walter's earlier recording (dating from the 1940s) was with the New York Philharmonic and the Westminster Choir. ∎

June 1975

BRAHMS: Sixteen Hungarian Dances. The London Symphony Orchestra conducted by Antal Dorati. Mercury SR175024, $6.98.

Mercury has again made available some of the best recordings in its catalog via a Golden Imports re-issue series. The quality of these "new" European pressings is clearly much better than that of the old. The original tapes seem to have been remastered, too; so much of the harshness that chronically afflicted Mercury recordings is now gone. This disc gives nearly ideal renderings of 16 of Brahms's 21 *Hungarian Dances,* originally composed for piano

(continued)

duet. Brahms himself arranged the first 10 dances for piano solo, and three of them (numbers 1, 3, and 10) for orchestra as well.

Dorati, who is Hungarian-born, responds beautifully to the spirit of each of these dances. The London Symphony Orchestra plays with verve. And the recorded sound testifies to the high technical standards the Mercury production crew set years ago and has adhered to.

Comment

This disc still affords the greatest pleasure—and it remains the most comprehensive single-disc collection of the orchestrated *Hungarian Dances*. ∎

May 1976

BRAHMS: Symphony No. 1 in C minor. The Chicago Symphony Orchestra under the direction of James Levine. RCA ARL11326, $6.98. ▲ ●

James Levine, music director of Chicago's Ravinia Festival and guest conductor with such prestigious orchestras as the Boston Symphony, the Los Angeles Philharmonic, the Philadelphia Orchestra, and the New York Philharmonic, will soon be the Music Director of New York's Metropolitan Opera Company, only the second musician in almost a century to hold that title. At 32, he is a veteran opera conductor for both Angel and RCA Records and is currently engaged in a long-term project to record all the Mahler Symphonies. In fact, Levine and the Chicago Symphony made this pressing of Brahms's *First Symphony* in the time they had left after recording Mahler's *Third Symphony*.

Their performance, straightforward and levelheaded, is a perfectly legitimate response to the score. If there is excessive sobriety here and there, Levine's reading is never exaggerated or overwrought. Magnificent playing by the Chicago Symphony and superlative reproduction by RCA's engineers are perhaps the chief glories of the performance. The sound is vibrant; the balance between the several choirs of the orchestra is outstanding in its naturalness. This most recent collaboration between Levine and the Chicago Symphony Orchestra is very impressive; still, among contemporary recordings of Brahms's *First Symphony*, those of Haitink, Kertész, and Stokowski seem preferable to me.

A grace note: The inferior quality of RCA's wafer-thin Dynaflex recordings appears to be a thing of the past. This disc is thicker, more substantial, and much better in quality than the earlier ones. The pressing is immaculate— one of the best I've heard in months.

June 1977

BRAHMS: Symphony No. 1 in C minor. The Cleveland Orchestra under the direction of Lorin Maazel. London CS7007, $6.98. ●

This is the first installment of what will soon be a complete cycle of the four

Brahms Symphonies as recorded by Lorin Maazel and the Cleveland Orchestra. My reaction to this release is mixed: part admiration for the precision of the ensemble playing, and part impatience with the very deliberate tempi Maazel has adopted.

The effect of those tempi has been to keep the music bogged down when it should soar. (One departure from the conductor's basically lethargic tempi is the glorious big tune: He handles that with remarkable haste in the last movement. Obviously, he means to avoid sentimentalizing that theme, but for me he goes too far in the other direction.) To his credit, however, Maazel is one of the very few conductors who habitually observes the exposition repeat in the symphony's first movement.

While one can respect the intent of Maazel's slow-tempo treatment—to probe the score deeply for possible subterranean meaning—one need not admire the result of that treatment.

Where Maazel fails, a recently released broadcast performance by the Berlin Philharmonic under Furtwängler in 1952 (Deutsche Grammophon 2530744) succeeds brilliantly with what is basically a similar approach. But Furtwängler, unlike Maazel, manages to invest his performance with a conviction that is genuinely overpowering.

Comment

The approaches of Maazel and Levine to this work are diametrically opposed: Maazel's is heavy, ponderous; Levine's is lean and transparently textured. Meantime, Deutsche Grammophon has released a recording of Brahms's *First Symphony* by Seiji Ozawa and the Boston Symphony Orchestra (DG2530889) that is one of the conductor's finest standard-repertory recordings to date; it has flexibility, propulsion, and an emotional involvement that is rare in Ozawa's music-making. ∎

September 1965

BRAHMS: Symphony No. 3 in F major; Variations on a Theme by Haydn. Cleveland Orchestra conducted by George Szell. Columbia MS6685, $5.98.

These are tensile, sharp readings, typical of Szell and the great, responsive orchestra he has brought to perfection. Szell's interpretations are always interesting and valid, and thus this umpteenth recording of the Brahms *Third* has its value. But though the recorded sound is certainly not bad, it is not up to the highest standards prevailing today, being a little gray and lacking the ultimate in color, presence, and vibrancy. The pressings, too, are rather noisy, with tape hiss and some unfortunate surface noise.

Comment

Sound reproduction is less satisfactory in the Klemperer–Philharmonia Orchestra account of the music (Angel S35545), but a more penetrating concep-
(continued)

tion is realized. Also worth investigating is the Giulini-Philharmonia Orchestra disc (Seraphim S60101), a deeply felt performance and well recorded. The same words apply with equal force to the excellent recording by Bernard Haitink directing the Amsterdam Concertgebouw (Philips 6500155). ■

July 1965

BRITTEN: Albert Herring. Sylvia Fisher, soprano (Lady Billows); Johanna Peters, contralto (Florence Pike); John Noble, baritone (Mr. Gedge); Owen Brannigan, bass (Police Superintendent); Edgar Evans, tenor (Mr. Upfold); April Cantelo, soprano (Miss Wordsworth); Joseph Ward, tenor (Sid); Catherine Wilson, mezzo-soprano (Nancy); Sheila Rex, mezzo-soprano (Mrs. Herring); Peter Pears, tenor (Albert Herring). English Chamber Orchestra conducted by Benjamin Britten. London 1378, 3 discs, $17.94.

Britten's comic opera concerns itself with the quest for a May Queen. But in this prim English village, no girl can be found who is good enough. Why not a May King? The spotless Albert Herring is selected. But somebody makes him drunk, and things happen. Britten has scored this amusing story for a very small orchestra. The opera received its premiere in 1947. It is typical of the composer's skill, smartness, and ability to parody older styles. Some advanced harmonies are occasionally in evidence, but Britten on the whole writes in a conservative style, though the opera is very much of our time.

The performance is simply spectacular. Because of the small orchestra, the singers have no trouble coming through clearly, and for once every word they sing can be understood. In addition, each member of the cast, presumably hand-picked by the composer, is a fine musician.

In the recording a good deal of separation is used. To cite one example, for the duet ending the fifth side each singer is confined to a specific location. Some special sound effects are incorporated, one or two of them unconsciously funny. In the opening scene, when Florence turns the leaves of her notebook, it sounds like the surf in a high gale.

Comment

London Records has systematically recorded all the major works of Britten under the composer's direction—a valuable project indeed. The present album is one of the most noteworthy in the series. ■

September 1972

BRITTEN: Piano Concerto; Violin Concerto. Sviatoslav Richter, piano; Mark Lubotsky, violin; with the English Chamber Orchestra conducted by Benjamin Britten. London CS6723, $5.98.

These two Britten scores were written when the composer was still in his mid-20s. Both exhibit Britten's rare craftsmanship, and both have a vibrant creativity that should have established them as concert staples. In this case, contemporary performers and public have been lacking in initiative. The works are rather unusual in form. The piano concerto opens with a percussive toccata and closes with a hearty march movement; in between come a bittersweet waltz and a brooding, mystical impromptu. The violin concerto opens and closes in a pensive, evocative mood, with a rhythmically exciting vivace movement in between. These two scores contain some of Britten's most engaging music. His greater fame as an opera composer should no longer eclipse his earlier accomplishments for the concert hall.

The performances of both scores are entirely satisfying. Britten has long been an expert conductor of his own and other music. The Soviet pianist Richter has become one of Britten's closest colleagues, and their association is evident in their sympathetic collaboration. And whoever Lubotsky may be (the record liner offers no clue), he is obviously a violinist of rare interpretive gifts.

Comment

These remain the only domestically available recordings of both scores, and their superior qualities continue to impress. Adventurous spirits may enjoy tracking down—in those few shops that specialize in imported records—the recording of Britten's violin concerto made for the (English) Classics for Pleasure label by Rodney Friend, the longtime concertmaster of the London Philharmonic Orchestra. Friend, now the New York Philharmonic's concertmaster, gives the concerto a searing performance.   ∎

November 1963

BRITTEN: War Requiem. Galina Vishnevskaya, soprano; Peter Pears, tenor; Dietrich Fischer-Dieskau, baritone; London Symphony Orchestra, Bach Choir, Highgate School Choir and Melos Ensemble, conducted by Benjamin Britten. London 1255, 2 discs, $11.96. ●

Britten composed the *War Requiem* to commemorate the opening of the rebuilt cathedral in Coventry. The result is one of the most ambitious choral works of the twentieth century. The score is really two pieces of music in one. A large section is devoted to a setting of the *Missa pro Defunctis*—the requiem mass for the dead. Almost equal in length are settings of poems by Wilfred Owen, the well-known English poet, who died in action a week before the 1918 Armistice. For the *Requiem* settings, Britten uses full orchestra, chorus, and soprano solo. For the Owen poems, the scoring is for chamber orchestra, tenor, and baritone. At the very end all groups are coalesced.

The *War Requiem* is a big, impressive work, which has been hailed in many quarters as a masterpiece (though a few dissenting voices have been raised). Its harmonic style is, on the whole, conservative and despite a few patches of dissonance should offer no problems to any listener. Indeed, the soprano

(continued)

solos, with their broad and almost Verdian melodies, could have been written by a composer active three generations ago, as far as harmonic innovation goes. Not that the *War Requiem* is derivative; it decidedly isn't. Even with the conservative harmonic approach, the mind of a very twentieth-century figure is at all times in evidence. The performance here is utterly brilliant—with the exception of Vishnevskaya, who is often extremely shaky in her singing. London has provided brilliant recorded sound, featuring extreme stereo separation.

Comment

Performances of this score are less frequent than when it was new, in the early 1960s. But the music still exerts a powerful emotional and philosophical impact. It is unlikely—Vishnevskaya aside—that we shall ever hear a more persuasive account of the *War Requiem* than in this recorded performance.■

August 1971

BRUCKNER: Symphony No. 1 in C minor. The Vienna Philharmonic Orchestra conducted by Claudio Abbado. London 6706, $5.98.

The "No. 1" is misleading. Before he composed this score, Bruckner wrote at least two other symphonies: one in F minor, known as the "Study Symphony," and one in D minor, identified as the "Symphony Number Zero." With two earlier works under his belt, it's small wonder that by the time he got around to his *First Symphony,* Bruckner had pretty well formulated his symphonic hallmarks. All the characteristic Bruckner traits are here to be heard: the epigrammatic rushing figures in the strings, answered by phrases from the woodwinds; the frequent use of tremolo in the strings; the emphasis on scoring for brass instruments, particularly trombones and tuba; and the attractive dancelike quality of the scherzo movement. Although not one of the most inspired of the Bruckner symphonies, *Symphony No. 1* still has much to recommend it.

It has been recorded previously a couple of times but not with the gentle grace and overall sprightliness that Abbado brings to it. In avoiding the ponderousness that characterizes Bruckner performances of many German-oriented conductors, Abbado sheds a new and welcome light on the music of the composer. At the same time, one could wish for a still brighter spotlight on the inner voices of the orchestration.

The Vienna Philharmonic, of which Abbado is now the principal conductor, plays splendidly for him; a special note of appreciation is due the orchestra's superlative French horn section. And London's recording engineers deliver another of their warm and resonant reproductions of distinctive tonal characteristics.

Comment

Despite the minor reservations, this is a major addition to the Bruckner discography—and a welcome one.   ■

BRUCKNER: Symphony No. 4 in E flat (Romantic). Chicago Symphony Orchestra conducted by Daniel Barenboim. Deutsche Grammophon 2530336, $6.98. ●

This new DG disc is an absolute marvel when heard on superior playback equipment. But the qualification must be emphasized; so great are the dynamic contrasts that any but the best reproducing equipment may have difficulty in handling the sound. But once the qualification has been met, this disc has glow, vibrancy and sonic spread that are impressive indeed.

Barenboim, despite his youth (he is 31), is one of the half-dozen or so most commanding and provocative conductors now before the public. Bruckner's *"Romantic" Symphony*, though gaining in public popularity, is not one of the composer's best. There are glaring structural weaknesses in all the movements, particularly the last one. Thus, it takes a conductor of special quality to hold the work together. Barenboim does so astonishingly well, so that the shifting moods of the work make a powerful impact in his performance. Partly, that is a result of wisely chosen tempos: The first movement and the slow movement have a wispy, dreamlike quality that matches their content beautifully, while the scherzo and the finale have a surging urgency that keeps them from bogging down. But mostly the success of this performance derives from Barenboim's personal commitment to the music and his ability to communicate that commitment to his players and to us the listeners.

Comment

A Barenboim-Chicago Symphony recording of Bruckner's *Ninth Symphony* (DG2530639) is now available; it has many of the strengths evident in the performance of the *Fourth* discussed above. The team of Barenboim and the Chicago Symphony, has in fact undertaken a project that will eventually embrace recordings of all nine Bruckner symphonies. Herbert von Karajan and the Berlin Philharmonic Orchestra also appear to be engaged in all-Bruckner recording cycle, and for the same company, too: Deutsche Grammophon. For all the excellence of the Barenboim Bruckner *Fourth,* it must be admitted that the Karajan–Berlin Philharmonic recording (DG2530674) has special qualities of structural cohesion and sensual splendor.   ■

BRUCKNER: Symphony No. 8 in C minor. The Cleveland Orchestra conducted by George Szell. Columbia M230070, 2 discs, $11.98.

This long, emotionally unkempt symphony reflects both the best and the worst of Bruckner. There are moments of ecstasy and serenity—mostly in the slow movement—as fine as any in symphonic literature. But there are also stretches of repetitive note-spinning, evidence of Bruckner's inability to sustain interest. The present release is one of the last of Szell's recordings with

(continued)

the Cleveland Orchestra before he died in July, 1970, and it does about as much as possible to make the most of Bruckner's virtues. Not everyone will agree with all of Szell's ideas; for example, his unusually slow tempo for the Scherzo movement makes the music lumbering and awkward. But he does manage to hold the whole thing together rather more successfully than most conductors.

Comment

Those who feel that Szell responds too casually to the weight and massive sonorities of this score may be more favorably impressed by the Haitink recording (Philips 6700020; two discs)—a much more traditional approach to the symphony, and one that benefits from fine orchestral reproduction. Karajan's mesmerizing account of the *Eighth*, with the Berlin Philharmonic (Deutsche Grammophon 2707085) is probably the finest recorded performance of a Bruckner symphony currently available. ■

January 1969

CAGE: Concerto for Prepared Piano and Chamber Orchestra; FOSS: Baroque Variations. Yuji Takahashi, piano (in the Cage), with the Buffalo Philharmonic Orchestra conducted by Lukas Foss. Nonesuch 71202, $2.98. ●

The listing above is inadvertently a perfect description of the concerto by John Cage. The solo instrument is indeed in an esthetic cage, completely constrained from its natural speech and music-making powers by the totally nihilistic and non-musical writing. The one-movement affair is divided into three parts, and the total running time of twenty-two minutes seems interminable. There is no form and no reason behind the seemingly random sounds conjured from the instruments in what must surely be a classic example of a musical put-on. It is distressing to find this nonsense treated respectfully by a fine orchestra, an extraordinary pianist, a distinguished conductor, and a dedicated recording company.

Foss' own *Baroque Variations* on the overside of the disc are a contemporary musical "happening." The fanciful and inventive Mr. Foss takes hold of three relatively familiar pieces by Handel, Scarlatti, and Bach and puts them through a musical meat grinder. What emerges is a bizarre mutation and distortion that does nevertheless have its moments of charm and humor. The ultimate in the dismembering of the original scores occurs at the climax of the third piece, *Phorion* (from the Greek word for "stolen goods"). The score directs the conductor to ad lib cues to the several sections of the orchestra successively. The musicians then create all manner of unstructured musical mayhem. The last few minutes of *Phorion* sound as though jack hammers and pneumatic drills were demolishing Buffalo's Kleinhans Auditorium, the site of the performance.

Both performances were recorded and processed with the Dolby audio noise-reduction system, and the two works benefit from it. Note: Only the most carefully balanced pick-up arms will be able to track the explosive ending of *Phorion*.

Comment

Whatever one may feel about these particular pieces, this disc is a reminder of the innovative programming Lukas Foss introduced for Buffalo Philharmonic audiences. Foss's successor in Buffalo, Michael Tilson Thomas, carried on the commitment to innovation. ∎

February 1975

CAGE: Three Dances (for two amplified prepared pianos); REICH: Four Organs (for four electric organs and maracas). Michael Tilson Thomas and Ralph Grierson, keyboards (in the Cage); Michael Tilson Thomas, Ralph Grierson, Roger Kellaway, and Steve Reich, keyboards, and Tom Raney, maracas (in the Reich). Angel S36059, $5.98.

Aficionados of far-out musical thought have a gold mine in this disc. John Cage is the daddy of contemporary Dada, and his *Three Dances*, though nearly 30 years old now, are among his most successful works. In experimenting with piano sonorities, Cage long ago devised his special technique of "preparing" the instrument to alter its sound. That is done by inserting a variety of foreign objects between the strings—nuts, bolts, screws, washers, felt, etc. The two prepared pianos of the *Three Dances* sound very much like a Balinese gamelan ensemble, particularly in the first of the dances. The second dance is a melodic reverie leading into the third, which is a pounding, mechanically rhythmic jungle rite.

Reich's *Four Organs* came about as close to causing riots in Boston's Symphony Hall and New York's Carnegie Hall in recent seasons as has any music composed since Stravinsky's *Rite of Spring* more than a half-century ago. The work consists of a single chord that is repeated over and over, gradually growing longer and longer in duration and subtly changing in rhythmic outline and expanding in chordal structure. Through the entire piece the maracas beat out a constantly repeated eighth-note pattern against the organs. There is no question that the steady repetition numbs the conventional senses after a while, but that is precisely what Reich intends. Those who can accept the premise of the music will enjoy a special, probably rapturous experience. Others may be unable to listen to more than a few minutes of *Four Organs*.

Both Cage and Reich are fortunate in the performances their works receive under the artistic impetus of Michael Tilson Thomas.

Comment

This disc is a unique experience. It will induce many reactions, but certainly not indifference. And there will probably be no middle ground: One will be either totally taken with the material or totally repelled! ∎

CAGE and HILLER: H p s c h d. Antoinette Vischer, Neely Bruce, and David Tudor, harpsichords; **JOHNSTON: Quartet No. 2.** The Composers Quartet. Nonesuch 71224, $2.98. ●

The string quartet by Ben Johnston, a member of the faculty at the University of Illinois, is the big news on this disc. Just under fifteen minutes long, the score is consistently fascinating. Johnston implements his own genuinely creative imagination with an engrossing sound structure of microtones— intervals with very little distance between them. The members of The Composers String Quartet have solved admirably all the problems posed by this very difficult score.

The Cage-Hiller work is another in the series of put-ons that Cage has been putting out for the better part of two decades. In this instance he has pasted fifty-one computer tapes together with harpsichord recordings—and he includes the added fillip of a printout sheet that gives directions for controlling the tone and volume of the separate sound channels in playback. Thus the listener can, to some extent, create his own performance each time he plays the disc by increasing or decreasing or eliminating various parts of the whole. Fun? Well, sure—somewhat like the fun little girls have when they dress their dolls in a variety of mix-and-match ensembles. But art it's not.

Comment

The rage for Cage that was something of a force during the 1960s has now pretty well subsided. What remains is a number of recordings that document Cage's Andy Warhol-like approach to the creation of sound—sometimes structured, sometimes unstructured. There is a certain curiosity value attached to the output of Cage, but his principal importance seems likely to be one of influence rather than accomplishment. ■

CANTELOUBE: Songs of the Auvergne (Vol. II). Netania Davrath, soprano, with orchestra conducted by Pierre de la Roche. Vanguard 2132, $5.98.

On the present disc are an additional fifteen Auvergne songs, which will come as a surprise to many listeners. Canteloube composed five books of these folk-song settings for voice and orchestra. In the 1930s, the Madeleine Grey recording of the Canteloube series achieved wide popularity, and most other singers used the Grey selection. So did Davrath in her first Vanguard set (plus a few songs that Grey did not record). Now we have all of them, and the music of the new recording is as evocative, sophisticated, and charming as the music of the old. Davrath's rather hard-sounding but responsive voice is clearly reproduced. A fine recording, one that will give constant pleasure through the years.

Comment

It is surprising that no other soprano or recording company has seen fit to enter the lists with these songs. One can imagine that a more seductive voice than Davrath's could serve the music, but her superior musical intelligence is welcome indeed. The disc continues to give pleasure. It has now been combined with the better-known first volume of Canteloube arrangements of *Songs of the Auvergne* in a two-disc album (Vanguard 713/4), selling for a bargain price. ■

September 1970

CHAUSSON: Poème for Violin and Orchestra; VIEUXTEMPS: Concerto No. 5 in A minor; SAINT-SAËNS: Introduction and Rondo Capriccioso; WIENIAWSKI: Concert Polonaise in D. Pinchas Zukerman, violin, with the London Symphony Orchestra conducted by Charles Mackerras. Columbia MS7422, $5.98.

This is the second recording by the dazzling twenty-one-year-old Israeli violin virtuoso, Pinchas Zukerman. His debut release on Columbia—the Tchaikovsky and Mendelssohn concerti—revealed him to be that most unusual of instrumentalists: a complete master of his craft whose performing wizardry is mated to a perceptive intelligence and a passionate emotional conviction.

The four works on this disc offer Zukerman an almost complete spectrum of technical display. He seems to meet without effort the manifold virtuoso challenges of the music and to concentrate entirely on the expressive content of each score. As a result, each performance is fully satisfying. Saint-Saëns' charming score comes through with an enchanting playful pixiness; Chausson's more somber work has a remarkable cumulative intensity; Vieuxtemps' lush, classic concerto glows with integrity; and Wieniawski's extroverted romp gets a rousing, no-holds-barred treatment.

Aiding Zukerman in his breathtaking accomplishment is a most sympathetic collaboration by Mackerras and the London Symphony Orchestra. Between them, soloist and conductor have worked out a unanimity of style rarely encountered in today's musical marketplace, where performances all too often seem casually thrown together. Finally, the sound is excellent, except that the solo violin is somewhat overemphasized. But that is a minor blemish in an otherwise extraordinarily successful release.

Comment

The promise implicit in this recording has now been dazzlingly fulfilled. Zukerman is clearly a superstar among today's virtuoso instrumentalists, and his recorded repertoire is constantly growing. He has also begun a promising career as a conductor. ■

March 1973

CHÁVEZ: Soli I, for oboe, clarinet, bassoon and trumpet; Soli II, for woodwind quintet; Soli IV for horn, trumpet and trombone.
(continued)

73

Carlos Chávez is seven years older than Dmitri Shostakovich, but unlike his Russian colleague, he has become increasingly less productive, and what work he has done has become increasingly less meritorious. The three works included on this disc cover a 34-year time span, from 1933 to 1967, but Chávez has apparently written nothing of any great consequence in recent years. Certainly the most recent of these *Soli* (Chávez uses the title *Soli* to describe a collection of solos), the one for brass trio, meanders aimlessly for much of its 11-minute playing time, and interest in its free-form scheme wears out long before the piece ends. The *Soli II*, composed for woodwind quintet in 1961, is more stimulating. But best of all is the *Soli I*, a jaunty, somewhat impertinent score for three winds and trumpet that Chávez wrote in 1933. It has some of the rhythmic and dynamic excitement of the composer's best-known work, his *Sinfonia India* that came three years later. But the piece hardly bears the weight for the expense of the disc as a whole.

Comment

Chávez remained reasonably active almost to the day of his death in August 1978. His performances as a guest conductor with orchestras in this country and abroad were invariably well received. ■

July 1960

CHOPIN: Ballades (4). Artur Rubinstein, piano. RCA LSC2370, $5.98. ▲

Now, all that remains for a complete Rubinstein discography of Chopin are the *B minor Sonata* and the *Études*. This disc marks his first recorded encounter with the *Ballades*, and all one can say is that the playing is prime Rubinstein: big in conception, musically warm and understanding, technically brilliant. The music of these four *Ballades* is among Chopin's greatest, and this disc is by far the preferred interpretation. While the stereo has color, it tends to be too big and even artificial-sounding.

June 1964

CHOPIN: Ballades (4). Witold Malcuzynski, piano. Angel S36146, $5.98.

Considering that the four *Ballades* are among Chopin's most popular compositions and that every pianist plays them, it is surprising how few complete recordings of them there are. Many pianists have recorded one or two, but only a few have taken on all four at a single sitting. Up to now the standard on LP has been the Artur Rubinstein disc. Malcuzynski is not the man to unseat Rubinstein. He offers steady, reliable performances, but they are performances noted more for strength and drive than for poetry and nuance. Rubinstein has the strength plus the poetry. Those who are interested in Malcuzynski, however, will find this disc well recorded (through marred by surface noise), with the music emerging without misrepresentation.

Comment

Malcuzynski's playing lacks the quality of youthful spontaneity that is such a joy in Rubinstein's performances—they are the ones to have.

Rubinstein's complete discography of Chopin piano music lacks only the two sets of *Études, Opus 10* and *Opus 25*. They remain unreleased, although he has undoubtedly recorded them. When they become available, one of the worthiest and most satisfying projects in all of recording literature will then be complete. ∎

September 1965

CHOPIN: Concerto No. 1 in E minor for Piano (Op. 11). Emil Gilels, piano, and Philadelphia Orchestra conducted by Eugene Ormandy. Columbia MS6712, $5.98.

In his way Gilels is a complete pianist—he can do anything at the keyboard. His performance of this popular Chopin concerto, though, has moments that are curiously sluggish. Gilels holds back, as though he does not want to be accused of virtuosity. Thus the passage work often does not have the sparkle and brilliance it should. On the other hand, the slow movement has mood and poetry, and the ending of the last movement goes with all the zip and celerity one can desire. On the whole a fine performance that in spots just misses greatness.

There is a slight trace of distortion at the end of side two that may show up markedly on all but the finest equipment.

March 1967

CHOPIN: Concerto No. 1 in E minor for Piano (Op. 11). Dinu Lipatti, piano, and orchestra. Seraphim 60007 (mono), $2.98.

There is a slight mystery about this record. Dinu Lipatti, the brilliant young Rumanian pianist, was already one of the great msuicians when he died at the age of thirty-three in 1950. Since his death a legend has grown around him. He made a few recordings, and after his death a few off-the-air items were released. Apparently this performance of the Chopin *E minor Concerto,* which is coming out for the first time, is another off-the-air performance. Presumably the conductor and orchestra are under contract to another record company; hence no names are mentioned. Whatever orchestra it is, it's a good one. Lipatti's playing is beautiful. He has an antivirtuoso approach, and the tempi are on the slow side, but the phrasing is aristocratic and the finger work impeccable. It is a very modern way of playing the work. Construction and logic, rather than romanticism, are featured. The recorded sound is clear and quite faithful, considering its date and source.

(continued)

Comment

The Gilels-Ormandy recording has now been transferred to Columbia's low-price Odyssey label (Y32369). A certain elegance and sophistication mark Lipatti's approach to this work, qualities well suited to the music. And considering the age and source of the recording, the sound is amazingly good. Of the many other recorded performances of Chopin's *E minor Concerto,* Rubinstein's (RCA LSC2575) has a rhythmic sparkle and vitality that set it apart, and Pollini's (Seraphim S60066) is a vigorous, headlong account. ∎

November 1959

CHOPIN: Concerto No. 2 in F minor for Piano (Op. 21); Andante Spianato and Grande Polonaise in E flat (Op. 22). Artur Rubinstein, piano, and Symphony of the Air conducted by Alfred Wallenstein. RCA LSC2265, $5.98.

Rubinstein and Chopin are by now synonymous, and there would be few to argue the fact that Rubinstein is the Polish composer's greatest living interpreter. His performances of the *Concerto* and the *Andante Spianato* and *Polonaise* (a work often heard on the concert stage but less familiar in its original form for piano and orchestra) have terrific musical authority and pianistic splendor. In the recording, the solo instrument is very much to the fore, perhaps to the detriment of the ensemble. But this is generally true of the Chopin concerti even in the concert hall. The piano itself is honestly reproduced.

July 1964

CHOPIN: Concerto No. 2 in F minor for Piano (Op. 21); Andante Spianato and Grande Polonaise in E flat (Op. 22); Nocturne in C sharp minor (Posth.). Tamas Vásary, piano, and Berlin Philharmonic Orchestra conducted by Janos Kulka. Deutsche Grammophon 136452, $6.98.

Up to now Vásary's few records have been devoted to Liszt; Vásary is a young Hungarian pianist. Now he turns to Chopin and makes a better impression. He does not have the uninhibited bravura flash for the grand style of Liszt playing, but he does have the poetry and style for Chopin's *F minor Concerto* and *Andante Spianato and Polonaise* (the latter more generally heard as a piano solo, though it was originally composed for piano and orchestra). Vásary displays a singing tone, an ability to color a phrase, flexible rhythm, and very fluent technical equipment (he even makes light of the coda to the last movement, a very tricky and difficult piece of writing). This kind of sensitive playing is not too common among today's young pianists, and one looks forward to more Chopin from this gifted young artist. The stereo sound has life and brilliance.

Comment

Rubinstein's performance clearly has more color, life, and sheer panache than

Vásary can offer. Rubinstein rerecorded the Chopin *F minor Concerto* with Eugene Ormandy and the Philadelphia Orchestra (RCA LSC3055). Strangely, the newer recording is not materially improved in sound; in fact, the 1959 recording is better balanced and suffers less from tonal constriction. Both Rubinstein performances are equally splendid. ∎

March 1966

CHOPIN: Eight Polonaises (Nos. 1-7); Four Impromptus (4) (complete). Artur Rubinstein, piano. RCA LSC7037, 2 discs, $11.96.

The veteran pianist is busy these days rerecording his repertoire. His recording experience with the *Polonaises* goes back to the 1930s, and his previous recording of the *Impromptus* was made some ten years ago. Of the four *Impromptus*, by far the most famous is the *Fantaisie-Impromptu*. Rubinstein has come up with a new edition of the popular work, which includes a few textual changes. He does not play all of the *Polonaises*. Chopin composed some in his youth that are seldom played. In common with most pianists, Rubinstein confines his attention to the first six *Polonaises*, the *Fantaisie-Polonaise*, and the *Andante Spianato and Grande Polonaise*.

He continues to amaze. Nearing eighty years of age, he still plays with the dash and ardor of a young man; and his technique remains a thing of wonder. No better performances of these pieces can be found. The recorded sound here is superb, full and colorful and having depth and quality.

Comment

As with all of Rubinstein's Chopin performances, this disc will continue to be a cherished collector's item. ∎

November 1966

CHOPIN: Fantaisie in F minor; Berceuse; Barcarolle; 3 Nouvelles Études; Bolero; Tarantelle. Artur Rubinstein, pianist. RCA LSC2889, $5.98.

For the most part, this disc contains music that Rubinstein has previously recorded. But it also contains two Chopin works he has never before touched in his long recording career (nor does he appear to have played them in concert for many years, if ever). These are the *Tarantelle* and the *Bolero*, both relatively obscure Chopin pieces, but no less attractive for that. By now, Chopin is almost completely represented by Rubinstein; only one area remains untouched, the two books of Études. If Rubinstein has not recorded them by now, the chances are he never will. This is a pity.

He plays the pieces on this disc with his usual authority, power, poetry,

(continued)

and technical command; nobody around can approach him in Chopin. The disc has subtlety and color but also surface noise.

Comment

Rubinstein, the most popular pianist in the history of recorded music, has given us very nearly his entire performing repertoire in recorded renditions that will constitute a precious legacy for posterity. The most important of all his recordings may well be his consummate interpretations of the Chopin piano music—models of emotional and intellectual insight and of pellucid piano playing. The performances on this disc prove the point. ∎

January 1967

CHOPIN: Nocturnes (21) (complete). Tamas Vásary, piano. Deutsche Grammophon 136486/7, 2 discs, $13.96. Records are available separately, $6.98.

Vásary displays his customary skill and taste in these two discs of all the Chopin *Nocturnes.* He has definite Romantic leanings that once in a while (as in the *F minor Nocturne of Opus 55)* are carried a little to excess. Generally speaking, though, his romanticism is marked by strong control and an avoidance of exaggeration. He gets a great deal of sentiment into his playing without ever becoming sentimental; his rhythm is flexible; and his limpid finger approach is a joy to experience. This young Hungarian pianist may turn out to be one of the great ones. Should you want just one of the discs, Volume I carries the more familiar *Nocturnes,* 1 through 10.

Comment

Vásary is more successful here than in the disc containing Chopin's *F minor Concerto* and several shorter works (see page 76). He captures the mood of each of the *Nocturnes* and communicates.it with conviction. ∎

March 1962

CHOPIN: Polonaise in A flat (Op. 53); Nocturne No. 17; Fantaisie in F minor (Op. 49); Études No. 23 in A minor (Op. 25), No. 11 and No. 3 in E major (Op. 10); Ballade No. 3 in A flat (Op. 47); Waltz No. 7 in C sharp minor (Op. 64, No. 2); Scherzo No. 3 in C sharp minor (Op. 39). Van Cliburn, piano. RCA LSC2576, $5.98. ▲ ●

Cliburn's first solo disc—up to now he has been heard only in concerti—is devoted to Chopin. It is a little disappointing. The playing itself is clear and accurate; Cliburn is a first-rate technician. But musically there is a lack of tension, of phrase build-up, of passion and conviction. One gets the feeling that Cliburn is divorced from the music, so objective is his approach. Why a person of his gifts should be so careful and even noncommittal in his Chopin playing is hard to figure out. The recording is good, though slightly heavy in the bass.

Comment

Time has not dealt more kindly with Cliburn's later solo discs: They all exhibit much the same quality of detachment evident here. How different is this playing from Rubinstein's total and passionate commitment to Chopin! ∎

July 1966

CHOPIN: Twenty-four Préludes (Op. 28, complete); Fantaisie in F minor (Op. 49); Berceuse. Jeanne-Marie Darré, piano. Vanguard 71151, $5.98.

Quite a few pianists, including the redoubtable Artur Rubinstein, have recorded the twenty-four Chopin *Préludes* and the *F minor Fantaisie* (which many consider Chopin's greatest work), but this version by Jeanne-Marie Darré is as good as any.

Her playing has character, personality, and the kind of honest technique (no smearing, no covering with the pedal) that is a joy to encounter. A veteran French pianist, Darré is a long way from the objective modern style. She is a Romanticist (and what other kind of pianist should approach Chopin?) who takes a good deal of liberty without being eccentric, who does not hesitate to follow her own instincts even against the instructions of the text. Since her instincts are never anything but musical, she makes the music convincing. Fine recorded sound, with some surface noise.

Comment

Darré is a highly individual performer infrequently represented as a recording artist. It is good to have her versions of these Chopin masterworks available for study and pleasure. ∎

July 1962

CILEA: Adriana Lecouvreur. Renata Tebaldi, soprano (Adriana); Mario Del Monaco, tenor (Maurizio); Giulietta Simionato, mezzo-soprano (Principessa); Giulio Fioravanti, baritone (Michonnet). L'Accademia di Santa Cecilia, Rome, conducted by Franco Capuana. London 1331, 3 discs, $17.94. ●

It has been years and years since *Adriana Lecouvreur* has been heard at the Metropolitan Opera. Chicago recently had a revival, however, thanks to Renata Tebaldi. The great Italian soprano loves the role, and why shouldn't she? It gives her an opportunity for a resounding death scene, for all kinds of pathos, for lyric singing, and for an unparelleled chance to emote. She
(continued)

wanted to sing it last season in New York, and one reason she did not return to the Met was that management said no. But management has reconsidered. Better Tebaldi with *Adriana* than the Met without Tebaldi.

And so New York will have Tebaldi *and* the Cilea opera next season. The chances are that, no matter how well Tebaldi is recieved, the opera will not be acclaimed. It is a tear-jerker of utterly no force or originality. It is, however, redeemed by one or two pretty tunes. And the Italian opera traditionalists—the hard core who respond to *Andrea Chénier* or *La Gioconda*—will have a field day. Francesco Cilea (1866-1950) knew the human voice and how to write for it.

Tebaldi is in beautiful voice here. The role exactly fits her, and she pours forth golden tone after golden tone. Another great singer in the cast is Simionato—a superlative artist who still retains more than enough voice to make her role of the Principessa convincing and even blood-curdling. Against this level, Del Monaco contributes nothing but a loud voice. Some might be unkind enough to describe his singing as bellowing. The others in the cast are capable, and Capuana is a fine conductor. The recorded stereo sound is extremely fine—resonant, mellow, unforced. As always, London has gone in for a great deal of separation, all of it legitimate here.

Comment

Perhaps even more convincing than the London set—now available as London 13126—is Columbia's recording of this opera, featuring Renata Scotto with James Levine conducting (M334588). It has a thrust and passion that are quite thrilling. The all-star cast includes Elena Obraztsova, Placido Domingo, and Sherrill Milnes—all in quite good voice. ∎

April 1964

COPLAND: Concerto for Clarinet and Orchestra. Benny Goodman and Columbia Symphony Orchestra conducted by Aaron Copland. **COPLAND: Old American Songs, Sets 1 and 2.** William Warfield, baritone, and Columbia Symphony Orchestra conducted by Copland, Columbia MS6497, $5.98.

The *Clarinet Concerto*—lyric, peppy, jazzy toward the end—is one of Copland's most attractive works. It was dedicated to Benny Goodman, who had commissioned the score; and here Goodman plays it with the technique, style, and humor it needs. Equally attractive are Copland's settings of a group of nineteenth-century American songs, some of them with folk characteristics. They are tender, lyric, spirited by turns. Warfield sings them sonorously, with keen musical intelligence. A perfect disc of its kind, and well recorded.

Comment

The concerto now also exists in an alternate coupling of works for clarinet by

Leonard Bernstein, Morton Gould, and Igor Stravinsky. All the works are played by Goodman and conducted by their composers (Columbia MS6805). The latter disc may come to have more historical interest than this release of the concerto with Copland's delightful *American Songs*. ∎

November 1969

COPLAND: A Lincoln Portrait. Gregory Peck, narrator. **KRAFT: Concerto for Four Percussion Soloists and Orchestra; Contextures: Riots-Decade '60.** Los Angeles Philharmonic conducted by Zubin Mehta. London 6613, $5.98.

Mehta conducts a heartfelt Copland performance and Peck is a dignified if somewhat understated narrator in this latest addition to the growing list of recordings of this affecting score. More than a quarter of a century has now passed since *A Lincoln Portrait* was written; it still is one of Copland's best works and this, surely, is one of its most satisfying performances. The two works by William Kraft that occupy the remaining space on the disc will serve to introduce this composer to a wide public. Both scores received their first performances within the past few years at the hands of Mehta and the Los Angeles Philharmonic (in which Kraft serves as principal percussion player); hence these recorded editions may be considered definitive. As befits the work of an expert player, the *Concerto* reveals a sure-handed and inventive imagination at work. The score consists of three brief movements, including a fanciful and rhythmically dazzling middle movement. This concerto is among the most beguiling recent scores by American composers.

The other work on the disc, *Contextures*, is much more self-conscious, dealing as it does with contemporary social unrest. The composer himself has written: "As the work progressed, the correspondence between the fabric of music and the fabric of society became apparent and the allegory grew in significance. So I found myself translating social aspects into musical techniques." During the course of his work on the score, Kraft decided to incorporate two films as accompaniments to parts of the music, so that a mixed-media production resulted. Finally, the news of the assassination of Dr. Martin Luther King came on the afternoon of the scheduled first performance and a new ending for the score was written to commemorate Dr. King's death. Kraft is now at work on a companion piece that will incorporate a spoken text taken from writings and speeches of Dr. King. *Contextures* lacks the conceptual unity of the percussion concerto, but it, too, is an impressive demonstration of Kraft's compositional abilities and his powers of communication on a level of great intensity. He is obviously a composer to watch.

London's engineers have contributed sound reproduction of wide dynamic range and great depth.

Comment

The Kraft concerto—an extraordinarily brilliant performance—has given listeners much pleasure since this review appeared. Kraft's output in recent years

(continued)

has become more prolific. Increasingly, his stature as a composer grows. ∎

March 1973

COUPERIN, François and Louis: Harpsichord Pieces. Albert Fuller, harpsichord. Nonesuch H71265, $2.98.

Included on this disc is some of the most inventive and colorful keyboard music of 17th-century France. The first side has music by François Couperin, called Couperin "Le Grand" to distinguish him from his illustrious uncle, Louis Couperin, whose music fills the second side.

The power and imagination of François Couperin are immediately in evidence on the first band on Side 1, which consists of two musettes. A musette is a dance in which a persistent bass note imitates the sound of a kind of French bagpipe, also called a musette. The harpsichord in these pieces manages to achieve an amazingly close resemblance to the sound of the musette and reminds the listener that the French countryside in the 17th and 18th centuries resounded to bagpipe playing.

The remaining items have perhaps less impact than the two opening musettes, but they nevertheless exhibit the wide range of expression of which both Couperins were capable. Louis Couperin even anticipated the improvisational features of jazz and some contemporary concert music by leaving to the performer some decisions regarding rhythm and meter.

Albert Fuller is one of America's leading scholars and performers, and he infuses these works throughout with enthusiasm, vitality and stylistic authority. The reproduction of the harpsichord is vivid.

Comment

Although this Couperin repertoire is rather esoteric, the disc is highly successful in projecting Fuller's stylistic mastery. The recorded sound of the harpsichord is larger than life as heard here, but it is immensely exciting. ∎

November 1972

DAVIDOVSKY: Synchronisms No. 6; Electronic Study No. 3; Synchronisms No. 5; Robert Miller, pianist, and The Group for Contemporary Music conducted by Harvey Sollberger. **KOLB: Trobar Clus; Solitaire for Piano and Vibes.** The Contemporary Chamber Players of the University of Chicago conducted by Barbara Kolb (in Trobar Clus); Cheryl Seltzer, piano, and Richard Fitz, vibraphone (in Solitaire). Turnabout TVS34487, $2.98.

Everything on this disc is informed with a sense of imaginative adventure. All the works except Barbara Kolb's *Trobar Clus* (the name comes from an early French antecedent of the rondo) include electronic sounds. Mario

Davidovsky's *Electronic Study No. 3* employs electronics only; the others have electronics in conjunction with instrumental sound.

Davidovsky's *Synchronisms No. 6* was awarded the 1971 Pulitzer Prize in Music. It is a fanciful combination of piano music and electronically synthesized sounds, and it may well be the composer's crowning achievement in the medium thus far. *Electronic Study No. 3* and *Synchronisms No. 5* (for percussion ensemble and electronic sounds) reflect some of the same compositional goals—combining of real and fantasy elements into a collage and then separating them, with the result that the works develop a high degree of tension that is then resolved.

One also finds tension and resolution in Kolb's *Trobar Clus*, but it is her *Solitaire* that leaves the most lasting impression. The work weaves an enchanting, dreamlike effect, the sonorities of piano, vibraphone and tape intermix and collide hypnotically, and through the piece there weaves from time to time quotations from a Chopin prelude that heighten the transitory, wispy feeling.

All the works are given first-rate performances and sound reproduction, so that this release adds impressively to Turnabout's catalog of contemporary American music.

Comment

This disc continues to be stimulating and absorbing. Both Davidovsky and Kolb have gone on to give us music of substantial merit, including some orchestral pieces without any electronic effects. However, the works included on this disc are important as way stations that trace the development of these particular composers. ∎

April 1974

DEBUSSY: Fantasy for Piano and Orchestra; Rhapsody for Clarinet and Orchestra; Rhapsody for Saxophone and Orchestra. Marylène Dosse, piano, Serge Dangain, clarinet, Jean-Marie Londeix, saxophone, with the Orchestra of Radio Luxembourg conducted by Louis de Froment. Candide CE31069, $3.98.

All three of these works are occasional pieces, minor manifestations of Debussy's genius. The *Fantasy for Piano and Orchestra* was written about six years before the composer's *Prelude to the Afternoon of a Faun*, the score that propelled him into celebrity. In all but title it is a piano concerto in three movements, the last two of which are connected without pause. Debussy was not satisfied with the *Fantasy* and did not allow it to be published during his lifetime, but his unmistakable style and color are readily identifiable.

The *Clarinet Rhapsody* is a fairly late work (1910), composed as an examination piece for clarinet students at the Paris Conservatory. It has far transcended the original intent and has become one of the basic staples of the still-meager repertory for clarinet and orchestra. The *Saxophone Rhapsody* resulted from a commission by Elisa Hall, a Boston-based saxophonist who

(continued)

wanted a new work for her instrument. So cavalier was Debussy about fulfilling the commission that he did not complete the piece. He merely sent Mrs. Hall a sketched but unfinished work with piano accompaniment instead of the contracted-for orchestral accompaniment. Not until a year after Debussy's death was the score completed and orchestrated by his younger colleague, Jean Jules Roger-Ducasse.

Performances of all three works on this disc are serviceable if not inspired.

Comment

The inspiration for putting these three works together came from this Candide pressing. The late Jean Martinon, in his recordings of the complete orchestral music of Debussy, followed Candide's lead. His performances, which benefited from far more detailed sound reproduction and better orchestra playing, are far more communicative. His piano soloist in the *Fantasy* is the accomplished Aldo Ciccolini; interestingly, in the *Clarinet* and *Saxophone Rhapsodies* he employs the same soloists who appear on the Candide disc—they are, though, far more inspired in their collaborations with Martinon (Angel S37065). ∎

November 1966

DEBUSSY: La Mer; Première rapsodie for Clarinet; Khamma. L'Orchestre de la Suisse Romande conducted by Ernest Ansermet, with Robert Gugholz, clarinet (in the *Rapsodie*). London 6437, $5.98.

The oddity on this record is *Khamma,* a work almost never heard (this is the only available recording of it). A "dance-legend," it was intended as a dance vehicle for Maud Allan. Debussy was profoundly uninterested in the score and even went so far as to tell Charles Koechlin that he should compose it and that he, Debussy, would sign it. (The program notes to this disc avoid that bit of information.)

As things went, Debussy did write a piano score, and Koechlin orchestrated it. Yet the work is curiously interesting, very Debussian in its harmonies, with some material that is extremely intense. A strange, moody, nebulous piece.

The *Première rapsodie for Clarinet* is also little known, though not the rarity that *Khamma* is, and it is well played here, by Robert Gugholz, presumably the first clarinet of Suisse Romande. *La Mer* is, of course, the big piece on this disc. It receives a fine, steady performance, though not a very exciting one. The sound is a little flat and muddy, without the brightness and presence that London has given to its best orchestral recordings.

September 1968

DEBUSSY: La Mer; Prélude à l'après-midi d'un Faune (Prelude to the Afternoon of a Faun); Jeux—Poème dansé. New Philharmonia Orchestra conducted by Pierre Boulez. Columbia MS7361, $5.98. ●

In his developing international career as a conductor, Boulez has specialized to some extent in the music of Debussy. But these performances are curiously unsatisfying. To be sure, all three works come through with unusual clarity: The rhythms are well defined and the orchestral textures are meticulously dissected. But somewhere along the way the essence of the music has been lost. The surge and drama of *La Mer,* the sensuous evanescence of the *Faun,* and the interweaving of disparate textures in *Jeux* are vitiated by Boulez' detached objectivity—an under-the-microscope treatment that renders the scores impotent.

Comment

It is curious how fads and fashions affect even concert repertoire. A decade or two ago *La Mer* was among the most frequently performed of all orchestral scores; today it is becoming something of a rarity in the concert hall. Both Toscanini (RCA VIC1246) and Giulini (Angel S35977) find more color and atmosphere in the work than does Ansermet, but in any case the principal interest in the London disc is the overside, particularly *Khamma.*

The analytical objectivity manifest in Boulez's Debussy performances continue to characterize his music-making. In certain repertoire, this objectivity has virtues. But here it is inappropriate, making the Boulez recording deficient in many of the most important areas of a conductor's responsibility: emotional communication, breadth, and warmth. ∎

September 1965

DEBUSSY: Pelléas et Mélisande. Camille Maurane, baritone (Pelléas); Erna Spoorenberg, soprano (Mélisande); George London, bass-baritone (Golaud); Guus Hoekman, bass (Arkel); Josephine Veasey, mezzo-soprano (Geneviève); Rosine Brédy, soprano (Yniold). L'Orchestre de la Suisse Romande and Geneva Grand Theatre Chorus conducted by Ernest Ansermet. London 1379, 3 discs, $17.94.

Those who do not know this opera must be warned that it is something special: delicate, without arias as such, with the singers operating in long stretches of recitative, with the orchestra supplying most of the commentary. To most Americans, the only well-known member of this cast will be George London—not counting, of course, the famous conductor Ernest Ansermet. It turns out that the other principals are very fine—idiomatic in style, convincing in characterization. This may not be one's dream performance of *Pelléas et Mélisande*—it lacks the magic and haunting color that would make it unforgettable—but it is a fine one. The major credit for its success must go to Ansermet, now eighty years old. He projects the delicate orchestral part with complete success. This music is in his very bones; he renders it with a degree of subtlety and imagination not shown by the singers, well as they handle their parts. This is the best-recorded *Pelléas et Mélisande* of the current versions, and the only one available in stereo. As usual with London discs, the engineers have taken full advantage of the stereophonic medium. There is a

(continued)

good deal of separation (Mélisande's first words, *"Ne me touchez pas,"* are heard from the extreme right) and even a bit of gimmickry, as in the grotto scene. None of this sounds artificial, though.

Comment

Ansermet is no longer with us, but this set of Debussy's vaporous opera can well stand as the conductor's finest memorial. A more recent Columbia stereo recording of the opera (Columbia M330119) has Pierre Boulez as conductor, but the Ansermet performance remains preferable, thanks to its personal involvement. ■

February 1971

DEBUSSY: Three Nocturnes; RAVEL: Rapsodie espagnole. The London Symphony Orchestra and the BBC Women's Chorus (in the Debussy) conducted by Leopold Stokowski. Seraphim S60104, $2.98.

These performances, among Stokowski's finest on discs, were recorded about ten years ago, when Stokowski was recording for Angel. They appeared at that time on the company's high-price label and now return as budget reissues. The shimmering sensuousness of both scores evokes from Stokowski a parallel response, which he transmits most tellingly to the orchestra.

Though generally well balanced, the reproduction in some places reveals its age. One wishes for more richness and resonance in the climaxes of both scores, and there is a patch of very obtrusive echo in *Fêtes,* the second of the Debussy *Nocturnes,* just before the street procession. No other budget label couples these works, however, and the blemishes are really minor in light of the very major attractions of Stokowski's interpretations.

August 1971

DEBUSSY: Three Nocturnes; Printemps; Première rapsodie for Clarinet. The New Philharmonia Orchestra conducted by Pierre Boulez, with the John Alldis Choir (in the third *Nocturne*) and Gervase De Peyer, clarinet (in the *Rapsodie*). Columbia M30483, $5.98.

This is the third volume of Debussy orchestral music recorded by Boulez. He has also recorded Debussy's only opera, *Pelléas et Mélisande.* He has stated that Debussy "is the only French composer who is universal, at least in the nineteenth and twentieth centuries." Add that all together and you get the idea that Debussy's music is something special to Boulez.

But not special enough, in our opinion, to bring out the best in Debussy. There can be little quarrel with the clarity of texture achieved in the Boulez performances. That clarity, however, is apt to strike the listener as cold and impersonal. In his preoccupation with orchestral timbre and color, Boulez produces a homogenization of ensemble sound lacking the sensual splendor that can be elicited from a symphony orchestra.

The superb English clarinetist, Gervase De Peyer, plays Debussy's *Clarinet Rhapsody* brilliantly, and Boulez' way with the orchestral portion of the work does it no damage. But there are many more colorful recordings available of the *Nocturnes*—among them those by Giulini, Monteux, and Stokowski. And the Munch recording of *Printemps* has greater vitality. To the credit of this recording, its sound is clean and well balanced.

Comment

The Stokowski is one of a series of extraordinary recordings produced in the glorious Indian summer of the Maestro's conducting career. Other remarkable recordings include his renditions of Tchaikovsky's *Fifth Symphony* (London 21017), Stravinsky's *Firebird Suite* (London 21026), and Ravel's *Second Suite* from his *Daphnis and Chloe Ballet* (London 21059).

July 1966

DELIUS: Concerto for Cello; Songs of Farewell; A Song Before Sunrise. Jacqueline Du Pré, cello; Royal Choral Society; Royal Philharmonic Orchestra conducted by Sir Malcolm Sargent. Angel S36285, $5.98.

Lesser-known Delius occupies this disc. The *Cello Concerto* is a long, rhapsodic, one-movement work very much in the spirit of the *Violin Concerto*. *Songs of Farewell* are settings of Whitman poems, and *A Song Before Sunrise* is a lovely picture for orchestra. Delius, one of the most personal of all composers, seems to arouse an equally personal reaction in most listeners. Some adore his music; others are thoroughly bored. It is music that requires a special taste, being Romantic, loosely organized, impressionistic, and richly sensuous. The performances here are splendid. There is a slight drift in the cello sound, which varies between dead center and left.

Comment

These are the only available recordings of these selections—and all are exemplary. If memory serves, this was the first performance by Jacqueline Du Pré to be released in this country; thus the disc has an added historical interest. ◾

March 1962

DONIZETTI: Lucia di Lammermoor. Joan Sutherland, soprano (Lucia); Renato Cioni, tenor (Edgardo); Robert Merrill, baritone (Ashton); Cesare Siepi, bass (Raimondo). L'Accademia di Santa Cecilia, Rome, conducted by John Pritchard. London 1327, 3 discs, $17.94.

(continued)

The primary interest here is, of course, in Joan Sutherland, who created a furor earlier this season in her Metropolitan Opera debut. She sang the role of Lucia, though in a slightly different version than she does on these records. London has done something of a restoration, with traditional cuts opened up. Included on a separate band on the last side of the album is a forgotten aria that sopranos used to sing in the first act of *Lucia*. Sutherland is in magnificient voice, and she brings back a vanished tradition of coloratura singing—a tradition in which the soprano has a big voice, an equally big technique, and a complete readiness to interpolate cadenzas and the like. Her singing in the famous "Mad Scene" puts in the shade the work of all contemporary sopranos who have essayed the role. The other singers in this recording are good, though the tenor is not the most polished or subtle of artists. And since the conducting is in competent hands (Pritchard is an English conductor who happens to know the Italian style very well), this *Lucia* is by far the best version ever recorded. The recorded sound is admirable.

Comment

Several performances recorded later have virtues that are absent here. Beverly Sills is a more affecting and moving Lucia (ABC ATS20006), but she lacks Sutherland's sheer sensual abandon. Sutherland, in her rerecording of the opera (London 13103) plays the role better than she did the first time around and enjoys Pavarotti, Milnes, and Ghiaurov, among others, as partners. Finally, Montserrat Caballé's recording (Philips 6703080), although deficient in drama, attempts to clear up and correct the many errors that have crept into the printed portions of the music over the years. ■

September 1967

DONIZETTI: Lucrezia Borgia. Montserrat Caballé, soprano (Lucrezia); Ezio Flagello, bass (Alfonso); Alfredo Kraus, tenor (Gennaro); Shirley Verrett, mezzo-soprano (Orsino). RCA Italiana Orchestra conducted by Jonel Perlea. RCA LSC6176, 3 discs, $17.94.

This is the first recording in history of the seldom-heard Donizetti opera; it has been washed ashore by the postwar interest in bel-canto opera. It is not a very good work, and its libretto is even more preposterous than the majority of its kind. It does provide an opportunity for florid singing—provided the singers are around. It cannot be said that the ones here are up to the task. Caballé has a fine lyric voice, but it is not flexible enough for coloratura singing, and when the music becomes difficult her singing is labored and uncomfortable. The same applies to almost everybody in the album. There's no point in singling out sinners. If bel-canto opera cannot have a combination of utmost technical brilliance coupled to utmost beauty of tone, it becomes a dismal bore, and that is the case here. Thus the album can be recommended only to the curious or to diehard bel-canto collectors.

Comment

Perhaps Caballé undertook this recording assignment too soon in her international career. One hopes that she may have an opportunity to rerecord the role, for it offers many musical and dramatic challenges. ∎

January 1973

DUKAS: The Sorcerer's Apprentice; SAINT-SAËNS: Danse Macabre; CHABRIER: España; MUSSORGSKY–RIMSKY-KORSA-KOV: A Night on Bald Mountain. The Philadelphia Orchestra conducted by Eugene Ormandy. RCA ARD10002, $5.98. ▲ ●

RAVEL: Bolero; TCHAIKOVSKY: Marche Slave; BIZET: Preludes to Acts 1 and 4 of Carmen; VERDI: Overture from La Forza del Destino; VON SUPPÉ: Poet and Peasant Overture. The Los Angeles Philharmonic Orchestra under Zubin Mehta. London XPS613, $5.98. ●

These two discs contain between them a veritable classical hit parade. The 10 works are all long-time favorites of concert audiences the world over, and all of them combine rich melodic invention with rhythmic vitality to create sparkling, exciting music.

It takes a virtuoso orchestra to do full justice to all these pieces. And fortunately, both the Philadelphia Orchestra and the Los Angeles Philharmonic rise to the occasion. In the matter of interpretation, Mehta is more uniformly successful than Ormandy. Mehta's *Bolero* is finely gauged and measured and he treats the score with the genuine respect that is too often absent from *Bolero* performances. His *Marche Slave* is straight-forward and robust. The preludes to the first and fourth acts of *Carmen* have dynamic thrust, and Mehta fully projects the dramatic values of the Verdi and von Suppé overtures.

Ormandy has his ups and downs. He gives his best performances in *A Night on Bald Mountain* and *Danse Macabre*; both are vigorous, colorful and uninhibited. Those qualities are emphasized in *Danse Macabre* by concertmaster Norman Carol, who plays the prominent violin solos. But one feels a curious remoteness in Chabrier's *España* and Dukas's *The Sorcerer's Apprentice*. And the *España* performance is further disfigured by a rhythmic rigidity that all but nullifies the music's bounce and élan.

The RCA disc, incidentally, is one of that company's first releases in its newly developed four-channel stereo system. The system is compatible in that records can be played on either four-channel or two-channel equipment. Since few readers are likely to have the new four-channel equipment, we listened to this disc on stereo equipment. Its sound in stereo is among the best yet accomplished in Philadelphia by RCA.

Comment

What was not known at the time of writing of the original review was the fact that this recording by Mehta and the Los Angeles Philharmonic Orchestra

(continued)

served as the musical soundtrack for the Academy Award-winning short film, *Bolero*. As examples of orchestral virtuosity, however, both of these discs are winners. ■

January 1967

DVOŘÁK: Carnival Overture; Slavonic Dances in C and A flat (Op. 46, Nos. 1 and 3); SMETANA: Overture and Three Dances from The Bartered Bride; Moldau. New York Philharmonic conducted by Leonard Bernstein. Columbia MS6879, $5.98. ▲ ●

Bernstein has put together a disc of popular Czech music: light, charming material. The music will hold no surprises for anybody, though occasionally the performances might. Here and there, as in the *A flat Slavonic Dance*, Bernstein takes overlanguishing tempi and goes in for wild exaggerations. The interpretations in such cases end up being merely cute. For the most part, though, Bernstein conducts with his usual bounce, and the disc is a very pleasant one. The recorded sound is vibrant and colorful.

Comment
Bernstein once remarked that in his early years of musical awareness he stood in awe of Arthur Fiedler, the conductor of the Boston Pops Orchestra, and of the repertoire normally regarded as Pops material. Since then, Bernstein has often taken trips into the Pops repertoire, generally with very happy results—as is the case here. ■

May 1976

DVOŘÁK: Cello Concerto in B minor. Lynn Harrell, cello, with the London Symphony Orchestra conducted by James Levine. RCA ARL11155, $6.98. ▲ ●

DVOŘÁK: Slavonic Dances (complete); Carnival Overture. The Cleveland Orchestra conducted by George Szell. Odyssey Y233524 (2 discs), $7.96. ●

In many ways, Antonin Dvořák is the most undervalued of 19th-century composers, because we know only a small part of his large musical output. These two releases represent some of his best-known work.

In tackling Dvořák's *Cello Concerto*, a touchstone of the literature for cello and orchestra, the team of Harrell and Levine is competing with some of the most formidable names in contemporary music: Casals and Szell (Seraphim 60240), Du Pré and Barenboim (Angel S36046), Fournier and Szell (Deutsche Grammophon 138755), Rose and Ormandy (Columbia MS6714),

Rostropovich and Boult (Seraphim S60136), and Starker and Dorati (Mercury SR75045). The approach of Harrell and Levine is thoughtful and penetrating, with special emphasis on the score's rhapsodic quality. Tempi tend to be generally slow. Some of the music's heroic vigor may be sacrificed in the process, but the interpretation is reasonable. The orchestra's playing and the recorded sound are fine. It must be added, though, that the Rostropovich-Boult and earlier Casals-Szell recordings on the budget-priced Seraphim label are both better buys.

This is the third time around for Szell's fiery treatment of the *Slavonic Dances*. First released as a two-disc set on Columbia's subsidiary Epic label, the dances were later reissued as a single Columbia disc minus the repeats. The latest two-disc incarnation with the repeats restored is best of all, and a distinct bargain at Odyssey's budget price. Szell is the master of every mood and color in these remarkable *Dances* and in the *Carnival Overture*, which rounds out the album. Performance and sound quality are good.

Comment

In a subsequent performance of Dvořák's *Cello Concerto*, Rostropovich enters the lists for the fourth time—this latest recording (Angel S37457) marking a collaboration with Carlo Maria Giulini and the London Philharmonic Orchestra. Harrell and Rostropovich both deliver thoughtful, impassioned accounts of the score, and Levine and Giulini both give penetrating orchestral performances. What probably tips the balance in favor of the Rostropovich disc is the fact that it includes a fine rendering by the same artists of Saint-Saëns's *First Cello Concerto* as a bonus. ∎

November 1972

DVOŘÁK: Czech Suite; VORISEK: Symphony in D. The English Chamber Orchestra conducted by Charles Mackerras. Philips SAL6500203, $6.98.

Though born in the United States, Charles Mackerras spent his youth in Australia and developed his career in Europe, where he is now music director of London's Sadler's Wells Opera. He has conducted in the United States occasionally, but his work is known here principally through recordings on various labels. His recorded work reveals him as a musician of broad scope, covering both operatic and concert literature. His particular favorites are preclassic music and Czech music of all periods. In the preclassic category may be listed his several superlative recordings of music of Handel (notably his account of *Messiah* —Angel S3705). His interest in Czech music is demonstrated by his championing of the operas of the Bohemian composer, Leos Janáček, who wrote in the late 19th and early 20th centuries.

The disc under consideration offers a happy combination of works from both areas of Mackerras's specialization. Jan Hugo Vorisek was a preclassic Czech composer who lived in Vienna from the age of 22 to his early death a dozen years later. This *Symphony in D* —his only symphony—shows Vorisek

(continued)

as an expert craftsman in the early 19th-century tradition; beyond that, the symphony is infused with a richness of invention and melodic inspiration that are reminiscent of Schubert. Vorisek possessed an uncommon ability to blend orchestral timbres, particularly those of strings and woodwinds. The *Symphony in D* is in the classical four-movement pattern: a vigorous, propulsive opening; a slow, meditative second movement; a robust, peasantlike scherzo; and a soaring concluding movement. This distinguished symphony deserves a place in the active symphonic repertory.

Dvořák's *Czech Suite*, though not so esoteric as the Vorisek symphony, is still something of a discovery also. Its five brief movements contain many folk-derived melodies, including such indigenous Czech dances as a polka and a furiant. This polka, incidentally, is one of Dvořák's most beguiling creations—a wistful D minor main section with a contrasting, lilting trio in D major.

To both works Mackerras brings exactly the right touch of elegance and ease, and the English Chamber Orchestra plays superlatively for him. This is one of the most worthwhile record releases of recent months.

Comment

Mackerras continues to be one of the most interesting conductors now active. An acknowledged master of baroque performing practice, he has enriched the recording catalogs with many illuminating performances of music from that period, particularly operas and oratorios by Handel. His other great specialty—Czech music—shows to brilliant advantage in this disc. In the same vein, Mackerras's sensitive and deeply felt conducting of Janáček's opera, *Katya Kabanova* (London 12109), may well reward the adventurous listener. ∎

April 1964

DVOŘÁK: Quartets (Vol. II). Kohon String Quartet. Vox SVBX550, 3 discs, $9.95.

Last year Vox started a series devoted to all of the Dvořák string quartets, played by the Kohon group. The recently issued Vol. II contains four additional quartets. One of them, the *American (Opus 96 in F major)*, is very familiar. Two of them, the *A flat (Opus 105)* and *G major (Opus 106)*, are less familiar. They were Dvořák's last two quartets, and most connoisseurs consider them his greatest. Then there is in this album the *A major (Opus 2)*, which should be a novelty even to Dvořák experts. It was published only as late as 1947 and is an early work, composed in 1862 (the *American* dates from 1893, the last two from 1895). The *A major* as originally written is a very long work, and Vox is very honest in its presentation. All of the cuts taken by the Kohon Quartet (most of these cuts sanctioned by the composer) are carefully detailed in the program notes. The *A major Quartet* has some lovely moments in it, though on the whole it lacks the spontaneity of Dvořák's best music. The *American*, which is much more Czech than American, needs no description. Both of the last two quartets are large-thewed, nationalistic, full of fine melody, rich harmony, and bracing rhythm. A highly recommended album, well played by the Kohon Quartet. The recorded stereo sound favors extreme separation, but the final blend is good and is an accurate reproduction of the Kohon sound—a little lacking in sensuous appeal but strong and direct.

Comment

Dvořák is perhaps the most underrated composer of the nineteenth century. The Vox albums devoted to recordings of all his string quartets are invaluable in demonstrating the real importance of Dvořák in the history of music. ∎

September 1966

DVOŘÁK: Quintet in A major. Peter Serkin, piano; Alexander Schneider and Felix Galimir, violins; Michael Tree, viola; David Soyer, cello. Vanguard S288, $2.98.

The loveliest of piano quintets, and one of the loveliest pieces of chamber music ever written, here receives a nice, free performance by a group of expert musicians. Schneider and his colleagues (Peter Serkin is the son of Rudolf, and all of the players are regulars at Marlboro, the chamber music center dominated by the elder Serkin) go about it with plenty of leeway in matters of phrase and rhythm. Some unorthodoxies are present, but these are unorthodoxies only in terms of the severe attitude characteristic of most present-day musicians. Schneider tries to spark a more Romantic view, and he and the others do not hesitate to make long ritards, or to use rubato effects, or to change tempo as the expression demands. As a result, some may call the performance mannered. But it seems to work up to the end of the last movement. Only there does an artificial feeling enter; the section before the coda is too drawn out. Elsewhere the playing is braced, and young Serkin's work is consistently spirited as well as pianistically elegant. The recorded sound is excellent.

Comment

There are nearly a half-dozen other recordings of this ebullient score, but none has greater joy and spontaneity. Now that this performance is available in Vanguard's low-price Everyman series, its attraction is even greater. ∎

September 1960

DVOŘÁK: Requiem. Maria Stader, soprano; Sieglinde Wagner, alto; Ernst Haefliger, tenor; Kim Borg, bass; Czech Choir and Czech Philharmonic Orchestra conducted by Karel Ancerl. Deutsche Grammophon 2707005, 2 discs, $13.96.

(continued)

Seldom heard, this *Requiem* is a work of dignity, strength, and tenderness. It also has a few passages of sheer academism, but not enough to take away from the score's good points. Dvořák composed this music in his international style; there is very little or none of the Czech nationalism for which he largely stands. The work receives an elegant performance. Nowhere does the solo singing fall below a high level; and Ancerl, who has been conducting the Czech Philharmonic since the war years (World War II, that is), is obviously a musician of imagination and technical command. The recorded sound is not so glamorous as in the Berlioz set also reviewed here (see page 43) but is in its way equally fine. It has velvety texture, smoothness, and brilliance without being overpowering. Some distortion creeps into the end of the *Quam olim Abrahae* fugue on side three; otherwise the recording can be highly praised. The Dvořák is a quieter, far less sensational and melodramatic work than the Berlioz *Requiem*, but in the long run it may prove more satisfactory as a musical experience.

Comment

This fine recording has been superseded by the more recent and even more convincing performance conducted by István Kertész (London CSA1281), which is luminescent in its tonalities. (Ancerl, by the way, became the conductor of the Toronto Symphony Orchestra after the Russian invasion of Czechoslovakia in 1968.) ■

November 1973

DVOŘÁK: String Quartet in C, Opus 61; Terzetto, Opus 74. The Guarneri Quartet. RCA ARL10082, $5.98.

Just as Dvořák is the most underrated symphonist of the 19th century, so is he perhaps the most underrated chamber-music composer of that period. In mastery of form, spontaneity, and directness of expression, the Dvořák string quartets rank as part of the foundation of the literature—and yet many of them are all but unknown.

The C *major Quartet* is one of the best of the lot. A profoundly lyrical and intense slow movement and a playful scherzo are framed by a vigorous opening movement and a finale of rhythmic and melodic charm. The *Terzetto*, a later work in four brief movements that ends in an impressive set of ten variations on a brief theme, is a trio (no cello). It is good to have available a virtuoso performance of this bit of real Dvořák esoterica, but the *Terzetto* cannot be called one of Dvořák's more inspired compositions.

The members of the Guarneri Quartet have been making something of a specialty of the music of Dvořák: With Artur Rubinstein they have recorded the composer's *Piano Quartet* and *Piano Quintet,* and they also have to their credit a passionate recording of the *Quartet in A flat, Opus 105*. To both the C *major Quartet* and the *Terzetto* they bring a nervous intensity that is fine in the febrile moments of the first and last movements of the quartet but is less appropriate when easy relaxation and charm are called for—as in the first movement of the *Terzetto*.

The members of the quartet, incidentally, played a game of musical chairs in the *Terzetto*. For violinist Arnold Steinhardt played the viola part, violist Michael Tree played second violin, and first violin was played by John Dalley, who normally plays second violin.

Comment

This quartet is obviously one of the most intense and personal of Dvořák's chamber music compositions. Therefore, it is especially puzzling that this disc should now be the only single-record account of this great score. Moreover, there is only one other performance available under any label: that of the Kohon String Quartet in a three-record Vox Box (SVBX549) containing four other Dvořák quartets. In flair and style, the Guarneri performance is superior to that of the Kohon. ■

August 1972

DVOŘÁK: Symphony No. 8 in G, Opus 88. The Hamburg Philharmonic Orchestra conducted by Charles Mackerras. Nonesuch H71262, $2.98.

Charles Mackerras is a Schenectady-born conductor who spent his formative years in Australia and then went to Europe to pursue his career. For a number of years he has been one of the principal conductors on the staff of the Hamburg State Opera, but his activities have expanded recently and next season he will make his debut with New York's Metropolitan Opera Company.

He has made a special study of the music of Czechoslovakia and is an expert on music by Czech composers. This disc of Dvořák's *G major Symphony* reflects the conductor's affinity and love for the music: It is a fine blend of rhapsodic lyricism and robust ardor. Unfortunately, however, it cannot compete with the best records of this work because the Hamburg Philharmonic Orchestra is not in a class with the world's best. The orchestra here sounds undermanned and sometimes strained by the requirements of Dvořák's score. Szell's recording of this work with the Cleveland Orchestra (Angel S36043), made just a few months before his death in the summer of 1970, remains the most recommendable.

Comment

Mackerras has not yet had the American career that his great gifts should earn him. It is probably only a matter of time before—as rumor has it—one of the country's leading symphony orchestras names him its music director. ■

February 1977

DVOŘÁK: Symphony No. 9 in E minor, "From the New World." Orchestre de Paris conducted by Georges Prêtre. Connoisseur Society CS2108, $6.98. ●

(continued)

About a dozen years ago Georges Prêtre seemed headed for an international career as a major conductor. His commitments in Europe were very impressive. He was a conductor at New York's Metropolitan Opera. He made guest appearances and recordings with the Boston Symphony and Chicago Symphony Orchestras. But then some disturbing tendencies began to mar his performances, chiefly a rhythmic slackness bordering on the perverse at times. His career went into rapid eclipse.

This disc, one of the first by Prêtre to be released here in some time, shows that he is once again a conductor to be reckoned with. His performance of Dvořák's best-known symphony is by turns tender, passionate, propulsive, and deeply felt. There is no trace of the willful and capricious wrong-headedness that had marked some of his earlier work. And he coaxes playing of superb discipline and intenstiy from the Orchestre de Paris.

The EMI engineers deliver sound that is detailed and extremely wide in range; the Connoisseur Society's processing is absolutely first-rate. Here, in short, is one of the best recordings of this work currently available—and from a most unlikely source.

Comment

Prêtre has recently come in for something of a rebirth as a recording conductor. He is responsible for a successful Columbia recording of Charpentier's opera, *Louise* (M334207) and the equally successful Angel recording of Bizet's *The Pearl Fishers* (SBLX3856)—both with the Roumanian born soprano Ileana Cotrubas in the central female role. ∎

September 1967

ELGAR: Concerto for Cello. Jacqueline Du Pré, cellist, and London Symphony Orchestra conducted by Sir John Barbirolli. Angel S36338, $5.98.

The Elgar *Concerto for Cello* is a very beautiful work—rich, post-Romantic, full of sweeping melodies and a very personal kind of harmony. It would not be going too far to call it a masterpiece. The more one hears it, the better it sounds, especially in this kind of warm, vital interpretation. Du Pré is a young English girl who is being hailed—and with good reason—as the most brilliant instrumental talent to have appeared in many a year. She and Barbirolli, that eminent Elgarian, join forces to present as perfect a performance as can be imagined.

But the record is terribly marred by the second side, which contains shoddy encore pieces by Bach, Saint-Saëns, Falla, Bruch, and others. The arrangment of the "Adagio" from Bach's *Toccata in C* with organ accompaniment is a horror; one wonders about the strange outlook of a musician like Du Pré, who plays the Elgar so beautifully and then lends herself to such an unmusical juxtaposition. Those encore pieces may have a place in the scheme of things, but not on this record.

In the concerto the recording is good, with the cello sounding a little to the right of center without drift. The solo instrument, though, does sound a little bigger than life.

Comment

In her tragically short playing career, Jacqueline Du Pré came to "own" the Elgar *Cello Concerto*. She played it with a rhapsodic abandon that was one of the glories of international concert life in the late 1960s and early 1970s. In defense of her "strange outlook," it must be said that she probably had no say in the juxtaposition of the concerto with the trivial encore pieces. (In England, the concerto was released with a different second side.)

There also exists on the Columbia label (M34530) a live concert recording of the Elgar concerto by Du Pré with her husband, Daniel Barenboim, conducting the Philadelphia Orchestra. If anything, that performance is even more impassioned than the studio version conducted by Sir John Barbirolli. The overside of the Columbia disc has a splendid Barenboim-conducted performance of Elgar's most popular orchestral work, the *Enigma Variations*. The combination makes the Columbia record indispensable. ∎

January 1969

ELGAR: Concerto for Violin (Op. 61). Yehudi Menuhin, violin, and New Philharmonia Orchestra conducted by Sir Adrian Boult. Angel S36330, $5.98.

Years back, Menuhin made a recording of this concerto with the composer leading the orchestra. The violinist has not played the concerto many times through the years, but it still is identified with him. It is a large-scale work, very attractive, even if the last movement does contain some thematic material uncomfortably close to the Brahms *Violin Concerto*. Elgar is coming back into favor once again, and he well deserves revival. Menuhin plays the concerto with his expected musical nobility, and also with a secure technique that has not always been evident in his recent recordings. The recording is admirable. There is no drift at all in the well-centered solo instrument, and there also is a great deal of color and orchestral detail.

Comment

Doubtless because of Jacqueline Du Pré's fiery devotion to the music of Elgar, her husband, Daniel Barenboim, has become one of the most perceptive interpreters of Elgar's music. Barenboim has transmitted this perception to many of his musical colleagues, including Zubin Mehta, Itzhak Perlman and Pinchas Zukerman. With Zukerman he has recorded a performance of the Elgar concerto (Columbia M34517) that is extraordinary in its inner conviction and deeply felt emotion. We are fortunate to have two such outstanding accounts of this great music as the Menuhin-Boult and Zukerman-Barenboim. ∎

January 1969

ELGAR: Enigma Variations; Cockaigne Overture. London Symphony Orchestra conducted by Colin Davis. Philips 900140, $5.98.

(continued)

At the age of forty-one Colin Davis is already the most important British conductor on the international musical scene. He has conducted all the major British orchestras, and he has appeared as guest conductor with many of the principal orchestras in this country. Last year, indeed, he is reported to have declined an offer from the Boston Symphony Orchestra to succeed Erich Leinsdorf as its music director. This season he served a lengthy engagement as guest with the New York Philharmonic.

Davis is currently in his first season as principal conductor of the BBC Symphony in London. But it is the London Symphony Orchestra with which he has been closely identified for about a decade.

That he has built up a particularly close and rewarding relationship with the London Symphony's musicians over the years is immediately apparent from the performances on this disc. Elgar's *Enigma Variations* are by now an integral part of standard symphonic literature, familiar in their contrasting moods and textures. Davis positively revitalizes them, however, delivering a performance of impressive strength and sensitivity. The overall attitude is broad and expansive, with careful attention to inner details of Elgar's orchestration. The *Cockaigne Overture*, a much slighter work, nevertheless receives the same careful treatment from the musicians.

Unfortunately, the record manufacturer appears to have been less careful. A whistle, like that of a tea kettle ready to be poured, was audible throughout side one on two different samples of the disc purchased by CU. It was particularly annoying during the soft passages. We would advise you to listen to the record in the store before you buy; if that's not possible, skip it. Another good version of the *Enigma Variations*, conducted by Sir John Barbirolli, is available on Angel (S36120).

Comment

By his own account, Colin Davis did not come by his affinity to Elgar naturally; at one time he considered Elgar's music to be pompous, inflated, and outdated. But more exposure to the Elgar aesthetic won Davis over. As this disc testifies, Davis now joins the ranks of this generation's most convincing Elgar interpreters. (Phillips's new number for this disc is 835317.) ∎

September 1963

ELGAR: Introduction and Allegro for Strings; Serenade in E minor for Strings; VAUGHAN WILLIAMS: Fantasia on a Theme by Tallis; Fantasia on "Greensleeves." Allegri Quartet and strings of the London Sinfonia conducted by Sir John Barbirolli. Angel S36101, $5.98.

British music for string orchestra. Both of the Vaughan Williams works are well known (*Greensleeves*, indeed, is a bestseller). Less familiar is the Elgar *Introduction and Allegro*. It is a fine, stately, well-written work and deserves much more popularity than has been its lot. The (1892) *Serenade in E minor* is a near-salon work, saved by a most expressive slow movement. This disc is decidedly worth having. Barbirolli is, of course, on familiar ground, and he conducts with his usual strength, color, and health. Good recorded sound.

Comment

Barbirolli's identification with this literature was complete: One remembers a Barbirolli recording of the Elgar *Introduction and Allegro* from way back in the late 1920s. The performance on this disc, representing his matured thoughts on the score, is memorable in every way—as are all the others in this splendid release. ∎

June 1973

ELGAR: Symphony No. 2 in E Flat. The London Philharmonic Orchestra conducted by Daniel Barenbolm. Columbia M31997, $5.98.

The same serenity and nobility infused in the four Vaughan Williams works reviewed on page 254 also characterize this work by Vaughan Williams's countryman and slightly older contemporary, Sir Edward Elgar. Indeed, among the markings in the score, one frequently encounters the word *Nobilmente* (nobly). And the symphony, conceived in early 1910 as a tribute to the reigning British monarch, is dedicated "to the Memory of His Late Majesty King Edward VII."

After years of being out of favor, the music of Elgar is making a spectacular recovery, perhaps because our world so desperately needs the qualities of affirmation expressed by his work. This symphony is a long and sprawling affair (it lasts nearly an hour), but into it Elgar poured some of his most deeply felt and fanciful music. The two outer movements are heroic in the grand manner (though the very end is contemplative), while the slow movement and scherzo, respectively, have an elegiac and an elfin quality.

Barenboim, a 30-year-old Israeli, has centered his musical activity in Britain during the last few years. And in the past year or so, he has emerged as one of the most perceptive of all Elgar interpreters. Sir Adrian Boult, the dean of British conductors, has done marvelously rich recordings of the two Elgar symphonies (Musical Heritage MHS 1285 and MHS 1335), but in this new release of the composer's *Second Symphony*, Barenboim yields nothing to Boult by way of authority or insight. The London Philharmonic plays very well indeed for him, and the British CBS engineers have captured full-bodied sound.

Comment

Sir Georg Solti, another "foreigner," has entered the lists with a recording of Elgar's *Second Symphony* (London CS6941), made with the London Philharmonic—the same orchestra as in the Barenboim recording. Before committing his own thoughts to the recording process, Solti had apparently made a study of Elgar's recording of the score. Solti delivers a tighter, less flexible account than Barenboim's, but it is no less convincing. The highest marks, though, must go to the noblest of all Elgar interpreters, Sir Adrian Boult;

(continued)

his most recent account of this symphony (Angel S37218)—also with the London Philharmonic—glows with the assurance of a master. ■

May 1972

ERB: Symphony of Overtures; The Seventh Trumpet; Concerto for Percussion and Orchestra. The Dallas Symphony Orchestra conducted by Donald Johanos, with Marvin Dahlgren, percussion soloist (in the Concerto). Turnabout. TVS34433, $2.98.

Donald Erb is an American composer in his mid-forties, currently composer-in-residence at the Cleveland Institute of Music. He has had grants from the Ford, Guggenheim and Rockefeller foundations, and his music has been performed by many of the country's leading symphony orchestras. Erb's principal stock in trade is his inventive ear: By asking his instrumentalists to employ unusual performing techniques, he comes up with a whole arsenal of new and unusual sounds. Much of his music has a fascinating pictorial quality.

Of all three works included here, the most successful seems to be the orchestral fantasy, *The Seventh Trumpet*, which was inspired by a section from the Book of Revelations that speaks of seven angels with trumpets who stand before God and accomplish all manner of natural and physical phenomena merely by the sounding of their trumpets. Erb summons a phantasmagoria of sounds from his orchestra in response to the Biblical verses and the whole thing is colorful, vibrant and stimulating.

The *Symphony of Overtures*, which has racked up an impressive number of performances in recent years, is made up of four separate overtures for plays from the Theater of the Absurd—"The Blacks" and "The Maids" by Genet, "Endgame" by Beckett and "Rhinoceros" by Ionesco. In this symphony Erb's imagination produces sounds that are alternately terrifying in their ferocity and hysterically funny in their strangeness. But they lack the unifying musical impulse that make *The Seventh Trumpet* such a fully rounded experience.

The *Concerto for Percussion and Orchestra* is the most closely knit of the three works on the disc, but its unusual sound spectrum seems to be an end in itself rather than the means toward a personal musical expression.

Erb's music requires much careful rehearsal and coordination of the orchestra's sections. For the most part, the Dallas Symphony Orchestra and its former music director, Donald Johanos, have admirably solved the problems presented to them by Erb. Marvin Dahlgren plays the percussion solos in the *Concerto* superbly, particularly the hallucinatory cadenza that ends the work.

Fine reproduction of the orchestra's playing has been captured by engineer Marc Aubort, and the mastering to disc has been very successful. This is one of Turnabout's most accomplished releases to date.

Comment

The works contained on this disc continue to be Erb's most frequently performed orchestral scores. Some of their popularity derives from the existence of this recording. Here, then, is further proof of the extraordinary contribution of recording to the vitality of contemporary music. ■

March 1962

FALLA: The Three-Cornered Hat; Interlude and Dance No. 1 from La Vida breve. Teresa Berganza, mezzo-soprano; L'Orchestre de la Suisse Romande conducted by Ernest Ansermet. London 6224, $5.98.

As Ansermet directed the world premiere of *The Three-Cornered Hat* in London, July 22, 1919, it can be safely assumed that he knows the music as well as anybody around. The gorgeous, colorful score is the very evocation of Spain, and Ansermet conducts it literally with a big bang, making much of the percussion (including castanets) sections. Highly recommended.

Comment

Those who crave a bit more seductive color in this score than Ansermet provides should consider the performance conducted by Rafael Frühbeck de Burgos, with Victoria de los Angeles as his soprano soloist (Angel S36235). And the Boulez-New York Philharmonic recording (Columbia M33970), with Jan De Gaetani as soprano soloist, reveals even more of the textural fabric of the brilliant orchestration. ■

September 1962

FAURÉ: Pelléas et Mélisande; Prelude to Pénélope; Masques et bergamasques; DEBUSSY: Petite Suite. L'Orchestre de la Suisse Romande conducted by Ernest Ansermet. London 6227, $5.98.

A lovely disc of quiet, charming music. The fairly well-known *Pelléas et Mélisande* is a suite of incidental music to the Maeterlinck play. *Pénélope* was an opera that never held the stage. *Masques et bergamasques* was incidental music for an entertainment at the Opéra-Comique. As for the popular *Petite Suite,* Debussy composed it as a two-piano work and it was later orchestrated by Henri Büsser. All of the Fauré music is marked by taste, elegance, and unusual melodic invention. The *"Sicilienne"* from *Pelléas et Mélisande* is one of the most exquisite things in French music. *Masques et bergamasques* is lighter and, in sections, actually frivolous. The deepest work is *Pénélope*, which is intense and dark-colored. Debussy's little suite is like a Watteau, gliding along in a pastoral landscape. Lovely performances and not so lovely recorded sound. The strings lack luster, and the orchestra in general sounds as though a veil has been thrown over it.

(continued)

Comment

Fauré's *Pelléas et Mélisande* is also available in two superlatively atmospheric performances: by Munch and the Philadelphia Orchestra (Odyssey Y31017), with works by Berlioz and Ravel; and by Andrew Davis with the New Philharmonia Orchestra (Columbia M34506), with the Franck *Symphony in D minor*. ■

March 1970

FRANCK: Sonata in A for Violin and Piano; BRAHMS: Trio in E flat for Horn, Violin, and Piano. Vladimir Ashkenazy, piano, and Itzhak Perlman, violin, with Barry Tuckwell, horn (in the Brahms). London 6628, $5.98.

The Franck *Sonata* is one of the lushest scores in the literature for violin and piano. The two distinguished young instrumentalists who perform it here are fully responsive to the lushness in the music, but they also do full justice to the work's classic structure and its improvisational qualities. Their performance has great strength and beauty, and they operate as sensitive collaborators. No finer version of the *Sonata* has yet been recorded.

In the Brahms *Horn Trio*, they are joined by the superb principal horn player of the London Symphony Orchestra, Barry Tuckwell. The three musicians together offer a beautifully lyrical performance of this calm and introspective score. There have been several recent releases of this piece—including a reissue on the Seraphim label of the classic performance of the early 1930s by Rudolf Serkin, Adolf Busch, and Aubrey Brain—but none has the conviction and tonal finesse of the performance by Ashkenazy, Perlman, and Tuckwell.

The London engineers provide recorded sound of great clarity and breadth. This is one of the most estimable recordings of recent months.

Comment

Perlman and Ashkenazy have also recorded the two Prokofiev *Sonatas for Violin and Piano* (RCA LSC3118) and the complete cycle of Beethoven *Violin and Piano Sonatas* (London CSA2501). They make a superb ensemble team—one looks forward to their further collaborations. ■

March 1977

FRANCK: Symphony in D minor; Redemption: Symphonic Fragment. The Orchestre de Paris under the direction of Daniel Barenboim. Deutsche Grammophon 2530707, $7.98. ●

Daniel Barenboim, in his relatively new role as music director of the Orchestre de Paris—Europe's latest virtuoso ensemble—has begun an extensive series of recordings for Deutsche Grammophon and CBS Records. The present disc is one of the first released in the series. I wish I could accord it a better reception.

The Franck *D minor Symphony*, with its lushly chromatic orchestration, is somewhat out of fashion. A convincing performance of it these days must combine enormous conviction with a degree of abandon. Those qualities are lacking here. What one gets instead is a rigid, tightly controlled reading that somehow manages to drain much of the music's tension and rhythmic vitality.

A particular case in point is the orchestra's statement of the very first theme after the groping introduction. What should be ferocious snap is reduced to wishy-washy tameness—the rhythmic bite is not clearly delineated. The fault recurs frequently. The recorded sound is on the harsh side, and a trumpet error at the very end should surely have been corrected in a retake.

Things go much better in the filler on the disc—the orchestral middle movement from Franck's oratorio *Redemption*. Here at least the performance succeeds in imparting the proper atmosphere, in a bold and vital musical statement. But the recorded sound still tends to the raucous. And why is there nothing in the liner note or on the jacket cover about this "Symphonic Fragment" from *Redemption?*

July 1977

FRANCK: Symphony in D minor; Symphonic Variations for Piano and Orchestra. The Royal Philharmonic Orchestra under the direction of Antal Dorati (with Ilse von Alpenheim, piano, in the Symphonic Variations). Vox Turnabout TVS34663, $3.98. ●

Strange indeed are the coincidences of duplication in the recorded repertory. The Franck *Symphony*, once one of the five or six most recorded and most played of musical works, had fallen from favor in recent years. Yet the past few months have seen four new recordings of it—by the Bournemouth Symphony Orchestra under Paavo Berglund, the Cleveland Orchestra under Lorin Maazel, the Orchestre de Paris under Daniel Barenboim, and by the Royal Philharmonic.

Dorati remains music director of London's Royal Philharmonic while becoming the new music director of the Detroit Symphony Orchestra this fall—and departing as the music director of Washington's National Symphony Orchestra. The Royal Philharmonic's performance of the Franck *Symphony* is less quixotic than Barenboim's (see above); it is an unruffled, uneventful excursion through the music. If that sounds like faint praise, it is. For if the *Symphony* is to make an impact these days, it needs a flat-out performance that stresses the sensuality and the great dynamic contrasts implicit in the score. Pierre Monteux and the Chicago Symphony Orchestra gave such a performance (RCA LSC2514) about 15 years ago; it still rates top honors, in my judgment.

The *Symphonic Variations* get pretty much the same orderly, efficient, uninvolved, and impersonal treatment as the *Symphony*. The pianist is conductor Dorati's wife, and this—along with a disc of Mendelssohn piano music just released by Philips—marks her introduction to the international recording scene. The sound quality is unexceptional throughout.

(continued)

Comment

The Boult performance, recorded in the early 1960s and recently given wide circulation in this country on the Quintessence label (7050), is a real challenge to the primacy of the Monteux recording. In his straightforward and unfussy way, Boult invests the score with new dynamism and drama. The filler on his disc is an equally, persuasive treatment of Liszt's *Les Préludes.* ∎

February 1975

FUX: Concentus Musico Instrumentalis: Serenada à 8; Rondeau à 7; Sonata à Quattro. Concentus Musicus of Vienna conducted by Nikolaus Harnoncourt. Telefunken SAWT9619A, $6.98.

Johann Joseph Fux was an Austrian theoretician and composer of the late 17th and early 18th centuries. His treatise on counterpoint, "Gradus ad Parnassum," served for generations as the official manual on the subject. He also composed music in many forms. His thoroughly baroque *Concentus Musico Instrumentalis* is a collection of sonatas and suites for various instrumental combinations. The opening piece on this disc, "Serenada à 8," is a suite from the *Concentus* consisting of 16 movements, most of them in the prevailing dance forms of the day. Prominent in several of the movements is the valveless trumpet, then in common use, which makes extraordinary demands on the performer; here the challenge is met brilliantly by soloist Don Smithers. But the suite itself cannot sustain interest. Periods of empty note-spinning far outnumber those of genuine musical interest.

The rondo and the sonata that fill out the disc are less pretentious, hence more rewarding—particularly the brief rondo, which is built on an engaging theme and offers interesting contrasts. The playing of the instrumentalists, who are specialists in the music of the period, is first-rate.

Comment

The playing is expert throughout, but that is frequently not enough to compensate for the long stretches of dullness in the music itself. For internal reasons best known to Telefunken, a new catalog number has been assigned to these performances: 641271. ∎

November 1971

GERSHWIN: An American in Paris; Rhapsody in Blue. The Hollywood Bowl Symphony Orchestra conducted by Felix Slatkin, with Leonard Pennario, piano (in the *Rhapsody in Blue*). Seraphim S60174, $2.98.

This disc, a budget-priced rerelease of performances recorded originally by Capitol Records, serves as a reminder of the riches that once made the Capitol Classics catalogue one of the most interesting and valuable in the industry. Both works are done with tremendous flair and vitality, and the recorded sound—a product of the early 1960s—is as vibrant and well balanced as if it had been accomplished with the latest recording technology. Both pieces are competitive with any other versions now on the market, at any price.

Comment

The disc also serves to remind us that Leonard Pennario has disappeared from recording activity. Formerly one of the best-sellers among recording artists, he had a repertoire that embraced a large part of the Romantic and post-Romantic piano literature. Two other Pennario recordings still extant and worthy of investigation are Angel S36049 *(Pennario Plays Favorite Classics)* and Angel S37303 *(Daydreams).* ∎

October 1974

GERSHWIN: Rhapsody in Blue; MILHAUD: Scaramouche; CHA-BRIER: Trois Valses Romantiques; BIZET: Jeux d'Enfants. Frances Veri and Michael Jamanis, pianists. Connoisseur Society CSQ2054, $5.98.

Although Gershwin's *Rhapsody in Blue* is best known in its arrangements for piano solo and jazz band and for piano solo and symphony orchestra, the work as originally composed was scored for two pianos. But not since the pioneer recording of the two-piano version (long since out of print) have record collectors been able to hear the score in this form. Veri and Jamanis, newcomers to the ranks of two-piano teams, play it affectionately. But they do lack the easy spontaneity and swaggering audacity of its finest interpreters (for example, Leonard Bernstein on Columbia M31804 or Earl Wild on RCA LSC2367, both using the piano/symphony orchestra version, or Eugene List on Turnabout TVS34457, with a sparkling account of the piano/jazz band setting).

The other three works on this disc are staples of the two-piano repertory, and in all of them Veri and Jamanis can stand comparison with the best. Milhaud's *Scaramouche*, derived from incidental music composed for a children's play, is great fun—with more than occasional influences of ragtime and jazz. Chabrier's *Waltzes* are crisp and elegant, and Bizet's suite of children's pieces is a delight.

This disc is a compatible quadraphonic recording, yielding four-channel sound when played through an SQ quadraphonic decoder. We listened to it on a high-quality stereophonic system, and the reproduction of the two pianos was first-rate.

Comment

One had expected to hear more from the team of Veri and Jamanis after this auspicious disc, but nothing else has been forthcoming. (They also made a companion disc—CSQ2067—released at about the same time.) A generation

(continued)

or so back several first-rate two-piano teams were active on our concert stages: Luboshutz and Nemenoff, Vronsky and Babin, Whittemore and Lowe, Appleton and Field, to name just a few. Duo-pianists are something of a rarity these days, which is a pity, given the wealth of fine literature available to be played and recorded. ■

March 1960

GILBERT AND SULLIVAN: H.M.S. Pinafore. George Baker and John Cameron, baritones; Richard Lewis, tenor; Owen Brannigan, bass; Elsie Morison, soprano; Monica Sinclair, contralto. Pro Arte Orchestra and Glyndebourne Festival Chorus conducted by Sir Malcolm Sargent. Angel S3589, 2 discs, $11.96.

Another in the series of Gilbert and Sullivan operettas from Angel: sung with style and spirit, with impeccable enunciation (so important in music like this), and with better voices than one usually encounters in G&S performances. Of course, there is always the definitive D'Oyly Carte series on London records to fall back on; but this *Pinafore* is better recorded than the London equivalent. It would be hard to make a choice, and most listeners should be content with either. The recorded sound is excellent. One amusing stereo touch: when Dick Deadeye is spying on Ralph and Josephine, his comments are confined to one speaker, and his voice is heard from the far right.

July 1960

GILBERT AND SULLIVAN: H.M.S. Pinafore. D'Oyly Carte Opera Company; New Symphony Orchestra of London conducted by Isidore Godfrey. London 1209, 2 discs, $11.96.

Only a short time ago—in the March 1960 issue, to be exact—this department recommended the Angel album of *Pinafore*. It is, therefore, with blushes and apologies that the new London album is brought into the picture here. When the previous review was written, however, there was no advance information that the D'Oyly Carte Company was going to bring out G&S recordings complete with dialogue for the first time in the history of the phonograph. That is what we have here, on these two discs: every last note of music *and* every last word of dialogue. We also get them in first-class stereo sound. For G&S fans there necessarily will be no alternative. There are, true, one or two points at which one might cavil. The music and the dialogue often have quite a disparity in sound character. And you'd think that London would give the names of the singers and their roles. All that is given are the singers' names on the record label. For those who are interested, here is a listing of the important roles: John Reed (Sir Joseph Porter); Jeffrey Skitch (Captain Corcoran); Thomas Round (Ralph Rackstraw); Donald Adams (Dick Deadeye); Jean Hindmarsh (Josephine); Gillian Knight (Buttercup).

June 1961

GILBERT AND SULLIVAN: Iolanthe. D'Oyly Carte Opera Company; New Symphony Orchestra of London conducted by Isidore Godfrey. London 1215, 2 discs, $11.96.

The D'Oyly Carte has started rerecording all of the G&S operettas with the spoken dialogue. *Pinafore* was issued a few months back. Now comes *Iolanthe*. All Savoyards will cheer. It may be that some of the singers in the D'Oyly Carte Company are not the vocal heroes and heroines they used to be ("silver'd is the raven hair"?); and the Fairy Queen in this recording has trouble singing the part. But she, like all the others in the cast, has the style down so perfectly that criticism tends to vanish. A libretto is provided with the album. Fortunately so, for one or two of the singers have sloppy diction. Plenty of stereo separation is present, often to amusing effect. For instance, the opening chorus of peers has half the singers in one speaker, half in the other. Presumably the chorus is divided into Liberals and Conservatives. And some of the dialogue, where the fairies bandy words with the peers, is really exciting. Voices come from various places along the wall, and the effect is quite startling.

January 1965

GILBERT AND SULLIVAN: Trial by Jury; Excerpts from Utopia Ltd. D'Oyly Carte Opera Company; Royal Opera House Orchestra conducted by Isidore Godfrey. London 1155, $5.98. ●

The chief interest here is the sampling from *Utopia Ltd.*, a Gilbert and Sullivan operetta that had its premiere in 1893 and was then dropped permanently from the repertoire. These excerpts are tantalizing. Capt. Fitzbattleaxe's big solo, "A Tenor, All Singers Above," is top notch G&S; however, the chorus's "Eagle High" is weak and flaccid. The duet "Words of Love Too Loudly Spoken" is charming, but the chorus's "O Make Way for the Wise Men" sounds routine. The chances are that *Utopia Ltd.* as a whole is not representative of G&S at their best; even so, there are surely enough Savoyards to support a complete recording. In the popular *Trial by Jury* the D'Oyly Carte singers operate at peak efficiency and humor. The stereo is unusually brilliant and lifelike.

September 1966

GILBERT AND SULLIVAN: Princess Ida. D'Oyly Carte Opera Company; Royal Philharmonic Orchestra conducted by Sir Malcolm Sargent. London 1262, 2 discs, $11.96.

Princess Ida has never been one of the all-time G&S favorites. But it should be. It was composed at the best period of the two collaborators—in 1884, between *Iolanthe* and *The Mikado*. It is the biggest of the operettas, in three acts as against the others' two. It is also the biggest in scoring and concep-
(continued)

tion. Some find its libretto, a parody on women's education, based on Tennyson's poem "The Princess" somewhat dated. It is hard to see why *Princess Ida* is any worse than any other G&S operetta. Some of the situations are as funny as anything in the G&S repertoire. As a matter of fact, all of the operettas are dated in spots, but that does not seem to faze any Savoyard. *Princess Ida* has some marvelous music in it. For pure melody, Sullivan never exceeded Hilarion's "Ida was a twelve month old," or the trio "Expressive glances." There is no better ballad in operetta than Cyril's "Would you know the kind of maid," or no better patter song than the Arac–Guron–Scynthius trio "For a month to dwell," or no better musical parody than Arac's "This helmet, I suppose," which sounds as Handel as Handel. *Princess Ida* is full of such delights. The album comes with complete text, including the dialogue omitted in the recording. Nice, lively sound.

January 1968

GILBERT AND SULLIVAN: The Sorcerer. D'Oyly Carte Opera Company; Royal Philharmonic Orchestra conducted by Isidore Godfrey. London 1264, 2 discs, $11.96.

Although *The Sorcerer* is the least popular of the Gilbert and Sullivan operettas, one shouldn't assume it is the worst. There are things in it to suit the most demanding Savoyard: the patter song of John Wellington Wells; the plangent "Time Was When Love and I Were Well Acquainted"; "Oh, Happy Young Heart," one of Sullivan's best waltzes; the chorus "With Heart and With Voice," which is as rousing as the Entrance of the Peers from *Iolanthe*; the Marmaduke–Sangazure duet, which prefigures the gavotte in *Gondoliers*. One could go on. It is true that the libretto of *The Sorcerer* deteriorates in the second act, but the score goes a long way toward compensating for this. As for the performance, it should be enough to report that the D'Oyly Carte singers are in perfect form. The sound of this recording is exceedingly brilliant.

Comment

All these performances are bound to become classics of their kind—including the Sargent-conducted recording of *H.M.S. Pinafore*, which is a thoroughly idiomatic account of the work, despite the absence of the D'Oyly Carte imprimatur. As for the other performances—all of which carry on the brilliant D'Oyly Carte tradition—they exemplify the special qualities that have made the D'Oyly Carte a unique performing group. ∎

January 1965

GLAZOUNOV: Concerto in A minor for Violin (Op. 82). Jascha Heifetz and orchestra conducted by Walter Hendl. **MOZART: Symphonie Concertante in E flat (K. 364).** Jascha Heifetz, violin, and William Primrose, viola, with orchestra conducted by Izler Solomon. RCA LSC2734, $5.98.

Heifetz, probably the most nearly flawless violin techñician since Paganini, has all but retired as a solo artist. But this does not mean his playing has slipped. His performance of the Glazounov *A minor Concerto*—that popular old war-horse—is spectacular. From any aspect—tonal, musical, technical—the playing is perfection. The Heifetz bow arm is as strong as ever, and the left hand is still infallible. In addition, Heifetz brings to the work, as he always has to this sort of virtuoso concerto, a kind of taste and aristocracy peculiarly his own. For the Mozart he joins up with one of his favorite partners, the celebrated violist, William Primrose. What results is a fine-textured performance of the lovely double concerto—a performance that is, on the whole, lean, fast, and objective. Instrumentally it is magnificent. Interpretively some may find it too dispassionate, perhaps a little too concerned with surface burnish.

It used to be that the piano was the most difficult instrument to record. Today, in stereo recordings, the violin poses some problems. Stereo has a tendency to spread the size of the violin. This is not noticeable when the violin is playing along with the orchestra, but in unaccompanied sections, such as the cadenza, the G string may sound as if it was six feet to the side of the E string. On this disc, in both concerti, the solo instruments occasionally come through bigger than life, although the stereo does have depth and orchestral color.

Comment

No other violinist has ever matched the absorption and fire of Heifetz in the Glazounov concerto—not even Nathan Milstein, whose recording of the score (Angel S36011) is otherwise exemplary. But there are a number of other recorded performances of the Mozart with greater personal involvement in the music—Grumiaux and Pelliccia (Philips 900130), or Stern and Zukerman (Columbia M31369), among others. ∎

September 1972

GLIÈRE: Symphony No. 3 in B minor (Ilya Murometz). The Philadelphia Orchestra conducted by Eugene Ormandy. RCA LSC3246, $5.98.

Leopold Stokowski and the Philadelphia Orchestra recorded a somewhat truncated version of Glière's sprawling *"Ilya Murometz" Symphony* in about 1940, proving that the rich juices of Glière's scoring are ideally suited to the Philadelphia Orchestra's sumptuous sound. That multi-disc RCA Victor album of 78s was a classic of its time. There have been other recordings of the score since then, including a performance by Stokowski and the Houston Symphony Orchestra (Seraphim S60089), in which the score was mercilessly cut to about 37 minutes, and an absolutely uncut version conducted by the late Hermann Scherchen (that is no longer available). But clearly the time has long been ripe for another Philadelphia recording of the music. Now that it has arrived (again somewhat cut), all expectations have been fulfilled.

This sort of colorful orchestral score draws from Ormandy a vivid re-
(continued)

sponse, and he extracts an appropriate performance from his players. Further, the RCA engineering team has here accomplished its best Philadelphia effort to date, producing sound that is vibrant, warm and intense. The symphony itself may impress some as gaudy and shallow, but whatever can be done on its behalf has here been done.

Comment

In reading the praise for the recorded sound achieved by RCA Records with the Philadelphia Orchestra, please remember that the words were written in mid-1972. Since then, the Philadelphia Orchestra has made many recordings for RCA that sound even better. And soon to be issued in this country on the Angel label are recordings engineered for the Philadelphia Orchestra by the expert technical staff of Britain's Electric and Musical Industries (EMI). ■

March 1973

GODARD: Concerto Romantique for Violin and Orchestra. Aaron Rosand, violin, with the Orchestra of Radio Luxembourg conducted by Louis de Froment: **CHAUSSON: Poème for Violin and Orchestra; SAINT-SAËNS: Introduction and Rondo Capriccioso for Violin and Orchestra; BERLIOZ: Reverie and Caprice for Violin and Orchestra.** Aaron Rosand, violin, with the Southwest German Radio Orchestra conducted by Rolf Reinhardt. Turnabout TVS34466, $2.98.

Godard's *Concerto Romantique,* written in 1876, clearly owes this, its first recorded performance, to the recent revival of interest in Romantic music. The piece—four brief movements that together last just over 20 minutes—was once prominent in the violin repertory but is now almost totally unknown. So the presentation of this ''new'' music might have held some interest as part of the overall Romantic revival. And indeed, Aaron Rosand, one of America's finest if most underrated instrumentalists, presents the concerto in the best possible light. But despite its elegance and grace, the piece itself is simply too insubstantial to sustain the interest aroused by its appearance. And the sound reproduction in this recording leaves something to be desired: It is strident and boxed-in, with little air space to give it mellowness.

Still, at its budget price, this disc would be well worth buying by those who would like to own the other three works contained herein. They are well-known staples of the literature for violin and orchestra, and Rosand's excellent playing makes these among the better recorded performances of each work. Curiously, the recorded sound in the Chausson, the Saint-Saëns and the Berlioz is considerably better than in the Godard, even though the Godard was presumably recorded more recently. The other three are all reissued from discs formerly released by Vox, the parent label of Turnabout.

Comment

Aaron Rosand may not enjoy the same international acclaim as Isaac Stern,

Itzhak Perlman, and Pinchas Zukerman, but he is in their league as far as artistry and technique are concerned. We are fortunate that he is in a sense the "house violinist" of the Vox Records family of labels; his many superlative performances—well represented by the four works reviewed above—are fine contributions to that firm's catalog. ∎

January 1965

GOLDMARK: Symphony, Opus 26 (Rustic Wedding). Utah Symphony Orchestra conducted by Maurice Abravanel. Vanguard 2142, $5.98.

Two generations or so ago, Karl Goldmark's *Rustic Wedding* used to be very popular. It is seldom heard in concerts anymore. This is a pity, for it is a charming, unpretentious, innocent, and highly melodic work. Beecham recorded it some years back, and now Abravanel has provided the first stereo version. He handles the symphony very well, with a good deal of color and rhythmic life. As a relief from the overplayed standard repertoire, this disc is highly recommended. Good recording.

Comment

A performance of this score by Bernstein and the New York Philharmonic (Columbia MS7261) is even more responsive to the gentle allure of this work. Vivid sound reproduction adds to its merits. ∎

April 1964

GOTTSCHALK: Nuit des Tropiques (A Night in the Tropics); Gran Tarantella for Piano and Orchestra; GOULD: Latin American Symphonette. Reid Nibley, piano, and Utah Symphony Orchestra conducted by Maurice Abravanel. Vanguard S275, $2.98.

Louis Moreau Gottschalk was an American (born in New Orleans) pianist and composer who died at the age of forty in 1869. In recent years a good deal of attention has been given him. He probably was America's first nationalist composer, the first to use dance and Negro themes of the United States and South America. *A Night in the Tropics* was composed in 1859 and is a two-movement "symphony." Vanguard is a little vague about the arrangement used here. The notes say that the performance is given in a "reconstruction" of the recently discovered piano score. But the orchestration sounds much too modern to be Gottschalk's own. We can assume that the melodic material, however, is Gottschalk's. Considering its date, *Tropics* is an amazing and even prophetic work. The first movement is a remarkable tone picture, and the second is even more remarkable: a sophisticated, rhythmically complex, lively Latin American dance. It is a much better score than the Gould work on this disc, a collection of commercial banalities. The

(continued)

Tarantella by Gottschalk has been orchestrated by Hershy Kay, and is a wonderful tintype. Splendid recording sound.

Comment

Gottschalk was a real American original; one might have expected his music to enjoy a new vogue during the Bicentennial celebrations. But such was not the case. In any event, this disc makes a good case for a Gottschalk revival. ■

September 1967

GOUNOD: Faust. Franco Corelli, tenor (Faust); Joan Sutherland, soprano (Marguerite); Robert Massard, baritone (Valentine); Nicolai Ghiaurov, bass (Mephistopheles); Monica Sinclair, mezzo-soprano (Martha); Margreta Elkins, mezzo-soprano (Siebel). London Symphony Orchestra, Ambrosian Singers, Highgate School Choir under Richard Bonynge. London 1433, 4 discs, $23.92.

Surprisingly few complete recordings of the most popular Gounod opera are available, and on paper the present album looked like a definitive winner, what with three such internationally famous singers as Sutherland, Corelli, and Ghiaurov in the three leading roles. But it does not work out that way.

Corelli shows little knowledge of French style; he belts out his role as though it were Manrico in *Il Trovatore*. Some of his singing does have animal impact, but his approach will grieve the purists. Sutherland seems miscast, singing a droopy kind of Marguerite, much too conscious of diction, technique, and tone projection and not conscious enough of characterization. The one who holds up his end is Ghiaurov, whose conception may be somewhat old-fashioned, but who has such presence and vocal command that he takes over the album. Minor roles are competently sung. Bonynge, the conductor, is accurate but unimaginative, and his tempi often are sluggish.

It should be mentioned that this is a more complete *Faust* than has ever been recorded or, indeed, heard on the stage. Not only are many cuts opened up (i.e., music traditionally cut is restored to the score), but some new material has been added from early versions. The recorded sound is very impressive. But those who want a better sung *Faust* should go back to De los Angeles, Gedda, and the others in Angel S3622.

Comment

The more recent recording in which Montserrat Caballé and Giacomo Aragall sing the principal roles (RCA FRL42493) is no better than this performance. Characterization is indifferent and the conductor, Alain Lombard, is excessively self-indulgent. ■

March 1970

GRIEG: Holberg Suite; WIREN: Serenade for Strings; GRIEG: Two Elegiac Melodies: No. 2, "The Last Spring." English Chamber Orchestra conducted by Johannes Somary. Vanguard Cardinal 10067, $3.98.

Grieg's *Holberg Suite* began its musical life as a work for solo piano, composed in honor of Ludwig Holberg, a distinguished Norwegian writer of the eighteenth century. Grieg himself transcribed the music for string orchestra, thus giving us one of his most appealing scores. Made up of a prelude and five succeeding dance sections, the *Holberg Suite* is full of rich melodic invention and captivating charm.

Delightful, too, is the *Serenade for Strings* by the contemporary Swedish composer, Dag Wiren. Its four brief movements illustrate the spontaneity, character, and rhythmic variety that should make Wiren and his music much better known in this country than they are. In England, the opening of this *Serenade* has served as theme music for one of the BBC's most popular programs, with the result that this work is a favorite with British audiences.

"The Last Spring" is one of two *Elegiac Melodies* that make up Grieg's *Opus 34*. It is exactly what its title suggests—a gentle, rhapsodic, bittersweet cameo that is most moving.

Vanguard Cardinal first presented Johannes Somary as conductor of the superlative English Chamber Orchestra in a memorable recording of Handel's *Theodora*. Again in this new disc, Somary secures brilliant playing from these virtuoso musicians, playing that is on a par with that elicited by Daniel Barenboim and Benjamin Britten. And the Vanguard engineers have captured these performances in meltingly beautiful sound, resonant and full-bodied, with especially vibrant bass reproduction. This disc is a gem.

Comment

This disc remains superlative on every level. Heard anew, its rich and cleanly balanced sound is especially enjoyable.　　　　　　　　　　　　　　　■

September 1976

GRIEG: Piano Concerto in A minor; FRANCK: Symphonic Variations for Piano and Orchestra. Gyorgy Cziffra, piano, with the Budapest Symphony Orchestra conducted by Gyorgy Cziffra Jr. Connoisseur Society CS2090, $6.98. ●

The Hungarian pianist Gyorgy Cziffra exploded on the international music scene 20-odd years ago with a series of recordings, usually made in England, of the splashiest virtuoso music that exists in piano literature.

A pianist of fiery temperament and great technical expertise, Cziffra rarely probed beneath the surface—most of his repertory depended for its effects on dexterous fingers and little else. Though Cziffra has not been in the American musical orbit recently, he has gone on concertizing and recording in Europe, principally in Paris, during the last dozen years or so. This disc is one of several recently released in this country under the Connoisseur Society label.

The mixture is pretty much as before. For Cziffra, technical problems seem

(continued)

nonexistent. But he and the conductor, his son, have some unusual—not to say strange—ideas about the works performed here. Unexpected slowdowns and speed-ups are common. Phrasing is sometimes choppy. The rhythmic pulse is not always as steady as it should be. And the Budapest Symphony Orchestra has some decidedly weak principal players. Other recordings do better by both of the works on this disc: for the Grieg, Richter (Angel S36899) and Rubinstein (RCA LSC3338); and for the Franck, Watts (Columbia M33072) and De Larrocha (London CS6818).

Comment

A recently released recording of Franck's *Symphonic Variations* played by the young French pianist Pascal Rogé, with Lorin Maazel conducting the Cleveland Orchestra (London CS7044), is excellent. It fills out the second side of an intense Maazel-Cleveland Orchestra account of the Franck symphony. ∎

September 1972

GRIEG: Piano Concerto in A minor; RACHMANINOFF: Rhapsody on a Theme by Paganini. Leonard Pennario, piano, with the Los Angeles Philharmonic Orchestra conducted by Erich Leinsdorf. Seraphim S60195, $2.98.

These performances are reissues of recordings originally made for Capitol about a dozen years ago. Pennario was then at his height as a recording artist, and with Leinsdorf he turned in vigorous accounts of both of these repertoire staples. The vigor, perhaps, has precluded the subtlety and variety to be found in the many competing recordings of both scores. Rubinstein's (RCA LSC2566) and Bishop's (Philips 6500166) Grieg concerto, for example, show greater feeling for the work; Graffman's Rachmaninoff performance (Columbia MS6634) makes more of the shifting moods in the music. But there is room in both works for healthy, uninhibited extroversion, which the team of Pennario and Leinsdorf supplies in abundance. Though the recorded sound is not the last word in sonic splendor, it is nevertheless more than acceptable even by today's standards.

Comment

A spellbinding recording of the Grieg concerto has been released on the low-price Quintessence label (7031) since the above was written. Earl Wild is the inspired pianist, and that dedicated disciple of Arnold Schoenberg, the late René Leibowitz, is the surprising—and surprisingly convincing—conductor. Wild also has a superb account of Rachmaninoff's *Rhapsody on a Theme of Paganini* on the Quintessence label (7006), with the late Jascha Horenstein doing a memorable job of conducting. ∎

June 1973

HAMILTON: Epitaph for This World and Time, for chorus and organs; Voyage, for French horn and chamber orchestra. Choruses and organists conducted by Alec Wyton (in the Epitaph); Barry Tuckwell, horn, with the London Sinfonietta conducted by David Atherton (in Voyage). Composers Recordings, Inc. SD280, $5.95.

Iain Hamilton—50-year-old native of Scotland, resident New Yorker, and regular commuter to Duke University in North Carolina, where he is on the music faculty—can take pride in a large catalog of music. It includes several works for large orchestra, two violin concertos (the second of which was premiered at last summer's Edinburgh Festival by American violinist Paul Zukovsky), a piano concerto and numerous works for smaller ensembles. Yet he has not had the worldwide fame and success he so richly deserves. This disc may bring his music to the attention of a wider public.

Both scores illustrate one of Hamilton's principal strengths—his ability to create dramatic and colorful effects, no matter what the performance medium. *Voyage,* for example, which is in everything but name a concerto for French horn and small ensemble, inventively covers a wide range of feelings and emotions. The horn soloist is asked to perform seemingly impossible feats of dexterity and breath control. The demands on the ensemble players are no less exacting. But the musical content is more impressive still. Within a framework of familiar devices—intervals bunched closely together, sections of improvisation and disparate rhythms clashing against one another—Hamilton has created a fascinating score.

Epitaph for This World and Time calls upon three choirs and three organs in the composer's setting of passages from the Revelation of St. John the Divine. There is an enigmatic quality to the text, and Hamilton requires his vocalists to scream and shout and whisper, as well as sing, while the organs supply veiled and mysterious background figures. The whole rises to moments of almost unbearable tension. The end returns to contemplative, restless searching.

Both scores are extremely well presented, in performance and in recording. It is to be hoped that this first major recording of music by Iain Hamilton will lead to others and to a much wider knowledge of his works.

Comment

Alas, the hope expressed in the last lines above has not been realized in the last several years—not in the United States, at any rate. Iain Hamilton's music is still almost totally unknown here, and that is our loss. Besides the orchestral and chamber works mentioned above, a number of powerful operas by Hamilton have been produced elsewhere—notably in Britain—with great success. Is it too much to hope that New York's Metropolitan Opera may one day mount Hamilton's spectacular *Royal Hunt of the Sun?* ■

May 1960

HANDEL: Concerti Nos. 13-16 for Organ. E. Power Biggs, organ, and London Philharmonic Orchestra conducted by Sir Adrian Boult. Columbia MS6439, $5.98.

(continued)

This album completes the Biggs-Boult sets of the Handel organ concertos. Two previous albums have been issued, and those who already own them will want to complete the series. Nothing can be added to what previously has been said. The music is magnificent, the performances admirable, the recording exceptionally realistic. (The thudding noises you may hear are not a defect in the recording but the sound of the tracker action of the old organ Biggs uses. It is an instrument designed by Handel himself.) Highly recommended. The stereo has color and depth.

Comment
The Biggs-Boult collection of all the Handel organ concertos is available in truncated form in a three-disc Columbia album (D3M33716). The performances by George Malcolm, as soloist, with the Academy of St. Martin-in-the-Fields (Argo D3D4) are far more stylish and lively than the Biggs-Boult collaborations. ∎

January 1960

HANDEL: Messiah. Eileen Farrell, soprano; Martha Lipton, contralto; Davis Cunningham, tenor; William Warfield, baritone; the Mormon Tabernacle Choir and the Philadelphia Orchestra conducted by Eugene Ormandy. Columbia M2S607, 2 discs, $11.96.

Those who are wondering how it is possible to get a *Messiah* on two discs are hereby reassured: it can't be done. Columbia has given us what amounts to an abridged performance here, with twenty-one of the fifty-three numbers (of the Prout edition) omitted. Thus, those who want a complete (or substantially complete) *Messiah* have to look elsewhere: say, in the direction of Boult (London 1329, three discs), or Sargent (Seraphim S6056, three discs). This department has not heard all of the stereophonic *Messiah* performances currently available, but of those that have been heard, the Bernstein (Columbia) and Beecham (RCA) performances are to be avoided. The Bernstein is artificial and the sections have been changed; the Beecham, reorchestrated in a vulgar manner. All the more pity that this Ormandy performance is not complete, for it is a very fine job as far as it goes. It has one of the best American choruses, a fine group of solo singers, and a wonderful orchestra. It also boasts one of the best choral recordings currently available. The pressings have only moderate tape hiss, the recorded sound is brilliant without being edgy, and the soloists come through with a lifelike impact. Especially impressive is the stereophonic *Hallelujah* chorus, with entries hurtling from every direction and a thrilling buildup.

March 1967

HANDEL: Messiah. Heather Harper, soprano; Helen Watts, alto; John Wakefield, tenor; John Shirley-Quirk, bass. London Symphony Orchestra and Chorus conducted by Colin Davis. Philips SC71AX300, 3 discs, $17.94. ●

HANDEL: Messiah. Judith Raskin, soprano; Florence Kopleff, alto; Richard Lewis, tenor; Thomas Paul, bass. Robert Shaw Chorale and Orchestra conducted by Robert Shaw. RCA LSC6175, 3 discs, $17.94.

These two *Messiah* performances have much in common. They use very small forces in an attempt to present a baroque performance—the kind of performance that avoids the massive Victorian tradition and instead goes back to the 1740s and 1750s. Davis uses a chorus of forty and an orchestra of thirty-two and Shaw uses a chorus of thirty-one and a small orchestra (the exact number is not specified). Heard this way, Handel's most popular work is going to sound different. There is a lithe quality instead of a heavy one. Tempi are faster, balances more carefully weighed, textures easier to hear. Both conductors try for musicological as well as musical authenticity, even letting their singers insert ornaments and cadenzas. Davis is especially free in this respect. Both conductors, too, have seen to it that the choral and solo singing is a model of clear diction.

Thus both *Messiah* performances are quite unusual, and are the most interesting and faithful ever recorded. With all the things the two performances have in common, there still remain some outstanding differences. Davis is more assertive and strongly rhythmic, and his tempi tend to be faster than Shaw's. Shaw uses eighteenth-century forces, but his thinking and approach are basically nineteenth century. Davis, on the other hand, has completely rethought the work, and approaches it as something entirely new. Perhaps the RCA set has the advantage in matters of pure voice; it has a superior vocal quartet. But the Philips singers have more style and spirit, and none of them is a weak vocalist. Thus the Philips album is recommended for its greater life, drama, and evocation of the eighteenth century. In both performances the recorded sound is absolutely tops.

Comment

The recording by Ormandy fills the bill nicely under the heading "Highlights from Handel's *Messiah.*" Current fashion has turned against the massive *Messiah* performances (such as the Boult and Sargent versions favored earlier), with the swollen choral and orchestral forces that were in vogue a generation ago. The later style, with small choruses and reduced orchestras, was pioneered by the recording industry. Other available recordings also present *Messiah* as a baroque entertainment, and two of them do so most satisfyingly. They are the performances superintended by Mackerras (Angel S3705) and Somary (Vanguard C10090/2). Choice among the four is pretty much a toss-up. ∎

January 1965

HAYDN: Quartets in E flat (Op. 33, No. 2), F major (Op. 3, No. 5), and D minor (Op. 76, No. 2). Janáček Quartet. London 6385, $5.98.

Each of these three works has a nickname. The *E flat Quartet* is *"The Joke"*

(continued)

because of the false end in the finale. The *F major* is *"The Serenade"* becaue of the famous slow movement. The *D minor* is *"The Quinten,"* or *"Fifths,"* because of the harmonic intervals of the first movement. All are fine pieces of music. Indeed, it is difficult to think of any dull ones among Haydn's eighty-two string quartets. Best of the three is the *D minor,* a masterpiece on a par with any of the Mozart quartets. The Janáček group plays these works superbly. It is one of the world's ranking chamber organizations, and it has not only the expected technical accomplishment one would expect from a modern group, but also a sober musicianship and feeling for the classic period that few contemporary groups do have. London has handled the stereo very well. For example, take the opening of the last movement of the *F major,* with the upper strings making the initial statement near the left and the lower strings responding at the right.

Comment

In the early days of long-playing records, the Haydn Society embarked upon a most ambitious project: the recording of all the Haydn string quartets by a quartet specially formed for the task under Alexander Schneider. The project was abandoned before it was even half finished. One complete edition of all the Haydn quartets, played by two different string quartets, exists today on the Vox label—but the performances are generally indifferent. For its part, the Janáček Quartet offers more secure ensemble, a more lustrous tone, and more inner vitality than the Schneider Quartet was able to bring to their recordings. The Aeolian Quartet of Great Britain has undertaken to record all the Haydn quartets (for Decca/London Records). Those released thus far are robustly played and recorded.   ∎

May 1969

HAYDN: Symphonies No. 93 in D and 94 in G (Surprise). The Cleveland Orchestra conducted by George Szell. Columbia MS7006, $5.98.

Szell and the Cleveland Orchestra have brought the scrupulous care for which they are famous to these performances of the *No. 94 (Surprise),* probably Haydn's best-known symphony, and the lesser-known but equally excellent *No. 93.* The results are felicitous. Szell pays great attention to the balance of the orchestral choirs, and within any given level of loud or soft the listener is rewarded with painstaking shadings and nuances. Subsidiary themes and figurations—particularly in the second violins and in the bassoon—are stated with great finesse, and the pervasive tympani part receives its proper emphasis. In both first movements Szell quite properly observes the repeat of the exposition. And there are many highlights as the symphonies progress: For example, in the *No. 93* the first statement of the slow movement's theme is played by a string quartet (as it was in the very first performance of the symphony) instead of by today's more usual massed strings; and near the end of the movement, the low-C belch on the bassoon is deliciously vulgar—just the effect Haydn must have sought. In the *Surprise*

Symphony, the surprise chord in the sixteenth bar of the slow movement is extraordinarily explosive; near the very end of the symphony the tympani is riotously eruptive. If only Szell could have combined such attention to detail with a more relaxed good humor, these performances would be ideal. As they are,though, they still merit a high recommendation. The Columbia engineers have contrived a very clear, if somewhat harsh, reproduced sound.

November 1973

HAYDN: Symphonies No. 93 in D and No. 94 in G (Surprise). The New York Philharmonic conducted by Leonard Bernstein. Columbia M32101, $5.98.

Having established himself as one of our most persuasive and perceptive Haydn conductors, with extraordinarily stylish recordings of the composer's "Paris" symphonies (Nos. 82 through 87, Columbia D3S769), Bernstein now seems to have embarked upon the cycle of the composer's last 12 symphonies, the so-called "London" symphonies. As before, the results are superlative. Bernstein invariably selects just the right tempo in each movement, and his rhythms have a resiliency that allows the music to breathe naturally and spontaneously. He maintains a superbly delicate balance between the winds and strings throughout.

The playing by the New York Philharmonic is exhilarating, and the recorded sound is as clean as a whistle. Columbia already has an unusually successful coupling of these two symphonies in its catalog by George Szell and the Cleveland Orchestra (MS7006). But this new Bernstein disc offers performances that are every bit as disciplined, with the added attraction of keener response to the wit and humor in both scores.

Comment

It's a pity that Szell recorded only seven Haydn symphonies with his great orchestra. The polish and sophistication he brought to his Haydn performances were delightful and they are qualities that are rare in today's musical marketplace.

Only two of Haydn's twelve "London" symphonies (Nos. 97 and 98) have yet to be recorded by the team of Leonard Bernstein and the New York Philharmonic. Surely Columbia will fill that gap before very long, for Bernstein's Haydn performances rank among his very best. ∎

February 1977

HAYDN: Symphonies Nos. 94 in G (Surprise), and 101 in D (Clock). The London Philharmonic Orchestra conducted by Eugen Jochum. Deutsche Grammophon 2530628, $7.98.

Eugen Jochum, now in his mid-70's, has had a long and distinguished career
(continued)

on the Continent with such institutions as the Hamburg State Opera, the Munich Radio Orchestra, the Berlin Radio, and the Amsterdam Concertgebouw Orchestra. Much of his current activity is concentrated in London; there his perceptions of Haydn, Mozart, Beethoven, Schubert, Mendelssohn, and Bruckner—the mainstream of German orchestral repertory—have led some to regard him as the natural successor to Otto Klemperer.

These performances of two of Haydn's best-known symphonies are models of the large-orchestra approach to that composer. Jochum's rhythms are ideally sprung. The textures are immaculately transparent—consider, in the last movement of the *Surprise Symphony*, the clarity of the flute doubling the strings in the repeat of the principal theme's first statement. The exposition repeats are observed in the first movements of both symphonies. And Jochum responds intuitively to the great good humor to be found in both scores. Listen, for example, to his superb, explosive pointing of the tympani roll near the end of the *Surprise*—it makes that moment as much of a musical surprise as the loud chord in the slow movement that gives the work its nickname. The members of the London Philharmonic are obedient to Jochum's every wish, and the Deutsche Grammophon sound is consistently rich and enveloping.

Comment

Four more of Haydn's "London" symphonies are available in Jochum-London Philharmonic performances on the Deutsche Grammophon label: Symphonies numbers 99 and 100 (DG2530459), and numbers 103 and 104 (DG2530525). All four scores benefit from the same felicities of Jochum's approach that are evident in numbers 94 and 101, reviewed above. ∎

May 1959

HAYDN: Symphonies No. 100 in G (Military) and No. 101 in D (Clock). Vienna State Opera Orchestra conducted by Mogens Wöldike. Vanguard S187, $2.98.

The stereo version is a mighty fine bargain. Wöldike has an easy, relaxed way with the music. He does not push it too hard, and some of his tempi are inclined to be slow (his pacing in the first movement of *No. 101* will take some getting used to). But he has musicianship, integrity, and style. He sees to it that the balances let the wind instruments be heard (almost always, conductors swamp the winds with overprominent strings), and he obviously is more interested in the music than in being a virtuoso conductor. Vanguard has presented him with as natural-sounding a reproduction of the orchestra as one is likely to hear in the present state of sonic development. The sound is bright and never soggy. There is a good deal of separation, none of which sounds artificial. The percussion in the *Military Symphony* has plenty of life but is presented with due proportion, not as a hi-fi gimmick. That, indeed, is what is outstanding about these performances and recordings: proportion.

Comment

No other single disc of Haydn symphonies offers these two brilliant scores from the composer's second *Salomon* set. Performances and recorded sound are still exemplary. ∎

July 1978

HAYDN: Symphonies Nos. 100 in G (Military), and 103 in E Flat (Drum Roll). The Academy of St. Martin-in-the-Fields under the direction of Neville Marriner. Philips 9500255. $8.98. ●

We live in an age of superlative Haydn conductors: Antal Dorati, Leonard Bernstein, and Eugen Jochum, among others. (For example, Dorati's recording of *all* the Haydn symphonies—more than 100 in number—is a landmark in recording history.) Now Neville Marriner joins the ranks of the masters in a project to record, for Philips, all the Haydn symphonies with nicknames. His earlier recording of Haydn's *Symphonies Nos. 52* and *53* (Philips 6500114) made it clear that his credentials were ample. The present disc, the first of the new series to be released, further demonstrates that Marriner has a most distinguished and persuasive way with Haydn.

Marriner gives the score suitable polish throughout and never allows the music's vital, surging pulse to slacken. The recorded sound is ideal—airy, clear, and lifelike, characteristics we almost take for granted with Philips these days.

Unlike some of Haydn's "name" symphonies, these works are among the best known in music. The *Symphony No. 100, Military*, gets its name from Haydn's use of such martial instruments as bass drum, cymbals, and triangle in the second and fourth movements. The *Symphony No. 103, Drum Roll*, derives its nickname from a role of kettle drums at the beginning of the Introduction to the first movement and again near the movement's end. While the musical dynamic of the drum passage lends itself to a variety of interpretations, Marriner chooses a very loud, imperious roll that commands immediate attention. I find it exactly right.

Comment

Marriner is becoming an increasingly familiar figure in American concert halls, and his appointment as Music Director of the Minnesota Orchestra holds great promise for that organization. ∎

November 1959

HINDEMITH: Concert Music for Strings and Brass (Op. 50); Symphony in B flat for Band (1951). Philharmonia Orchestra conducted by Paul Hindemith. Seraphim S60005, $2.98.

(continued)

Any time a leading composer conducts his own music the results are of more than routine interest. Here Hindemith leads a great orchestra in two examples of his fine, sturdy writing. Neither of these is a particularly dissonant score (as dissonance is measured nowadays), and each has the typical Hindemithian fluency, brilliant technique, and wry melodic lines. The stereo has a fullness and subtlety representative of modern recording at its best.

Comment

Since Hindemith's death in 1963, this disc has assumed even greater historical interest—particularly since becoming available in the low-cost Seraphim series. ■

HOLST: The Planets. The Boston Symphony Orchestra and the New England Conservatory Chorus conducted by William Steinberg. Deutsche Grammophon 2530102, $6.98. ▲ ●

In these days of heightened interest in space travel, Gustav Holst's fanciful orchestral suite of 1914–16, *The Planets*, has assumed hit proportions in the orchestral repertoire. This Steinberg-Boston Symphony recording of the score is the third to be released in recent months (the other two were conducted by Bernard Herrmann and Bernard Haitink); a Mehta-Los Angeles Philharmonic performance is scheduled for early release on the London label; and in the next few months *The Planets* is scheduled for further recordings by Leonard Bernstein and the New York Philharmonic (on Columbia) and Eugene Ormandy and the Philadelphia Orchestra (on RCA).

During the 1950s, Steinberg served simultaneously as music director of the London Philharmonic Orchestra and the Pittsburgh Symphony Orchestra. Thus there is a measure of appropriateness to his selection of this landmark of British orchestral literature for his first recording with the Boston Symphony Orchestra on the DG label. While he does not erase memories of Sir Adrian Boult's extraordinary identity with this music—Boult recorded *The Planets* no fewer than four times, the most recent of which (Angel S36420) is a brilliant stereo reproduction—Steinberg nevertheless presents an admirable straightforward account. If he misses the menace that Boult brings to the opening "Mars" section or the beefy character of the middle theme in the "Jupiter" section, there is a beguiling quality of tenderness to Steinberg's performances of such sections as "Venus" and "Mercury." And his treatment of the concluding "Neptune" section, with its wordless chorus and final fadeout to nothingness, is most compelling.

Comment

A combination of circumstances—including his own frail health—conspired to limit the number of recordings Steinberg made during his three seasons (1969-72) as music director of the Boston Symphony Orchestra. This performance of *The Planets* is near the top of his recorded output and should be a valued memento of the Steinberg era in Boston. ∎

August 1972

HUBAY: Violin Concerto No. 3 in G minor; ERNST: Violin Concerto in F sharp minor; YSAYE: Chant d'Hiver in B minor for Violin and Orchestra. Aaron Rosand, violin, with the Orchestra of Radio Luxembourg conducted by Louis de Froment. Candide CE31054, $3.98.

The piano—both solo and with orchestra—has been the main focus of the current revival of Romantic and post-Romantic music. This disc comprises Romantic and post-Romantic music for violin and orchestra, by three distinguished violinist-composers. Two of them, Hubay and Ysaye, lived into the 1930s and were world-famous touring virtuosi. Ernst, who died in 1865 was a contemporary and colleague of Berlioz and Paganini.

Hubay's concerto is the longest and most formally structured of the three works on the disc. It has four movements—a fantasia, a scherzo, a lyrical adagio and a stunningly virtuosic finale. A pleasant and engaging score, this work is a welcome addition to recorded literature. The concerto by Ernst is a one-movement affair with an extended cadenza for the solo instrument and a full-blooded ending that could almost be an aria out of a Donizetti opera. The slightest of the three works is Ysaye's brief *Chant d'Hiver*, the third of seven tone poems that he composed, mostly for violin and orchestra. Ysaye has previously been represented in the record catalogs by other works—notably *Sonata for Unaccompanied Violin*—that do him greater justice. This work is a trifle.

All three scores are played with superb taste and artistry by Rosand, one of today's most expert violinists and a specialist in the Romantic and post-Romantic literature. The Orchestra of Radio Luxembourg may be somewhat deficient in technical polish, but it makes up for that lack, in some measure, by its enthusiasm and spontaneity. One has the feeling that it would do better under a more demanding conductor.

This disc is valuable for the Hubay concerto and for Rosand's playing throughout.

Comment

Two other discs of music for violin and orchestra from the Romantic era are of interest: Candide 31064 and Turnabout 34629. They contain, respectively, works by Joachim and Hubay, and by Arensky, Rimsky-Korsakov, and Wieniawski—all played superlatively by the soloist, Aaron Rosand. ∎

August 1972

HUSA: String Quartets Nos. 2 and 3. The Fine Arts Quartet. Everest 3290, $4.98.

(continued)

From the opening bouncing-bow motif of Karel Husa's *Third String Quartet*, it is evident that a major work is in the offing. Husa, a 50-year-old native of Prague, has been a member of the faculty at Cornell University for nearly 20 years. He teaches composition there and is in charge of the university's symphony and chamber orchestras. His musical output embraces a wide variety of forms and media, but he had gone largely unrecognized until his *Third String Quartet*, commissioned by the Fine Arts Quartet, was awarded the Pulitzer Prize in Music in 1969.

Highly textured instrumental effects are a hallmark of the *Third String Quartet*, with tremolos, slides, bouncing bows and close harmonics abounding. But those effects are used to further the overall musical scheme rather than as ends in themselves. The Quartet is marvelously vital and imaginative, most welcome at this time of musical faddism and gimmickry.

Husa's *Second String Quartet* has the same vitality as the *Third*, but its means are more conventional. The four instruments toss themes or fragments of themes from one to the other, and they interact more or less according to classical patterns. Although the *Third Quartet* is the bolder work, the *Second* is nevertheless a stimulating and vibrant one. The Fine Arts Quartet, one of Chicago's most valued cultural institutions, gives masterful accounts of both scores.

Comment

Husa's most frequently played orchestral score is the intense and passionate *Music for Prague*, composed to protest the brutal Soviet invasion of his native city in 1968. A recording of *Music for Prague* by the Louisville Orchestra conducted effectively by Jorge Mester (Louisville S722) is available, but the score cries out for a dazzling recorded performance by a major virtuoso ensemble—Solti–Chicago Symphony, say, or Mehta–New York Philharmonic. ■

November 1972

IVES: Orchestral Set No. 2; MESSIAEN: L'Ascension. The London Symphony Orchestra and (in the Ives) Chorus conducted by Leopold Stokowski. London SPC21060, $5.98.

Stokowski, the wizard, here turns in another of his prodigious recording accomplishments. His performances of both scores are toweringly dynamic, with an overall power and sweep that defies description. Neither work is very well known, though both have been recorded previously—the Ives in a good but much less penetrating account by Morton Gould and the Chicago Symphony (RCA LSC2959), and the Messiaen in a long-unavailable earlier Stokowski recording (Columbia ML4214) with the New York Philharmonic. In the Messiaen, the nonagenarian Stokowski summons from his players greater vitality and more passion than he could evoke a quarter of a century before. Indeed, for sheer intensity the playing of the London Symphony strings in the final section (The Prayer of Christ Ascending to the Father) is quite overwhelming.

124

Both scores are characteristic of their composers. Ives's *Orchestral Set*, just now coming into its own some 60 years after it was written, is a complex work of extraordinary invention and cumulative power, with some considerable pictorial effect. (The last movement, for example, is a musical evocation of the mood aboard a crowded New York City train on the day of the sinking of the Lusitania.) And the Messiaen deals with that composer's concern for the mysticism and traditions of the Roman Catholic Church.

The London Phase 4 engineers have provided sound of enormous dynamic range and great clarity. Here is another extraordinary offering in the remarkable late-flowering period of Stokowski's activity.

Comment

This disc remains one of the glories of recording literature, a riveting memento of that glorious Indian summer of Leopold Stokowski's life, when he contributed some of the greatest performances of his career. ∎

November 1966

IVES: Symphony No. 1 in D minor; The Unanswered Question; SCHUMAN: Variations on "America" after Charles Ives. Chicago Symphony Orchestra conducted by Morton Gould. RCA LSC2893, $5.98.

This is a first recording of the *Symphony No. 1* by Charles Ives, that strange American nationalist ignored during his life and all but canonized during the last fifteen years. It was composed in 1896–98 and is a student work that shows Ives could be as academic as the next composer if he so desired. Completely eclectic, the work is a mélange of ideas stemming from Beethoven, Dvořák, Brahms, the French school, and, in the second movement, apparently Mahler. The presence of that last name is curious. The chances are that in 1898 Ives had not heard Mahler's music, and yet here he was, composing one of those long-phrased slow movements that breathe the very world of Gustav Mahler. Even more curious, the *Symphony No. 1*, derivations and all, makes an extraordinary impact. From it an original mind, full of ideas, emerges. The melodic materials, too, are highly attractive. This work is a good introduction to the spiky, problematic Ives we find in the later works.

The Unanswered Question, on the second side of this disc, is a moody, mystic little masterpiece. *Variations on "America"* will be a novelty to most. Originally composed as an organ piece, and presented here in an orchestration by William Schuman, it is an irreverent sort of affectionate spoof on "My Country, 'Tis of Thee."

Morton Gould, not usually associated with this kind of music, conducts with a great deal of style and knowledge. RCA has provided fine recorded sound. There is total separation for *The Unanswered Question*, thus allowing the "questions" to sound in an antiphonal manner, as they do in the concert hall.

(continued)

Comment

In November 1966, it was still possible to write that Morton Gould was "not usually associated with this kind of music." Since then this distinguished composer-conductor has carved out a secure niche for himself as one of America's most open-minded and adventurous musicians. This Ives disc is one of Gould's finest accomplishments—and still one of the most notable in the recent history of recording. ■

March 1967

IVES: Symphony No. 2; "The Fourth of July" from Symphony: Holidays. New York Philharmonic conducted by Leonard Bernstein. Columbia MS6889, $5.98.

The *Second Symphony* was issued some years back. Now Columbia has repackaged it, adding to the disc *"The Fourth of July"* and, as a bonus, an attached seven-inch disc in which Bernstein discusses Ives in general and these two works in particular. The *Second Symphony* is the best introduction to the music of Ives. It is full of the essential Ives spirit, yet is relatively uncomplicated until the end of the last movement, where suddenly everything goes on at once in a wild and unforgettable mélange. *"The Fourth of July"* is a strange and wonderful evocation of America in the last century. The recorded sound in the symphony remains good, despite some background noise and tape hiss.

Comment

It was back in 1951 that Bernstein conducted the world premiere performances of the Ives *Second Symphony* with the New York Philharmonic—fifty years after the symphony's completion. Bernstein's association with the score is thus almost proprietary, and his recording of it is superb. ■

June 1966

IVES: Symphony No. 4. Members of the Schola Cantorum and the American Symphony Orchestra conducted by Leopold Stokowski. Columbia MS6775, $5.98.

About a year ago Stokowski conducted the world premiere of the Ives *Fourth Symphony*, a work that had been completed in 1916. Ives left the score in a mess, and several experts had to work quite a few years putting it into shape. Part of their problem was that of renotation, so that players could read the difficult parts. At that, the *Fourth Symphony* is so complicated that it needs the help of two additional conductors (David Katz and José Serebrier, on this disc). It is one of Ives' typical wild mélanges, with all kinds of polyrhythms, with simple passages set against passages of fearsome complexity, with direct quotations from the American hymnody interspersed with patriotic tunes going along loudly in every key at once.

Many have hailed the Ives *Fourth* as a masterpiece, and it probably is. Some of it may sound awkward, but it is a real evocation of an aspect of America, expressed in music of overwhelming force and imagination. Stokowski, as much as one can gather, conducts brilliantly. Fine recorded sound. Large sections of the score involve antiphonal effects, and these the stereo delivers.

Comment

After conducting the 1965 premiere of Ives's *Fourth Symphony*, Stokowski included the score in the repertory seasons of the American Symphony Orchestra and made a television film with the orchestra rehearsing and performing the score. Stokowski's recording of the *Fourth* is definitive—as is Bernstein's of Ives's *Second Symphony.* Equally persuasive is the RCA recording (ARL10589) of the *Fourth Symphony.* The RCA disc, which is astonishingly clean-textured, was conducted by José Serebrier, who was one of Stokowski's assistants in the world premiere performance and recording of the score. ∎

June 1971

JANÁČEK: Sinfonietta; LUTOSLAWSKI: Concerto for Orchestra. The Chicago Symphony Orchestra conducted by Seiji Ozawa. Angel S36045, $5.98. ●

The *Sinfonietta,* written in 1926, is probably the best-known orchestral work by the Czech composer, Leos Janáček. The colorful, five-movement score begins and ends with brass fanfares that Janáček had composed some time before for an open-air athletic meet. In between Janáček has composed vital and unique music with bubbling woodwind harmonies, stabbing brass chords, and high-register strings.

Lutoslawski composed his *Concerto for Orchestra* in 1954, modeling it after Bartók's *Concerto for Orchestra* of a decade earlier. There are Polish folk elements in Lutoslawski's score, just as there are Hungarian folk elements in Bartók's, in both cases thoroughly integrated into the musical fabric of the piece. Each of the three movements of the score is itself divided into several sections, so that the work—less than thirty minutes long—succeeds in producing a kaleidoscopic effect. The overall effect is brilliance, but there are also tenderness and serenity. Since Lutoslawski wrote the *Concerto for Orchestra,* he has produced music that is stylistically very different, but he has yet to duplicate the power and sweep of the *Concerto.*

Both scores are given clear-headed and carefully shaded interpretations by Ozawa, but they lack the ultimate authority that would have given the two scores their inherent virtues—Janáček's its unity and Lutoslawski's its vitality.

(continued)

Comment

Be that as it may, the stunning performances by the Chicago Symphony Orchestra deserve special attention. In the 1960s Ozawa spent a number of summers as Artistic Director of the Chicago Symphony's Ravinia Festival concerts, and the close rapport developed between conductor and orchestra during that period is everywhere evident in these performances. ∎

September 1965

JANÁČEK: Slavonic Mass (M'sa Glagolskaja). Evelyn Lear, soprano; Hilde Rössl-Majdan, mezzo-soprano; Ernst Haefliger, tenor; Franz Crass, bass; Bavarian Radio Symphony Orchestra conducted by Rafael Kubelik. Deutsche Grammophon 138954; $6.98.

In recent years there has been something of a Janáček renaissance. His operas are in the repertoire of many European houses, and even in America his works are being played with increasing frequency. He was a Czech composer who died in 1928, a nationalist in the tradition of Dvořák. The outstanding Czech composer of his day, he wrote strong music that, though it had its roots in the nineteenth century, was nevertheless modern in its frequent tonal clashes, economy of means, and general philosophy.

This mass was composed in 1926 to celebrate the tenth anniversary of the Czech republic. The text honors the two Czechoslovakian patron saints, St. Cyril and St. Methodius, who had translated much of the Bible into Glagolitic script (a precursor of the modern Latin script). Hence the title of the mass. The music is rough-hewn, uncompromising, with tremendous power and a great deal of personality. Definitely it is an important score, an exciting one, and very much worth getting to know.

The performance is all one could ask for. Kubelik, a Czech, knows the tradition, and his soloists are solid and dependable. Very bright recorded sound.

Comment

The only other available recording, conducted by Kempe (London OSA26338), is a smoother, less craggy performance. But its sonics are considerably richer than the Kubelik-DG version. ∎

September 1965

KODÁLY: Háry János: Suite; Galanta Dances. London Symphony Orchestra conducted by István Kertész. London 6417, $5.98.

What a bang-up recording! At audio shows this fall you can be sure that the stereo version of this disc will be resounding from all booths. The volume is high, but there is never any distortion. Instruments stand clearly separated from the orchestral fabric, and the entire orchestra has unusual gloss and color. Toward the end of the *Galanta Dances,* listen to the trumpets ripping through the curtain of sound.

The disc contains Kodály's two most popular scores, and both are minor masterpieces. Examples of Hungarian nationalism, they are melodious, lively, colorful, scored with unusual brilliance and resource. Highly recommended. The disc also contains a bonus—two arias for soprano from *Háry János.* One is a love lament, of haunting beauty, and the other is a fast, more traditional kind of folk song. Both are unfamiliar; both are worth knowing. They are sung by a Hungarian soprano named Olga Szonyi, who has all of the good and bad points associated with Slavic singers today. Together with flair, rhythm, and temperament is an unsteady vocal production that makes the voice emerge shrill and tremolo-ridden.

Kertész is a young Hungarian conductor who has been making a big splash in Europe in recent years. On this disc he conducts with drive and energy, and his work is most impressive.

Comment

This disc has kept its luster over the years. It makes even more tragic the death of István Kertész, who drowned some years ago in an accident off the coast of Israel. ∎

October 1975

KORNGOLD: Violin Concerto in D; Suite from "Much Ado About Nothing"; Theme and Variations. The Stuttgart Radio Orchestra conducted by Willy Mattes, with Ulf Hoelscher, violin (in the concerto). Angel S36999, $5.98.

Before Erich Wolfgang Korngold became a Hollywood film composer in the 1930's, he had already carved out for himself a distinguished reputation as a prodigy composer of concert and operatic music, which was played and sung by all the great performers of the time. Then, in 1947, he turned his back on film composition entirely and until his death in 1955 at the age of 60 devoted himself once again to music for the concert hall.

One of the major works of Korngold's later years was his *Violin Concerto,* a brilliant, three-movement display vehicle for the solo instrument. It is one of very few recent violin works that treat the instrument in its traditional, singing capacity. Throughout, Korngold incorporates themes he had initially created for film scores, but they fit hand in glove in the fabric and formal structure of the piece. The concerto is done full justice in a particularly well-played performance by the young German violinist, Ulf Hoelscher.

Korngold's suite for *Much Ado About Nothing* dates from 1918. It is boisterous, extroverted, and good-humored music and consists of five sections; the third of them, a droll march, depicts Dogberry and Verges, the two comical officers of the watch in Shakespeare's play. The *Theme and Variations,* composed two years before Korngold's death, was intended for school orches-

(continued)

129

tras. Korngold characterized the theme as having the quality of "an Irish folk tune," and the seven variations that follow are full of color and contrast.

In all the pieces, Mattes and his Stuttgart instrumentalists offer expert performances, and the recorded sound is fine.

Comment

The *Suite from "Much Ado About Nothing"* is also available in a fine recording by the Westphalian Symphony Orchestra conducted by Siegfried Landau (Candide 31091). If the Stuttgart Radio's performance is smoother, the Westphalian account has more bite and sparkle. The *Violin Concerto* performance has formidable competition indeed: Heifetz, for whom Korngold composed it, recorded the music many years ago—in monophonic sound, to be sure—and that disc is still available (RCA LM1782). Splendid as Hoelscher's playing is, Heifetz remains in a class by himself. ∎

March 1971

KOUSSEVITZKY: Concerto for Double Bass. Gary Karr, bass, with the Oslo Philharmonic Orchestra conducted by Alfredo Antonini; **BLOCH: Sinfonia breve.** The Minneapolis Symphony Orchestra conducted by Antal Dorati. CRI S248, $5.95.

Serge Koussevitzky directed the Boston Symphony Orchestra between 1924 and 1949. Those twenty-five years represent one of the most glorious periods in American symphonic life. Koussevitzky came to Boston from conducting triumphs in Europe, but his musical career had begun as a virtuoso on that most unlikely of virtuoso instruments, the double bass. He composed this concerto for the instrument in 1902, for his own use, and he performed it extensively during the early years of the century. After many years of neglect, the score was revived some years ago by Alfredo Antonini for his series of televised concerts on CBS. The soloist then, as on this recording, was the prodigy Gary Karr, who is still an astonishing young bass virtuoso. Incidentally, he has inherited and plays Koussevitzky's own superb Amati instrument.

The *Concerto* clearly indicates the influence of Tchaikovsky. The opening motif, given to horns in unison, is strikingly reminiscent of the opening of Tchaikovsky's *B flat minor Piano Concerto*; and the motif returns again to herald the opening of the last movement. But Koussevitzky as composer had his own strongly lyrical strain. Thus, the score has more than curiosity interest, and it is good to have it available in this stunning performance.

The overside, *Sinfonia breve* by Bloch, was recorded originally by Mercury about ten years ago. It has been out of the catalog for some time and returns now as part of a project by Composers Recordings, Inc., that consists of acquiring and releasing important contemporary recordings not otherwise available. The score, a product of the early 1950s, was one of Bloch's last important orchestral works. It is tightly organized and full of power and tension. Dorati is superlative, and the recorded sound is a tribute to the excellence of Mercury's decade-old quality standards.

Comment

Composers Recordings, Inc., is one of the most valuable of all recorded catalogs currently on the market. The CRI list includes much contemporary music that is not otherwise available. This disc is particularly rewarding, but there are many others under the CRI imprint that are equally deserving of wide circulation. The astute collector should investigate the CRI catalog and mine its riches. ■

June 1971

KUHLAU: Concerto in C for Piano (Op. 7); CLEMENTI: Concerto in C for Piano. Felicja Blumental, piano, with the Salzburg Symphony Orchestra conducted by Theodore Guschlbauer (in the Kuhlau); with the Prague New Chamber Orchestra conducted by Alberto Zedda (in the Clementi). Turnabout 34375, $2.98.

Kuhlau and Clementi, as composers of teaching-music, are names that generations of aspiring pianists have had to cope with. Their performing works, however, are appropriate fodder for Blumental, a distinguished pianist who has made a career out of recording forgotten music of the past. This record features two rather substantial concerti for piano and orchestra by these minor nineteenth-century figures.

The Kuhlau *Concerto* is at once the more arresting and diverting. The principal theme, stated at the outset by the orchestra, has more than a passing resemblance to the principal theme of the opening of Beethoven's *First Piano Concerto*, written a few years earlier, and Kuhlau's orchestration and interweaving of piano and orchestra are also similar. But where Beethoven's *Concerto* is full of the unexpected, Kuhlau's is highly predictable—indeed, almost formula-ridden. With it all, though, the Kuhlau has a period charm that makes its revival worthwhile.

Clementi's *Concerto*, on the other hand, has little to recommend it. It is conceptually barren, its elaboration is tedious, and its melodies are commonplace. Clementi may have been a colorful operator in his contemporary society, as the jacket notes point out, but this example of his work shows him as esthetically dull.

Comment

Also worth investigating are some of Kuhlau's brief sonatinas for piano solo, engagingly played by Philippe Entremont in an interesting two-disc album of sonatinas (Columbia MG33202) by a number of composers—some important and some not. ■

January 1960

LISZT: Concerti No. 1 in E flat major and No. 2 in A major for Piano and Orchestra. Philippe Entremont, piano, and the Philadelphia Or-
(continued)

chestra conducted by Eugene Ormandy. Columbia MS6071, $5.98.

It is always pleasant ot hear the work of an up-and-coming young artist. Entremont is an extremely talented young French pianist who seems to have a flair for the Romantics. He turns in idiomatic, red-blooded performances of these two bravura concerti, reveling in the difficulties and playing with a surprising degree of style for one of his years. He does not approach the stature of a Rubinstein in the E *flat*, but Rubinstein has not recorded the *A major*, and Entremont's pairing of these two concerti is as good as any available. There is a slight glassiness to the upper register of the solo instrument. There also is some tape hiss. Nevertheless, the balance between piano and orchestra is fine and the sound in general is acceptable.

March 1973

LISZT: Piano Concertos Nos. 1 in E flat and 2 in A. Ivan Davis, piano, with the Royal Philharmonic Orchestra conducted by Edward Downes. London SPC21081, $5.98.

Ivan Davis is a young American pianist—artist-in-residence at the University of Miami (Fla.)—who has not had the performing career in this country that his enormous ability warrants. He is a pianist of the old school, with a brilliant virtuoso technique and a Romantic temperament. His métier, not surprisingly, is the piano literature of the Romantic masters, from Chopin through Rachmaninoff, and London Records has been sponsoring him in a series of recordings of that music—to the vast benefit of listeners.

The present coupling of the two Liszt piano concertos joins in excellence such previous Davis recordings as the Tchaikovsky *First* and Rachmaninoff *Second Piano Concertos*. To these two Liszt virtuoso showpieces Davis brings qualities of derring-do and fanciful imagination that present the scores in the best possible light. These are eminently worthy alternative performances to the cooler but equally brilliant recordings of the works by Richter (Philips 835474). Davis is matched every step of the way by the hair-trigger response of the Royal Philharmonic Orchestra and conductor Edward Downes, of London's Covent Garden Opera and the recently installed music director of the emerging Australian National Opera in Sydney.

Comment

Dazzling though the Davis-Downes performances may be, two of the many available recorded pairings of these scores stand out above all the rest: Sviatoslav Richter's, with Kondrashin conducting (Philips 835474), and Lazar Berman's, with Giulini conducting (Deutsche Grammophon 2530770). Both pianists bring prodigious technical virtuosity to their playing—and poetic sensitivity as well. ∎

September 1973

LISZT: Mountain Symphony. Music for Westchester Symphony Orchestra conducted by Siegfried Landau. **Malédiction for Piano and String Or-**

chesta; The Funeral Gondola. Alfred Brendel, piano, with a string orchestra conducted by Michael Gielen (in the *Malédiction*). Turnabout TVS34518, $2.98.

The three works on this disc represent Liszt at three stages in his creative career. The *Mountain Symphony,* the first of his dozen-or-so symphonic poems, is a middle-years piece composed when Liszt was in his 40s. The *Malédiction* is a very early work that anticipates the single-movement, formal structure that characterizes the composer's symphonic poems for orchestra. The short piano solo, *The Funeral Gondola,* was written in 1882, when Liszt was already into his 70s.

The *Mountain Symphony* is the longest and least interesting of the three. Its sprawling nature and diffuse architecture make it seem an endless bore. New York's suburban but fully professional Music for Westchester Symphony Orchestra is expert but could have benefited by more imaginative conducting.

The *Malédiction* is inherently more interesting, with a rather wide emotional range and an early demonstration of Liszt's interest in esoteric harmonic combinations. But ultimately it, too, tends to discursive rambling. Liszt gave full range to his harmonic daring—far in advance of its time—in *The Funeral Gondola,* probably the best-realized of the three pieces. Brendel plays both works expertly; and Gielen and his string ensemble are worthy collaborators in the *Malédiction.* The stereo reproduction for *The Funeral Gondola* has been electronically contrived from a monophonic master tape, which may account for the rather metallic piano sound.

Comment

A few years ago a geniune revival of interest in the less-known and rarely performed orchestral works of Liszt seemed to be under way. That revival now appears to have run its course, at least insofar as concert performances are concerned. All the more reason, then, to regret the reserved character of this performance of Liszt's *Mountain Symphony.* Much more convincing is the Haitink-London Philharmonic recording (Philips 6500189). Its advantages include superior sound reproduction and two more of Liszt's symphonic poems on the second side: *Battle of the Huns* and *From the Cradle to the Grave.* ∎

May 1974

MACDOWELL: Suite No. 2 for Orchestra (Indian); Piano Concerto No. 2 in D minor. Westphalian Symphony Orchestra conducted by Siegfried Landau (with Eugene List, piano, in the concerto). Turnabout TVS34535, $2.98.

Edward MacDowell, the American composer, studied music in Germany when he was between the ages of 17 and 27. While there, he was a pupil of Joachim Raff and a protégé of Liszt. He returned to the U.S., settling in Boston, and spent the next decade composing a series of orchestral works.

(continued)

Most of those, including the two on this disc, were first played by the Boston Symphony Orchestra.

These two works are perhaps MacDowell's most enduring orchestral scores. The concerto is by turns lyrical and dramatic, and it has an exhilarating spontaneity. It has been somewhat neglected in recent years; perhaps this new recording and the forthcoming Bicentennial of the American Revolution will renew interest in it. The *"Indian"* Suite smoothly incorporates American Indian melodies—Iroquois, Chippewa, Iowa, Kiowa—within the framework of traditional European music. The fourth of its five movements, a searing Dirge, is one of MacDowell's most inspired creations. It is a deeply moving lament that has lost none of its emotional appeal after more than 75 years.

Both performances are most persuasive. List is an old hand at the concerto; some dozen years ago he recorded MacDowell's two concertos with the distinguished Mexican composer-conductor, Carlos Chávez (still available on Westminster 8156). Now his approach has ripened, and his performance is even more assured. Throughout the concerto and the suite, Landau and the Westphalian Symphony Orchestra are exemplary. In the growing catalog of American music on the Turnabout label, this MacDowell disc is a special highlight.

February 1975

MACDOWELL: Suites for Orchestra Nos. 1, Opus 42, and 2, Opus 48 (Indian). The Eastman-Rochester Orchestra conducted by Howard Hanson. Mercury SR175026, $6.98.

With the approaching American Bicentennial, the music of Edward Mac-Dowell (1861-1908) and other composers of his generation is sure to come in for some special attention. MacDowell's output includes many works for piano solo, songs, choral works, two piano concertos, a *Romance* for cello and orchestra, three symphonic poems, and the two suites on the present disc.

The *First Suite* is rarely performed—a pity since it is a real charmer. Its five brief movements are titled "In a Haunted Forest," "Summer Idyll," "In October," "The Shepherdess' Song," and "Forest Spirits." The music as well as those titles are reminiscent of Grieg, but MacDowell's score also has a sincerity and a secure craftsmanship of its own.

The *"Indian"* Suite is much better known. True to its name, it actually does incorporate music of the Iroquois, Iowa, and other tribes. It, too, is in five movements, and the fourth, the Dirge, was MacDowell's own favorite among all his works. It is a powerful and haunting lament of a mother over the death of her son. The other movements are titled "Legend," "Love Song," "In Wartime," and "Village Festival."

Both scores are given masterly performances under Hanson's direction. And though the recordings themselves were made a dozen years ago and more, they are remarkably vivid in their present reincarnation.

Comment

The Vox-Turnabout catalog has a fair number of recordings of American music played by this German orchestra under the direction of Siegfried Landau. This disc is doubtless one of the very best of them—on many levels: orchestral performance, interpretation, and sound reproduction.

The Hanson performance is another of the resurrected recordings that now form the bulk of Mercury's "Golden Imports" line. As is usually the case, the remastering of the tapes has warmed up, expanded, and generally improved the sound compared with what we hard on the original recordings more than a dozen years ago. ∎

March 1961

MAHLER: Das Lied von der Erde; Adagietto from Symphony No. 5. Dietrich Fischer-Dieskau (baritone), Murray Dickie (tenor); Philharmonia Orchestra conducted by Paul Kletzki. Angel S3607, 2 discs, $11.96.

In every previous recording of *Das Lied von der Erde,* from the very first in the 1930s, a mezzo-soprano (or contralto) and tenor have been used. Mahler did specify that a baritone could replace the female singer, but conductors have felt that not enough vocal contrast would be provided if two males were used. Now Angel has taken the plunge. Fortunately it has assigned as fine an artist as Fischer-Dieskau to the performance. He is one of today's great stylists, a singer with a good voice, unparalleled musicianship and taste, and a high degree of sensitivity. Thus, the experiment turns out to be not an experiment but a solid accomplishment. Fischer-Dieskau is completely convincing as the low-voiced singer in *Das Lied*, phrasing with his expected artistry and underlining the meaning of the words with extraordinary art and perception. Dickie is a good singer, though as a stylist he is not on Fischer-Dieskau's level; and Kletzki conducts understandingly. This is an important release. The stereo records are handled tactfully. The singers are separated—the tenor at the right, the baritone closer to left center—but there is no gimmickry involved.

June 1973

MAHLER: Das Lied von der Erde. René Kollo, tenor, and Yvonne Minton, mezzo-soprano, with the Chicago Symphony Orchestra conducted by Sir Georg Solti. London OS26292, $5.98. ●

In everything but name, Mahler's *Das Lied von der Erde* (The Song of the Earth) is a symphony. Its six sections are settings of Chinese poems a thousand years old, translated into German by Hans Bethge. They all convey deep feelings of world-weariness and cynicism, which Mahler obviously shared. In setting the poems, Mahler created an intensely passionate and poignant work.

Das Lied von der Erde does not lack for convincing recorded performances: London Records itself has the searing account conducted by Bernstein (OS26005); Angel has the monumental Klemperer performance (S3704); and

(continued)

Columbia has Walter's direct and spontaneous presentation (Odyssey Y30043, an incredible bargain at the budget price of $2.98). Solti's new version takes its place right beside those superlative recordings. He delivers an intense, though firmly controlled, performance.

The Chicago Symphony Orchestra has never played better than it does here, and the two vocal soloists characterize their music most effectively — particularly Miss Minton and particularly in the long and demanding final section, the *Abschied* (Farewell). If any one element gives this release its special distinction, however, it is the reproduction of the sound. The engineers have outdone themselves in clarifying the textures of Mahler's ripe orchestration. Indeed, the purity of sound may seem to deprive the end of the *Abschied* of some of its veil of mystery. But the magic of the orchestration at that point is really enhanced by pellucid reproduction. In an uncommonly successful recording series made by Solti in Chicago, this is one of the best.

Comment

Kletzki's performance with the Philharmonia Orchestra has now been transferred to the budget-price Seraphim line, and it is all on a single disc (S60260). Those in search of an even more passionate rendering with two male soloists may consider the Bernstein-conducted performance (London 26005), which also benefits from extremely vivid recorded sound. Fischer-Dieskau repeats his superbly sensitive account of the low-voice solos, and the tenor is James King. Solti's success with this music comes as something of a surprise, since he generally is most comfortable with music of blazing colors and febrile intensity. *Das Lied von der Erde* is, in the main, a work of inward expression. Solti responds to it with rare and rapt conviction. Also recommended is Haitink's version (Philips 6500831), with Dame Janet Baker as mezzo-soprano soloist and James King, again, as tenor. ∎

May 1963

MAHLER: Symphony No. 1 in D major (The Titan). Columbia Symphony Orchestra conducted by Bruno Walter. Odyssey Y30047, $2.92. ●

Walter always brought something special to Mahler. As is well known, the late conductor was one of Mahler's disciples. Then, as one of the grand old men of music, Walter became Mahler's chief propagandist. In this Mahler symphony, Walter conducts *mit Liebe*. What he brings to the music, and what so few contemporary conductors can bring, is relaxation. Walter never hurries, and yet his tempi always seem perfect. There is something spacious and of a previous century about the way he leans into a phrase, lovingly outlining it. No recording of the Mahler *First* can approach this one. Even the handicap of a break in the third movement is scarcely enough to prevent this disc from heading the list.

February 1971

MAHLER: Symphony No. 1 in D major (The Titan). The London Symphony Orchestra conducted by Jascha Horenstein. Nonesuch 71240, $2.98. ●

This is the second release in the new Nonesuch series by Jascha Horenstein recorded in England by the Unicorn Record Company. As in the recording of Nielsen's *Fifth Symphony* (see page 163), Horenstein is here at the top of his form. He first demonstrated his special feeling for Mahler more than forty years ago in an excellent recording of the *Kindertotenlieder*. Perhaps Horenstein's greatest strength is his ability to give an unsuspected logic and coherence to the very loose structure of much of the *First Symphony* score, particularly the long and somewhat disjointed final movement. Throughout are flashes of genuine interpretive inspiration.

As in the Nielsen recording, Horenstein has elicited beautifully articulated and responsive playing from his orchestra. But the recorded sound is much more natural and well balanced than it was in the Nielsen. In this recording, Horenstein has opted to omit the "Blumine" movement that Mahler himself discarded soon after he wrote the symphony. It is included in the recordings by Brieff and Ormandy, but this listener agrees with Mahler and Horenstein in its omission.

September 1972

MAHLER: Symphony No. 1 in D (The Titan). The Royal Philharmonic Orchestra conducted by Erich Leinsdorf. London SPC21068, $5.98.

One of the first works Erich Leinsdorf recorded in Boston a decade ago when he became music director of the Boston Symphony Orchestra was Mahler's *First Symphony* (RCA LSC2642). It is tightly organized, superlatively played and microscopically exact, but it lacks the charm and tenderness that other conductors have brought to the music—most notably Jascha Horenstein (Nonesuch 71240).

Given an opportunity to rerecord the symphony, Leinsdorf has obviously tried to temper his earlier tendency to rigidity. He succeeds to some degree. This new performance is certainly more intimate and relaxed. But one can't escape the feeling that ease and informality simply do not come naturally to Leinsdorf. Despite a fine orchestral performance and a superlative reproduction of it, this new Leinsdorf recording does not displace several other available versions of Mahler's magnificent *First Symphony*—Solti's (London CS6401) and Walter's (Odyssey Y30047), as well as Horenstein's.

September 1973

MAHLER: Symphony No. 1 in D (The Titan). The Concertgebouw Orchestra conducted by Bernard Haitink. Philips SAL6500342, $6.98. ▲ ●

After a 10-year project in which Haitink and the Amsterdam Concertgebouw Orchestra recorded all of Mahler's completed symphonies for Philips, it has been decided to go back and redo the *First Symphony* to allow Haitink to express his latest views on the score. In the earlier recording, Haitink omitted the exposition repeat in the first movement; here he observes it, thus broadening the architectural span. And he does hold the rambling structure of the last movement in tighter control in the current issue. As with Haitink's Mahler in general, the music unfolds naturally and easily, with spontaneity

(continued)

137

and nicely adjusted tempos. As usual, the Concertgebouw Orchestra plays superbly for Haitink and the recorded sound is richer and more voluptuous than has been the recent norm in Philips's Concertgebouw releases.

This release surpasses all but a very few of its rivals. However, CU still prefers the unique blend of poetry and passion in the recording conducted by the late Jascha Horenstein (Nonesuch 71240)—and it comes at the budget price of $2.98.

Comment

Our preference for the Horenstein recording persists. It is a vibrant, dynamically expressive account of the music; since its relase, it has acquired the status of a classic. Walter's recording is also special, although some of the tempo changes—particularly in the last movement—verge on the capricious. But Walter's performance gives the music a special authenticity. The Haitink recording benefits from the smoothest and warmest sound reproduction of all recordings of the Mahler *First*.

Of the two versions that include Mahler's discarded "Blumine" movement, which may be of special interest to musicologists, the more consistently alive recording of the five-movement score is Ormandy's (RCA LSC3107); strangely, though, it is less compelling than Brieff's (Odyssey 32160286). ■

July 1960

MAHLER: Symphony No. 4 in G major. Lisa Della Casa, soprano; Chicago Symphony Orchestra conducted by Fritz Reiner. RCA LSC2364, $5.98.

The music world is celebrating the hundredth anniversary of Mahler's birth. When all the results are in, the present disc should emerge as one of the really important—and, of course, permanent—tributes. Reiner and his orchestra do a remarkable job with this work. The shortest, and the most accessible, of the Mahler symphonies, this *G major* has some marvelous ideas in it. And its unconventional last movement, nothing less than a song for soprano and orchestra, is one of the most enchanting pieces of writing that the entire post-Romantic movement has to show. It is a pleasure to report that this is among the most realistic recordings RCA or any other company has brought out. The sound is brilliant but natural, well balanced, with quiet surfaces and no distortion even in the loudest passages.

September 1966

MAHLER: Symphony No. 4 in G major. Judith Raskin, soprano, and Cleveland Orchestra conducted by George Szell. Columbia MS6833, $5.98.

Like *The Dream of Gerontius*, the Mahler *Fourth Symphony* was composed in 1900. But where the Elgar work is seldom performed in this country, Mahler and his symphonies are all but overplayed. The last twenty years have seen an incredible reappraisal of the Austrian composer, and today he has emerged as one of the heroes of the late Romantic movement. All of his nine symphonies (actually there are ten, including the unfinished) have been recorded more than once, and the popular *Fourth*—the shortest and melodically the most appealing—has an imposing list of conductors on records: Reiner, Bernstein, Walter, Klemperer, and Solti. Now comes Szell and his great orchestra in the kind of clear, pinpointed, precise, and intelligent performance so typical of this conductor. This is one of the best of all available recordings, and it also has the virtue of Judith Raskin's sensitive and sweet-sounding delivery of the soprano solo in the last movement. Excellent recorded sound. Spatial effects come through without gimmickry.

May 1969

MAHLER: Symphony No. 4 in G major. Utah Symphony Orchestra conducted by Maurice Abravanel, with Netania Davrath, soprano, in the last movement. Vanguard Cardinal C10042, $3.98.

Abravanel's Mahler series for Vanguard Cardinal is a mixed bag, this *Fourth Symphony* being one of the less successful performances. It lacks the sensitive interpretation necessary to keep the music from sounding contrived and banal. Davrath, too, disappoints: Her singing of a child's fantasy of heaven is rather leaden, and she has some surprising difficulties with intonation.

The *Fourth* has the lightest instrumentation of all the Mahler symphonies (trombones and tuba are dispensed with entirely). Shortly before his death Mahler further clarified the balances and textures of the scoring with subtle adjustments in the instrumentation. Those adjustments were first published in the 1963 critical edition of the score, and Abravanel's recording is the first to incorporate them. It thus takes on an importance by virtue of which it transcends, somewhat, the performance's deficiencies; not sufficiently, though, to dislodge Bernstein and Szell as this listener's preferred conductors of Mahler's *Fourth*.

Comment

Since the Mahler centennial in 1960, we have had other and more persuasive accounts of this idyllic music. In the full-price category, the Szell wins top honors for an all-around noteworthy performance of Mahler's *Fourth.* In the low-price department, Kletzki's performance (Seraphim S60105) is probably the most satisfying, and his soprano, Emmy Loose, handles her assignment most affectingly. The Reiner-Chicago Symphony account has now moved to RCA's low-priced Gold Seal label (AGL11333). ∎

March 1961

MASCAGNI: Cavalleria Rusticana. Giulietta Simionato, mezzo-soprano (Santuzza); Mario Del Monaco, tenor (Turiddu); Raquel Satre, mezzo-soprano (Lola); Cornell MacNeil, baritone (Alfio); Orchestra and Chorus of L'Accademia

(continued)

di Santa Cecilia, Rome, conducted by Tullio Serafin. London 1213, 2 discs, $11.96.

Three sides of this album are devoted to *Cav.* On the fourth, Del Monaco loudly sings a group of popular Italian songs. The opera, of course, needs no description, and remains one of the finest *verismo* pieces ever composed. In many respects this is a fine performance. Simionato here may have provided the greatest characterization of Santuzza ever put on records. She does not emote all over the album, but she sings with dignity, clarity, imagination, and formidable vocal resource. Her low notes especially are a delight. Usually the role is sung by a soprano. Simionato, being a mezzo with a remarkably secure range, takes in the bottom as well as the top of the tessitura. Turiddu is one of Del Monaco's best roles, and MacNeil sings a splendid Alfio. The conducting, however, is on the dull side. Serafin seldom livens things up, and the Sicilian fire simmers low in this fiery opera. If you hear some fading in and out of singers and chorus, do not let it disturb you; the engineers are following the score. Thus, when Lola enters, she is first heard offstage, as per the libretto. Finally she reaches the microphones.

The stereo is highly directional and has plenty of color.

Comment

A later London album, with Silvio Varviso conducting (1266), provides more fire than Serafin was able to offer. Del Monaco repeats his Turiddu in the same loud fashion; Tito Gobbi is a more arresting Alfio, but Elena Suliotis does not measure up to Simionato in the role of Santuzza. That Santuzza might be enough to give the nod to the earlier set. Also available is a recording (London 12101) with Tebaldi as Santuzza, Bjoerling as Turiddu, and Bastianini as Alfio. Vocally the set is splendid, although Tebaldi's characterization is somewhat pallid and Erede's conducting is routine. ∎

September 1960

MENDELSSOHN: Concerti No. 1 in G minor (Op. 25) for Piano and No. 2 in D minor (Op. 40) for Piano. Rudolf Serkin, piano, and Philadelphia Orchestra conducted by Eugene Ormandy (in the *G minor*); Columbia Symphony Orchestra conducted by Ormandy (in the *D minor*). Columbia MS6128, $5.98.

Serkin has the reputation of being a stern classicist, and the public is apt to forget how well he plays Romantic music, and also what a brilliant virtuoso he can be when he wants to. The virtuoso element in his nature is very much to the fore in these two concerti—the very popular *G minor*, the almost unknown *D minor*. Serkin unleashes his strength in passionate performances. He does not conceive of the concerti as polite salon music, as many pianists do. Rather he plays them with unusual force, and with prestissimo finger work that positively glitters. The *D minor Concerto* is not so good a piece of music as its companion, though it does generate plenty of excitement in the first and last of its three movements. Serkin's fiery performance alone is worth the price, and this despite a quality of recorded sound that is a long way from the best being accomplished today. Serkin seldom has had good luck in his recording sessions, and this is no exception. His tone in the concert hall is nowhere near as rough-sounding as it is on this disc.

Comment

Recordings of these two works by Murray Perahia, with Neville Marriner conducting the Academy of St. Martin-in-the-Fields (Columbia M33207), present a serious challenge to the Serkin-Ormandy team. These performances are gentler and more lyrically oriented than the rather ferocious Serkin-Ormandy approach—but either account of both scores is superlative. ■

March 1977

MENDELSSOHN: Symphony No. 4 in A (Italian); Overture, Scherzo, Nocturne and Wedding March from "A Midsummer Night's Dream." The Boston Symphony Orchestra under the direction of Colin Davis. Philips 9500068, $7.98. ●

Over the last four decades the Boston Symphony has enriched record libraries with several classic renderings of Mendelssohn's *"Italian" Symphony*: two conducted by Serge Koussevitzky (in the 30's and 40's) and one by Charles Munch (in the 50's). This version, directed by Colin Davis, the orchestra's principal guest conductor, is the Boston Symphony's latest recording of the work. It is as much of a classic as the earlier pressings.

Exuberance is perhaps the hallmark of the *"Italian" Symphony*. Certainly it is of this performance. At the same time, Davis is very successful at relaxing tensions, creating a gentler flow in those sections where a light touch is required—as in the third movement, for example. (Davis also observes the all-important exposition repeat in the first movement.) The performance of the Boston Symphony Orchestra is dazzling throughout, and the recorded sound is rich and detailed.

The excerpts from "A Midsummer Night's Dream" are less successful. The performance is largely lacking in the vitality and spontaneity of the-*"Italian."* Instead, we have careful, almost cautious, readings of the excerpts—especially of the "Nocturne," which sounds stiff and unyielding. Even the "Wedding March" is deficient in buoyancy and sparkle.

Though the orchestra's playing and the recorded sound are again technically first rate, this disc is to be recommended only for its exuberant performance of the *"Italian" Symphony*.

Comment

An especially ebullient recording of the *"Italian" Symphony* is now out on the RCA label (ARL12632) played by the English Chamber Orchestra conducted by Raymond Leppard. Its second side, also most perceptively rendered, is Mendelssohn's *"Reformation" Symphony*. ■

MENDELSSOHN: Symphony No. 5 in D minor (Reformation); SCHUBERT: Symphony No. 5 in B flat major. The New York Philharmonic conducted by Leonard Bernstein. Columbia MS7295, $5.98.

The Mendelssohn is the more interesting performance; the Schubert, the more satisfying. In the Mendelssohn, Bernstein invests the second movement with an unusually strong feeling of sylvan reverie, the two outer movements with an appropriate feeling of urgency. And yet one is conscious of a heavy calculation that robs the performance of spontaneity. Not so with the Schubert, which flows freely and naturally, with an easy geniality. Though the two scores were recorded at different times and with different producers, they are consistently excellent both in the playing and in the recorded sound.

Comment

Even so, the calculations of Bernstein are infinitely more interesting than many conductors' superficial run-throughs. And no other disc offers both these symphonies together—so there is much to be said in favor of this release. ■

MENDELSSOHN: Violin Concertos in D minor and E minor. Yehudi Menuhin, violin, with the London Symphony Orchestra conducted by Rafael Frühbeck de Burgos. Angel S36850, $5.98.

Yehudi Menuhin has now been in the public spotlight for nearly a half-century, ever since that evening in 1927 when as a lad of 11 he stepped onto the stage of New York's Carnegie Hall to play the Beethoven *Violin Concerto* with Fritz Busch and the New York Symphony Orchestra. In the intervening years his artistry developed and seasoned, and his performances are consistently informed with a rare insight.

Unfortunately, though, the years have exacted their toll with respect to technical security. Menuhin never was a blinding virtuoso, and now there are times in the concert hall when his playing exhibits growing signs of strain under the sheer physical demands of playing; he struggles when he should be relaxed, assured and in tune. Perhaps that accounts in some measure for his increasing activity as a conductor, and one can only speculate that the day may not be long off when he will devote all his performances to conducting.

Menuhin has recorded both these Mendelssohn concerti before. Perhaps his most notable recording of the *E minor Concerto* was made with Wilhelm Furtwängler and the Berlin Philharmonic Orchestra in the late 1940's. That performance was subsequently reissued back-to-back with the *D minor Concerto*, a youthful Mendelssohn work that Menuhin discovered in manuscript in 1951 and recorded soon after he played its premiere performance. One has only to compare the earlier disc (RCA LM1720, no longer available) with this

Angel recording of two decades later to notice that the 35-year-old Menuhin could command much more repose, assurance and spontaneity than the older Menuhin is able to deliver today.

Nor do the EMI-Angel engineers live up to their own general level. The sound reproduction is harsher than one has been led to expect from them.

Comment

In recent years Menuhin has cut down on both his concert and recording performances. Only in his early sixties, Menuhin has much to offer. One can only hope that he will emerge from a rather difficult time in his performing life with renewed powers of technical security and command. ∎

August 1975

MENNIN: Symphony No. 4, "The Cycle," for Chorus and Orchestra; CZERNY: Concerto in C for Piano (four hands) and Orchestra. The Camerata Singers (in the Mennin), Jean and Kenneth Wentworth, pianos (in the Czerny), with a Symphony Orchestra conducted by Abraham Kaplan. Desto DC7149, $6.98.

Peter Mennin and Carl Czerny make one of the oddest couples in the record catalogs. Czerny, pupil and friend of Beethoven, is remembered chiefly for the many exercises he composed for piano practice, while Peter Mennin has been president of New York's famed Juilliard School of Music for more than a decade. Pedagogy would appear to be their only common denominator.

The Czerny concerto is a minor work, predictable and rather undistinguished. The same may be said of Mennin's symphony; stylistically it is in the quick, busy style characteristic of American composers during the 1940's and 50's. Since Mennin wrote the music, he apparently thought he was competent to write the words, too. Not so. He chooses a cosmic theme and treats it with breathtaking banality. Both works are effectively performed here, though the recorded sound has a cramped quality—the result, no doubt, of the record's having been taped in a smallish studio.

Comment

Long in the forefront of record companies concerned with contemporary American compositions, Desto built up a rich catalog of works. The company has now been absorbed by a conglomerate, but it is good to find that many Desto recordings are still available. ∎

January 1970

MESSIAEN: Quartet for the End of Time (Quatuor pour la fin du temps). Michel Beroff, piano; Gervase De Peyer, clarinet; Erich Gruenberg, violin; William Pleeth, cello. Angel S36587, $5.98.

(continued)

Olivier Messiaen, now sixty-three, has been called the father of French avant-garde music. He burst upon the international music scene right after World War II, and there is hardly a French musician of the past quarter-century who has not come under his influence. However, his pupils and imitators took off in other musical directions after a short period when his music was in great vogue. Messiaen's music is exotic—often religiously inspired—and it can be highly affecting.

This quartet, for example, was inspired by a passage from Chapter 10 of The Revelation of St. John (" . . . there should be time no longer . . ."). It was composed in 1941, when Messiaen was a prisoner of war in Silesia, and is typical of his style and technique. The eight short sections of the score cover a wide range of sounds and images and moods that are further varied in texture by the unusual instrumental combinations.

The performance is exceptionally perceptive. The violinist, the cellist, and the clarinetist are among Britain's most distinguished musicians. The pianist, a very young Frenchman (not yet twenty), has already built a European reputation as one of the most discerning of the new generation of instrumentalists. Add Angel's finely graded sound, and you have a disc of unusual interest and excellence.

Comment

The instrumentation of this unusual quartet prompted the creation of the group called Tashi, whose guiding spirit is pianist Peter Serkin. Tashi has recorded the Messiaen quartet (RCA ARL11567) in a performance that displays perhaps even more insight than does the Angel disc. Some may find this score pretentious with its mystical implications but there is no denying it has a riveting quality. ∎

October 1975

MILHAUD: The Four Seasons. Szymon Goldberg, violin, Ernst Wallfisch, viola, Geneviève Joy and Jacqueline Bonneau, pianos, and Maurice Suzan, trombone, with the Ensemble of Soloists of the Lamoureux Orchestra of Paris conducted by the composer. Philips 6504111, $7.98.

The late Darius Milhaud composed an enormous amount and variety of music during his 82-year lifetime. Some of it will surely stand the test of time and will continue to be performed as part of music's standard repertory.

The four works on this disc are brief concertos for different solo instruments and different ensemble forces. Thus, Milhaud's The Four Seasons differs from Vivaldi's work of the same name, which consists of four concertos, all for violin with string accompaniment. Vivaldi's The Four Seasons can easily be performed in concert. But with Milhaud's, a recording is virtually the only opportunity one can have to hear the four pieces in one sitting.

"Spring," for violin, was composed in 1934; "Summer," for viola, and "Autumn," for two pianos, date from 1951; and "Winter," for trombone, was written in 1953. They are not all of equal interest, to be sure. Impeccable craftsmanship is a steady feature of all Milhaud's output. The hallmarks of his most successful works—lightness and rhythmic buoyancy—are evident mainly in "Spring." Its improvisatory grace and elegance perhaps serve to emphasize the labored quality of the "Summer" and "Autumn" concertos. Some of the sparkle returns in the "Winter" concerto, perhaps because of the challenge posed by the trombone as solo instrument. With full orchestra the solo trombone must be very assertive to be heard. Milhaud solved the problem by scoring the orchestral accompaniment for strings only. That allows the trombone a wider range of dynamism and results in an unexpectedly intimate effect. The performances are uniformly excellent.

Comment

This is no earth-shaker, but a pleasant disc that groups four typical examples of the skill and compositional facility of a major creative figure of the twentienth century. ■

August 1977

MUSSORGSKY-RAVEL: Pictures at an Exhibition; PROKOFIEV: "Classical" Symphony in D. The Chicago Symphony Orchestra under the direction of Carlo Maria Giulini. Deutsche Grammophon 2530783, $7.98. ●

These performances by the Chicago Symphony were under the direction of Carlo Maria Giulini, who served as that group's principal guest conductor during Sir Georg Solti's tenure as music director. (Giulini will succeed Zubin Mehta in the fall of 1978 as music director of the Los Angeles Philharmonic Orchestra.)

Ravel's orchestration of Mussorgsky's *Pictures at an Exhibition* has been a sort of benchmark among recordings by the Chicago Symphony over the past quarter-century. In 1952 the orchestra's celebrated recording of that score can be said to have marked the coming of age of high-fidelity recording techniques. The Chicago Symphony made new recordings of the work in 1957, with Fritz Reiner conducting, and again 10 years later under the direction of Seiji Ozawa. Now, after a decade, is this effort with Giulini conducting.

Mussorgsky originally wrote the music in the form of a suite for piano as a memorial to a friend, the painter Victor Hartmann. Nearly half a century later, Serge Koussevitzky invited Maurice Ravel, the great French composer, to orchestrate the work. The result was one of the greatest orchestral showpieces in the musical repertoire.

Giulini doesn't slight its virtuosity—far from it—but the cultivated elegance of his reading is most welcome. Each section is characterized and delineated with care, so that the whole becomes a magnificent sum of many splendid parts. The 100-odd players of the Chicago Symphony again perform magnificently, with the anonymous saxophone and tuba soloists especially deserving of laurels. The sound reproduction is splendid: rich, vibrant, and clear in its details.

(continued)

In Prokofiev's "*Classical*" *Symphony*, Giulini's manner is leisurely, almost casual, and his tempi are generally slower than the norm. If some momentum and propulsion are lacking, there is a gain in detail and clarity of texture. Giulini's approach may not square with your ideas about this score, but if you can adjust to it, there is a unique pleasure to be derived from Giulini's treatment of this music. As usual, the musicians are at the top of their form. The sound is luminous. This disc is very special.

Comment

Giulini is now a contract artist whose services will be available exclusively to Deutsche Grammophon. A series of operatic recordings is planned for him, and we can hope for a string of performances by Giulini and the Los Angeles Philharmonic. ∎

September 1973

MOZART: Adagio and Fugue in C minor (K. 546); BEETHOVEN: Great Fugue, Opus 133; STRAUSS: Metamorphosen for 23 Solo String Instruments. The Strings of the Berlin Philharmonic Orchestra conducted by Herbert von Karajan. Deutsche Grammophon 2530066, $6.98.

Here, three great masterpieces for strings are given highly charged, emotional performances. Mozart's *Adagio and Fugue* is a terse, anguished statement that is one of the composer's most moving. Beethoven's *Great Fugue* started out as the final movement of the composer's *String Quartet No. 13 in B flat*. Its massive structure, however, so overburdened the other movements of the *Quartet* that Beethoven was persuaded to compose a new final movement for the composition and to let the *Great Fugue* stand as an independent work. It is often performed—as it is in this recording—by massed strings. The multiplying of performing forces from the original four players serves to clarify and strengthen the huge form of the work.

The *Metamorphosen* by Richard Strauss is a work composed in the twilight of his life (he was over 80 in 1945 when he wrote it). It is an extraordinary one-movement elegy that seems to sum up the aesthetic that motivated Strauss during his most productive period: the thirty years between 1885 and 1915 when all his symphonic poems were written, along with the operas *Der Rosenkavalier, Salome, Electra* and *Ariadne auf Naxos*. The *Metamorphosen* is a backward look not only at Strauss by Strauss, but also at the crumbling of the Nazi-inspired hopes for German world domination. It is this latter that is seemingly in the mind of Strauss when, at the very end of the piece, he introduces a reference to the Funeral March from Beethoven's *Eroica Symphony*, labeling it "In Memoriam."

Karajan conducts with great care and devotion. The strings of the Berlin Philharmonic are positively luxuriant. And the Deutsche Grammophon engineers have caught it all in voluptuous sound.

Comment

Many savants regard the Berlin Philharmonic as the finest orchestra performing today. A special glory of the orchestra is its string section, and this disc lets us hear those strings in all their splendor. ■

November 1973

MOZART: Piano Concertos No. 11 in F (K. 413) and No. 12 in A (K. 414). Rudolf Serkin, piano, with the Marlboro Festival Orchestra conducted by Alexander Schneider. Columbia M31728, $5.98. ●

This release brings to four the number of Mozart piano concertos recorded by Serkin and Schneider. As before, their collaboration is a total joy. Too many performers approach the Mozart piano concertos as though they were treading on eggs, reducing the music to dainty posturing. Not so Serkin and Schneider, whose approach is hearty and robust. The result is that both scores bubble along with exhilarating buoyancy and vitality.

Neither concerto ranks among Mozart's greatest, but both have their very attractive features—particularly the *A major,* with its uncommonly solemn slow movement and its exuberant last movement. A warmer acoustical environment than the Marlboro concert hall would have made the performance even more alluring. But that is a minor blemish on an otherwise outstanding release.

Comment

The number of Mozart piano concertos recorded by Rudolf Serkin with Alexander Schneider conducting has not increased. But Serkin's son, Peter, with Schneider conducting has recorded six concertos from what may be loosely termed Mozart's Middle Period (numbers 14 through 19) (RCA ARL30732). The results are superlative; abundant warmth and virility, splendid technical facility, and absolutely pellucid recorded sound. ■

September 1969

MOZART: Concerti No. 15 in B flat major for Piano (K. 450) and No. 17 in G major for Piano (K. 453). Robert Casadesus, piano, with members of the Cleveland Orchestra conducted by George Szell. Columbia MS7245, $5.98.

With the appearance of this disc, there are now eight Mozart piano concerti available in performances by Casadesus and Szell. These two are among the greatest of all Mozart's works; all the more unfortunate, then, that the team of Casadesus and Szell functions at less than its excellent best. The performances are sprightly and efficient, and, as always when Szell is conducting Mozart, the woodwinds are given their proper prominence in relation to the

(continued)

strings. But one misses the joyful and spontaneous music-making that has informed some of the previous Casadesus-Szell collaborations, notably their performances of Mozart's *Concerti Nos. 21* and *24*. The recorded sound on the new disc is clear.

No other disc on the market presents these two concerti together. The recommended versions are Bernstein's for *No. 15* (London 6499) and Barenboim's for *No. 17* (Angel S36513).

Comment

Despite the disappointing elements in this disc, it is a pity that the team of Casadesus and Szell did not record many more of the Mozart piano concerti. The generally vigorous, springy approach they brought to most of their performances is a precious quality in Mozart music-making. ∎

September 1962

MOZART: Concerti No. 17 in G major for Piano (K. 453) and No. 21 in C major for Piano (K. 467). Geza Anda, pianist and conductor of the Salzburg Mozarteum Camerata Academica. Deutsche Grammophon 138783, $6.98. ▲ ●

Into every pianist's life must come the urge to play and conduct at the same time. Generally the results are bad (in most cases, the orchestra simply ignores the pianist's wavings when there are some free bars, and plays the score the way the musicians know it should be played; but one feels the lack of a coordinating force). The results are no better in these routine performances. Anda is a skillful enough pianist, but he should be sticking to what he does best—playing the piano. These two concerti, among Mozart's very greatest, fail to lift off the ground. Part of the trouble is due to Anda's tendency to sentimentalize, and to his Romantic ideas about the music. Another part is due to the lack of a strong presence on the podium.

Comment

This performance of the *Concerto, No. 21*, used for the sound track of the Swedish film, *Elvira Madigan* earned legions of new admirers for the work. Better renderings of both concertos may be had from Barenboim (who serves as both pianist and conductor, but without the problems that beset Anda): *No. 17* on Angel S36513, and *No. 21* on Angel S36814. ∎

June 1973

MOZART: Piano Concerto No. 19 in F (K. 459); Piano Concerto No. 23 in A (K. 488). Alfred Brendel, piano, with the Academy of St. Martin-in-the-Fields conducted by Neville Marriner. Philips SAL6500283, $6.98. ●

Alfred Brendel is a 42-year-old Viennese pianist who has gained international respect largely through a series of recorded performances of the music of the Viennese masters—Mozart, Beethoven and Schubert. This disc (along with simultaneously released performances of Schubert sonatas) marks his Philips-label debut in this country.

These two concertos are among the most genial and easygoing of all Mozart's works. Brendel plays them with enormous finesse and assurance. Unfortunately, though, the sparkle and whimsy inherent in both scores is in short supply. Brendel and Marriner are very proper and correct in their approach, so much so that a little lighter touch from both would have been welcome. That marvelous collection of British instrumentalists who call themselves the Academy (or ensemble) of St. Martin-in-the-Fields play superbly, and the Philips recording team has captured bright and clearly defined sound.

Comment

The team of Brendel and Marriner now have available four other discs, offering seven more of Mozart's piano concertos. Fortunately, in nearly every case the response to the fun in these works is more frank and spontaneous than in the two concertos on this disc. So much the better, then, if this team plans to record all the Mozart piano concertos. ∎

August 1978

MOZART: Piano Concerto No. 20 in D Minor (K. 466); Two-Piano Concerto in E Flat (K. 365). André Previn, pianist and conductor, with the London Symphony Orchestra, and Radu Lupu, piano (in the *Two-Piano Concerto*). Angel S37291, $7.98.

During the past quarter-century, André Previn has had an amazingly varied career as a recording pianist. He has performed with many jazz combos and classical chamber music groups. He has accompanied soprano Eileen Farrell in blues and torch songs. He has played Gershwin with André Kostelanetz and his Orchestra, Shostakovitch with Leonard Bernstein and the New York Philharmonic, and Mozart with Sir Adrian Boult and the London Symphony. But to the best of my knowledge this is only the second recording for which he has served both as pianist and conductor—a dual role he assumes increasingly often in the concert hall. (The first such disc was his debut for Angel Records, about 1970, with Gershwin's *Concerto in F* and *Rhapsody in Blue*.)

Last season, Previn devoted one of his "Previn and the Pittsburgh" telecasts to an analysis and performance of Mozart's *D minor Piano Concerto*. This time his piano playing is more polished and secure than it was in the telecast, and the same intelligence and love that went into that program pervade this recording. His account of the orchestral part is also carefully judged and shaded; witness, for example, the perfect balance of the trumpet line that punctuates the piano-orchestra dialogue near the end of the last movement. Previn takes that last movement at a good clip, but the music can stand it.

(continued)

And in the last movement Previn plays a cadenza of his own devising that contains some surprising harmonic modulations and melodic progressions.

The *Two-Piano Concerto,* surely one of Mozart's sunniest inventions, receives a somewhat cautious performance, notable more for clarity of articulation than for unconstrained spontaneity. But the orchestral performance is alert, and the team of Previn and Lupu (the record label suggests that Lupu is playing Piano I) makes for a finely integrated ensemble. With both works, the sound reproduction is exemplary for its balance and definition.

Comment

Although other, more passionate individual recordings of each work probably exist, this recording brings a certain distinction: It is the only available disc that combines both these irresistible scores. ∎

February 1977

MOZART: Piano Concertos Nos. 21 in C (K. 467) and 23 in A (K. 488). Ilana Vered, piano, with the London Philharmonic Orchestra conducted by Uri Segal. London SPC21138, $6.98. ●

This is Ilana Vered's second recording of Mozart's *C major Piano Concerto* in just a couple of years. On the first, the Mozart was almost an afterthought to the performance of the notorious "Yellow River" Concerto composed by a "team" of Chinese musicians. Since then Vered has become an intriguing and stimulating recording personality, with excellent accounts of music by Chopin, Rachmaninoff, and Tchaikovsky, among others, to her credit. On the evidence of this disc, she is a persuasive interpreter of Mozart as well.

Spontaneity is perhaps the most immediately winning trait of her collaboration with Uri Segal, the conductor. Together, the two Israeli musicians breathe a lively vitality and improvisational quality into their interpretations. In the slow movement of the *C major Concerto* Vered adopts a dangerously slow tempo—the marking after all is andante, not adagio. (It is the slow movement of the other concerto on this disc that bears an adagio marking.) This, incidentally, is the movement that figured so prominently in the sound track of the Swedish film *Elvira Madigan.* Far from wallowing in sentimentality with their slow tempo, however, Vered and Segal imbue the music with an appropriate feeling of tragedy and pathos.

The London Philharmonic plays superbly, and aside from occasionally over-microphoned woodwinds (reversing the usual complaint in Mozart recordings) the recorded sound is all one could wish.

Comment

Vered is an artist whose every recording has special qualities. She seems to be the pianist of Decca/London's choice for the Phase 4 series of recordings; the company has chosen wisely and well. ∎

MOZART: Divertimento No. 17 in D major (K. 334); March in D major (K. 445). The Esterhazy Orchestra conducted by David Blum. Vanguard Cardinal C10066, $3.98.

Mozart's divertimenti were composed as entertainment music for the garden parties of Austrian society. That Mozart, under such casual circumstances, was able to produce some of his most inspired music, is one of the imponderables of the creative process. The divertimenti cover a variety of moods, and some of them plumb surprisingly profound emotional depths. This *D major Divertimento* is one such—a deeply probing and lyrically passionate work despite its rather informal structure.

The *March* that precedes the *Divertimento* on this disc most probably was composed as a companion piece, as music to accompany the arrival of the guests. It is a brief, ceremonial piece full of the appropriate flourishes.

David Blum and his Esterhazy Orchestra (made up of many of the leading free-lance musicians in New York) have contributed several splendid discs to the Vanguard catalog, including four of various Haydn symphonies. In this Mozart disc, too, the playing is extremely stylish and polished, and Blum reinforces his position as a perceptive interpreter of eighteenth-century music.

The Vanguard sound is a full, rich, vibrant complement to the performances.

January 1974

MOZART: Divertimento in D (K. 334); Notturno in D (K. 286). The Academy of St. Martin-in-the-Fields conducted by Neville Marriner. Argo ZRG705, $5.98.

These two works are among the finest in Mozart's entire output. The six-movement *D ·major Divertimento* is a delight from beginning to end. The *Notturno*, a brief three-movement affair, bubbles with gracious music. In the baroque concerto grosso format (which obviously served as Mozart's model) two contrasting instrumental groups are pitted against one another. Mozart's *Notturno* has no fewer than four separate small "orchestras" in competition. As such, the *Notturno* would make an ideal vehicle for quadraphonic reproduction, with each of the four different groupings playing through a separate sound source. But this Marriner-conducted performance is now available only in two-channel (albeit highly expert) stereo reproduction; presumably, a quadraphonic master of the performance exists and will be released later.

For some years, Marriner and his superlative body of musicians have been enriching the record lists with extraordinarily fine performances of music from the baroque and classical periods. This Mozart disc continues the long string of successes. By now Marriner has honed his musicians to a fine point of sensitivity and suppleness, and he himself has become one of the most authoritative stylists on the international scene. Incidentally, the word "Academy" in the name of the orchestra is used to mean "ensemble."

(continued)

Comment

The Vanguard record and a companion disc (Vanguard 10082) containing two more divertimenti *(K. 138 and K. 287)* represent high accomplishment indeed: performances of outstanding excellence with crystal-clear recorded sound. One wonders what has become of David Blum and the Esterhazy Orchestra.

Marriner's greatest recordings in a long series of outstanding achievements may well be the music of Mozart. The Argo disc is a fine example of Marriner at his best. ∎

May 1959

MOZART: Don Giovanni. Cesare Siepi and Fernando Corena, basses; Anton Dermota, tenor; Suzanne Danco, Lisa Della Casa and Hilde Gueden, sopranos; Walter Berry, baritone; Kurt Böhme, bass. The Vienna Philharmonic Orchestra and the Vienna State Opera Chorus conducted by Josef Krips. London 1401, 4 discs, $23.92.

As is London's companion set of *The Marriage of Figaro*, this performance of *Don Giovanni* (released monophonically several years ago) already is a classic. It has a cast as strong as any that can be assembled in the world today, its recorded sound is exceptionally clear, and the orchestral playing is beyond reproach. Many critics through the years, including such composers as Wagner and Gounod, have considered *Don Giovanni* to be the greatest of all operas. It well may be, and it is basic to any record collection. The stereophonic version is good but not so successful as the *Figaro* set. Most of the sound is concentrated in one channel; there could have been much more legitimate separation. But the reproduction is mellow, the surfaces quiet, and the singers' voices are realistically captured. Those who have not heard Siepi, Corena, and the others in the opera house will have a very good idea of what their voices really sound like. The stereo is quite good in terms of color and instrumental definition.

October 1974

MOZART: Don Giovanni. Ingvar Wixell, baritone (Don Giovanni), Martina Arroyo, soprano (Donna Anna), Stuart Burrows, tenor (Don Ottavio), Luigi Roni, bass (Commendatore), Kiri Te Kanawa, soprano (Donna Elvira), Wladimiro Ganzarolli, bass (Leporello), Richard Van Allan, bass (Masetto), Mirella Freni, soprano (Zerlina). Chorus and Orchestra of the Royal Opera House, Covent Garden, conducted by Colin Davis. Philips 6707022, 4 discs, $27.92.

Colin Davis came to international attention in 1959 as a result of a concert performance in London of *Don Giovanni*, for which he served as a last-minute substitute conductor. Since then, he has steadily gained prominence. In this country, he has led memorable performances at New York's Metropolitan Opera, has guest-conducted many of our leading symphony orchestras, and serves as principal guest conductor of the Boston Symphony Orchestra. He is currently music director of London's Royal Opera in Covent Garden. The present recording of *Don Giovanni* derives from a widely admired new production of the opera at Covent Garden, though only a few of its principals actually sing their roles here.

Don Giovanni is considered by many to be the greatest opera ever composed. Mozart and his librettist, Lorenzo da Ponte, did more than chronicle a centuries-old story of a rake. Their antihero is also a symbol of man in hapless pursuit of unattainable goals and thus represents a great human tragedy. Even in Mozart's own miraculous output, the mating of music and drama makes *Don Giovanni* unique.

This opera poses a strenuous challenge to performers, and the present catalog contains several recordings of unusual merit. One of the best is the performance under the direction of the late Otto Klemperer (Angel S3700). Klemperer's approach is extraordinarily powerful and intense, though some may find it too monolithic. This new Davis-conducted recording is also strong, but it is gentler and more relaxed—a human approach as contrasted with Klemperer's superhuman vision.

The men in the new cast are by and large more convincing than the women. Ingvar Wixell as Don Giovanni is well-nigh perfect—a rich and lyric baritone voice at the service of a perceptive characterization. As his servant Leporello, Wladimiro Ganzarolli is worldy-wise and comic without descending to the burlesque excesses that some have brought to the part—and he sings his role beautifully. And Stuart Burrows, in the largely unrewarding role of the country bumpkin, brings grace, elegance, and a silky tenor sound to his portrayal. Martina Arroyo, as the vengeful Donna Anna, is highly intense, but her vocal line is occasionally disfigured by some hooting. Kiri Te Kanawa, the Maori singer who scored a great personal success in Verdi's *Otello* at the Metropolitan Opera, is a rather superficial Donna Elvira. She does not encompass the complexity of the role, but her singing does have a lovely lyrical quality. As Zerlina, Mirella Freni repeats the innocent and fragile performance that was one of the distinguishing characterizations in the Klemperer recording.

The album comes with an attractive booklet containing the libretto and a perceptive essay on Mozart and *Don Giovanni* by the producer, Erik Smith. All in all, this new *Don Giovanni* is a most welcome addition.

Comment

Those who object to some of the lethargic tempos chosen by Krips may prefer the Angel set conducted by Carlo Maria Giulini (S3605). A generally excellent cast, including Joan Sutherland as Donna Anna, and Elisabeth Schwarzkopf as Donna Elvira, gives a spirited, articulate, and highly polished performance. The recorded sound is still quite acceptable, despite its age. The Davis-conducted *Don Giovanni* was one of the first recordings to acquaint us with the strengths of baritone Ingvar Wixell; he has since become one of the busiest opera singers on the contemporary scene, both on stage and in recordings. Although Kiri Te Kanawa is not at her best in the Philips album, she, too, has gone on to big things since she made this recording. It is good to learn that she figures prominently in CBS/Columbia's plans for operatic recording. ∎

MOZART: The Marriage of Figaro (Le Nozze di Figaro). Cesare Siepi, bass (Figaro); Hilde Gueden, soprano (Susanna); Lisa Della Casa, soprano (Countess Almaviva); Alfred Poell, baritone (Count Almaviva); Suzanne Danco, soprano (Cherubino); Fernando Corena, bass (Dr. Bartolo); Hilde Rössl-Majdan, mezzo-soprano (Marcellina). The Vienna Philharmonic Orchestra and the State Opera Chorus conducted by Erich Kleiber. London 1402, 4 discs, $23.92.

When this performance was released several years ago, it was rightly greeted as a classic: a superb cast, paced by a great conductor and orchestra. Rehearing these discs of Mozart's incomparable opera confirms the impression; and hearing them in stereo cements it down. Not only is the singing and orchestral playing of a quality equal to the best the world today has to offer, but the stereo sound has turned out extremely successful. *Figaro* is, above all, an ensemble opera abounding in trios, quartets, and other concerted numbers. It was just made for stereo. Listen to the Act III sextet (toward the end of side five), where the voices virtually line up along the entire wall: Figaro and Susanna out of one speaker (that crack you hear is Figaro getting his face slapped by Susanna—the libretto says "boxing his ear"), the Notary stuttering along somewhere in the middle, the other singers at the right adding their comments proportionately. Or listen to the great quartet in Act II, again with the voices well separated. The biggest climaxes are smoothly taken, without any suspicion of "shatter," nor is there any inner-groove distortion. Anybody desirous of starting an opera collection on stereo should begin with this recording. It is one of the greatest of all operas in as great a performance as one is ever likely to hear.

Comment

This performance is still a *sine qua non* where recordings of *The Marriage of Figaro* are concerned. And as time passes, the radiance of this album shines brighter and brighter.   ■

MOZART: "Great" Mass in C minor (K. 427). The London Symphony Orchestra and Chorus conducted by Colin Davis, with Helen Donath and Heather Harper, sopranos, Ryland Davies, tenor, and Stafford Dean, bass. Philips SAL6500235, $6.98. ●

Mozart's *K. 427* is not a complete mass: It only goes through the first part of the Credo (so that from the Crucifixus onwards is missing, including the entire Agnus Dei). But what we do have is a towering masterpiece. Even in Mozart's own terms, this work has a rare spiritual quality, with unusually profound passion and drama.

There have been a number of fine recordings of this music in the past, but none to equal the overall excellence of this new one. Davis is authoritative and inspired, his vocal and instrumental forces are first-class, and the sound of the Philips disc is vibrant.

Comment

The most arresting and affecting recording performance of this great work currently available belongs to Davis. Expert Mozartean though he is, Davis is also thoroughly at ease with Berlioz, Sibelius, Tippett, and many other composers of the nineteenth and twentieth centuries. ∎

November 1966

MOZART: Quartets No. 22 in B flat major (K. 589) and No. 23 in F major (K. 590). Guarneri Quartet. RCA LSC2888, $5.98. ▲

Some of the strongest musical talent in the United States turns up every summer at Marlboro, the center in Vermont established by Rudolf Serkin. The four players in this string quartet are Marlboro alumni, as it were. They met there and decided to pool their talents. The result is the most impressive string quartet to have come along since the Juilliard was formed about 1950.

Each of the four players is a powerhouse instrumentalist, and each is also a good musician. The two do not always go together. If one complaint can be levied against the group, it is that its businesslike, exact playing has everything but charm. The boys as yet do not know how to relax. But this complaint may be made about most music-making today, and it may be that in a few years the Guarneri Quartet will have learned how to ease up. In any case, Mozart's last two quartets receive driving, polished, rhythmically precise performances.

The recorded sound in stereo provides a perfect example of what modern techniques can do for recorded chamber music. Listen to the beginning of the third movement of the *F major Quartet*, with the violin entrance on the left, the cello on the right. On high-quality equipment it's close to the real thing.

Comment

Since the release of this disc, the Guarneri Quartet has become one of our most active concert and recording quartets. And over the years, the players have indeed learned how to ease up. Their performances now have a gentler shape; that, and the perfection of ensemble that they habitually display, makes them clearly "the most impressive new string quartet to have come along since the Juilliard was formed around 1950." ∎

January 1967

MOZART: Requiem. Elly Ameling, soprano; Marilyn Horne, mezzo-soprano; Ugo Benelli, tenor; Tugomir Franc, bass. Vienna Philharmonic Or-

(continued)

chestra and State Opera Chorus conducted by István Kertész. London 1157, $5.98.

Lyric, tender, and melodious, the *Requiem* was Mozart's last score, and there is quite a mystery about it. On his deathbed, Mozart gave his pupil, Franz Süssmayer, instructions about completing the score. Ever since, scholars have been wondering how much of the *Requiem* is Mozart and how much Süssmayer. Süssmayer himself claimed a great deal, but modern scholarship tends toward the belief that Mozart dictated all of the thematic elements and also told Süssmayer how the orchestration was to go. In any case, what has come down is a beautiful score; and the Lacrimosa section has a poignance and intensity rare even for Mozart.

The present performance is, unfortunately, disappointing. There is some good solo singing, especially from Ameling (a Dutch soprano), but the chorus makes shrill sounds, the conducting is routine, and the recorded sound is muddy. Those who want a good performance of the Mozart *Requiem*—and all music lovers should—can turn to several prior versions. The best of the modern stereo versions is by Karajan (DG 138767).

Comment

Today, however, the Colin Davis recording (Philips 802862) is the clear leader in the field: It is a straightforward, deeply felt performance, with good solo singers, a fine chorus, and detailed recorded sound. ∎

May 1962

MOZART: Serenade No. 7 in D major (Haffner, K. 250). Willi Boskovsky, violin, with the Vienna Philharmonic Orchestra conducted by Karl Münchinger. London 6214, $5.98.

The *Haffner Serenade* was commissioned of the nineteen-year-old Mozart for the wedding of Elizabeth, daughter of Salzburg Burgomaster Sigmund Haffner. Mozart also composed a march (*K.249*) to precede and follow the *Serenade*; its absence here is fully compensated by the *Serenade's* rich performance. Mozart put some of his most endearing music into these nine movements for a joyous occasion. The performance by Münchinger, Boskovsky, and the Vienna Philharmonic is another occasion for joy, to which the engineers contribute, too. In breadth and quality of sound, in instrumental texture and balance, in its revelation of the colorful palette of Mozart's orchestration, the *Haffner Serenade* is here rekindled. Stereo has seldom been employed with such faithful results, as in a figure passing from one section of the strings to the other or a soloist against full orchestra. This is the *Haffner* to live with.

Comment

This superlative performance and recording now belongs to London's lower-price Stereo Treasury label (STS15375). ∎

MOZART: Serenade No. 10 in B flat major for 13 Wind Instruments (K. 361). London Wind Soloists conducted by Jack Brymer. London 6346, $5.98.

This is the *Serenade for Thirteen Winds*, and it is a masterpiece. A long work in seven movements, composed in 1781, it is one of those transparently scored Mozart pieces in which idea follows idea. The crown of the *Serenade* is the slow movement. Even for Mozart these long melodies and rich harmonies are unusual; and the middle part, with its sudden shift to minor, is excruciatingly sad. The last movement is an enchanting romp. But, then, every movement is wonderful. The present disc presents a straight, unmannered performance, secure rhythmically, smooth technically. Each of the players knows his business. Beautiful sound.

April 1974

MOZART: Serenade in B flat for Thirteen Winds (K. 361). The Netherlands Wind Ensemble conducted by Edo de Waart. Philips SAL839734, $6.98.

This monumental score is one of Mozart's towering masterpieces. It is called *"Gran Partita,"* written as it is on a grand scale in seven movements. Though Mozart composed many woodwind serenades and divertimentos, this one is blessed with special reserves of divine inspiration. In melodic invention, harmonic interest, profundity, and sheer good spirits, this serenade is one of the creative miracles of Western musical thought.

The work has not lacked for excellent recordings: Koussevitzky led a memorable version in the 1940's, and currently available editions include splendid performances conducted by Karl Böhm (DG2530136), Otto Klemperer (Angel S36247), and Leopold Stokowski (Vanguard 71158). This new version by the rising young Dutch conductor, Edo de Waart, is smooth and carefully prepared with sonics of extraordinary clarity. Klemperer plumbs greater depths, but de Waart deals very successfully with the elements of fun in the music. This is a welcome release.

Comment

The Brymer-London Wind Soloists performance, formerly available as a single disc (London 6346), now exists only as part of the five-disc Stereo Treasury series (London STS15377/81) devoted to Mozart's complete music for woodwinds. Klemperer's recording (Angel S36247) is well reproduced, and the performance is more personal, more probing. The extraordinary account of this score conducted by Wilhelm Furtwängler (European Unicorn WFS10) is also now available in this country, but in monophonic sound only; it is worth hunting for in specialty shops. ∎

January 1965

MOZART: Sinfonia Concertante in E flat major for Violin and Viola (K. 364). Yehudi Menuhin, violin, and Rudolf Barshai, viola. **HAYDN:**

(continued)

Concerto No. 1 in C major for Violin. Yehudi Menuhin, violin. Bath Festival Orchestra conducted by Menuhin in both works. Angel S36190, $5.98.

A comparison with the Heifetz-Primrose performance of the Mozart (see page 108) is interesting. (That RCA disc, by the way, uses the French spelling of "symphony" and this Angel disc the Italian.) Menuhin and Barshai take a much more personal approach to the music than do Heifetz and Primrose. Their vibrato is faster; the orchestra sounds fuller; the tempi are considerably slower. It is a Romantic and even a stressed reading—the RCA is more classic and objective. This listener prefers the RCA although Menuhin is in good form and his Russian partner is obviously a superior musician. The coupling also comes into consideration. Haydn's *Concerto in C* is a rather weak, routine work, whereas the RCA disc has Heifetz's dazzling performance of the Glazounov *Concerto.* Angel, in the stereo disc, has done a little better than RCA in holding down the spread of the solo instruments, but a careful listener will still tend to be bothered.

January 1973

MOZART: Sinfonia Concertante in E flat for Violin, Viola and Orchestra; STAMITZ: Sinfonia Concertante in D major for Violin, Viola and Orchestra. Isaac Stern, violin, and Pinchas Zukerman, viola, with the English Chamber Orchestra conducted by Daniel Barenboim. Columbia M31369, $5.98.

Mozart's *Sinfonia Concertante* for two solo string instruments and orchestra is one of his most sublime works. Mozart's biographer, the late Alfred Einstein, wrote of "the living unity of each of the three movements, organic in every detail, and the complete vitality of the whole orchestra, in which every instrument speaks its own language." Within the framework of that "organic unity," it is nevertheless proper to single out the slow movement of the *Sinfonia Concertante* as containing some of the most deeply felt and elegiac music Mozart ever wrote.

Karl Stamitz, whose *Sinfonia Concertante* for similar performing forces shares this disc with Mozart's great work, was an older Mozart contemporary and one of the principal figures of the Mannheim School of musical composition that paved the way for the music of the Classical era. The Stamitz *Sinfonia Concertante* is a pleasant enough score, but it lacks the stunning genius of Mozart's. Its formal outlines may well have served Mozart as a model, however, for structurally the two works have much in common. Mozart's score, a staple of the concert repertory, has been recorded many times; the Stamitz is a rarity both in the concert hall and in recording.

This is Stern's third recorded performance of the Mozart. The first, one of the glories of recorded literature, was made in France during the early 1950's, with the violist, William Primrose, and Pablo Casals conducting the Perpignan Festival Orchestra. Their collaboration resulted in a performance that was a rhapsodic adventure from beginning to end. Unfortunately, that monophonic disc (Columbia ML4564) is no longer available. Much less successful—indeed a sorry disappointment—was a later recording with Walter Trampler playing the viola solo, while Stern himself did double duty as violinist and conductor. Whatever the reasons, the Stern-Trampler version (Columbia MS7251) is relatively hard-driven and tense. Now this latest disc again makes available a supreme artistic performance. As in the earlier, Casals-conducted recording, Stern plays the violin part with an intensity that is truly hyponotic, and as his viola partner, Zukerman is equally persuasive. Their ensemble is remarkable, as is the orchestral support by the English Chamber Orchestra under the vibrant and supple direction of Daniel Barenboim.

The same qualities of rare collaborative musicianship inform the performance of the lesser work, the Stamitz *Sinfonia Concertante*.

Comment

The Columbia has afforded great dividends in listening pleasure over the years. Stern, Zukerman, and Barenboim, the three principals in these two works, are individually unique; together, they have deep personal bonds that lend special luster to their artistic collaboration. ∎

November 1968

MOZART: Symphonies No. 32 in G major (K. 318); No. 35 in D major (Haffner, K. 385); No. 38 in D major (Prague, K. 504). The English Chamber Orchestra conducted by Daniel Barenboim. Angel S36512, $5.98.

Barenboim is the twenty-six-year-old musician who has enjoyed a spectacular international career as a pianist for about half his lifetime. During the past several years he has also been conducting orchestras in Europe, Israel, and Australia. Last April he made his conducting debut in the United States, unexpectedly, as a last-minute substitute for István Kertész in four Carnegie Hall concerts by the London Symphony Orchestra. Since then he has been back as a conductor, touring with the English Chamber Orchestra and also at several leading summer festivals.

This disc confirms the fine impression he has made generally. He is a conductor with a distinct point of view, and he molds individual but highly persuasive accounts of these three Mozart symphonies. The slender *Symphony No. 32* is invested with a highly charged dramatic tension, the *Haffner* bubbles along with joyous abandon, and the *Prague* is powerful in its seriousness. Barenboim has obviously established a special rapport with the players of the English Chamber Orchestra; they respond to his direction as though intuitively. And it is a pleasure to hear these symphonies played by an orchestra of chamber proportions: The instrumental balances are much truer than when the music is tackled by a full-sized symphony orchestra. Angel's recorded sound is clear and clean.

Comment

In the years since these words were written, Barenboim has become a superstar on the international conducting circuit. A familiar figure to all the world's

(continued)

major orchestras, he has recorded as a conductor with the New York Philharmonic and the Chicago Symphony. Clearly, he is marked for an increasingly important role in American musical life. The *Haffner* whose name identifies *Symphony No. 35* is the same Viennese gentleman for whom Mozart, some years earlier, composed his *D major Serenade* (see page 156). ■

November 1977

MOZART: Symphony No. 38 in D (Prague, K. 504); SCHUBERT: Symphony No. 8 in B minor (Unfinished). The English Chamber Orchestra under the direction of Benjamin Britten. London CS6741, $7.98.

The release of this record is a posthumous tribute to Benjamin Britten—the conductor, not the composer. As a conductor, Britten was drawn to a wide range of music from the Classical and Romantic periods. He performed much of that music at his annual Aldeburgh Festival on the English coast, and recorded a good deal of the music as well. This disc seems to have been made sometime in 1972, judging by the copyright date shown on the record label.

These are performances of two staples of the repertory that deserve to be cherished. Britten approaches both scores with genuine love, and is rewarded with warm, responsive playing. Out of respect for the composers, he observes the indicated repeats of the expositions in both works' first movements, and also in the last movement of the Mozart *Symphony.*

Britten is also very sensitive to the other markings in the score. As an example, his ferocious attack in the opening of the development section of the Mozart *Symphony's* last movement gives the music uncommon urgency, which is precisely the effect Mozart wanted at that point. The playing is in the best tradition of the English Chamber Orchestra, and the recorded sound is a model of definition and richness.

Comment

Britten was basically a Romantic at heart—not only in his compositions but also in his conducting. The two performances on this disc represent some of his finest interpretive efforts. ■

November 1965

MOZART: Symphonies No. 40 in G minor (K. 550) and No. 41 in C major (Jupiter, K. 551). Philharmonia Orchestra conducted by Otto Klemperer. Angel S36183, $5.98.

Mozart's two most popular (and oft-recorded) symphonies are conducted here by an an eighty-year-old legend. Otto Klemperer is the last of the great band of German conductors who came to fame shortly after the turn of the century. His performances here, though, are a little disappointing. Dignity is

160

present, and so is an obvious dedication to the music. But Mozart was a more volatile composer than these rather heavy readings would indicate. There is not enough tempo variation among the movements of the G minor Symphony; and, while Klemperer's deliberate pacings are better in the Jupiter, the overall effect here, too, is stolid. Excellent recorded sound has been achieved.

Comment

Klemperer gives dignified readings, but Giulini (London 6479), with brio and contrast, provides much more volatile performances. A barbarically cut version of the G minor Symphony's first movement achieved some currency in the pop field not long ago by virture of a recording by Waldo de los Rios and his Orchestra. The music is far more effective uncut and "un-Riosized." ∎

May 1974

MOZART: Symphony No. 41 in C (Jupiter, K. 551); SCHUBERT: Symphony No. 8 in B minor (Unfinished). The Boston Symphony Orchestra conducted by Eugen Jochum. Deutsche Grammophon 2530357, $7.98. ▲ ●

Eugen Jochum is a distinguished elder statesman among European conductors. Last season he appeared for the first time as a guest with the Boston Symphony Orchestra and is scheduled to return to the orchestra in July at Tanglewood. These two symphonies were recorded shortly after concert performances of them were given in Boston's Symphony Hall.

Both performances demonstrate Jochum's characteristic solidity of approach. He leaves nothing to chance, displaying a professionalism that well might serve as a model to some of his younger colleagues. The recording of Schubert's "Unfinished" Symphony is one of the best around—warm, expansive, and dramatic in exactly the proper proportions, with splendid playing by the orchestra and rich, lustrous reproduction.

The "Jupiter" Symphony fares even better. Jochum's concept and tempi are on the deliberate side, but everything works, and the grand arc of the score is characterized most effectively with an impressive and fiery last movement. Again, the engineers have provided finely detailed and impressively rich reproduction.

The recent recording history of the Boston Symphony has been spotty. Here is one of its best records in a long time.

Comment

Jochum is now the laureate conductor of the London Symphony Orchestra, and has recorded all nine of the Beethoven symphonies with them for the British EMI record company (Angel in this country). He is in the process of recording the Bruckner symphonies, and there are plans for other extensive recording projects under his direction. ∎

MUSSORGSKY: Songs and Dances of Death; BRAHMS: Ernste Gesänge. George London, bass-baritone, accompanied by Leo Taubman. Columbia Special Products CMS6734, $5.98.

The Mussorgsky work is the greatest of Russian song cycles, and London sings it in the original. The Brahms, of course, is sung in German. There are several recordings of the Brahms, but few of *Songs and Dances of Death*, and this is the only available one in stereo. The vocal performance is not very good. The singer's voice is now an unwieldy instrument, rough-sounding with virtually no top. But London does have intelligence, musicianship, and style, and the Mussorgsky, not a pretty cycle, can take his kind of sound. For the Brahms, it is less appropriate, but here too London's fine musical instincts make up for many vocal sins.

MUSSORGSKY: Songs and Dances of Death; Seven Other Songs. Kim Borg, bass; with Prague Radio Symphony Orchestra conducted by Alois Klima (in *Songs and Dances of Death*); with Prague National Theater Orchestra conducted by Zdenek Chalabala, and Alfred Holecek, piano (in the *Seven Other Songs*). Nonesuch 71215, $2.98.

Songs and Dances of Death is among the most heartfelt and moving works in the vocal literature. Each part describes death triumphant under a particular circumstance. The cycle demands a singer of unusually persuasive powers and dramatic urgency. The Finnish bass, Kim Borg, is too gentle and reserved to give the songs their full impact.

The seven songs include some of Mussorgsky's best, notably "Song of the Flea," "The Classicist," and "The Seminarist." All seven were written with piano accompaniment (as, indeed, was *Songs and Dances of Death*), but orchestral transcriptions are used—not very successfully—for four of the seven. Particularly offensive is the "Flea" orchestration, a virtual syllabus of misapplied "imaginative" touches. For his part, Borg is more effective in the gentle songs than in the robust or dramatic ones.

The sound, a product of Czechoslovakia's Supraphon Records, is vivid and clear, and the surfaces are very quiet.

Comment

George London's primacy has now been seriously challenged in both these extraordinary cycles: by the team of Fischer-Dieskau and Barenboim with the Brahms (Deutsche Grammophon 2707066), and by Vishnevskaya, with Rostropovich conducting the Shostakovitch orchestration of the Mussorgsky songs (Angel S37403). ∎

NIELSEN: Symphony No. 3 (Sinfonia Espansiva). Royal Danish Orchestra conducted by Leonard Bernstein. Columbia MS6769, $5.98.

In recent years this country has seen a great deal of interest in the music of Carl Nielsen, Denmark's most important composer, who died in 1931. The *Third Symphony* was composed in 1912 and is in the traditional symphonic, post-Romantic idiom, with big, soaring melodies (especially in the first movement), rich orchestration, and the rest of the trappings. Nielsen was a strong composer who worked in absolute music with a great deal of individuality. It is true that this symphony has a title, but it is only a clue to the mood, and no program is suggested. Bernstein, who has been one of the chief instruments of the Nielsen revival, conducts magnificiently. The stereo opens up the orchestral spectrum.

Comment

This magnificent symphony—in this equally superb performance—is wholeheartedly recommended to anyone who values heroic nobility and the grand gesture in music. The score abounds in these virtues, and Bernstein revels in them. ∎

July 1963

NIELSEN: Symphony No. 5 (Op. 50). New York Philharmonic conducted by Leonard Bernstein. Columbia MS6414, $5.98.

Carl Nielsen was a Danish composer who died in 1931 without ever having achieved an international reputation. Nor has he yet. But his music is becoming more and more talked about, and he is beginning to get performances outside his homeland. He deserves them. This *Symphony No. 5,* composed in 1922, is an unusually powerful and individual piece of writing. Nielsen was a traditionalist whose roots were in the late Romantic period (Mahler was one of the composers who influenced him), but he was not afraid to use dissonance and to break the rules when he felt like it. In a way, his music is to Denmark what Vaughan Williams's music is to England. He is an important figure, and this noble, dramatic symphony should be investigated by the alert music lover. Bernstein is a convincing exponent of the music, and the recorded sound is unusually full and colorful.

September 1970

NIELSEN: Symphony No. 5 (Op. 50); Saga-Dream (Op. 39). The New Philharmonia Orchestra conducted by Jascha Horenstein. Nonesuch 71236, $2.98. ●

Jascha Horenstein is a Russian-born, European-based conductor now in his early seventies who has never had the glamorous international career to which his extraordinary gifts should have entitled him. During the early 1950s he was given the chance to record a rather wide orchestral repertoire, but despite the general excellence of those early LPs (especially of sympho-

(continued)

nies by Mahler and Bruckner), Horenstein somehow never really made his mark in international musical life. The present disc is the result of the personal enthusiasm for the art of Horenstein by an English record buff, John Goldsmith, who has underwritten the initial cost of a series of Horenstein's recordings in a variety of repertoire.

Goldsmith's series is off to a notable start with this Horenstein performance of Nielsen's *Fifth Symphony*. A masterpiece of twentieth-century symphonic composition, the score has had its share of recordings, notably Columbia's dynamic performance by Leonard Bernstein and the New York Philharmonic. But Horenstein brings to his reading a measured control that discloses the work less as a series of episodes than as a unified totality. The joyous assertion of life in the last part becomes the inevitable result of the chaos in the first part. All told, Horenstein invests the symphony with a rich spiritual meaning.

The *Saga-Dream* tone poem that fills out the second side is a warmly poetic score that was inspired by an old Icelandic legend. Again, Horenstein is most convincing, delivering a performance of sensitive nuance. Unfortunately, the recorded sound in both the symphony and the tone poem suffers somewhat from excessively close microphoning, with a resultant lack of warmth.

Comment

The Nielsen *Fifth Symphony* is represented in these recordings by two superlative performances—the Bernstein and the Horenstein. Points of distinction between them: Bernstein employs a revised edition of the score made in 1950 by two eminent Nielsen advocates, Erik Tuxen and Emil Telmanyi; Horenstein uses the original score, which has a somewhat thicker orchestral texture. The association between Nielsen's *Fifth Symphony* and Horenstein goes back nearly fifty years, to 1927, when he rehearsed the score for a performance given in Frankfurt, under Wilhelm Furtwängler's direction, for the International Society for Contemporary Music. ∎

September 1968

NIELSEN: Symphony No. 6 (Sinfonia Semplice). Music for Westchester Symphony Orchestra conducted by Siegried Landau. **SIBELIUS: Six Humoresques for Violin.** Aaron Rosand, violin, with Southwest German Radio Symphony Orchestra conducted by Tibor Szöke. Turnabout 34182, $2.98.

The Music for Westchester Symphony Orchestra, here making its recording debut, is an all-professional group that includes many of New York City's leading instrumentalists. They're good. And the high quality of their playing shows up well in this performance of the last symphony by Denmark's great composer, Carl Nielsen, whose music only now—nearly four decades after his death—is beginning to make its way in the international repertoire. The *Sinfonia Semplice* is full of characteristic Nielsen traits: prominent scoring for glockenspiel, xylophone and other percussion instruments; sudden contrasts between loud and soft; and pungent irony. Landau has not yet solved all the problems posed by the score: The phrasing should be more incisive and his interpretation more consistent. The quality of the recorded sound, however, is excellent.

The Sibelius *Humoresques*, which fill out the second side of the disc, are slight trifles. They were originally released by Turnabout's parent company, Vox Records, more than half a dozen years ago. The surfaces on the disc tested were somewhat noisy.

Comment

With the withdrawal of the Ormandy-Philadelphia Orchestra recording (Columbia MS6882), this recording of Nielsen's last symphony is the only one available as a single disc. (The other recorded version—Seraphim S6098—is the Blomstedt-conducted performance included in the three-disc album devoted to Nielsen's last three symphonies.) Until a new "single" of Nielsen's *Sixth Symphony* is released, this disc will have to do. ∎

November 1966

OFFENBACH: Gaité Parisienne. New Philharmonia Orchestra conducted by Charles Munch. London 21011, $5.98.

This one is for sound bugs only, preferably sound bugs with tin ears. The record, one of London's Phase 4 Stereo releases, is the kind of disc that used to titillate the buffs in the early days of hi-fi. It has extreme separation, close-up miking, big surges of volume, and a glossy, superficial brilliance. The only trouble is that the orchestra does not sound like an orchestra. Strings are hard and edgy; other instruments are picked up and emphasized to the detriment of the general ensemble. When the volume is turned down to a bearable level, all of the little real quality there is vanishes.

The performance of the popular ballet score (done in its entirety) is interesting. Munch, not usually a conductor of pop material, conducts with a good deal of individuality, with some surprisingly slow tempi but also with a good deal of effervescence throughout most of the score.

June 1978

OFFENBACH-ROSENTHAL: Gaité Parisienne; OFFENBACH: Overture to "La Fille du Tambour-Major." The Monte Carlo Opera Orchestra under the direction of Manuel Rosenthal. Angel S37209, $7.98. ▲ ●

Last year marked the 40th anniversary of one of the most sparkling ballets in all of music: *Gaité Parisienne*. This effervescent score, made up chiefly of music by Jacques Offenbach, was created in 1937 by Manuel Rosenthal, then a rising young French composer-conductor. (Rosenthal composed some of the music himself.) Offenbach, the most representative composer of late 19th-century Paris, where the ballet's lively action takes place, contributes

(continued)

music from such sources as *The Tales of Hoffmann*, *La Périchole*, *La Belle Hélène*, *Orpheus in the Underworld*, and *La Vie Parisienne*.

Since *Gaîté Parisienne* was originally created for the Ballet Russe de Monte Carlo, it seemed a happy inspiration to have the Monte Carlo Opera Orchestra make this new recording of the score with Rosenthal himself as conductor. Unfortunately, this promising endeavor is not completely successful. Despite its respectable credentials, the Monte Carlo Opera Orchestra can't match the verve and virtuosity of the Boston Pops, which has made several recordings of the entire *Gaîté* score. Rosenthal delivers less of the work's high spirit than did Arthur Fiedler, the Boston Pops conductor. And the recorded sound of this Angel disc becomes rather raucous. The Fiedler-Boston Pops recording (RCA LSC2267) is no model in that respect, but there is less incipient distortion apparent in the American recording. The Rosenthal disc begins with the *Overture to La Fille du Tambour-Major*, an engaging work, but performance and recording are not engaging enough to make up for my disappointment with the *Gaîté Parisienne*.

Comment

The sound of the Fiedler-Boston Pops recording (RCA LSC2267) is closer to that of a symphony orchestra, but Munch invests his reading with many interesting facets. Although not normally associated with this kind of repertoire, Munch delivers a thoroughly perceptive, persuasive account of the score, bringing out its poetry and contrasts more successfully than any conductor who has ever recorded this music—including Rosenthal himself. ∎

March 1961

ORFF: Carmina Burana (Scenic Cantata). Janice Harsanyi, soprano; Rudolph Petrak, tenor; Harve Presnell, baritone; the Rutgers University Choir and the Philadelphia Orchestra conducted by Eugene Ormandy. Columbia MS6163, $5.98. ●

By now, *Carmina Burana* is almost a classic. Despite some "modern" touches, it is really very simple and very enjoyable music—lusty, melodious, rhythmically exciting. And humorous, too. The music should be followed with the words before the listener's eyes. Ormandy has been making a specialty of this score and it is perfectly suited to his talents. The singers and the Philadelphia Orchestra respond brilliantly. And yet the stereo has a few fortissimo passages where the forces might have been more clearly defined. A good recording, in short, but not an overwhelming one.

Comment

Among the available recordings of this infectious score, the Ozawa-Boston Symphony performance (RCA LSC3161) is a virile and sensitive reading and a brilliant recording of massed choral and orchestral forces; we recommend it highly. Ozawa's soloists are Evelyn Mandac, soprano; Stanley Kolk, tenor; and

Sherrill Milnes, baritone. More garish and perhaps more viscerally exciting is the recording by the Cleveland Orchestra conducted by Michael Tilson Thomas (Columbia M33172). ■

August 1971

PAGANINI: The Twenty-Four Caprices for Solo Violin. Paul Zukofsky, violin. Vanguard-Cardinal 10093/4, 2 discs, $7.98.

Zukofsky is a demon violinist, not yet thirty, who already has an enviable career; his principal reputation is as a performer of the most difficult and advanced violin music by composers on the contemporary scene. He is equally at home with some of the most demanding music of the past, as is demonstrated in this extraordinary account of the Paganini *Caprices for Solo Violin*—works designed to exploit all the possible technical challenges with which composers and performers of nineteenth-century violin music were acquainted.

In the documentation that accompanies this two-record album, Zukofsky explains some of the problems he faced and how he solved them—particularly the vexing questions of tempo (on the whole, he opts for tempi that are considerably slower than we are accustomed to) and of which repeats to observe and which to ignore. The result of his study is not only this recorded edition of his performances, but also a printed edition of the *Caprices* scheduled for publication soon. And his "semi-private ramblings" on each of the *Caprices* provide interpretive insights.

In addition to mastering all the technical problems posed by Paganini, Zukofsky manages to invest these virtuoso show-off pieces with a degree of musical worth not often discovered by violinists. Vanguard's recorded sound is close-up and brilliant.

Comment

Those who feel that Zukofsky's performances may be too idiosyncratic should consider the recording by Ruggiero Ricci (London 6163)—a single disc with all twenty-four *Caprices*, though with little of Zukofsky's observance of the repeats. Ricci's performances are brilliant throughout, but Zukofsky is consistently the more thoughtful and probing interpreter. The performances by Itzhak Perlman (Angel S36860) are somewhere between the audacious approach of Zukofsky and the more traditional manner of Ricci. ■

November 1972

PAGANINI: Violin Concerto No. 1 in D; SARASATE: Carmen Fantasy. Itzhak Perlman, violin, with the Royal Philharmonic Orchestra conducted by Lawrence Foster. Angel S36836, $5.98. ▲ ●

(continued)

Itzhak Perlman is an extraordinary young Israeli violinist. He and his even-younger compatriot, Pinchas Zukerman, have become two of the most sought-after artists on the international scene. The choice of the Paganini *D major Concerto* for this record appears to be a happy one; Perlman has more than the requisite digital and bowing technique, and his lush tone endows the music with a warmth and fluidity that are a pleasure to hear. Lawrence Foster, the new resident conductor of the Houston Symphony Orchestra, conducts a sympathetic accompaniment, and the members of the Royal Philharmonic deliver a sensitive, secure performance.

The only trouble is that still another Israeli violinist, Shmuel Ashkenazi, has made a recording of the same concerto (DGG 139424). Like Perlman, Ashkenazi completely conquers the technical hurdles of the work, and he is very well partnered by his musical and technical collaborators. But Ashkenazi turns in a performance that is just a bit more dashing and impetuous than Perlman's. And Ashkenazi's disc accommodates the entire concerto on one side, so he was able to put on the other a much more significant disc-mate than was Perlman. Perlman chose Sarasate's brilliant but superficial *Carmen Fantasy* (on themes from the Bizet opera). Ashkenazi couples Paganini's *D major Concerto* with the same composer's *Second Concerto*—the B minor, which has as its finale Paganini's fanciful rondo movement with its interplay between violin harmonics and the percussion section's triangle, thus giving the movement its subtitle "La Campanella" ("The Little Bell"). Perlman plays the Sarasate *Fantasy* very well indeed, but the combination of Ashkenazi's more abandoned performance of the *D major Concerto* and his more substantial disc-mate gives his offering the edge.

Comment

This disc marked Perlman's debut for Angel Records after about a half-dozen years of recording for RCA Records. He has now built up a sizable catalog for Angel that includes extraordinary recordings of the Mendelssohn *E minor* and Bruch *G minor* concertos (Angel S36963), Bartok's *Second Concerto* (Angel S37014), and the Brahms *Concerto* (Angel S37286). ∎

July 1962

POULENC: Piano Music. Grant Johannesen, piano. Golden Crest S4042, $5.98.

Johannesen, engaged by Golden Crest to record the complete piano music of Fauré, temporarily breaks into his task to offer a disc of piano music by a later French composer—Francis Poulenc. On this disc are heard the *Humoresque*, *Improvisations (Book II)*, *Suite française*, *Valse in C*, *Les Animaux Modèles*, and *Villageoises*. The disc is a charmer. Poulenc's piano music is sophisticated and elegant, witty and always pianistic. As a pianist himself, Poulenc knows how to treat the instrument; and, like the Romantic composers, he goes for a singing line rather than percussive devices. The music itself is a combination of music hall tunes, folk themes, dances, and whatnot. All of it is light music, but it is the light music of a fine, inventive musical mind. There should be very few listeners who will fail to respond to the good fun, high workmanship, and melodic appeal of this music, Johannesen plays it "straight." That is to say, he is at all times responsive to the musical needs, but he does not paint the lily by becoming coy or arch. A fine musician and a thoroughly equipped technician (the music is not easy), Johannesen, with his French training, is just the man for the disc. His tone fits, too; it is clear, unsullied by too much pedal, yet never dry. As for the recorded sound, it is a little too close-up, making the piano sound rather hard. Johannesen is not one of the great piano colorists, but he is not *that* bleak. Some background noise is present, too, though not disturbingly prominent.

Comment

Much of this repertoire enjoys more atmospheric performances and more colorfully recorded sound in the recording by Gabriel Tacchino (Angel S36602). The Johannesen and Tacchino discs offer some of the same pieces, but each pianist plays music that the other does not. For a single-disc survey of some of Poulenc's most ingratiating piano music, Tacchino's is the one to have. ■

November 1965

POULENC: Sextuor for Piano and Woodwind Quintet; Trio for Oboe, Bassoon, and Piano; Sonata for Flute and Piano. Jacques Février, piano; Michel Debost, flute; and Paris Wind Ensemble. Angel S36261, $5.98.

These are peppy performances of peppy music. It may be that in his chamber music Poulenc wrote the same piece again and again, but it was a pretty good one to begin with. These three pieces have much in common: sophistication, wit, lightheartedness, sentimentality. The second subject in the first movement of the *Sextuor* is one of the juiciest, prettiest, sexiest themes in the music of this century. Of course, it's all light and fluffy; but it is also neosalon music of craftsmanship and originality. The performances can be summed up briefly: beautiful playing from expert French instrumentalists. The recorded sound is good, though not outstanding—a little lacking in mellowness. The stereo has depth and presence.

Comment

An equally diverting account of the *Sextuor* is to be found in a performance by the Philadelphia Woodwind Quintet (Columbia CMS6213), along with woodwind works in a similar vein by Françaix and Milhaud. If the *Sextuor* is all you require of Poulenc's woodwind wit, then the Columbia disc may be the one to get. ■

POULENC: Stabat Mater; Quatre Motets pour un temps de pénitence (Four Motets for a Time of Penitence). Régine Crespin, soprano, and René Duclos Choeurs and Orchestre de la Société des Concerts du Conservatoire de Paris conducted by Georges Prêtre. Angel S36121, $5.98.

The *Stabat Mater*, composed in 1951 for the death of Christian Bérard, is scored for soprano, chorus, and orchestra. The *Four Motets for a Time of Penitence* (1939) are for a cappella chorus. Both are among the more important liturgical works of the century. For most people the *Stabat Mater* will make the more immediate impression because of its greater textural variety. The unaccompanied motets are more severe, austere, abstract. Both works receive fine performances by the French musicians. Crespin, in her solos in the *Stabat Mater*, is altogether beautiful. Unfortunately the recorded sound is not what it should be. Often the chorus sounds mushy and in the distance. But these are the only available recordings of the music; so sonic considerations are secondary.

Comment

This is still the only recording of the *Stabat Mater*, and until a more detailed recorded performance comes along, this is the version with which we shall have to live. ■

PROKOFIEV: Concerti No. 1 in D flat for Piano (Op. 10) and No. 3 in C for Piano (Op. 26); Sonata No. 3 for Piano. Gary Graffman, piano, and the Cleveland Orchestra conducted by George Szell. Columbia MS6925, $5.98.

The *Piano Concerto No. 3* by Prokofiev is well known, but *No. 1* is less familiar. It is typical: full of rhythm, anti-Romantic, and whimsical, with a ferociously difficult solo part. The difficulties mean nothing to Graffman, who was born to play this kind of music. His fingers are infallible, he has strong rhythm, and he accents the modern sound of both scores by playing with very little pedal. This is honest playing, without any bluff or cover-up. It is also exciting, especially in the short *Piano Sonata No. 3* which fills out the second side of the disc. The recorded sound is clear and brilliant, pinched just a bit at the end of side one.

Comment

Others—notably Argerich (DG139349) and Janis (Mercury 75019)—have managed to find just a bit more headlong propulsion in the *Third Concerto*, but this performance of the *First Concerto* has more sheer bravura than any other recorded version, including the much admired disc by Ashkenazy (London CS7062). ■

PROKOFIEV: Concerto No. 3 in C for Piano (Op. 26); MACDOWELL: Concerto No. 2 in D minor for Piano (Op. 23). Van Cliburn, piano, and the Chicago Symphony Orchestra conducted by Walter Hendl. RCA LSC2507, $5.98.

Whatever Cliburn plays always has at least one consistent virtue—tone. He produces a full, resonant, large-size tone that never sounds jagged or forced. Along with this, he is an unusually strong technician, even in this day of brilliant virtuosos. His performance of the MacDowell is easily the best on records. Not that he has much competition in the three previous versions, but his recording would be superior in any company. His ideas of the Prokofiev do raise a few questions. Most pianists try for a fairly percussive, strongly rhythmic approach. Cliburn is basically a Romanticist, and he does not modify his tonal attack. Thus, the concerto may sound too smoothed-out, too tame, for some listeners. This reviewer likes its warmth and Romantic dash as played by Cliburn.

Comment

Cliburn's disc remains the choice among the available recordings of the Mac-Dowell concerto. Prokofiev's *Third Concerto* does have other, more convincing recorded interpretations (see previous Comment, page 170). ■

July 1963

PROKOFIEV: Concerto No. 4 for Left Hand (Op. 53); BARTÓK: Piano Concerto No. 1 for Piano. Rudolf Serkin, piano, with the Columbia Symphony Orchestra conducted by George Szell (in the Bartók) and the Philadelphia Orchestra conducted by Eugene Ormandy (in the Prokofiev). Columbia MS6405, $5.98.

Two modern works, the Bartók composed in 1926, the Prokofiev in 1931. The Bartók is savage, rhythmic, driving, exciting; the Prokofiev also has drive, but a much more pronounced melodic cast. Serkin, not normally associated with this kind of repertoire, plays both works brilliantly—with dash, virtuosity to burn, and his own sensitive musicianship. Both pieces are splendidly recorded, with plenty of stereo separation but with the piano dead center. A wonderful disc.

Comment

No other single disc offers both these works, so it would be idle to compare the performances on the several alternative versions of both scores. In any case, the preferred versions of both concertos are those by Serkin. ■

May 1965

PROKOFIEV: Concerti for Violin No. 1 in D major and No. 2 in G minor. Isaac Stern, violin, and the Philadelphia Orchestra conducted by Eugene Ormandy. Columbia MS6635, $5.98.

(continued)

It is hard to think of a violinist who could do a better job with these concerti than does Isaac Stern. His playing here is a model of strength, rhythm, technique, and identification with the music. Both works are very difficult, but Stern whizzes through them, making them sound easy. This combination of dash, electricity, and control is representative of the modern school of violin playing at its best. The music itself remains exciting, especially the *D major Concerto*, a work not heard as often as the *G minor*. And Stern's virtuoso playing is backed up by the virtuosity of Ormandy and his orchestra. An important and highly recommended disc.

As for the recorded sound, the stereo is impressive *in toto*, but the disc still makes the violin sound bigger than life.

Comment

Two extraordinary young women—Soika Milanova (Monitor S90101) and Kyung-Wha Chung (London CS6997) challenge Stern's supremacy in this repertoire. Both deliver strong, impassioned performances of these remarkable scores. If price is a factor, the Monitor disc, an outstanding value, is the recording of choice. ■

March 1959

PROKOFIEV: Peter and the Wolf (Op. 67); Lieutenant Kijé Suite (Op. 60). Boris Karloff, narrator; Vienna State Opera Orchestra conducted by Mario Rossi. Vanguard S174, $2.98. ▲

As an introduction to music for the younger set, *Peter and the Wolf* remains the nonpareil. Many composers have imitated the formula; none has come anywhere near its humor and musical invention. And *Lieutenant Kijé*, the score that Prokofiev composed in 1934 for a film, is still one of the great examples of wit in music. These two scores, of course, represent the lighter side of the composer, but they are none the less valuable or important for that. Both receive their first stereo interpretations on this disc. The orchestra is listed in heavy type as the Vienna State Opera Orchestra and immediately after that designation, in parentheses and very small type, comes "Volksoper." The Volksoper is, in a way, a state opera, in that it is subsidized by Austria. But the Volksoper is to the Staatsoper what the New York City Center is to the Metropolitan Opera. Its building is old and stuffy; its orchestra nowhere near the equal of the Staatsoper, and its repertoire is confined to operetta. What all this leads to is that the Staatsoper uses the great Vienna Philharmonic, and when the designation "Vienna State Opera Orchestra" appears on a record, one takes it for granted that it is the Vienna Philharmonic. Thus, Vanguard's designation is misleading, though technically the company may be within its rights. Not that the Volksoper has a bad orchestra. It is a well-disciplined group, and Rossi handles it quite well. (And it may even have VPO players in it.) This interpretation of *Peter and the Wolf* is admirable. It has some unorthodoxies, including an unusually deliberate closing march, but it also has superb instrumental definition and a nice, relaxed quality. The clarinet really sounds like a clarinet; the bassoon like a bassoon; strings like strings. Karloff's genial and mellow voice is well placed; there is no wandering. He recites the narrative better than anybody since the original Serge Koussevitzky recording with Richard Hale. Hale's spectacularly melodramatic delivery used to scare the kids; Karloff will soothe them. These are well-balanced, natural-sounding recordings that are not juiced up and should sound fine on any equipment.

August 1975

PROKOFIEV: Peter and the Wolf; BRITTEN: The Young Person's Guide to the Orchestra. Will Geer, narrator, with the English Chamber Orchestra conducted by Johannes Somary. Vanguard VSD71189, $6.98.

Will Geer, who has had a long and distinguished career as a character actor, has keen musical interests and is something of an authority on American folk music. We remember him as narrator, with Serge Koussevitzky and the Boston Symphony, in memorable performances of Copland's *A Lincoln Portrait* in the 1940's. So he would seem an ideal choice to narrate these "classics" by Prokofiev and Britten. Unfortunately, he doesn't live up to all our expectations.

To be sure, Greer is probably the best narrator for a recorded *Peter and the Wolf* since Richard Hale's legendary first recording of it. Hale brought a marvelous pomposity and disingenuous wonder to his reading, and Geer starts out in somewhat the same fashion. But along the way he retreats and reins in his spontaneous, childlike awe. The effect is disappointingly restrained. The text for *The Young Person's Guide*, originally written for an educational film, is didactic and hopelessly bland. Still, it need not be spoken with the degree of detachment Geer brings to it. Musically, however, both works get first-rate performances, with marvelous playing by the English Chamber Orchestra, sensitive and responsive conducting from Somary, and superbly rich and clean sound reproduction.

Comment

Among current *Peters*, the recording narrated by Michael Flanders is perhaps the least histrionic and hysterical. It has been reissued on the Seraphim label (S60172). Leinsdorf's *Kijé* is the most unusual (Seraphim S60209) since it provides a baritone to sing the "Romance" and "Troika."

A challenge to Geer's narration of *Peter and the Wolf* has come from a most unlikely source: David Bowie, the freak of rock music, has recorded the story to a musical performance by Eugene Ormandy and the Philadelphia Orchestra (RCA ARL12743). The result is, surprisingly, convincing. The overside of that disc also contains a performance of Britten's *The Young Person's Guide to the Orchestra*, which is mercifully without narration. ■

March 1965

PUCCINI: La Bohème. Mirella Freni, soprano (Mimi); Nicolai Gedda, tenor (Rodolfo); Mario Sereni, baritone (Marcello); Mariella Adani, soprano (Mus-
(continued)

etta). Chorus and Orchestra of Rome Opera House conducted by Thomas Schippers. Angel S3643, 2 discs, $11.96. ●

There are quite a few *Bohème* recordings available, but no excuse need be made for this new version. It is one of the very best, thanks to Freni and Gedda. Mirella Freni is a young Italian soprano who has been hailed as the best of the newcomers, and she lives up to her advance billing here. She has a warm, appealing voice, produced easily and confidently, and a good deal of sensitivity to go with it. One can safely predict that in a few years she will be one of the world's important singers. The big surprise is Nicolai Gedda. He has always been a competent tenor, but never in the past has he sung with such fervor, brilliance, and color. It is hard to think of a tenor today who can produce such a full-throated top C. Sereni and Adani are competent in their roles, and Schippers conducts with a good deal of sweep—except in the second act, when he is surprisingly stodgy.

Clear recorded sound, very quiet surfaces. The ending of side two, with its big climax for chorus and orchestra, is handled without strain or inner-groove distortion.

Comment

Recorded in 1956 under the direction of Sir Thomas Beecham, a uniquely youthful, vivid account of this perennial favorite is again available—this time in authentic stereo. All the principals (Victoria de los Ángeles, Jussi Bjoerling and Robert Merrill, among others) sing splendidly. The recorded sound is fine. This album (Seraphim S6099) would certainly merit recommendation, especially at its budget price.   ■

May 1959

PUCCINI: Madama Butterfly. Anna Moffo, soprano (Madama Butterfly); Cesare Valletti, tenor (Pinkerton); Rosalind Elias, mezzo-soprano (Suzuki); Renato Cesari, baritone (Sharpless); Fernando Corena, bass (The Bonze). Rome Opera House Orchestra and Chorus conducted by Erich Leinsdorf. RCA VICS6100, 3 discs, $8.94.

The oft-recorded *Butterfly* reaches us in a new RCA recording that is supposed to be a restudied version, musically speaking—a version that eschews the "grand opera" approach and stresses the lyricism. That does not prevent Moffo and Valletti from bawling out their high notes at the climax of the duet. (It would take more than a restudied version to keep Italian high voices in check—though, to be accurate, Moffo is American-born.) Nevertheless, this *Butterfly* does contain a quality of grace and elegance that no other version can match. Moffo really sings her role, and she also throws in an exciting high D flat, ending with a decrescendo (this is in the first-act Entrance Scene) that no other soprano on LP has duplicated. Leinsdorf does not whip the orchestra to a frenzy, and he sees to it that his singers engage their roles with a certain amount of musicianship. The result is a beautifully sung and integrated *Butterfly*. This is the only stereophonic version available at the time of writing. The monophonic version has several challengers, notably the Angel set with Callas. Callas is not the sumptuous-voiced singer that Moffo is, and some of her fortissimo attacks above the staff are painful; but she does have intelligence, musicianship, and a haunting quality of voice in soft passages. In the Richmond album, Tebaldi uses her voice prodigally, but the result is anything but subtle. Little of the character of Butterfly is suggested. De los Angeles, in the EMI Angel set, sings with beauty but her conception is tame; she lacks temperament. And the old Columbia set with Steber in the title role (no longer available) presents a steady version lacking color and style. It is unfortunate that the new RCA stereo recording does not match its musical values with tonal ones. The sound tends to be somewhat thin and even shrill in spots. Strings have an unpleasant edge. Voices often are too strong and blot out the orchestra. Heavily modulated fortissimo passages may cause many pickup cartridges to "shatter." There also is some inner-groove distortion. Reducing the treble frequencies was a great help, though at no time was there a quality of sound that the best stereo discs can give.

Comment

Many new *Butterfly* recordings have been released since this one first saw the light of day in the late 1950s. Angel's Barbirolli-conducted performance, with Renata Scotto in the title role (S3702), is probably the most warmly touching and lyrical. But the availability of this Leinsdorf-Moffo collaboration on RCA's low-price Victrola label may be an overriding attraction to budget-minded opera lovers. ∎

January 1968

PUCCINI: La Rondine. Anna Moffo, soprano (Magda); Daniele Barioni, tenor (Ruggero); Mario Sereni, baritone (Rambaldi); Graziella Sciutti, soprano (Lisette); Piero De Palma, tenor (Prunier). RCA Italiana Opera Orchestra conducted by Francesco Molinari-Pradelli. RCA LSC7048, 2 discs, $11.96.

Of all the mature Puccini operas, this is heard least often. It is hard to see the reason. *La Rondine* is sweet—even bittersweet—and may well be the most charming opera Puccini ever composed. It was originally a Viennese operetta, which accounts for its large number of waltzes. Indeed, Magda's aria, *"Oggi lascia amore,"* is uncomfortably reminiscent of Lehár's *Merry Widow*. There are some very beautiful things in *La Rondine*. Magda's *"Che il bel sogno"* ranks with anything Puccini ever wrote. Also in the top Puccini idiom are the Lisette-Prunier duet ending Act I, the Magda-Ruggero duets, the Quartet in Act II and the ending of the opera. Those alone should be more than enough to recommend *La Rondine*. The work is recorded in stereo here for the first time, and the sound is good. The role of Magda lies very well for Anna Moffo, and she turns in her finest performance to date, singing not only with a clearly focused voice but also passion. Her work seems to set the pace for
(continued)

the entire cast, which has been chosen with unusual care. Special honors should go to the fresh-voiced Barioni and to Sciutti, whose soubrette singing is appealing. Molinari-Pradelli's conducting reflects his wide experience in opera. The recorded sound is rich and undistorted. Extreme separation effects promote the illusion of being in an opera house.

Comment

This recorded performance is not likely to be superseded for some time to come—a fact that apparently has been taken for granted by RCA's competitors, since no alternative recording exists. ∎

September 1965

PUCCINI: Tosca. Maria Callas, soprano (Tosca); Tito Gobbi, baritone (Scarpia); Carlo Bergonzi, tenor (Cavaradossi); Giorgio Tozzi, bass (Sacristan). Orchestre de la Société des Concerts du Conservatoire and Théâtre National de l'Opéra Chorus conducted by Georges Prêtre. Angel S3655, 2 discs, $11.96.

Callas and Gobbi made a widely heralded *Tosca* for Angel about ten years ago. Now they collaborate in an up-to-date stereo version. In Gobbi's case the years between have not made much difference. He was always a great singing-actor with a rather dry voice, and that he remains. Even with a certain shortening in his top range, he still has enough pure voice to put his conception across with enormous dramatic projection. Many consider him the greatest Scarpia alive, and he lives up to his reputation in this album.

But Callas! These days her voice is actually painful to hear. In her recent *Carmen* recording she was able to handle the notes because of the low tessitura, but she runs into all kinds of vocal troubles in *Tosca*, at times having to drive her voice, which is sometimes shrill and unsteady and occasionally displays a wobble that is all but enough to make the listener seasick. The famed Callas temperament and brains are present, but here these qualities are not enough to compensate.

The best singing in the album is contributed by Bergonzi, a sure-voiced, stylish tenor. Tozzi also does fine work as the Sacristan, and Prêtre leads the orchestra in a dependable though not very striking manner. Very fine recorded sound. But for those who demand good singing from the soprano in the title role, this album is not the answer. The earlier Callas (Angel 3508, mono only) is better, and better still are the more recent versions by Price (London 1284) or Tebaldi (London 1210).

Comment

An error in the original review ascribes the role of the Sacristan to that estimable American bass, Giorgio Tozzi. It is not Tozzi who sings the part in this recording, but a little-known Italian second-stringer named Giorgio Tadeo. It speaks well of his performance that he could have been mistaken for Tozzi! Another worthy entry in the recorded *Tosca* sweepstakes is the later Price version (RCA ARL20105), with Domingo as Cavaradossi and Milnes as Scarpia. Zubin Mehta conducts an impassioned presentation of the score. ∎

May 1963

PUCCINI: Il Trittico. (1) Il Tabarro. Robert Merrill, baritone (Michele); Renata Tebaldi, soprano (Giorgetta); Mario Del Monaco, tenor (Luigi). **(2) Suor Angelica.** Renata Tebaldi, soprano (Suor Angelica); Giulietta Simionato, mezzo (Princess); Lucia Danieli, mezzo (Mother Superior). **(3) Gianni Schicchi.** Fernando Corena, bass (Gianni Schicchi); Renata Tebaldi, soprano (Lauretta); Lucia Danieli, mezzo (Zita); Agostino Lazzari, tenor (Rinuccio). Each opera with Chorus and Orchestra of the Maggio Musicale Fiorentino conducted by Lamberto Gardelli. London 1364, 3 discs, $17.94.

Il Trittico means The Triptych. Puccini composed three one-act operas intended for an entire evening's entertainment. As things turned out, only one of the three operas—*Gianni Schicchi*—ever attained status as a repertory opera. *Suor Angelica*, which is a novelty in that it does not have a man in the cast, has always been a failure. Recently, however, *Il Tabarro* has been attracting attention, as well it might. It is Puccini's one *verismo* opera, and is a taut little shocker, with a good deal of prime Puccini melody and some amazing orchestral effects. It is a masterpiece. So is *Gianni Schicchi*, which is to Puccini what *Falstaff* is to Verdi. Thus *Il Trittico* is at least two-thirds very much worth hearing. In this album Tebaldi sings leading parts in each opera. She no longer has the sweetness of tone she had a few years ago, but even in her present state she makes most sopranos sound pallid. *Tabarro* and *Suor Angelica* receive very good performances. Merrill is especially impressive in the former; and while Del Monaco bellows, as always, he at least has a voice to bellow with. And in *Angelica* the great Simionato is a stylish, knowledgeable artist. But in *Gianni Schicchi*, Corena is in competition with Tito Gobbi in the Angel disc of several years back (S35473; no longer available) and he comes off second best. Fortunately, London is releasing each opera of the triptych separately. Thus listeners can get the London *Tabarro* (1151), the Angel *Gianni Schicchi* (S35473), and (if they so desire) the London *Suor Angelica* (1152). An opera lover can live without the last-named, but the two others in the triptych are mandatory for any collection.

Comment

These recordings retain their excellence. But they must give way to the generally more theatrical performances of the triptych recorded in London under Lorin Maazel with such stalwarts as Renata Scotto, Placido Domingo, Ileana Cotrubas, Marilyn Horne, and Tito Gobbi in featured roles. *Gianni Schicchi* is Columbia M34534, *Suor Angelica* is Columbia M34505, and *Il Tabarro* is Columbia M34570. ∎

PUCCINI: Turandot. Inge Borkh, soprano (Turandot); Renata Tebaldi, soprano (Liù); Mario Del Monaco, tenor (Calaf). Chorus and Orchestra of L'Accademia di Santa Cecilia, Rome, conducted by Alberto Erede. London 1308, 3 discs, $17.94.

Most experts regard *Turandot* as Puccini's masterpiece. It does not have the immediately appealing quality of *Bohème* or *Tosca*, but its breadth, novel (for Puccini) harmonies, striking use of the chorus, and power of musical idea set it apart from all his other operas. One reason why it is not heard more often is the lack of sopranos to sing the title role. Puccini wrote a near-impossible vocal part here, and it takes a dramatic soprano on the order of a Raisa to handle it. Borkh is no Raisa, and she often has to force to carry over the orchestra. The tessitura lies a little high for her, too. But in this generation there are few who can sing the role, and Borkh is as good as any. Del Monaco sings lustily, as always, and brings animal excitement to the role of Calaf. Some exquisite singing is contributed by Tebaldi, though much of it is a little too stately for Liù. Nevertheless, this cast probably is as good as could be gathered today. As for the conductor, Erede is steady and competent, little more. Stereo effects are not obtrusive, but they are there. At the beginning of the final duet, Del Monaco is heard from a point between the speakers, with Borkh at his left. And the Ping-Pang-Pong trio (those are the names of the characters; no reference to stereo "ping pong" is meant) at the beginning of side three has a nice, realistic spread. Until Birgit Nilsson gets around to recording *Turandot*, this will be the preferred version.

Comment

Birgit Nilsson has not only managed to record *Turandot*, she has done it twice: first for RCA with Erich Leinsdorf conducting (LSC6149), later for Angel with Francesco Molinari-Pradelli conducting (S3671). The RCA recording has more of a feeling of theater; the performance for Angel is marginally smoother in its singing. But the most striking of all *Turandot* recordings, in this writer's opinion, is the later London album (CSA13108) with Joan Sutherland as an astonishingly convincing Princess, Montserrat Caballé lavishly playing Liù, and Luciano Pavarotti soaring into the stratosphere as Calaf—all directed with fire by Zubin Mehta. ∎

RACHMANINOFF: Concerti No. 1 in F sharp minor (Op. 1); No. 4 in G minor for Piano (Op. 40). Philippe Entremont, piano, and the Philadelphia Orchestra conducted by Eugene Ormandy. Columbia MS6517, $5.98.

Of the four piano concerti by Rachmaninoff, *Nos. 1* and *4*, in F sharp minor and G minor respectively, are the least played. The composer himself was uneasy with them. He composed *No. 1* in 1891 and made a thorough revision in 1919; and the *G minor Concerto* of 1926 was revised in 1942. The *G minor* never has had much play, and it is a tired-sounding and uninspired work (though the piano writing is fascinating). In recent years, by contrast, *No. 1* has been coming up. It is quite a lovely work, altogether representative of the composer in its pianistic brilliance and heartfelt melodic content; and today's young pianists seem attracted to it. Entremont, a very talented young man, plays both concerti with unusual spirit and dash. His is the playing of youth: glittering, rhythmically fluent, somewhat percussive tonally but altogether exciting in its exuberance and flair. In years to come Entremont will display more repose in his work. Right now he is impulsive, a little too anxious to overpower the music. Nobody would go wrong getting this disc, though. Fine recorded sound.

Comment

One of Entremont's most successful performances, this is now the only one-disc recording available of the two Rachmaninoff concertos. Entremont is an ardent partisan of both these works. The quality of the recorded sound remains respectable. ∎

September 1973

RACHMANINOFF: Piano Concerto No. 2 in C minor. Artur Rubinstein, piano, with the Philadelphia Orchestra conducted by Eugene Ormandy. RCA ARD10031, $6.98. ▲ ●

Rubinstein has recorded the most popular of the Rachmaninoff concertos at least twice previously—once with Vladimir Golschmann conducting the NBC Symphony Orchestra back in the days of 78-rpm discs, and later, in the early days of stereo, with Fritz Reiner conducting the Chicago Symphony Orchestra (a performance still listed in the RCA catalog as LSC2068). This new release was recorded in quadrasonic sound a little more than a year ago. From the executant standpoint, the result is nothing short of phenomenal.

Rubinstein, after all, is well into his eighties, but his stamina and concentration remain incredible. His playing on this new disc is infused with a vibrancy and dynamism that surely are the envy of every other performing pianist, young and old alike. And his technical facility is awesome; the Rachmaninoff *Second Concerto* is certainly not an easy piece, and yet Rubinstein tosses it all off effortlessly. In the bargain, he invests the score with a rare lucidity and dignity that are as welcome as they are rare. Ormandy and the Philadelphia Orchestra are the perfect collaborators in this extraordinary performance.

RCA is now releasing nearly all of its classical recordings in its "Quadradisc" format, a compatible four-channel disc that can be played on either regular stereo or quadraphonic reproducing equipment. Since the overwhelming majority of listeners do not yet own quadraphonic reproducing equipment, it should be emphasized that, even in regular stereo, this recording of Rachmaninoff's *C minor Concerto* has a richness of sound that is consonant with the highest standards prevailing in the industry.

(continued)

RACHMANINOFF: Piano Concerto No. 2 in C minor. Artur Rubinstein, piano, with the Philadelphia Orchestra conducted by Eugene Ormandy. RCA ARL10031, $6.98.

This is a stereo reduction of the four channel disc RCA released a few years ago as one of its first Quadradiscs (ARD10031). The performance is heroic, monumental—one of the best recordings of this music ever made. The stereo sound is vibrant, full-bodied, and much richer than that of the quad version played with stereo equipment.

But RCA has offered scandalously poor value in spreading this 34-minute work over an entire disc. Pianist Ilana Vered's performance of the same concerto for London Records's Phase 4 series runs 37 minutes and takes just one side of the record (SPC21099); that leaves room on the other side for Rachmaninoff's *Prelude in C sharp minor* and his *Rhapsody for Piano and Orchestra on a Theme by Paganini.* And RCA itself has released a recording with more than twice the music on this one—Tchaikovsky's *Piano Concerto in B flat minor* and Prokofiev's *Second Piano Concerto* (ARL10751), both brilliantly played by the young American pianist, Tedd Joselson, in his recording debut. Finally, the disc we bought was so badly warped that almost half of one side was unplayable. We fixed that by storing the disc for a few days under a pile of records. But a curse on RCA's wafer-thin Dynaflex discs!

RACHMANINOFF: Piano Concerto No. 2 in C minor; Rhapsody on a Theme of Paganini. Abbey Simon, piano, with the St. Louis Symphony Orchestra under the direction of Leonard Slatkin. Turnabout QTVS34658, $3.98. ●

This is an early release in a projected series of the complete Rachmaninoff piano concertos to be recorded by Abbey Simon with the St. Louis Symphony under Leonard Slatkin's direction. I can pay this disc no finer compliment than to say that it recalls the classic recordings of these works made by the composer himself with the Philadelphia Orchestra under Leopold Stokowski. Simon plays both the *Concerto* and the *Rhapsody* effortlessly and with enormous control. He also resists the temptation to highlight the brilliance of the writing for piano at the expense of its poetic quality; there is warmth and color in his playing.

Slatkin, the music director of the New Orleans Philharmonic Orchestra, conceives the orchestral parts of both scores as richly Romantic. The recording and playing of the St. Louis Symphony, which seems to get better and better, are full-blooded and expressive.

Comment

RCA's pioneering efforts in the production of a compatible stereo/quad disc were rather short-lived, doubtless because of public indifference to the whole concept of quadraphonic reproduction. About the only major company still in the compatible stereo/quad business is Angel Records (the American releasing arm of Britain's EMI).

Mercifully, RCA has now also abandoned the Dynaflex aberration. By and large, though, the current RCA disc is still on the thin side when measured against discs such as Philips or Deutsche Grammophon. Rubinstein's account of Rachmaninoff's *Second Concerto* with Ormandy may well be in a class by itself; still, Simon's effort remains uncommonly satisfying—as does his over-side account of the composer's *Rhapsody on a Theme of Paganini*. ∎

September 1959

RACHMANINOFF: Concerto No. 3 in D minor for Piano (Op. 30).
Van Cliburn, piano; Symphony of the Air conducted by Kiril Kondrashin. RCA LSC2355, $5.98. ▲

Cliburn is, of course, the most publicized young pianist of the generation. He made his great reputation with the Tchaikovsky *Piano Concerto in B flat minor* and this Rachmaninoff *Third*, both of which he played in Carnegie Hall on May 19, 1958, on his return from the Soviet Union. He already has recorded the Tchaikovsky for RCA. Now comes the Rachmaninoff and this is not the result of a studio session. Rather it is a record of the actual Carnegie Hall performance, complete with audience noises. Naturally a certain amount of documentary importance invests the disc, and it quite possibly could develop into a collector's item. Extrinsic factors aside, the young pianist's performance is splendid. He is in complete command of the notes, and he handles the music with a combination of power and sensitivity that very few pianists could duplicate. The recording is quite good. Surfaces are fairly quiet, the balance between piano and orchestra is first-rate, and on the whole many worse concerto recordings have been released. It is true that this disc does not have the brilliance it might have, but it more than gives the idea of the historic occasion it represents.

November 1963

RACHMANINOFF: Concerto No. 3 in D minor for Piano (Op. 30).
Vladimir Ashkenazy, piano; London Symphony Orchestra conducted by Anatole Fistoulari. London 6359, $5.98.

All the Russian pianists dote on the Rachmaninoff *D minor*. Ashkenazy, no exception, gives the music a lyric, highly emotional performance backed by clear finger work. It is beautiful playing. Those who want overwhelming drive and sonority will turn to the Horowitz disc (RCA LM1178); and there is always Rachmaninoff's own, obsolete in sound but noble and brilliant in performance. But the Ashkenazy, by virtue of its poetry and sensitivity, will surely make a place for itself in the public's esteem.

Comment

Rachmaninoff's *Third Piano Concerto* has become *the* work for piano and orchestra of the 1970s. From among the many new recordings available, three
(continued)

strike this listener as being particularly meritorious. Cliburn's disc (RCA LSC2355) has mellowness and warmth. The latest of Ashkenazy's three recordings of the score (RCA ARL11324, with Ormandy conducting the Philadelphia Orchestra), combines poetry and power; the Horowitz performance recorded at the January 1978 Carnegie Hall concert celebrating the fiftieth anniversary of the pianist's American debut (RCA CRL12633, with Ormandy conducting the New York Philharmonic), which gives us electrifying tension and personality. ∎

April 1974

RACHMANINOFF: Symphony No. 2 in E minor (complete version). The London Symphony Orchestra conducted by André Previn. Angel S36954, $5.98.

The centennial of the birth of the Russian-American pianist-composer-conductor, Sergei Rachmaninoff, occurred in 1973. It was celebrated by concerts, by the rerelease of all of Rachmaninoff's recorded performances of his own piano music, and by new recordings of several of his most important compositions. This new recording of the composer's *Second Symphony* is a late entry, but it is by no means the least of them. Indeed, by shedding new light on Rachmaninoff's abilities as a symphonist, this disc may be the most important of all the centennial observances.

Rachmaninoff composed his *Second Symphony* early in this century. It is an expansive, melodic work richly scored for a large orchestra and full of lush harmonies. Like other symphonies of its era, the *Second* is long, taking nearly an hour to perform, In later years, Rachmaninoff sanctioned what came to be regarded as "official cuts" in the score, and nearly every conductor observed them over the years—including Previn himself in an earlier recording with the London Symphony Orchestra. Now, however, Previn has rethought the score, has repudiated the shorter version he was "guilty" of playing and has reinstated every note of Rachmaninoff's original creation. Previn writes, "It makes the Symphony undeniably long, but I feel that its honesty, its power, its heart-felt lyricism can stand it."

The love of conductor and orchestra for this score is instantly apparent. The playing itself is vibrant and spontaneous, and the sound is splendidly full, with particularly rich reproduction of the low strings. There still exist those who denigrate Rachmaninoff the composer as too obvious and sentimental; this totally convincing performance should make some converts.

Comment

If I were asked to single out one of André Previn's many recordings, this would undoubtedly be my choice. It contains conducting of utter conviction, playing of great nuance and sensitivity, and recorded sound of outstanding depth and clarity. In short, this is unquestionably a great recording. ∎

RAFF: Symphony No. 5 in E ("Lenore"). The London Philharmonic Orchestra conducted by Bernard Herrmann. Nonesuch H71287, $2.98.

Joachim Raff was one of the most important and frequently performed composers in the late 19th-century period of musical Romanticism. His compositions covered a wide spectrum of formats, including solo works, chamber music, a total of 11 symphonies, and six operas.

This *Fifth Symphony*, inspired by a famous contemporary German ballad by Bürger called "Lenore," was especially guaranteed to send listeners of a century ago into rapture. But until the Romantic revival of the past few years, Raff had become little more than a name in the history books. Now, a few of his works have become available in recordings, including the *Third Symphony* (*"In the Forest"*) on the Candide label.

In releasing this London-derived production by Unicorn Records of Raff's *Fifth*, Nonesuch continues its unique service to the American record-buying public. And it is fitting that Bernard Herrmann should be the conductor, for some 30 years ago it was he who dug around in the CBS music library and introduced radio listeners to some music by Raff and other exotic composers.

The Bürger ballad tells a tale of lost love: A damsel whose beloved has fallen in war goes off on a terrifying horseback ride with a mysterious, spurred stranger. He, of course, turns out to be the specter of the lost lover. Raff expands the story backwards; the first three movements of the symphony deal with the joys of love and the parting of the lovers. Only in the last movement does the composer address himself to Bürger's eerie ride on horseback.

The music is reminiscent of much that is familiar from standard 19th-century German composition: Mendelssohn, Schumann, Weber, and especially Liszt are obvious influences. This symphony will not replace any of the great basic repertoire symphonies. But Raff handles his material with such a secure mastery that it is easy to understand why this music was impressive to audiences of the past. And it is a welcome diversion from the recordings of well-established classics.

The performance by the London Philharmonic Orchestra under Herrmann's direction is responsive, with a sympathetic feel for the music. The recorded sound, however, is not quite so vivid and full-bodied as one might hope for.

Comment

Before Bernard Herrmann devoted most of his energies to creating some of the finest film music ever written (*Citizen Kane, North by Northwest, Psycho, and Vertigo*, among others), he was the staff conductor for the CBS Radio Network, director of the CBS Symphony Orchestra and responsible for such distinguished broadcasts as "Invitation to Music." In that role he introduced an entire generation to rare and unusual scores from the whole range of music history. This recorded performance of Raff's *"Lenore" Symphony* is a case in point. ∎

RAVEL: Boléro; Rapsodie Espagnole; La Valse. The Boston Symphony Orchestra conducted by Seiji Ozawa. Deutsche Grammophon 2530475, $7.98 ▲

This is the first installment of a scheduled multidisc release of Ravel's orchestral music by Ozawa and the Boston Symphony to celebrate the centennial of the composer's birth last year. (Vox Records has already released a four-disc boxed set, QSVBX5133, of the orchestral music played by the Minnesota Orchestra under Stanislaw Skrowaczewski.)

The three works on this record are staples in the Boston Symphony's repertory; the orchestra recorded them many times in years past under Serge Koussevitzky and Charles Munch. The new performances under Ozawa attest to the current splendor of the Boston Symphony, which plays with elegance, discipline, fine tonal shadings, and nice internal balances. But where are the fire and passion of these works? *Boléro*, taken at a very brisk pace, builds little cumulative tension. The *Rapsodie Espagnole* gets a curiously detached performance. And *La Valse*, that shattered, convulsive evocation of the vanished 19th century, emerges as tame and matter-of-fact. Distant-sound microphone placement doesn't help much either, though there is considerable textural clarity.

Comment

Here is another example of Ozawa's failure to come to grips with the fundamental responsibilities of the conductor's art. To be sure, these three works are colorful and imaginative in structure and sound. But Ozawa is content to ride the surface of the music and seems to be uninterested in its interior life and vitality. ■

RAVEL: Boléro; DEBUSSY: Prelude to the Afternoon of a Faun; La Mer. The Chicago Symphony Orchestra under the direction of Sir Georg Solti. London CS7033, $7.98. ●

For several years in the early 70's, Solti served simultaneously as music director of the Orchestre de Paris and of the Chicago Symphony. He therefore conducted a great deal of French orchestral music—far more, probably, than he would have otherwise. One recalls his way with two works by Berlioz: the *Symphonie Fantastique* (London CS6790), and his Chicago and New York performances in concert of *The Damnation of Faust*. This disc further illustrates the lasting effects of Solti's French connection.

Performance and recording of *Boléro* are quite remarkable. Solti establishes and works excitingly, at that tempo. *Boléro* is a great vehicle for orchestral set in his own recording. But Solti needs no justification: The music works, and works excitingly, at that tempo. *Boléro* is a great vehicle for orchestral virtuosity, and the Chicago Symphony musicians—rank and file as much as soloists—rise magnificently to the occasion. The sound reproduction is a model of clarity and brilliance that helps make this one of the greatest *Boléro* recordings ever.

The two Debussy scores fare well, if less spectacularly than Ravel's tour de force. The *Prelude to the Afternoon of a Faun* has sensuality and sensuousness to spare, and the unnamed flute soloist (Donald Peck, surely) plays beautifully. Still I wish the whole thing gave more evidence of spontaneous feeling. *La Mer*, which is superbly played and recorded, strikes me as rather deficient in mystery and atmosphere. But the *Boléro* performance is peerless.

Comment

The *Boléro* reviewed above is the recording to have. But if the Debussy pieces are your prime concern, try the Monteux performances. His *La Mer* is with the Boston Symphony Orchestra on Quintessence 7027, and his *Prelude to the Afternoon of a Faun* is with the London Symphony Orchestra on London STS15356. ∎

September 1966

RAVEL: Gaspard de la Nuit; DEBUSSY: L'Isle Joyeuse; CHOPIN: Scherzo No. 4 in E (Op. 54); Nocturne in B major (Op. 62, No. 1). Vladimir Ashkenazy, piano. London 6472, $5.98.

Ashkenazy is a great pianist, and it would be hard to imagine a better performance of the impossibly difficult Ravel work. Notes roll from his fingers in predestined patterns; he has a subtle sense of color and just as good a sense of musical proportion. His Debussy is also beautiful. It is the Chopin that raises some questions. Here the Russian pianist sometimes tends to over-interpret, and he is especially fussy in the *B major Nocturne*. But the Ravel remains the finest performance on records. Ashkenazy has not been treated well by the engineers of this disc. The stereo contains surface noise, is over-monitored and in fortissimo passages has a clangorous tone that is not a true representation of Ashkenazy's art.

Comment

Other sterling recordings of the Ravel are those of Alicia De Larrocha (Columbia M30115, with *Alborada* and *Valses Nobles*) and Ruth Laredo (Connoisseur Society S2005, with *La Valse* and *Valses Nobles*). Along with Ashkenazy's, these are thoroughly realized conceptions and performances of one of the most dazzling works in piano literature. Also highly recommended is the Ravel recital by Emanuel Ax (RCA ARL12530), which presents finely chiseled versions of *Gaspard de la Nuit*, the *Valses Nobles et Sentimentales*, and the four-hand piano version of the *Mother Goose Suite* (in which the other hands belong to Ax's wife, pianist Yoko Nozaki). ∎

May 1965

RAVEL: Valses Nobles et Sentimentales; POULENC: Mouvements Perpétuels; Intermezzi in A flat and D flat; FAURÉ: Nocturne in A

(continued)

flat; CHABRIER: Scherzo-Valse. Artur Rubinstein, piano. RCA LSC2751, $5.98.

A French program, and one that contains quite a few items never before recorded by the veteran pianist. Indeed, all is new except the Fauré *A flat Nocturne* and the Poulenc *Mouvements Perpétuels*, and Rubinstein last recorded these works more than twenty years ago. The playing is beautiful—everything one has come to expect of the great artist: poise, maturity, a spacious line, the big tone, the rhythmic plasticity, the sheer aristocracy. Good recorded sound.

Comment

A special pleasure is Rubinstein's marvelously colored and atmospheric account of the Ravel waltzes. But in everything on the disc, Rubinstein is in top form.

As mentioned above, there also exists a refined and sensitive account of the Ravel *Valses Nobles et Sentimentales* by Ruth Laredo (Connoisseur Society S2005), but where Rubinstein addresses a miscellaneous program of French piano music, Laredo's disc is devoted entirely to piano music by Ravel (*La Valse* and *Gaspard de la Nuit* complete the disc). Other atmospheric accounts of the *Valses Nobles et Sentimentales* are those by Ax (RCA ARL12530), De Larrocha (Columbia M30115), and Simon (Turnabout 34397). ∎

April 1974

RHEINBERGER: Organ Concertos in F major, Opus 137, and G minor, Opus 177. E. Power Biggs, organ, with the Columbia Symphony Orchestra conducted by Maurice Peress. Columbia M32297, $5.98. ●

Josef Rheinberger (1839-1901) was almost an exact contemporary of Brahms. Rheinberger was greatly admired during his lifetime as organist, teacher, conductor, and composer. But like many of the Romantics, he is largely unknown today. This disc of his two colorful organ concertos should bring him to a wider public. The earlier of the two works, the *Concerto in F*, is scored for the solo organ with string orchestra and three horns. The later *Concerto in G minor* is more festive and ceremonial, and it calls for an orchestra of strings, two horns, two trumpets, and tympani. The two works are very much of their time and place—late 19th-century Germany—with resemblances to the music of Brahms and Richard Strauss. Both concertos abound in the opulence of Romanticism at its height, showing Rheinberger's mastery of organ technique and color.

In the golden days of live radio music in the forties and fifties, E. Power Biggs had a weekly Sunday morning series on CBS radio; he performed these and other works from the vast but too-little-known repertory of organ music. He is thus ideally prepared to champion these two concertos, and he plays them with sweep and authority. He receives first-rate orchestral support by the Columbia Symphony Orchestra under the direction of Maurice Peress,

186

the conductor of the Corpus Christi (Tex.) Symphony Orchestra. Included is a seven-inch disc in which Biggs rather stiffly discourses on the organ-orchestra combination, with musical examples.

Comment

Biggs, alas, has died since this disc was released. But Peress has moved from his duties in Corpus Christi to a more important assignment: As the music director of the Kansas City Philharmonic Orchestra; he enriches the life of that community and its surroundings. ∎

February 1975

RIEGGER: String Quartet No. 2; HARRIS: Fantasy for Violin and Piano; MOSS: Elegy for Two Violins and Viola; Timepiece for Violin, Piano and Percussion. The New Music Quartet (in the Riegger), and various other instrumentalists in the Harris and Moss works. Composers Recordings Incorporated CRI SD307, $5.95.

The performance of the Riegger quartet was once available on the Columbia label. Its reappearance here is another of CRI's restorations of valuable recordings from other sources that otherwise would languish in the twilight zone of catalog withdrawal. The work itself is one of the composer's strongest, and the performance and recording (even the electronic stereoizing) are satisfying.

Donald Harris's *Fantasy for Violin and Piano*, composed in Paris during 1956-57, is a brief one-movement work that manages to cover a wide spectrum of moods and colors. It makes great demands upon the virtuoso powers of both the performers, and those demands are met with ease by the artists of the present performance—Paul Zukofsky, violin, and Gilbert Kalish, piano.

The two pieces by Lawrence Moss are more ambitious and stimulating, especially the *Elegy*. It is dedicated to the memory of the composer's brother, who died suddenly shortly after the music was begun. In performance, two of the players are required to move about stage, but the work is engrossing and moving even without the visual component. *Timepiece* is constantly shifting but always intriguing, with the three instrumentalists sometimes playing in very close ensemble, sometimes in total independence of one another. Moss, too, is fortunate in his performers—Paul Zukofsky and Romuald Teco, violins, and Jean Dupouy, viola, in the *Elegy*, and Zukofsky again, along with Gilbert Kalish, piano, and Raymond Des Roches, percussion, in *Timepiece*. In the latter work there is extreme stereo separation in the recorded sound, with the violin distinctly in the left channel, the piano in the right and the various percussion instruments spread across the center.

Comment

Composers Recordings recently changed its status from commercial venture to nonprofit undertaking. It is a valuable enterprise and deserves widespread support. ∎

TERRY RILEY: In C. Terry Riley, leader and saxophone, with members of the New York State University Art Center Orchestra. Columbia MS7178, $5.98.

In this age of the widespread artistic put-on, Terry Riley's *In C* may well be the ultimate in musical infantilism. The jacket notes inform us that the score consists of fifty-three numbered musical figures and a piano part, called the Pulse, made up entirely of even octave eighth notes to be played steadily on the top two C's of the keyboard throughout the entire performance. Any number of players may participate, and each member of the ensemble plays all fifty-three numbered figures consecutively, in synchronization with the Pulse. Each player decides for himself when he will move from one figure to the next, where he will place his downbeat and how often and how long he will rest. The performance comes to an end after all the players have finished figure 53. The result is not only chaotic, it is a stupefying bore as well. When Ravel deliberately assaulted the sensibilities of his listeners with his *Boléro*—a quarter of an hour of a single theme reiterated in a steadily mounting crescendo—he wondered if the human nervous system could tolerate such abuse. But any such problem with the *Boléro* becomes pale indeed when compared with the inanities of *In C*. Imagine, if you can, forty-five minutes of rhythmic monotony, combined with the elementary harmonic structures and incessant repetition of the note C. It's a musical version of the Chinese water torture. The recording consists of a series of electronic over-dubbings that convey a sonority reminiscent of the gamelan, an exotic Balinese instrument. The various textures are clearly and cleanly reproduced.

Comment

The vogue that this sort of thing enjoyed in some quarters during the 1960s now seems, mercifully, to have ended. ■

July 1976

RIMSKY-KORSAKOV: Scheherazade. The Los Angeles Philharmonic Orchestra conducted by Zubin Mehta. London CS6950, $6.98. ●

One would expect Zubin Mehta to be an ideal conductor for this colorful and dramatic score. His flair and generally extroverted approach to music-making would seem tailor-made for this evocation of the Arabian Nights. But what we get in three of the four movements is a curious sense of detachment. (The third movement, "The Young Prince and Princess," is the exception; it fairly swoons with exaggerated sighs and heavings.) Nor is the orchestra's playing up to its own standards. The recorded sound is on the boomy side. In short, there are many other *Scheherazade* recordings around preferable to this one. Among them are discs under the direction of Beecham (Angel S35505), Haitink (Philips 6500410), Monteux (London STS15158), and Reiner (RCA LSC3312).

Comment

To the list of preferred *Scheherazade* recordings must now be added the last of the many Stokowski accounts of the score (RCA ARL11182). This performance is the summation of Stokowski's lifelong experience with *Scheherazade*: It throbs with youthful passion and exhilaration—and the recorded sound is voluptuous. ∎

November 1969

RIMSKY-KORSAKOV: Symphony No. 1 in E minor. Moscow Radio Orchestra conducted by Boris Khaikin. **Poem of Oleg the Wise.** Mark Reshetin, bass, and Vladimir Petrov, tenor, with the Bolshoi Theater Chorus and Orchestra conducted by Boris Khaikin. Melodiya/Angel S40094, $5.98.

Rimsky-Korsakov's symphonic suite, *Antar*, is sometimes labeled the composer's second symphony, which has given rise to the assumption that there must have been a first symphony. Well, here it is in a release imported from the Soviet Union. However, this recording is of the composer's revised version of the score, made nearly a quarter of a century after its composition. So instead of being an example of musical juvenilia, the score represents the mature reworking of a composition begun during the composer's teens.

Truth to tell, there is very little to distinguish the symphony from any number of similar scores by lesser composers of the later nineteenth century. It has an unmistakable Russian character, but the musical materials are commonplace and their development routine. The Moscow Radio Symphony Orchestra is an unpolished ensemble and it gives a rough-and-tumble performance. But there is a vigorous exuberance emphasized by the resonant and full-bodied sound reproduction.

The cantata, *Poem of Oleg the Wise*, dates from a much later period, after Rimsky-Korsakov had already written *Scheherazade, Capriccio espagnol*, and most of the other scores for which he is chiefly remembered today. It is a musical setting for Pushkin's ballad version of an ancient Russian legend about the fulfillment of a prophecy concerning the death of Oleg the Wise, ruler of Kiev. The cantata offers little that is fresh and new; rather, it seems a tired exercise in familiar sounds and patterns. The performance and the recording seem to do all that can be done for the music.

Comment

Both scores are from the bottom of the pile of Rimsky-Korsakov's creative works. The disc is recommended only to those with a special interest in the (justly) forgotten repertoire. ∎

January 1970

RIMSKY-KORSAKOV: Antar (Symphony No. 2); IPPOLITOV-IVANOV: Caucasian Sketches; GLIERE: Russian Sailors' Dance.

(continued)

189

The Utah Symphony Orchestra conducted by Maurice Abravanel. Vanguard C10060, $3.98.

About a year ago Morton Gould and the Chicago Symphony Orchestra made the first stereo recording of Rimsky-Korsakov's lively and colorful *Antar* (Victor LSC3022). The performance is extremely good, communicating as it does the kaleidoscopic moods of the music. Abravanel, too, is similarly successful. Although his orchestra is hardly the equal of the Chicago Symphony, his players nevertheless give a powerful and passionate performance.

Thus, a listener might choose according to what is on the other side of the disc. Gould's disc couples the Rimsky-Korsakov score with the brooding and mystical *Symphony No. 21* of the Russian composer Miaskovsky. Abravanel's flip-side performances of the much more familiar rousers by Ippolitov-Ivanov and Glière may or may not sway the case in his favor. At any rate, they are invested with a high level of artistry and excitement, and the Vanguard engineers have come up with rich, well-balanced, and clearly defined sound.

Comment

In contrast with the routine *First Symphony*, Rimsky-Korsakov's *Antar* is an intriguing illustration of his meticulously developed sense of orchestral color; the scoring could well serve as an object lesson in orchestration. RCA has unaccountably chosen to withdraw the excellent Gould-Chicago Symphony recording. ∎

January 1974

ROCHBERG: String Quartet No. 3. The Concord String Quartet. Nonesuch H71283, $2.98.

George Rochberg's *Third String Quartet* may well be the most masterful musical composition to appear in the last 20 years. The Concord String Quartet performs the work superbly, the work of its members being characterized by the composer himself as what "a composer dreams of . . . with performers who miraculously understand what he is trying to say. . . ." And, technically, the Nonesuch sound does full justice to both the work and the performance.

Rochberg, now 55, has had a distinguished career as academician, teacher and composer. During the past 25 years, his musical style and philosophy have undergone profound changes. He was once a dedicated adherent of musical atonalism and the 12-tone scale. But he has since emerged as a partisan of 19th-century classicism and romanticism, showing in particular the influence of Beethoven and Mahler in some of his recent works. The *Third String Quartet*—completed two years ago—may represent the crystallization of Rochberg's new-found individuality within the tonal-music framework he once rejected.

This quartet begins with a ferocious Introduction, labeled a Fantasia, with clashing dissonances and angular rhythms. A contrasting mood of tranquility soon takes over, but with a sinister air of expectancy that is resolved when the brusque restlessness of the opening returns. Next comes a headlong and urgent March, with much solo material assigned to the first violin and the cello. The Fantasia and the March form Part A of the quartet.

Part B—the spiritual core of the quartet—is a remarkable series of Variations (on an original theme) that explores the exalted, late-Beethoven terrain. The four instruments engage in a genuine dialogue throughout, with the first violin often sent to the uppermost limits of the instrument's range. The music has an extraordinary serenity almost unknown in contemporary serious compositions.

A second March—also dramatically charged—ushers in the third and concluding part. This March leads without interruption to an extended Finale that alternates Scherzos and Serenades. The ghost of Mahler hovers over the Serenades, while in the Scherzos the Sibelius of the *Seventh Symphony* and the Schoenberg of *Transfigured Night* can be heard. Near the end, Rochberg brings back the dissonances and rhythms of the opening March, and the work concludes with a figure—many times repeated—of summation and resolution.

This astonishing composition succeeds in transforming the sublime concepts of traditional music into contemporary language.

Comment

In returning to traditional musical concepts, Rochberg generated a swirl of controversy. Some have labeled him a turncoat revisionist, one who has betrayed the cause of contemporary music. Others—this writer among them—see Rochberg as a guiding force in shaping the direction of music in the last quarter of the twentieth century. This quartet may well be a seminal work in that respect. ∎

November 1973

ROCHBERG: Tableaux; RAN: O, the Chimneys. Jan de Gaetani, soprano, with the Penn Contemporary Players conducted by Richard Wernick (in the Rochberg); Gloria Davy, soprano, and Shulamit Ran, piano, with the New York Philomusica Chamber Ensemble conducted by A. Robert Johnson (in the Ran). Turnabout TVS34492, $2.98.

George Rochberg and Shulamit Ran are among the most original and creative composers on the contemporary scene. Though of different generations— Rochberg is 55 and Ran is in her early 20's—both of them create music with irresistible force and drama. Both scores included on this disc date from the late 1960's, and both have an intensely personal meaning to their creators. The text for Rochberg's work is taken from a surreal tale of terror and love written by the composer's son, Paul, who died just as his literary gifts were beginning to be realized. Miss Ran, an Israeli, has taken her texts from

(continued)

poems by Nelly Sachs that deal with the Nazi atrocities suffered by European Jews. The chimneys of the title refer to the smokestacks in the concentration-camp crematoria.

Both composers have here concerned themselves mainly with sounds and sound combinations, yet both scores are splendidly structured in content and form. Both leave the listener profoundly moved. Some of the credit unquestionably belongs to the performing artists, who conquer all the challenges presented to them by the composers, and to the superlative sound of the recording engineers. This is a most rewarding disc of contemporary music, from a source (Turnabout Records is a division of Vox) that is rapidly becoming a leader in the field. And note the bargain price.

Comment

The power of both these scores remains undiminished. We strongly recommend them to anyone with an interest in the music of our time. The conductor, Richard Wernick, is Rochberg's colleague on the music faculty of the University of Pennsylvania and a distinguished composer—winner, in fact, of the 1976 Pulitzer Prize for Music.   ∎

July 1978

RODRIGO: Guitar Concerto; Fantasia para un Gentilhombre. Angel Romero, guitar, with the London Symphony Orchestra under the direction of André Previn. Angel S37440, $7.98. ●

The much-recorded Guitar Concerto ("Concierto de Aranjuez"), composed in 1939 by the blind Spanish composer Joaquin Rodrigo, has become *the* classic work for guitar and orchestra. Thanks to a popular London recording (London STS15199) by Narciso Yepes, and an evocative arrangement of the work's second movement by Bill Evans for Miles Davis, the *Concerto* had become quite well-known in this country even before its American concert premiere in the summer of 1964, with Angel Romero in the Hollywood Bowl.

The reasons for the score's popularity are plain. The music abounds in rhythm and melodic vitality. It blends the slender sound of the guitar with that of a reduced orchestra perfectly. And it serves as an ideal showcase for the talents of contemporary classical guitarists.

In his *Fantasia para un Gentilhombre*, written for and dedicated to Andrés Segovia in 1954, Rodrigo tried to repeat the formula of the *Guitar Concerto*. While the work is charming, it doesn't quite have the zest and bite of the *Concerto*—which are precisely the qualities emphasized by Romero and Previn in both these performances. These pieces have only rarely enjoyed the élan apparent here, and the sense of sheer joy they convey. Romero had recorded the *Concerto* earlier with Victor Alessandro and the San Antonio Symphony Orchestra (Mercury 75021), but good as it was, that recording is not up to the new one. The sound captured in the studio is crisp and transparent.

Comment

Another first-rate recorded performance of Rodrigo's *Guitar Concerto* is that of John Williams, with Daniel Barenboim conducting the English Chamber Orchestra (Columbia M33208). The recording also includes the flavorful *Guitar Concerto* by the Brazilian Heitor Villa-Lobos. ∎

November 1959

ROSSINI: The Barber of Seville. Cesare Valletti, tenor (Almaviva); Robert Merrill, baritone (Figaro); Roberta Peters, soprano (Rosina); Fernando Corena, bass (Dr. Bartolo); Giorgio Tozzi, bass (Basilio). Metropolitan Opera Orchestra and Chorus conducted by Erich Leinsdorf. RCA LSC6143, 4 discs, $17.98.

If nothing else, this is the most complete *Barber* ever recorded. Many standard deletions have been restored, including the last-act tenor aria *"Ah, il più lieto"* (more familiar as *"Non più mesto"* from Rossini's *Cenerentola*; Rossini often cribbed from his own music). The performance of this great *opera buffa* is, on the whole, good, with honors going to the male side of the cast. Merrill, Corena, and Tozzi sing resplendently. Valletti, though, is a little weaker. He produces some strained notes (rare with him) and actually struggles with his opening *"Ecco ridente."* Peters is puzzling, ripping off some imposing coloratura passages in some sections, becoming shrill and forced in others. She has a fine musical grasp of her role, however, and she sings the lyric moments quite beautifully. Leinsdorf conducts accurately and with steady rhythm. The recorded sound is successfully realized. Stereo is, of course, ideal for opera, and in episodes like the big ensemble number ending Act II (on side five), the spread is very realistic. The voices are lined up along the wall (stage), and the listener gets a feeling of individual placement. Elsewhere the sound is lively. And the orchestra has not been neglected; its balance with singers is unusually precise. RCA has packaged the opera in a silly box with a protruding metal hasp. Just try sliding it into a shelf and see what happens. As a recompense, the four discs are being offered for the price of three.

November 1963

ROSSINI: The Barber of Seville. Victoria de los Angeles, soprano (Rosina); Luigi Alva, tenor (Almaviva); Sesto Bruscantini, baritone (Figaro); Carlo Cava, bass (Basilio); Ian Wallace, baritone (Bartolo). Royal Philharmonic Orchestra and Glyndebourne Festival Chorus conducted by Vittorio Gui. Angel S3638, 3 discs, $17.94.

The greatest of all *buffa* operas here receives a smooth, clear, well-integrated performance that just misses greatness. It misses because the entire conception is a shade too careful. Thus the effervescent, Italianate, extroverted quality is lacking. This is especially true of two singers—Sesto Bruscantini as Figaro and Victoria de los Angeles as Rosina. Bruscantini is certainly compe-

(continued)

tent enough, but basically he lacks imagination. Though he takes full charge of the vocal qualities, his conception and characterization of the role are gray. And charmingly as De los Angeles sings, she is much too ladylike for the best interests of so pert a character as Rosina. The Spanish soprano, by the way, sings the role in the original mezzo-soprano register, and she sings it most beautifully. It is a shame that she does not have more temperament. Of the other singers, Alva is a smooth lyric tenor, Cava a well-routined bass, and Wallace a baritone with a fine command of the patter and also the *fioritura*. Gui conducts with accuracy, but here again more of a flair was needed to capture the sheer fun of the opera. The recorded sound is lifelike. Take the ending of Act I, where the singers are lined up: Almaviva at the left, Bartolo at the right, the other in between. No monophonic recording could ever begin to suggest an equivalent feeling of stage presence.

March 1966

ROSSINI: The Barber of Seville. Teresa Berganza, mezzo-soprano (Rosina); Manuel Ausensi, baritone (Figaro); Ugo Benelli, tenor (Almaviva); Fernando Corena, bass (Bartolo); Nicolai Ghiaurov, bass (Basilo). Rossini di Napoli Chorus and Orchestra of Naples conducted by Silvio Varviso. London 1381, 3 discs, $17.94.

Probably the greatest *opera buffa* ever written, *The Barber of Seville* has been immensely popular for well over a century. But seldom does it receive good performances any more. Rossini composed for a breed of virtuoso singers long extinct. Very few singers today have the technique to sing the florid coloratura and to make the equally florid interpolations expected of a singer in the 1820s. All current recordings of the opera are deficient in one way or another, and this new one is no exception. Ausensi, a lively enough Figaro, is a sloppy technician who tries to achieve his results by lung-power rather than finesse. The highly touted Berganza is disappointing. She does have more ability at coloratura work than most sopranos, but her singing is peculiarly lacking in temperament. There are also noticeable off-pitch attacks on exposed high notes. Benelli, smooth-voiced and flexible, is an asset; and so is Corena, about the best *buffo* around. But, judged purely on voice, the sensational singer here is Ghiaurov, the new Bulgarian bass. He produces a sound of immense size, and he handles his beautifully colored voice with ease and freedom. Obviously he is an important singer. Varviso conducts well.

The engineers have had a little fun with the stereo effects. At the beginning of side three, during the Bartolo-Basilio recitatives, the sound of pacing footsteps comes through the left speaker. In the second-act quintet, each voice is heard from a different location. All of this is, of course, perfectly valid, providing lively and naturalistic touches.

Comment

Of the several recordings of this sparkling score currently available, the most vital and exuberant performance is perhaps the one conducted by Abbado (Deutsche Grammophon 2709041), with Berganza, Luigi Alva, and Hermann Prey in the pivotal roles. The set that may exude the most fun is the version on

Angel (S3559) conducted by Alceo Galliera, with Maria Callas, Luigi Alva, and Tito Gobbi. ∎

April 1974

ROSSINI: Humorous Piano Music (Pleasures and Peccadillos).
Aldo Ciccolini, piano. Seraphim S60216, $2.98.

Having carved out an international career for himself as the principal expo-nent of the piano music of Erik Satie, that eccentric of the late 19th and early 20th centuries, Aldo Ciccolini has now gone back a few years in musical history to examine some of the "Sins of Old Age" and other compositional transgressions of another irreverent creator, Gioacchino Rossini. By the time he was 37, Rossini had produced about three dozen operas in an incredibly prolific outpouring of works for the lyric stage. Then, unaccountably, he composed no more operas, although he lived another 40-odd years. There was an occasional foray into music for the church. Then in his 60s and 70s he composed a series of nearly 200 instrumental and vocal pieces whose prin-cipal characteristic is satirical and pungent humor. Ciccolini has chosen wisely among the piano pieces and has come up with a delightful disc. Several of the pieces will be familiar to those who know the ballet score *La Boutique Fantasque*, arranged for orchestra by Respighi. Note that Respighi did little but orchestrate; all the charm and deviltry is in the Rossini originals.

Ciccolini plays the pieces with exactly the right innocent abandon, and the piano reproduction is fine. Undoubtedly Ciccolini will treat the listening public to additional discs of these captivating Rossini miniatures.

Comment
No further additions to the Rossini piano literature have been forthcoming from Ciccolini—a pity, for as shown here, Ciccolini is as persuasive a pianist with Rossini as with the music of Satie. (His recordings of Satie have restored the music of that strange and eccentric composer to currency.) We continue to hope for more Rossini from Ciccolini. ∎

July 1976

ROSSINI: Overtures. The Academy of St. Martin-in-the-Fields under the direction of Neville Marriner. Philips 6500878, $7.98. ●

St. Martin-in-the-Fields, a church in London's Trafalgar Square, has for nearly 20 years been home for one of the world's finest chamber orchestras, the Academy of St. Martin-in-the-Fields. The Academy's recordings and tours under the direction of Neville Marriner, its founder and conductor, have earned it fame throughout the world. Its repertoire ranges from baroque music for small groups to the latest in 20th-century music for small

(continued)

orchestras. This disc is the Academy's first venture in recording Rossini's *Overtures*, and it is a revelation.

By using fewer musicians than usual, Marriner gets his orchestra to play with crispness and sparkle that are as rare as they are right for this music. It is as though these eight overtures—familiar favorites such as those for *The Barber of Seville* and *La Scala di Seta*, and less familiar ones, as those for *La Cambiale di Matrimonio* and *L'Inganno Felice*—had been scrubbed clean of accumulated tradition; they emerge as newly discovered treasures. And this is, indeed, a disc to treasure.

Comment

Another Philips recording of Rossini is of related interest—a collection of arrangements for winds of three *Overtures* and highlights from *The Barber of Seville*. The performances, by the expert Netherlands Wind Ensemble (Philips 9500395), are alive with vitality and good humor. ∎

May 1967

ROSSINI: Semiramide. Joan Sutherland, soprano (Semiramide); Marilyn Horne, mezzo-soprano (Arsace); Joseph Rouleau, baritone (Assur); John Serge, tenor (Idreno); Spiro Malas, bass (Oroe). London Symphony Orchestra and Ambrosian Opera Chorus conducted by Richard Bonynge. London 1383, 3 discs, $17.94.

The search for Sutherland "vehicles" continues, and thus *Semiramide* gets its first recording in history. It is a bel-canto opera of tremendous difficulty. Every singer has to have a virtuoso technique. But such a cast is impossible to put together from this generation of singers. Aside from Sutherland and Horne, the singers in this album merely go through the motions. Their parts are simplified or cut (this is especially true of the tenor). However, the cuts actually help the opera. An uncut *Semiramide* would run forever, and it is not that strong a work. There are some lovely bits of music in the score, but most of it is conventionally florid writing intended to give the singers a chance to unfurl their voices. After a while, one has the feeling of being drowned in vocal froth, but it must be admitted that when Sutherland and Horne are singing, the results are tremendously exciting. They take liberties, interpolate cadenzas, change keys (Sutherland takes the most famous aria of the opera, *"Bell raggio,"* down to A flat from the original A major), and indulge in all kinds of vocal pyrotechnics. No other living singers could approach these two in this kind of repertoire.

Bonynge conducts well, though without much personality. His role is that of *maître d'hôtel* to the two great stars, and he politely ushers them this way and that. The recorded sound is extremely brilliant and spacious. Some big climaxes, at the end of almost every side, are handled smoothly without a trace of shatter or innergroove distortion.

Comment

Semiramide is unlikely to be recorded again very soon. What a pity, then, that the others in this set cannot approach the style and vocalism of the two leading singers. For that matter, what a pity that the conducting was entrusted to so bland a conductor as Bonynge. ∎

March 1973

RUBINSTEIN: Ocean Symphony. Westphalian Symphony Orchestra conducted by Richard Kapp. Candide CE31057, $3.98.

Anton Rubinstein was one of the most powerful and influential figures in the musical life of 19th-century Russia. He was a phenomenal pianist, and he enjoyed considerable success as a composer. The *"Ocean" Symphony* was his second, completed in 1854 when he was 25. Some years later he added two more movements to the original four-movement format, and stll later a seventh. It is the enlarged six-movement work, minus the Adagio movement of the original four-movement format, that is recorded here. The obvious influences on the *"Ocean" Symphony* are Schumann and Mendelssohn. The symphony is an interesting period piece, but hardly an unjustly neglected masterpiece.

Kapp and Candide Records have been exploring 19th-century symphonic music, and this release of the *"Ocean" Symphony* joins their earlier recording (Candide CE31063) of the symphony, *"In the Forest,"* by Rubinstein's contemporary, Joachim Raff. In both instances Kapp works with the Westphalian Symphony Orchestra of Recklinghausen in Germany—a provincial orchestra in every sense. In each case, what emerges is a likeness of the score, but without the invigorating spark that might have been applied by an outstanding combination of conductor and orchestra, such as Bernstein and the New York Philharmonic in their recording of another symphony from the period, Karl Goldmark's *"Rustic Wedding Symphony"* (Columbia MS7261).

Comment

The rush to record the forgotten Romantic favorites of a century ago has slowed in recent years. Yet how good it is to have works like this available for listening. This disc fills in our knowledge of the works of one of the nineteenth century's most important musical influences. ∎

October 1974

SAINT-GEORGES: Symphony No. 1 in G; String Quartet No. 1 in C; Symphonie Concertante in G for Two Violins and Orchestra; Scene from Ernestine. The Juilliard Quartet (in the *Quartet*), Miriam Fried and Jaime Laredo, violins (in the *Symphonie Concertante*), Faye Robinson, soprano (in the *Ernestine*), with the London Symphony Orchestra conducted by Paul Freeman. Columbia M32781, $5.98.

(continued)

With this disc, Columbia inaugurates its Black Composers Series, a project being carried out in conjunction with the Afro-American Music Opportunities Association. The series will encompass two centuries of symphonic music composed by blacks.

Chevalier de Saint-Georges (1739-1799) was an almost exact contemporary of Haydn. Born on the Caribbean island of Guadeloupe, he had a French father and an African mother. At an early age he showed considerable musical talent, and he became an accomplished violinist. He lived most of his life in Europe, where he composed a considerable body of music and enjoyed great social popularity.

The four works on this disc reveal a musical personality very much of its period. The *First Symphony* and the *String Quartet* are unremarkable examples of 18th-century patterns and formulas. Both are pleasantly uninteresting. The *Symphonie Concertante* for two violins and orchestra, one of eight scores for that combination written by Saint-Georges, is better. Best of all is the short scene from Saint-Georges's opera, *Ernestine*, a dramatic recitative and aria in which the heroine laments her separation from her lover. The music is a powerful evocation of longing and despair, and suggests that the composer's true métier may well have been music for the theater. If more of Saint-Georges's operatic music is available, we should be given an opportunity to hear it.

All the performances carry the stamp of authority. One complaint: The text of the *Ernestine* scene should have been included with the documentation, particularly since the (presumably French) diction of Faye Robinson is largely unintelligible.

The recording was done in London—except for the quartet, which was recorded in Columbia's New York studios—and the sound quality is uniformly excellent throughout. The long-range goals of the Columbia/AAMOA project are certainly laudable despite the variable merits of the selections of this initial release.

Comment

The Black Composers Series has apparently ended as far as Columbia Records is concerned. The project drew attention to a number of deserving works. Principal among them, perhaps, are Roque Cordero's *Concerto for Violin and Orchestra* (Columbia M32784), and the *Piano Concerto* (M34556) and the *Concerto for Trombone and Orchestra* (M32783) of George Walker. ■

March 1963

SAINT-SAËNS: Concerto No. 4 in C minor for Piano and Orchestra; FAURÉ: Ballade for Piano and Orchestra; Préludes in D flat major, G minor, and D minor. Robert Casadesus, piano, and New York Philharmonic conducted by Leonard Bernstein. Columbia MS6377, $5.98.

Casadesus has recorded this concerto and the *Ballade* in the past, but not to such good effect. He is a specialist in this music, and one honestly wonders if any other living pianist could bring to it equal flexibility, elegance, and style. And what virtuosity Casadesus displays! The writing is very difficult, but Casadesus scampers through it with a touch no heavier than a snowflake. Fauré's *Ballade* is the prize on this disc. The Saint-Saëns *C minor Concerto* has dated a bit, but the Fauré is as delicate, individual, and chaste as ever. As a bonus, Casadesus plays three Fauré *Préludes* with his usual style and taste. The piano sound is colorful, the balance is good, and the orchestra is faithfully reproduced.

Comment

The Saint-Saëns piano concertos seem to be coming back in fashion. Now available are two complete integral sets of all five of them: The Ciccolini-Baudo performances (Seraphim S6081) have more fire and character than do the Tacchino-Froment collaborations (Vox SVBX5143). Another sensitive account of the Fauré *Ballade* is that of John Ogdon, with Louis Frémaux conducting the City of Birmingham Symphony Orchestra (Klavier 527). ∎

November 1971

SAINT-SAËNS: Symphony No. 3 in C minor (Op. 78, Organ). The Los Angeles Philharmonic Orchestra conducted by Zubin Mehta. London 6680. $5.98. ●

In the dozen or so years since stereo sound reproduction has become standard for home listening, Saint-Saëns' *Third* (or *"Organ"*) *Symphony* has been a test piece fòr playback equipment. The score is loaded with orchestral effects, from the wispiest of soft passages to loud, heavily scored climaxes. Included in the orchestral forces are two pianos and a prominently scored organ. There is bombast and vulgarity in this music, to be sure; in the hands of the right conductor, however, Saint-Saëns' *Third Symphony* can transcend its trivialities and become an exciting and moving experience. Mehta is almost—but not quite—the "right" conductor. He avoids some of the excesses indulged in by other conductors in this music, and he secures a heads-up performance from his players. But he does not rival the excitement and bravura Charles Munch brought to his stereo recording of the score with the Boston Symphony Orchestra (RCA LSC2341). And, curiously, the decade-old RCA recording has a richer, more vibrant reproduction of the orchestral performance.

February 1975

SAINT-SAËNS: Symphony No. 3 in C minor (Op. 78, Organ). Virgil Fox, organ, with the Philadelphia Orchestra conducted by Eugene Ormandy. RCA ARL10484, $5.98. ▲

Saint-Saëns' *"Organ" Symphony*, though nearly 100 years old, has come into its own only in recent years, largely as a result of the opportunities it affords
(continued)

for spectacular sound reproduction. The 78-rpm recording by Charles Munch and the New York Philharmonic signaled the modern-day interest in the symphony. Since it was made, and especially following the introduction of stereo technology, recordings of the score have proliferated. They include a rerecording by Munch, this time with the Boston Symphony Orchestra (RCA LSC2341).

RCA has again entered the lists with this new recording of the symphony made with its resident forces of Eugene Ormandy and the Philadelphia Orchestra. The result, sonically, is splendid—perhaps the best reproduction RCA has ever given the Philadelphia Orchestra. Organist Virgil Fox, eschewing here his customary and vulgar role as clown prince of the instrument, contributes playing that is vital and bold. And Ormandy has the measure of this score, as he previously demonstrated in a Columbia mono recording no longer available. Yet the performance doesn't have quite the last measure of authority of the Munch recording—which, incidentally, still sounds remarkably good.

Anyone interested in buying the Ormandy/Philadelphia record may have trouble finding it. The jacket is so bizarre, and the identification so obscured that one would not readily spot the presentation as that of serious music.

September 1976

SAINT-SAËNS: Symphony No. 3 in C minor (Organ). The Chicago Symphony Orchestra under the direction of Daniel Barenboim, with Gaston Litaize, organ. Deutsche Grammophon 2530619, $7.98. ▲ ●

Daniel Barenboim, a young Israeli musician who is currently one of the world's most sought-after conductors, has developed a special relationship with the Chicago Symphony Orchestra in recent years. The orchestra's musicians and its public eagerly await his visits to Chicago, which have yielded some outstanding recordings on both the Angel and Deutsche Grammophon labels. This rendering of Saint-Saëns's most popular symphony is the latest in a chain of successes produced by this conductor-orchestra team.

Musically, the work is among the richest of romantic symphonies, with roughly equal proportions of power, poetry, and passion. Its demands are many: a very high level of orchestral virtuosity, responsiveness on the part of the conductor to the music's varying shades and moods, and, in recording, sound that is at once detailed and full-bodied.

The presentation on this disc meets most of those demands admirably. The musicians respond vibrantly to Barenboim's authority; the sound reproduction is vivid and lively. (Litaize's organ playing, incidentally, was dubbed so adroitly from a performance in the great cathedral of Chartres that the two-step recording is virtually undetectable.)

All in all, this is the first serious challenge to the extraordinary recording of the *"Organ" Symphony* made nearly two decades ago by the Boston Symphony Orchestra under Charles Munch (RCA LSC2341). Though I still prefer the Munch version (for its power, poetry, and passion), my respect for this fine performance by Barenboim, the Chicago Symphony, and the Deutsche Grammophon engineers is very great indeed.

Comment

The Mehta and Barenboim accounts of this score have many points in their favor; also worthy of note is the performance conducted by the late Jean Martinon (Angel S37122). But the sheer vitality and exuberance of the Munch performance sweeps everything before it. And the reproduction given Munch and the Boston Symphony Orchestra—labeled a "Stereo Spectacular" when it was new—is no less spectacular today. ■

September 1965

DOMENICO SCARLATTI: Twelve Sonatas for Piano. Vladimir Horowitz, piano. Columbia MS6658, $5.98.

Horowitz makes no attempt in these flawless, diamond-bright performances to "harpsichordize" the music, and he is not afraid to use the big sonorities and the color effects of which the modern piano is capable. Naturally, the pianist being Horowitz, the performances are under rigid technical and rhythmic control, with dazzlingly even fingerwork. The pianism is amazing, the interpretations thoughtful and brilliant in turn. Surfaces are not as quiet as they should be.

Comment

This disc is the perfect showcase for the other side of Horowitz—the "nonthunderer" who etches delicate and elegant sound images. As examples of the pianist's refined artistry, the performances are most welcome. ■

November 1968

SCHOECK: Notturno (Op. 47); BARBER: Dover Beach (Op. 3). Dietrich Fischer-Dieskau, baritone, and the Juilliard Quartet. Columbia Special Products AKS7131. $5.95.

Fischer-Dieskau's voice is a mellow and beautiful one, thoroughly under the singer's control at all times. He is the master of color and shading, and his way with words, no matter what the language, must be the envy of his colleagues. Fischer-Dieskau and the Juilliard Quartet introduced the long Schoeck song cycle *Notturno* to the United States in April 1967. This recording, made immediately after that premiere, is the baritone's first venture before American recording microphones. Both in the *Notturno* and in Samuel Barber's moving setting of the Matthew Arnold poem, the Columbia engineers have provided sound of radiant warmth. And Fischer-Dieskau's collaboration with the members of the Juilliard Quartet is a partnership in the truest sense of the word: The four string players are given an equal share of the musical burden, and they carry it with great distinction. Some listeners may find themselves more attracted to the concentrated drama of *Dover*

(continued)

Beach than to the more diffuse and problematical Schoeck settings of poems by Nikolaus Lenau and Gottfried Keller. The disc is strongly recommended, however, to all listeners who cherish vocal art on the highest level.

Comment

One cannot help feel that this disc will come to be regarded as a classic of recorded literature. ■

SCHOENBERG: Gurre-Lieder. Herbert Schacht-schneider, tenor (Waldemar); Inge Borkh, soprano (Tove); Hertha Töpper (Waldtaube). Symphony Orchestra and Chorus of Bavarian Radio conducted by Rafael Kubelik. Deutsche Grammophon 2707022, 2 discs, $13.96.

This is probably the most immense work ever scored for symphony orchestra; it leaves even Mahler's *Symphony of a Thousand* well in the rear. Schoenberg, then a young man whose days of atonalism and dodecaphonism were still ahead of him, was out to eclipse Wagner and Mahler. He calls for four flutes, four piccolos, five oboes, seven clarinets, three bassoons, two contrabassoons, ten horns, seven trumpets, four harps, eleven percussion players, and an enormous body of strings. Small wonder that the score is so seldom performed. Deutsche Grammophon took advantage of a live performance to make this recording. As such, it lacks some of the refinement and control of studio recordings. There is a good deal of separation and plenty of color and the sound is, on the whole, satisfactory despite some pinched climaxes (the ending of side four, for example, does not open up as it should).

In any case, this is the only version currently available, and the music is very much worth having. It is an intensely chromatic, rich-sounding example of post-Romantic gigantism. Wagner, and especially the Wagner of *Tristan and Isolde*, is the main influence, with Mahler also playing a part. But there is enough force and personality in the *Gurre-Lieder* to overcome its derivations, and anybody responsive to romanticism in music should have a marvelous time with this album. The performance, especially the contribution from the podium, is admirable. Kubelik handles the gargantuan forces with style and finesse.

Comment

Vitality and conviction are perhaps the principal elements in this performance, now assigned a new number in the DG catalog (2726046). A later Boulez-conducted recording of the *Gurre-Lieder* (Columbia M233303) reveals more of the inner details of the scoring, but Kubelik's remains the more impassioned reading. ■

March 1967

SCHUBERT: Fourteen Songs. Dietrich Fischer-Dieskau, baritone, and Gerald Moore, piano. Angel S36342, $5.98.

In this Schubert song recital, Fischer-Dieskau has selected some of the most popular songs (such as *"Auf dem Wasser zu singen"* and *"Der Jüngling und der Tod"*) and set them off against others not so well known. The disc provides a most attractive Schubert song recital. Fischer-Dieskau is, of course, the ranking exponent of this material. By now he has developed into a supreme stylist, one who handles the song texts with the musical line in mind and sings the notes with the texts always in mind. Few singers of any age have so achieved a fusion of word and note. The recorded sound is realistic.

Comment

These songs have since been rerecorded by Fischer-Dieskau in his massive project of recording *all* six hundred or so of the songs of Schubert. But the performances on this disc cannot be bettered. In top form, too, is that supreme piano accompanist, Gerald Moore. ∎

June 1970

SCHUBERT: Grazer Fantasie; Ländler Suite; MOZART: Fantasia in C minor (K. 475); Fantasia in D minor (K. 397). Lili Kraus, piano. Odyssey 32160380, $2.98.

This disc contains the world premiere recording of the *Grazer Fantasie* by Schubert, which was discovered only a year or so ago and is so called because it turned up in a trunk in Graz, Austria. Though the discovered score was not in Schubert's own hand, there seems little question that the piece is an authentic Schubert creation. In its short span—less than fifteen minutes—the *Fantasie* is an ingratiating and gently lyrical work with surprising permonitions of Chopin's piano writing. There is also an improvisatory quality that is beautifully conveyed by Mme. Kraus. Knowing of the turmoil in which Schubert left his personal effects, one can only hope that other missing works will turn up in due time—especially the two missing symphonies that he is known to have composed in the 1820s, toward the end of his life.

The *Ländler Suite* is a collection of dances assembled by Mme. Kraus from the many that Schubert composed. It makes a delightfully diverting encore piece. The two Mozart *Fantasias*, on the other hand, are among that composer's most profound piano pieces.

To everything on this disc, Mme. Kraus brings dedication, serenity, and appropriate simplicity. With playing of this caliber, fine engineering, and the low price, this is indeed a welcome addition to the recording literature.

Comment

Other pianists have incorporated the *Grazer Fantasie* into their concert reper-
(continued)

toire, but Kraus is still the only one to have recorded it. The performance sets a high standard for any pianist who may be inclined to enter the lists. ∎

March 1960

SCHUBERT: Quintet in A major (The Trout). Clifford Curzon and members of the Vienna Octet. London 6090, $5.98.

Schubert's *Trout Quintet* is one of the most popular pieces of chamber music ever written. At its best the present disc is an example of polished, accurate playing, with good ensemble and fine tonal virtue. But some of the ideas are on the eccentric side, such as the impossibly fast tempo of the third movement or the rather lagging pace that ends the second one. Nor is the recorded sound all that it might be. There are patches of surface noise, as shortly after the beginning of side two, and the piano tends to be too much to the fore. String tone is good, however; and despite the imbalance, the piano is reproduced realistically. A possible alternative to this performance is a disc of the *Trout* played by Denis Matthews and the Vienna Konzerthaus Quartet (Vanguard S151).

Comment

But best of all the available recordings of the *Trout* is another Vanguard release (71145), an absolutely exhilarating performance with Peter Serkin as pianist and Alexander Schneider as violinist, among other musical luminaries. This performance, in Vanguard's full-price line, has more youthful élan and generosity of spirit than the later recording by Peter Serkin with his Tashi group and guest artists (RCA ARL11882). ∎

September 1966

SCHUBERT: Sonata in A major for Piano (Op. Posth.). Rudolf Serkin, piano. Columbia MS6849, $5.98.

It is surprising that the only other available recording of this great piece of music is an inadequate presentation by Charles Rosen. A generation or so ago the big Schubert sonatas were seldom heard, and Schnabel was virtually the only major international pianist who featured them. But our generation has taken the Schubert sonatas to its heart, and they are not only the common property of all pianists, but also popular with audiences. One would have thought that the posthumous *A major Sonata*, one of the very best, would have attracted many recording companies. At least, this new Serkin disc will take care of the problem for a long time to come. The distinguished pianist plays with his usual force and character, and with an unusual amount of lovely detail. Serkin always has been identified with the Austro-German school, and he brings to this music stringent musicianship and discipline. But he is more than a scholar. He takes a free point of view toward the music, phrasing with considerable latitude, avoiding any kind of pedantry and in general bringing a good deal of romanticism to his interpretation. This broad, moving, grand sonata could not be in better hands. Serkin must be a difficult pianist to record (and it is said that he does not like recording sessions). In the concert hall his tone is big, noble, and full of nuance. On records, though, it tends to be clanging and hard, as it is here.

Comment

Notable new recordings of this great sonata have come in recent years from Alfred Brendel (Philips 6500284) and Radu Lupu (London CS6996). Both offer recorded sound that is much warmer than on the Serkin disc. But in the end one comes back to Serkin and his epic vision of this music—a more totally realized conception. ■

November 1972

SCHUBERT: String Quartet No. 13 in A minor; Quartet Movement in C minor. The Guarneri Quartet. RCA LSC3285, $5.98.

Schubert's four-movement *A minor quartet* is a sublime masterpiece whose seraphic beauty is ennobling to the listener. Schubert used the principal melody of the second movement as the *Entr'acte* after the third act of *Rosamunde* and in his B-flat *Impromptu* for piano.

The *Quartet Movement in C minor* is the opening movement of a quartet that Schubert began in 1820 but then put aside. Like the *Unfinished Symphony* that he composed two years later, Schubert simply never returned to the work. The single movement that we have is breathtakingly beautiful, a piece of easy-going melodic warmth interrupted occasionally by stormy passion.

The Guarneri Quartet has sometimes been criticized for playing with too much intensity. No such charge, however, can be leveled against their playing on this disc; it is warm, gentle and perceptive, with a rosy glow to the string sound.

Comment

The Guarneri Quartet, which was still relatively new in 1972, has now firmly established itself as one of the finest string quartets on the international scene. Its growing catalog of recordings includes several performances with Artur Rubinstein of the piano quartet and quintet literature. Chief among them are the three Brahms quartets and the Schumann quintet (RCA LSC6188), and the two Mozart quartets (RCA ARL12676). ■

June 1973

SCHUBERT: Symphonies Nos. 4 in C minor (Tragic) and 6 In C. The Philadelphia Orchestra under Eugene Ormandy. Columbia M31635, $5.98.

(continued)

One does not ordinarily associate Ormandy with early 19th-century orchestral music, but it is a pleasure to report that his performances of these two Schubert symphonies are most satisfying. The key to Ormandy's success, perhaps, lies in his buoyant rhythmic treatment: Both scores benefit from a clear delineation of the underlying pulse in each movement, and Ormandy chooses tempos that work well everywhere. The question of the proper tempo is particularly crucial in the last movement of the *Sixth*, where some conductors have indulged in wildly exaggerated extremes. Beecham, for example, used to take it impossibly slowly, while Maazel (in his recording of a dozen or so years ago) races it mercilessly. Ormandy, for his part, adopts a bouncy and vivacious tempo that emphasizes the music's grace and good spirits without ever degenerating into a mad dash. The Philadelphia Orchestra responds to Ormandy's every wish, with some particularly sensitive gradations in dynamics.

Comment

Although concert performances of both these symphonies remain comparatively rare, many first-rate recordings of each are available. Ormandy's is the only disc to combine these two works—others offer the *"Tragic"* Symphony with either Schubert's *Third* or *Fifth Symphony*—so this recording is well worth investigating. ∎

August 1972

SCHUBERT: Symphony No. 9 in C (The Great). The New York Philharmonic conducted by Leonard Bernstein. Columbia M31012, $5.98. ●

Bernstein has been a recording artist for a quarter of a century now, and over the years he has contributed some of the most inspired performances available. Unfortunately, this is not one of them. Bernstein drives the music mercilessly; not only is the tempo fast, but Bernstein unleashes a relentless nervous energy that ultimately robs the score of its expansiveness and breadth and vitiates the long arches of Schubert's melodic inspiration.

There are many far more satisfying recorded accounts of Schubert's sublime *Ninth Symphony*; among them are those by Furtwängler (Turnabout 4364, mono only), Krips (London STS 15140), Szell (Angel S36044) and Walter (Columbia MS6219).

Comment

To the list of outstanding recorded performances of Schubert's *"Great"* C *major Symphony* we may now add the thoughtful, carefully measured account of Carlo Maria Giulini with the Chicago Symphony Orchestra (Deutsche Grammophon 2530882). ∎

August 1975

SCHUBERT: Vocal Quartets. Elly Ameling, soprano; Janet Baker, mezzo-soprano; Peter Schreier, tenor; Dietrich Fischer-Dieskau, baritone; with

Gerald Moore, piano. Deutsche Grammophon 2530409, $7.98.

This record is another installment in Deutsche Grammophon's presentation of the total song output of Schubert. Fischer-Dieskau is mainly responsible for the project; he has already recorded hundreds of Schubert's songs—principally in two albums (DG 2720006 and 2720022) that together comprise a total of 25 discs. Schubert's songs for four voices are relatively unknown, even to Schubert scholars, so that this new disc is welcome indeed, particularly since the performances are so superb. Each of the artists is an acknowledged master of the repertoire; together they form a superstar ensemble. And that paragon of piano collaborators, Gerald Moore, is once again at the top of his form.

Nine quartet songs are included here, each with its own special virtue. Perhaps the most lastingly impressive is "Gott im Ungewitter" (God in the Storm). Its text powerfully depicts an awesome, mighty, and ultimately merciful God. Schubert responds by producing one of his most moving song settings.

The four voices and the piano are beautifully balanced. This is an uncommonly rewarding release.

Comment

The collaboration of these five great performers—pianist Gerald Moore is integral to the success of this venture—has produced a precious record of rare and unusual repertoire. ∎

July 1964

SCHUBERT: Die Winterreise. Dietrich Fischer-Dieskau, baritone, and Gerald Moore, piano. Angel S3640, 2 discs, $11.96.

We have had several fine *Winterreise* recordings in recent years, but this probably is the best. Fischer-Dieskau, the finest active male Lieder singer, has everything working for him—a big, resonant voice, a thorough knowledge of style, unusual musical intelligence. All of these attributes are necessary for *Die Winterreise*, the greatest of all song cycles. It is a long, moving, even bitter collection of twenty-four songs. The first of the cycle, *"Gute Nacht,"* is sad, and Schubert never really lightens the mood. Throughout, the feeling is one of bleakness, and it culminates in the final *"Leiermann,"* so chilly, sorrowful, and intense that it could well be the most frightening song ever written. Fischer-Dieskau uses more voice here than he has in some previous albums. That is, he uses almost none of the crooning effects that sometimes have marred his work. This adds greatly to the dignity of his interpretation. He has thought through every song, and he deftly underlines the basic mood of each, building to the climax with unerring taste. Gerald Moore is a worthy partner.

(continued)

Comment

Fischer-Dieskau has rerecorded this entire cycle for Deutsche Grammophon (2707028). The voice in the DG set is slightly darker and some of the songs are invested with even greater inner tension, but otherwise there is little to choose between the two editions. There is also available a superlative account of this cycle and the Schumann *Dichterliebe* by the team of Peter Pears and Benjamin Britten (London 1261). ■

August 1972

SCHUMAN: Symphony No. 7; ROREM: Third Symphony. The Utah Symphony Orchestra conducted by Maurice Abravanel. Turnabout TVS34447, $2.98.

For the past 25 years or so, Maurice Abravanel and the Utah Symphony Orchestra have been making America's most consistently adventurous and stimulating recordings. A subsidy from the Ford Foundation, enriched by Abravanel's enthusiasm, has led to the first recordings of both the Schuman and the Rorem symphonies. As a result, one of the finest recent American orchestral scores—Schuman's *Seventh Symphony*—has finally been committed to records, and in a performance quite worthy of it.

William Schuman, among others, was commissioned by the Boston Symphony Orchestra to compose a score for its 75th anniversary season in 1955-56. But the work, which was to become the *Seventh Symphony*, was so slow in coming that it was not ready in time for performance during the anniversary season. Indeed, it was not until five years later—in October 1960—that Charles Munch conducted the world premiere in Boston. The wait was well worthwhile.

The *Seventh Symphony* is a big work, in Schuman's formal pattern—four sections alternating slow-fast-slow-fast—progressing from a contemplative, brooding opening to an exhilarating and boisterous conclusion. In between is some of Schuman's most deeply inspired music. The sound and the spirit are unmistakably Schuman's, with his characteristic use of unison string passages, brass punctuations and woodwind solos; but the overall emotional framework places this symphony squarely in the victory-through-struggle mold of such classic symphonies as Beethoven's *Fifth*, Brahms's *First* and Tchaikovsky's *Fifth*.

Ned Rorem's *Third Symphony*, completed in 1958, is much less compelling. Its emotions are much more superficial and its patterns much more predictable. In the second and fifth movements, there is a casual jazz flavoring. The score is pleasant, diverting and lightweight.

Both works receive here devoted care and attention. The Rorem performance comes off less well, lacking all the abandon and panache that would present it in its best possible light. But Abravanel's real understanding of the form and substance of the Schuman symphony does credit to the material. It is true that the Utah Symphony Orchestra cannot summon the sheen or the sensual splendor of the Chicago Symphony or the Philadelphia Orchestra. But it is an alert and responsive instrument nonetheless. Abravanel has every reason to be proud of his Salt Lake City accomplishments.

Comment

Since this review first appeared, we have had many more splendid recordings from Maurice Abravanel and the Utah Symphony Orchestra: Bloch's *Sacred Service* and Roy Harris's *"Folksong" Symphony* on the Angel label (S37305 and S36091, respectively) and the four Brahms symphonies on Vanguard (10117/20) are particularly noteworthy. We can also look forward to forthcoming Abravanel-Utah Symphony recordings of music by French and American composers, as well as a cycle of the seven symphonies of Sibelius. ∎

September 1963

SCHUMANN: Carnaval (Op. 9); Fantasiestücke (Op. 12). Artur Rubinstein, piano. RCA LSC2669, $5.98.

Rubinstein has recorded the *Carnaval* once before, but that record has been withdrawn. In any case, this is a better performance—all the more amazing in that Rubinstein is a man well in his seventies. But he still plays with complete technical freedom, plus the authority, singing line, and athleticism that always have been his. No better performance of the *Carnaval* can be had, and the same applies to Rubinstein's poised, poetic performance of the *Fantasiestücke*. Good recorded sound, on the whole, though the tone does become hard at the end of the *Carnaval*. And surely RCA could supply better program notes than the advertising copy it has used for this disc.

Comment

What was true nearly two decades ago is still true: No better performance of the *Carnaval* or the *Fantasiestücke* is to be had. This disc, along with nearly all those made by Rubinstein during the 1960s when he was in his seventies and eighties, is remarkable testimony to his unique artistry. ∎

May 1972

SCHUMANN: Cello Concerto in A minor; BLOCH: Schelomo for Cello and Orchestra; BRUCH: Kol Nidrei for Cello and Orchestra. Christine Walevska, cello, with the Monte Carlo Opera Orchestra conducted by Eliahu Inbal. Philips 6500160, $5.98.

Christine Walevska is a young American cellist, still in her early twenties, who has studied with Piatigorsky in California and with Maurice Maréchal at the Paris Conservatory. In this, her debut recording, she reveals admirable musicianship and technical security. The inclination to compare her with Jacqueline du Pré, that other extraordinary international cello virtuoso who is also still in her twenties, is irresistible. Walevska seems more reliable than du Pré in intonation, and her tone is more silkily refined, but as yet her playing seems to lack the fiery commitment and intensity of du Pré's.
(continued)

Perhaps this quality will come as she gains more experience.

As it is, this disc presents us with estimable if not quite overpowering accounts of all three works. Perhaps the *Kol Nidrei* performance is the most successful. Conductor and soloist have managed a beautifully rich and expansive treatment of Bruch's setting of the traditional Hebrew chant for the Day of Atonement, successfully avoiding exaggerated bathos or melodrama. Other cellists have made more of the drama inherent in *Schelomo* or the lyrical effulgence in the Schumann *Concerto*. But young Miss Walevska is clearly an important new artist, worth watching closely. The Philips engineers have done their jobs well: The sound is well-focused and full-bodied.

Comment

As a recording debut, this release promised much—and much of that promise has been fulfilled in Christine Walevska's subsequent recordings, particularly a disc devoted to all the music for cello and orchestra by Saint-Saëns (Philips 6500459). Unaccountably, however, she is not heard from as often as her great gifts would seem to warrant. ■

March 1961

SCHUMANN: Concerto in A minor for Piano and Orchestra (Op. 54). Van Cliburn and Chicago Symphony Orchestra conducted by Fritz Reiner. RCA LSC2455, $5.98. ▲ ●

It is good to know that Cliburn can play something else besides the Tchaikovsky and Rachmaninoff concerti. He gives a beautiful account of himself in the Schumann, playing with manliness, poetry, and without exaggeration. This is one of the very finest performances of the familiar concerto ever put on records. Young Cliburn is on his way toward becoming a very great pianist. The stereo disc is warm and undistorted in sound. An objection should be entered against the skimpy program notes RCA has provided.

Comment

In the nearly two decades since this performance was released, Cliburn has displayed very little artistic growth, and his behavior, sometimes undependable, has become increasingly erratic. The pianist who recorded this performance while in his twenties should today be a titan of stimulating artistry. Unfortunately, he is not. ■

July 1966

SCHUMANN: Dichterliebe; Liederkreis (Op. 24). Dietrich Fischer-Dieskau, baritone, accompanied by Jörg Demus, piano. Deutsche Grammophon 139109, $6.98.

The fantastic Fischer-Dieskau, who has already made more recordings than any singer in history (and he is only in his forties, with many productive years ahead of him), now turns his attention to one of the supreme song cycles in history, Schumann's *Dichterliebe*. The *Opus 24, Liederkreis*, with which he fills out the disc, is not to be confused with the *Opus 39 Liederkreis* set, which he previously recorded (on Angel S36266). As a matter of fact, Fischer-Dieskau is represented by an earlier recording of the *Dichterliebe*; but, great artist that he is, he continues to grow, and this new album is better than its predecessor. If nothing else, he now avoids the crooning effects that used to mar his work. Everything is done by pure voice and voice alone, without any artificial expressive aids.

Fischer-Dieskau enters into the world of each song, outlining its mood and expressing its emotion with infallible taste and style.

Comment

Also superlative is the performance of the *Dichterliebe* cycle by Peter Pears and Benjamin Britten; it occupies the fourth side in their magnificent account of Schubert's *Winterreise* (London 1261). ■

September 1962

SCHUMANN: Fantasia in C major (Op. 17); BEETHOVEN: Sonata No. 17 in D minor for Piano (Op. 31, No. 2). Sviatoslav Richter, piano. Angel S35679, $5.98.

Richter's performance of the *D minor Sonata* is certain to arouse a good deal of talk in pianistic circles. Some will call his performance dramatic, effective, close to what Beethoven had in mind. Others will describe it as affected, overdone, and arbitrary. Certainly it is different. Tempi are slow and deliberate; there are many pauses intended to heighten the drama; a lavish use is made of color resources. This observer felt a little uncomfortable with the Richter interpretation, and even more so in the large-scale Schumann *Fantasia*. The latter has its moments of grandeur, but these are not maintained. Often Richter seems to pick at the notes rather than get into them. Fair recorded sound, with some background rumble in the stereo. There is still no great recorded LP performance of the Schumann work.

Comment

The recordings by Arrau (Philips 802746), Ashkenazy (London CS6471), and Pollini (Deutsche Grammophon 2530379) are all more convincing than Richter's. But the best is the Horowitz concert recording (Columbia M2S728), with its inimitable sweep, fancy, and invention. ■

August 1971

SCHUMANN: Frauenliebe und Leben, and Other Songs. Leontyne Price, soprano, and David Garvey, piano. RCA LSC3169, $5.98.

(continued)

Leontyne Price restricted her American appearances during the recent season to the concert stage rather than the opera house. In her recital programs, the songs of Schumann figured prominently; she apparently feels an affinity for them. She certainly takes great pains with her diction throughout this recorded recital, and her enunciation of the German texts could well serve as a model to all who essay these songs.

But her voice conveys an excess of *sangfroid*. In the second song of the *Frauenliebe und Leben* cycle—the ecstatic *"Er, der Herrlichste von allen"* ("He, the noblest of them all")—her sense of emotional reserve negates much of the joy and exultation of this expression of the first flush of young love. And as the cycle goes on, the blandness of conception is disappointing. Lotte Lehmann had nothing like the vocal beauty and security of Miss Price, but as she traversed the rapture and heartbreak of Schumann's songs she made the listener live those feelings along with her.

Similarly, the songs on the reverse side of the disc are sung with great beauty and care, but they are rather bloodless. Bloodless, too, are the piano accompaniments; perhaps a more assertive pianist might have drawn more impassioned performances from Miss Price. Despite the beauty of the vocalism and the expert reproduction of it, the disc is a letdown.

Comment

Now that Leontyne Price gives American audiences fewer and fewer opportunities to hear her in an opera house, it seems as though she is beginning to phase out the operatic aspect of her career. This disc demonstrates that her true strength as an artist is on the opera stage rather than as a recitalist. ∎

July 1978

SCHUMANN: Symphonies Nos. 1 in B Flat (Spring) and 4 in D minor. The Vienna Philharmonic Orchestra under the direction of Zubin Mehta. London CS7039, $6.98. ●

This is the first disc of a complete cycle of Schumann symphonies planned for release by London Records with the Vienna Philharmonic Orchestra under Zubin Mehta. London's earlier release (London CSA2310) of the Schumann symphonies with the Vienna Philharmonic under the baton of Georg Solti was one of the rare artistic failures in that conductor's long and distinguished recording career. Solti's intensity and the constant pressure he brought to bear on the music were completely at odds with the rich warmth of the composer's ripe Romanticism.

Calm is hardly the distinguishing trait of Mehta's conducting—and, truth to tell, both of the works recorded here contain passages of overstress. But nowhere does the urgency become oppressive, as it all too often was in the Solti performances. In fact, more propulsiveness and drive would have been welcome at that point in the *First Symphony* where the first movement's first theme emerges from the Introduction.

On the whole, however, these are perceptive, affectionate accounts of both scores, well played and vividly recorded. By the time these words reach print, Deutsche Grammophon—which also plans to release the Schumann symphonies in their entirety—will have issued its readings of these works by the Chicago Symphony Orchestra with Daniel Barenboim, a great friend of Mehta's. Comparisons should be interesting.

Comment

Comparisons are now in order since Deutsche Grammophon also offers Schumann's *First* and *Fourth Symphonies* on a single disc in the Barenboim-Chicago Symphony series (DG2530660). In general, the orchestras have little in common except excellence. Barenboim's is the more studied approach, Mehta's the more spontaneous. Barenboim strives for light textures, Mehta for opulent ones. These two symphonies are also available on Deutsche Grammophon (2530169) with Karajan and the Berlin Philharmonic in performances that combine energy and tenderness. ∎

January 1969

SCHUMANN: Symphonies No. 3 in E flat (Rhenish) and No. 4 in D minor. Vienna Philharmonic Orchestra conducted by Georg Solti. London 6582, $5.98.

This is apparently the first installment in an integral series of the four Schumann symphonies recorded for London by Solti and the Vienna Philharmonic. The enterprise is off to a very good beginning. Both performances have an engaging quality of lyricism, the orchestra is in top form, and the sound reproduction by the engineers is mellow. Solti was recently engaged as music director of the Chicago Symphony Orchestra beginning with the 1969–70 season; evidently Chicagoans can look forward to music-making on an exalted level.

Comment

The Vienna Philharmonic recordings of the Schumann symphonies (London CSA2310, three discs) are not among Solti's conspicuous successes as a conductor. His generally rigid musical approach does not suit these very personal, Romantic scores. Among other complete recordings of these four symphonies, those of either Bernstein (Columbia D3S725) or Szell (Odyssey Y330844) offer much more natural affinity with the music. ∎

March 1970

SCRIABIN: Symphony No. 1. The USSR Symphony Orchestra and the RSFSR Russian Chorus conducted by Yevgeny Svetlanov, with Larissa Avdeyeva, mezzo-soprano, and Anton Grigoriev, tenor. Melodiya/Angel S40113, $5.98.

(continued)

The late 1960s saw a reawakening of interest in the mystical Russian composer of the early years of the century, Alexander Scriabin. The interest will probably continue into the seventies, for Scriabin's esthetic principles seem peculiarly in tune with some of the artistic currents of today. For example, more than half a century ago, Scriabin sought a union between sounds and colors and asked that certain of his works be given with a light and color accompaniment. When Stokowski thus performed some of Scriabin's orchestral works with the Philadelphia Orchestra in the 1920s, he was branded a charlatan; earlier this season, when Seiji Ozawa did the same thing with the New York Philharmonic, he was considered very responsive to contemporary thought.

This disc presents the first recording of Scriabin's *First Symphony*, a rambling, rhapsodic work in six movements that takes about fifty minutes to perform. In the last movement, Scriabin introduces a poem of his own—sung by two soloists and, briefly, chorus—that glorifies art as a kind of religion. The music demonstrates many influences, particularly those of Wagner and Tchaikovsky, yet the score is still Scriabin's own—fiery and soaring, with a demonic fervor.

Svetlanov seems to have a full grasp of the symphony, but alas, his performing forces are not quite equal to the job. The orchestra sounds routine, and the two solo voices are pinched and nasal. Despite those reservations, however, the disc is recommended to listeners with a lively musical curiosity.

Comment

What appeared to be the start of a Scriabin renaissance has apparently faded and obscurity seems once again to have overtaken the composer. This symphony, however, will still pay listening dividends to the curious collector. ∎

May 1972

SHANKAR: Concerto for Sitar and Orchestra. Ravi Shankar, sitar, with the London Symphony Orchestra conducted by André Previn. Angel SFO36806, $5.98. ▲ ●

The sitar is the long-necked, multi-stringed instrument of Indian classical music that has been enjoying such a vogue among some of the more impressionable younger musicians in the West, thanks principally to the interest expressed in the instrument by, among others, George Harrison, late of The Beatles. The sitar has a quality of eerie mysticism and hypnotic power, but unless one is ready to submit totally to the intricate formal patterns of the music of India, a little sitar sound goes a long way.

Shankar, in his *Concerto*, has attempted to fuse the characteristic melodic and rhythmic devices of Indian classical music with the varied tonal spectrum projected by a Western symphony orchestra. What emerges, unfortunately, is surprisingly bland. The musical content is exceedingly slight, and soon boring. Of the four movements in the *Concerto*, the third (and shortest) is by far the most engaging, for here at least Shankar does compose music of propulsive rhythmic interest.

The performance and recordings do all that can be done to support the composition, but there is little here to engage the enthusiasm of any but out-and-out fanciers of exotic sound for its own sake.

Comment

Unfortunately, the passage of time has not revealed previously unsuspected treasures in this score. Our verdict is still that the concerto wears out its welcome long before its conclusion. ∎

November 1963

SHOSTAKOVICH: Symphony No. 4 (Op. 43). The Philadelphia Orchestra conducted by Eugene Ormandy. Columbia MS6459, $5.98.

Shostakovich composed this work in the 1930s but withdrew it before its first performance. He was under attack at the time for "bourgeois formalist tendencies" and probably decided that this symphony was too advanced for the taste of a Stalin. But now, with a somewhat more relaxed attitude in the Soviet Union, the *Fourth Symphony* has come to light. If you respond to Shostakovich's idiom, there will be much to admire in this long, often intense work (with its curiously Mahlerian touches, especially in the third movement). By 1963 standards, the writing is anything but "advanced," though it naturally has its share of twentieth-century techniques. Ormandy's performance is strong and colorful. He is almost unbeatable in music like this. The recorded sound is superb.

Comment

The brief flurry of performances this score enjoyed here and abroad in the early 1960s has largely subsided. Seen in perspective, the *Fourth Symphony* now seems considerably less impressive, with its length and bombast far more noticeable. ∎

September 1972

SHOSTAKOVICH: Symphony No. 5. The USSR Symphony Orchestra conducted by Maksim Shostakovich. Melodiya/Angel SR40163, $5.98.

It was Shostakovich's *Fifth Symphony*, first performed in 1937, that reconciled the composer with the arbiters of Communist Party art in the Soviet Union. For the previous half-dozen years, he had been harassed by the authorities because of what they called the "bourgeois decadence" of his work. But his *Fifth* was greeted by the Moscow Daily News in these words: "The com-
(continued)

215

poser, while retaining the originality of his art in this new composition, has to a great extent overcome the ostentatiousness, deliberate musical affectation, and misuse of the grotesque, which had left a pernicious print on many of his former compositions." Shostakovich had deliberately set out to produce a work that could be understood by the musically unsophisticated and at the same time would fulfill the demands of literate musicians. He succeeded brilliantly, as has been proven by the continuing success of the score, one of the most popular 20th-century orchestral works.

The *Fifth Symphony* has not lacked for successful recorded performances, beginning with the pioneering effort by Leopold Stokowski and the Philadelphia Orchestra. Perhaps the most successful until now has been Leonard Bernstein's with the New York Philharmonic (Columbia MS6115).

This latest recording is conducted by the composer's son, Maksim, a pianist originally who has become increasingly prominent as an adept interpreter of his father's works. The younger Shostakovich conducts this performance with a thrust and passion that are quite overpowering. Some listeners may object to the surface gloss of this performance, but its mounting impetuosity seems most appropriate to the heart-on-the-sleeve emotional qualities of the music. The USSR Symphony Orchestra has much improved in tone quality and virtuosity in recent years, and the Soviet engineers have provided vivid reproduction. All in all, this new disc is probably the best recording of Shostakovich's *Fifth Symphony* currently available.

Comment

This is probably still the most commendable of currently available recordings of this twentieth-century classic. A good alternative might be André Previn's performance with the Chicago Symphony Orchestra (Angel S37285). A recording planned by Leonard Bernstein and the New York Philharmonic, which would have superseded their 1958 disc, was canceled when Bernstein bowed out of some concert commitments with the orchestra in 1978. Eventually, that recording should be made since Bernstein is a particularly perceptive interpreter of this music. ∎

April 1974

SHOSTAKOVICH: Symphony No. 8 in C minor, Opus 65. The Moscow Philharmonic Symphony Orchestra conducted by Kiril Kondrashin. Melodiya/Angel SR40237, $5.98.

The *Eighth Symphony* of Shostakovich is a product of the brutal war year, 1943. Like the celebrated *Seventh ("Leningrad") Symphony*, it is a massive, panoramic score, and it is regarded by many knowledgeable listeners as one of the best of all the Shostakovich symphonies. Curiously, however, the *Eighth* is now one of the composer's least known works in this country despite the flurry of performances it originally received here by such conductors as Koussevitzky and Stokowski. Even the present recording was made about a decade ago and is only now finding its way to these shores. (A recent recording made by André Previn with the London Symphony Orchestra will presumably also be made available over here.)

The *Eighth* has a Mahler-like master plan. A long and brooding opening adagio is followed by a brief and grotesque scherzo (called allegretto). The last three movements are connected organically and without pause. There is a perpetual-motion, fiercely driving allegro succeeded by a largo consisting mainly of the second subject from the first movement treated in widely varied passacaglia form. The concluding allegretto, a lighter, sometimes humorous movement, at last subsides into an enigmatic, deeply felt ending. The symphony does have its moments of banal military propaganda, but as a whole it is extraordinarily moving.

The performance under Kondrashin is dedicated and perceptive, and the reproduction—despite its age—is quite vivid. This is an important addition.

Comment

The Previn recording (Angel S36980) has indeed been made available in this country. It is, in fact, even more persuasive than that of Kondrashin, by virtue of finer orchestral playing, superior recorded sound, and an even more penetrating insight into the music. ■

August 1971

SHOSTAKOVICH: Symphony No. 12 in D minor (Op. 112; In Memory of Lenin). The Leningrad Philharmonic Orchestra conducted by Yevgeny Mravinsky. Melodiya/Angel 40128, $5.98.

When CU earlier in 1971 reviewed recorded works by this composer we commented that, in attempting to accommodate to the official Soviet line, "Shostakovich has had to dilute much of his creative energy." Nowhere is there better support to be found for that comment than in the composer's *Twelfth Symphony*. The score, completed a decade ago, celebrates the October Revolution of 1917. Once before, in his *Second Symphony* of 1927, Shostakovich drew inspiration from the revolution. But whereas the *Second Symphony* is a work of imagination, vitality, and individuality, the *Twelfth* is trashy and vulgar—a vast hodgepodge of effects, with climax piled upon climax until the listener's sensibilities rebel. One wonders whether Shostakovich was deliberately reflecting the corruption and perversion of ideals that followed the Bolshevik ascent to power. At any rate, the artistic bankruptcy of his *Twelfth Symphony* cries out for some extra-musical explanation.

Leningrad, the city of Shostakovich's birth (when it was still called St. Petersburg), has played an important part in his professional life. He attended that city's conservatory and composed his witty, sardonic *First Symphony* as his graduation exercise. Over the years, it has been the Leningrad Philharmonic that has played the first performances of nearly all his symphonies. And Mravinsky, who has conducted the orchestra for more than three decades, has established something of a priority claim on the interpretation of Shostakovich. So the performance on this disc, sadly, must be

(continued)

regarded as definitive. It reveals a rather serious erosion in the quality of the Leningrad Philharmonic Orchestra since it was last heard in this country; the decline is particularly noticeable in the strings. The reproduction is strident and coarse. But given the nature of the music, perhaps that was unavoidable.

Comment

The *Twelfth Symphony* represents the artistic nadir of the late years of Shostakovitch. In many of the works that followed this score, particularly the last three symphonies and the last quartets, he was able to produce music that may well prove to be of lasting value.　　　　　　　　　　　　　　　■

March 1973

SHOSTAKOVICH: Symphony No. 15 in A, Opus 141. The Moscow Radio and Television Symphony Orchestra conducted by Maksim Shostakovich. Melodiya/Angel SR40213, $5.98.

The *Fifteenth Symphony* of Shostakovich is puzzling, profound and highly provocative. When Eugene Ormandy and the Philadelphia Orchestra gave the work its American premiere last September, the music aroused conflicting reactions: Some listeners dismissed the score as inconsequential and barren of ideas; others hailed it as a masterwork. CU's critic tends toward the latter point of view.

Throughout his career Shostakovich has been plagued by ill health and political harassment. It is possible to discern in the *Fifteenth Symphony* reflections of both. The first movement's toy-shop atmosphere (so characterized by Shostakovich himself) may well be one of the composer's attempts to create "proletarian" music for the musically untutored. But the movement is laced with quotations from the composer's earlier symphonies—particularly the *First*, an audacious, nose-thumbing score that Shostakovich produced at the age of 19. Are we to infer that the 65-year-old Shostakovich wants to tell us that the style and esthetics of the *First Symphony* represent the "real" Shostakovich? And what is the significance of the repeated quotation of the trumpet call (the theme of "The Lone Ranger") from Rossini's *William Tell* overture—a reference to the struggle for freedom in the face of political oppression?

After the first movement, the symphony progresses to a somber funeral march, then to a brief and unsettling scherzo-like movement, and finally to a concluding adagio that begins, extraordinarily enough, with a direct quotation of the "Fate" motive from Wagner's *Ring* operas, followed by the tympani playing the same rhythmic pattern that accompanies the death of Siegfried in Wagner's *Götterdämmerung*. The final movement then develops into an extended passacaglia whose bass figure resembles that in the passacaglia from Benjamin Britten's opera, *Peter Grimes*. The end is an extraordinary and protracted string chord that is finally resolved by the entrance of bells and celesta. It is as if thoughts of death, and perhaps death itself, have caused a purification to take place. The *Fourteenth Symphony* of Shostakovich, which appeared in 1969, was a vocal symphony set to texts that all dealt with death; is Shostakovich anticipating his own death?

The performance on this disc is conducted by the composer's son, Maksim, who has emerged in recent years as a perceptive interpreter of his father's music. Maksim delivers a hair-raising account here, by turns demonic, mystical and desolate. The Moscow Radio and Television Symphony Orchestra sounds perhaps better than it ever has before on records, and the Russian engineers have given us as brilliantly reproduced sound as has ever come out of Soviet recording studios.

This disc, in short, is a triumph for all concerned.

Comment

Shostakovitch died in August 1975, leaving unsolved the enigmas of the *Fifteenth Symphony*. But the music continues to fascinate. The symphony has begun to make a place for itself in the active repertoire of orchestras around the world and audiences are receptive. In this writer's opinion, it is a genuine masterwork. ∎

January 1961

SIBELIUS: Concerto in D minor for Violin (Op. 47). Jascha Heifetz and Chicago Symphony Orchestra conducted by Walter Hendl. RCA LSC2435, $5.98.

The very first violinist in history to record this concerto was Heifetz, back in the late 1930s. This is his third recording of the score, and he still "owns" it. No violinist in our time has conquered the ungrateful solo writing with such ease and elegance; no one else has brought equivalent power and understanding. (That includes the great David Oistrakh, whose recent Columbia disc of the concerto has nowhere near the authority that Heifetz brings.) Heifetz is fortunate in his new recording. The solo instrument is steady, with no wandering from speaker to speaker, while the orchestra sounds full, resonant, and distortion-free. On the whole, this is a brilliant achievement, musically and technically.

November 1965

SIBELIUS: Concerto in D minor for Violin (Op. 47); BRUCH: Concerto in G minor for Violin (Op. 26). Zino Francescatti and the New York Philharmonic, conducted by Leonard Bernstein (for the Sibelius) and by Thomas Schippers (for the Bruch). Columbia MS6731, $5.98.

Both of these popular violin concerti have been recorded umpteen times before. The only reason for mentioning this entry is that it is played so well. Francescatti is the Romantic violinist par excellence, with a resplendent technique, a tone that is sheer damask, and a throbbing vibrato that extracts every bit of sentiment from the music. His performances here are well up in

(continued)

the Heifetz-Oistrakh class. And Columbia has supplied extremely rich recorded sound that is easily as good as these two concerti have ever received and much better than most. The solo instrument is well forward (though not annoyingly so), and it is well maintained in one position in the stereo version.

June 1971

SIBELIUS: Concerto in D minor for Violin (Op. 47); **TCHAIKOVSKY: Concerto in D major for Violin.** Kyung-Wha Chung, violin, with the London Symphony Orchestra conducted by André Previn. London 6710, $5.98.

In 1967 the prestigious Leventritt International Competition in New York was won jointly by two young violin students at the Juilliard School of Music—the Israeli Pinchas Zukerman and the Korean Kyung-Wha Chung. Zukerman immediately embarked upon an international career that has already made him one of today's foremost concert artists. Chung's career has been slower in gaining momentum, but with the release of this debut recording, one feels certain that she, too, will very quickly attain stardom.

These two performances mark Chung as that rare virtuoso who has conquered all the technical demands of her instrument and, at the same time, possesses a refined and highly sensitive musical consciousness. Her playing here is totally secure, with a degree of elegance that is unusual in any performer of any age and quite astonishing in one only twenty-two years old. Her intonation is impeccable; her tone has an attractive silken quality.

In both performances, the execution is smaller-scaled than usual. The works thereby gain a measure of gentle intimacy that casts them in a new light and affords a refreshing change from the *wow* technique more commonly employed. The London Symphony plays beautifully. All told, this is the most important recording debut by a violinist in several years—since Zukerman's.

Comment

The Heifetz recording of the Sibelius concerto is still unique for its propulsion, technical mastery, and tonal suavity. It has been remastered and reissued on one side of a disc that also contains the violinist's imperious account of Prokofiev's *Second Concerto* (RCA LSC4010). Perlman, with Erich Leinsdorf and the Boston Symphony Orchestra (RCA AGL11529), plays the Sibelius and Prokofiev concertos vibrantly and with brilliant virtuosity. The recording offers smooth sound reproduction.

Chung's lyrical and rhapsodic account of the Sibelius concerto in her London disc is a must for any lover of superior violin interpretation. Stern's recording (Columbia M30068) is more impassioned and at the same time more urbane. The Zukerman-Barenboim collaboration (Deutsche Grammophon 2530552) tries hard but is ultimately rather too studied. The Francescatti recording is now available only on the budget-price Odyssey label (Y33522). ∎

January 1966

SIBELIUS: The Swan of Tuonela; Valse Triste; En Saga; Finlandia. Philadelphia Orchestra and Mormon Tabernacle Choir conducted by Eugene Ormandy. Columbia MS6732, $5.98.

A Sibelius potpourri. Ormandy has brought together four of Sibelius' most popular pieces. Most popular of all is, of course, *Finlandia*, to which a chorus has been added in this recording. The result is quite vulgar (though there are those who say that *Finlandia* is pretty much of a potboiler to begin with). The *Valse Triste* remains an attractive *morceau*, the *Swan of Tuonela* is a moody and unusual bit of tone painting, and the long *En Saga* (so popular only twenty years ago, but now virtually unplayed) is still an impressive work, full of the bardic content that meant so much in its day. From the Philadelphia Orchestra in this kind of repertoire we expect glowing, voluptuous sounds, and these are what we get. The stereo is detailed and nuanced.

Comment

This disc—still highly desirable—is a collection of some of the shorter Sibelius orchestral scores, sumptuously played and recorded. ∎

July 1977

SIBELIUS: Symphony No. 1 in E minor; Finlandia. The Boston Symphony Orchestra under the direction of Colin Davis. Philips 9500140, $7.98.

Interest in the music of Jean Sibelius, the great Finnish composer, is again on the rise after a period of relative decline in the 1950s and 60s. Today, with such conductors as Colin Davis, Lorin Maazel, and James Levine to champion his work, and the founding of a Sibelius Society in New York City, Sibelius is regaining the eminence he has always merited as a giant in the world of music.

This disc is the second in what will eventually be the complete cycle of the seven Sibelius symphonies to be recorded by the Boston Symphony Orchestra under Colin Davis. It is masterly. From the plaintive opening clarinet solo played by Harold Wright to the quality of exultation at the work's end, this reading of the *Symphony* is personal, poetic, dramatic, and deep with feeling. Davis eloquently underlines the Romantic passion of the music, written at the very end of the 19th century, and also the individuality of the Sibelius sound. Though the *First Symphony* was very much of its time, it also anticipated what might be called the "cellular" structure of melodic development that was to become so pervasive in 20th-century music.

As always, the Boston Symphony's superlative musicians do their best for Davis, their principal guest conductor. The reproduction is fine, aside from a touch of muddiness. The performance of *Finlandia* is surprisingly tame; more impassioned and heroic recordings of it abound—among them, those conducted by Barbirolli and Ormandy. Be that as it may, this new performance of the *First Symphony* would be hard to surpass.

(continued)

Comment

Some may prefer the more voluptuous recording of this symphony made by Leopold Stokowski less than a year before his death (Columbia M34548). Stokowski's filler is not *Finlandia* but *The Swan of Tuonela*, which is given an absolutely riveting, atmospheric treatment. ∎

June 1970

SIBELIUS: Symphony No. 2 in D (Op. 43). The New York Philharmonic conducted by Leonard Bernstein. Columbia MS7337, $5.98.

The *Second* is the most played and at the same time the most abused of Sibelius' seven symphonies. Composed in the heroic-dramatic tradition of Beethoven's *Eroica* and *Ninth*, and Tchaikovsky's *Fifth*, its frequent posturings and excesses demand the most sympathetic of conductors if the work is not to sound banal and pompous. Such a conductor was Serge Koussevitzky, whose performances of the score with the Boston Symphony Orchestra were among the great glories of American concert life during the 1930s and '40s. Leonard Bernstein absorbed much of his early musical orientation and philosophy at the feet of Koussevitzky; hence it might be anticipated that he would bring to Sibelius' *Second* Koussevitzky's grandeur and eloquence.

That expectation is only partially fulfilled, unfortunately. The first two movements in Bernstein's performance heave and sigh with exaggeration. The third movement is somewhat better. But it is not until the finale that Bernstein delivers the direct and impassioned statement that one had been hoping for all along. But the superb treatment of that last movement cannot atone for the earlier waywardness. Orchestral playing and recorded sound are of the highest quality.

September 1973

SIBELIUS: Symphony No. 2 in D. The Philadelphia Orchestra conducted by Eugene Ormandy. RCA ARL10018, $5.98.

Ormandy and the Philadelphia Orchestra are old hands with Sibelius. The composer has found a consistent champion in Ormandy for nearly four decades, whereas he has been seriously neglected in most other musical centers for over 10 years—even during the 1965 centennial celebrations of Sibelius' birth. An earlier recording of the *Second Symphony* by Ormandy and the Philadelphia Orchestra (Odyssey Y30046) is first-rate. But this new release is even more authoritative and perceptive, and the reproduction is absolutely glorious. This disc, like all new RCA recordings, is quadraphonic, playable on stereo or RCA quad equipment. Our judgment of this disc's rich, stunning sound is based on stereo listening; it is a most rewarding issue.

November 1977

SIBELIUS: Symphony No. 2 in D. The Boston Symphony Orchestra under the direction of Colin Davis. Philips 9500141, $7.98.

This disc is the fourth Sibelius symphony to be released by Colin Davis and the Boston Symphony Orchestra. (The other three—numbers 3, 4, and 6—have been recorded and will be released shortly.) As his concert perform-ances and recordings have made plain, Davis has a powerful affinity for Sibelius; he is highly responsive to the rich scoring, lush harmonies, and rhythmic vibrancy of the *Second Symphony*. The high strings have a most beautiful sheen, and the conductor and his team of recording engineers exult in the many opportunities this particular work affords to underline the low strings and the tympani.

Some of the musicians heard here recorded this work with Koussevitzky in 1935 and 1950, when the Boston Symphony was perhaps the world's greatest Sibelius orchestra. Koussevitzky's way with this score was inimitable. Good as it is, the Davis performance must yield to Koussevitzky in rendering the mystery and icy loneliness of the second movement, and the ecstatic aban-don of the last. RCA has reissued Koussevitzky's 1950 recording several times—most recently as Victrola VIC1510 (mono only). I recommend that disc to anyone interested in fully exploring the nobility and unique power of this music.

Comment

Davis and the Boston Symphony, Abravanel and the Utah Symphony, Or-mandy and the Philadelphia Orchestra, and Karajan and the Berlin Philhar-monic all either have completed or are in the process of completing integral recordings of the seven Sibelius symphonies. Clearly, the pendulum of popu-larity is swinging back to Sibelius after a couple of decades of disfavor. The Davis performances, incidentally, are available not only on single discs but also as a five-disc album (Philips 6709011), which includes a recording of the symphonic poem *The Swan of Tuonela* that is downright hypnotic in mood. That account is not otherwise available. ∎

September 1966

SIBELIUS: Symphony No. 4 in A minor (Op. 63); The Swan of Tuonela. Berlin Philharmonic Orchestra conducted by Herbert von Karajan. Deutsche Grammophon 138974, $6.98. ▲

Many consider the *No. 4 in A minor* the best of the seven Sibelius sympho-nies. It certainly is the most cryptic, the most interesting, and the one that is closest to the stripped-down feeling characteristic of the mature Sibelius. Herbert von Karajan's approach is interesting, and altogether different from that of Serge Koussevitzky, who used to be the great Sibelius exponent. Where Koussevitzky was interested in color, even in so enigmatic and bleak a work as the *Fourth Symphony*, Karajan's interpretation is ultramodern: un-sentimental, businesslike, with tempi on the fast side and a concentration on smoothness of delivery rather than expressive content. Those who seek a more traditional view of the score can go to the Ansermet disc (London 6387). But the Karajan is well worth considering, and the solo bits are played (as
(continued)

they are on *The Swan of Tuonela*, which fills out the last side) with exemplary finesse by the fine Berlin musicians. Deutsche Grammophon has provided its customary noiseless surfaces and clear recorded sound.

Comment

Karajan has since rerecorded the *Fourth Symphony* (Angel S37462) in a performance not markedly different from the one discussed above. Of the currently available recordings of this remarkable and underplayed score, the version conducted by Colin Davis with the Boston Symphony Orchestra (Philips 9500143) strikes this listener as full of insight and the most consistently satisfying. ∎

July 1966

SIBELIUS: Symphony No. 5 in E flat (Op. 82); Pohjola's Daughter. New York Philharmonic conducted by Leonard Bernstein. Columbia MS6749, $5.98.

For some twenty years the music of Sibelius was allowed to slip from the repertoire, and only recently has it been coming up again. In fact, we are in the middle of a Sibelius renaissance, sparked by the hundredth anniversary of the composer's birth in 1865. Bernstein has had a good deal to do with the Sibelius revival, and the composer is in his blood. Bernstein, after all, was a protégé of Serge Koussevitzky, and Sibelius was one of Koussevitzky's favorite composers. Bernstein conducts Sibelius very much in the Koussevitzky manner—broadly, spaciously, with emphasis on the drama and the pictorial elements. His reading of the fine *Fifth Symphony* is typical in its extroverted enthusiasm.

Bernstein, being Bernstein, is apt to overstress the obvious at times, and in the slow movement he leaves little to the imagination, adopting a slow tempo and twisting the melodic elements dry. Nevertheless, a vital, well-integrated reading, and the same applies to the symphonic poem *Pohjola's Daughter*. There is something very appealing about the heart-on-sleeve conducting of Bernstein in these two works. And he elicits wonderful sound from the Philharmonic, sound that is brilliantly captured in the stereo disc.

Comment

Karajan's most recent recording of the *Fifth Symphony* (Angel S37490) is the only real rival to that of Bernstein. Indeed, Karajan presents an icily terrifying account of the music, which seems especially convincing. ∎

August 1972

SKROWACZEWSKI: Concerto for English Horn and Orchestra; MAYER: Two Pastels; Andante for Strings. The Minnesota Orchestra conducted by Stanislaw Skrowaczewski, with Thomas Stacy, English horn (in the Concerto). Desto DC7126, $5.98.

William Mayer is an American composer in his mid-forties whose principal claim to fame may be the score for a work titled *Hello, World!* a musical trip around the world once recorded by RCA Victor with Eleanor Roosevelt as narrator. Mayer's *Two Pastels* and *Andante for Strings* date from the late 1950's, and are atmospheric, impressionistic pieces well crafted with a keen ear for sonority.

The major interest of the disc, though, is the English horn concerto by the conductor of the Minnesota Orchestra, Stanislaw Skrowaczewski. In it the composer eschews the traditional sound spectrum of the instrument in favor of a wholly unexpected array of sounds ranging from guttural outbursts to explorations in the upper and lower extremes of the English horn's range. Much of the effectiveness of the score lies in the extraordinary artistry of young Mr. Stacy, who handles all the technical demands with ease. This concerto is recommended to anyone in search of exotic but intriguing contemporary music.

Comment

Since this recording was made, Stacy moved on from the Minnesota Orchestra to become the much-admired English horn soloist of the New York Philharmonic. Skrowaczewski, who also resigned from the Minnesota Orchestra, now devotes himself to composing and guest conducting. On the evidence of this English horn concerto, this composer has significant things to say. His future creative efforts should prove to be interesting. ∎

March 1973

SMETANA: Four Symphonic Poems; Richard III; Wallenstein's Camp; Haakon Jarl; Carnival in Prague. The Bavarian Radio and Television Symphony Orchestra conducted by Rafael Kubelik. Deutsche Grammophon 2530248, $6.98.

It was Franz Liszt who invented the symphonic poem as a musical form. Free and structurally open, it served as an ideal medium of expression for a number of 19th- and 20th-century composers. One was the Bohemian Bedrich Smetana, who composed ten symphonic poems (including the six of his cycle, *My Country*).

The first three of these four Smetana symphonic poems were composed between 1858 and 1861. The fourth, *Carnival in Prague*, dates from 1883 and was the last score the composer did before he succumbed to mental illness, dying within a year in a Prague asylum.

Given the facts, it is easy to find in *Carnival in Prague* a slackening of the imaginative and creative powers that inform the earlier three scores; or was the literary and historical inspiration for those pieces responsible for their
(continued)

greater merit? In any case, *Richard III, Haakon Jarl,* and especially *Wallenstein's Camp* are prime examples of Smetana's work.

These pieces are hardly known outside Czechoslovakia, but they obviously are very close to the heart of conductor Kubelik. He has transmitted his devotion to the Bavarian Radio and Television Symphony Orchestra, who play with conviction. The recorded sound, particularly in *Carnival in Prague,* is a bit harsh but not enough to interfere seriously with enjoyment of this worthy record.

Comment

Kubelik has performed a great service in recording most of the principal orchestral works of Smetana and Dvořák, the two major nineteenth-century figures of Czech music. It would be an equally great service should he ever turn his attention to the two giants of twentieth-century Czech music, Janacek and Martinu. Without special advocacy, the extraordinary Martinu symphonies will probably continue to languish in neglect. They need the devoted care and attention Kubelik could undoubtedly bring to them. ■

January 1965

JOHANN STRAUSS: Die Fledermaus (excerpts). Anna Moffo, soprano (Rosalinda); Sergio Franchi, tenor (Alfred); Risë Stevens, mezzo-soprano (Orlofsky); Jeanette Scovotti, soprano (Adele); Richard Lewis, tenor (Eisenstein); George London, baritone (Falke); John Maxwell, baritone (Franke). Vienna State Opera Orchestra under Oscar Danon. RCA LSC2728, $5.98.

This hop, skip, and jump through *Fledermaus,* in English, with a cast that contains several big names, may fill a need for those who want an introduction to the greatest of all operettas or for those who insist on hearing opera in English. Otherwise there is not much to recommend. The singing is spotty (Stevens, indeed, almost talks much of her role instead of singing it), and the translation sounds insipid next to the original. Much preferred is the complete work on Angel S3581. A very good buy is Richmond 62006, mono only. Both are two-disc sets.

Comment

Astonishingly, there are only two discs of excerpts available from this greatest of all Viennese operettas: the Danon reviewed above and one conducted by Karajan (London OSA25923), taken from Karajan's recording of the full score. Of the two, Karajan's outclasses Danon's in every respect. But where are the competing versions? ■

March 1977

JOHANN STRAUSS: Overtures to "Die Fledermaus" and "The Gypsy Baron"; On the Beautiful Blue Danube and Emperor

Waltzes; Tritsch-Tratsch and Annen Polkas. The Berlin Philharmonic Orchestra conducted by Herbert von Karajan. Angel S37144, $6.98.

Columbia Records recently released some of these same selections as performed by the New York Philharmonic under Leonard Bernstein. This disc has a clear advantage over the Columbia-Bernstein release, besides offering more music for the money—the recorded sound is richer, mellower, and better balanced, particularly in the all-important bass drum and cymbal parts in these scores.

On the negative side, however, one must point to Karajan's apparently irresistible need to overinterpret. That trait is most flagrant in the coda of the *Emperor Waltz*, where Karajan indulges in a drastically slowed-down, almost dreamlike tempo, possibly in the interest of drawing a very sharp musical contrast. But for this listener the result strains credence. Another instance: the *Annen Polka*, which in Karajan's hands becomes too cutesy for words. But the disc does include some glorious moments, since the Berlin Philharmonic plays magnificently, and the recording engineers provide exemplary sound. A conditional recommendation, then, for this effort.

Comment
In general, the most idiomatic of currently available performances of the Strauss repertoire belong to Boskovsky. By and large, his earlier recordings on the London label are preferable to his more recent ones for Angel. ■

March 1963

JOHANN STRAUSS: Vienna Blood; Artists' Life; My Life Is Love and Laughter; Treasure Waltz; Thunder and Lightning Polka. Chicago Symphony Orchestra conducted by Fritz Reiner. RCA LSC2500, $5.98. ▲ ●

Reiner was Hungarian-born, and Hungary lies next to Austria. Every Hungarian gets Strauss waltzes with his mother's milk. Reiner brings to the music an authentic-sounding rhythm, a flexible approach, and, often, a delightful feeling of lassitude. His feeling produces a lovely disc. And the recording is good, though with intermittently noisy surfaces.

May 1976

JOHANN STRAUSS: Favorite Waltzes, including Wine, Women and Song; Tales from the Vienna Woods; Emperor Waltz; Roses from the South; On the Beautiful Blue Danube; and Vienna Blood. The Johann Strauss Orchestra of Vienna conducted by Willi Boskovsky. Angel S37070, $6.98.

Admirers of Johann Strauss the Younger, the Waltz King, will welcome this collection of a half-dozen of the master's most popular waltzes played by an

(continued)

orchestra lineally descended from the composer's own, conducted by a man who for more than two decades has been *the* reigning conductor for that music. Strictly speaking, the recordings are not new; all but *Vienna Blood* have been released in recent years by Angel in various collections of Viennese music.

There is little here of the Viennese "lingering" that, judiciously applied, can give these waltzes a very special character and quality. For the most part, Boskovsky favors brisk tempi. Some works respond nicely to his approach— for example, *Roses from the South* and *On the Beautiful Blue Danube*, which move along merrily, with a fine lilt. On the other hand, *Wine, Women, and Song* and *Tales from the Vienna Woods* lose something of their mood and magic in Boskovsky's handling. Playing and recording are excellent.

Comment

Perhaps the finest of all available recorded anthologies of Strauss waltzes are the several discs in the "New Year's Eve in Vienna" series, with Willi Boskovsky conducting the Vienna Philharmonic Orchestra (London 6008, 6485, 6641, 6707, and 6731). Boskovsky has the authentic Viennese style and his traditional performances have marvelous enthusiasm. ■

October 1964

RICHARD STRAUSS: Also Sprach Zarathustra. Philadelphia Orchestra conducted by Eugene Ormandy. Columbia MS6547, $5.98.

Also sprach Zarathustra ("Thus Spake Zarathustra") is one of Strauss' later tone poems and one of the biggest—but not one of the best. Nevertheless, when played by a great orchestra, it can provide exciting moments. The Philadelphia Orchestra is a great group, and Ormandy is a virtuoso conductor; thus the piece is heard under the best auspices. A tremendous orchestra is used, and there are some spectacular climaxes. If your system can take the opening measures and the end of side one without distortion, you have nothing to worry about.

May 1969

RICHARD STRAUSS: Also Sprach Zarathustra. The Los Angeles Philharmonic conducted by Zubin Mehta. London 6609, $5.98. ●

Zubin Mehta has several times expressed an affinity for the large-scale orchestral canvases of Richard Strauss; this disc and a recent recording of Strauss' *Ein Heldenleben* confirm Mehta's very special way with the Strauss symphonic poems. He conceives of the sprawling score, inspired by the Zarathustra of Nietzsche, as a single sweeping span, rather than as a series of disjointed episodes. Consequently, he is more successful than most conductors in holding the listener's interest through the entire vast pattern.

Mehta's concept is enriched by superb execution from his players and by meticulously clear sound reproduction. Definition and differentiation of the separate tones are established right at the very beginning of the work, in the sustained bass accompaniment. And throughout the disc the overall sound has a real physical bite, particularly with the low instruments—tuba, contrabassoon, cellos, and basses.

To those listeners who were intrigued by hearing the opening of *Also sprach Zarathustra* in the film *2001: A Space Odyssey*, this new Mehta recording offers a sumptuous opportunity to become familiar with the entire score.

August 1972

RICHARD STRAUSS: Also Sprach Zarathustra. Boston Symphony Orchestra under William Steinberg. Deutsche Grammophon 2530160, $6.98.

And still they come, the flood of new recordings of Richard Strauss' philosophical treatise on Nietzsche's *Zarathustra* set in motion by Stanley Kubrick's use of the opening fanfare from the score in his film *2001: A Space Odyssey*. With its thunder and massed sonorities, Strauss' music also lets recording engineers flex their technical muscles toward producing brilliant sound reproduction. This release may be Deutsche Grammophon's finest technical accomplishment yet in recording the Boston Symphony Orchestra. It has the full-throated, open sound fully representative of the mellow brilliance of the orchestra in its home auditorium, Boston's Symphony Hall. And the orchestra's concertmaster, the formidable Joseph Silverstein, plays the prominent violin solos in Strauss' score with an equal blend of technical mastery, tonal opulence and interpretative elegance.

Steinberg's conception of the score is all of a piece: steady and unflappable. Other conductors among those who have recorded *Also Sprach Zarathustra* have made of it more of a raging, surging emotional experience—most notably Henry Lewis (London 21053), Lorin Maazel (Angel 35994), Zubin Mehta (London 6609) and (particularly noteworthy since his historic recording of the mid-fifties is now available on a budget label) Fritz Reiner (RCA Victorola 1265).

August 1977

RICHARD STRAUSS: Also Sprach Zarathustra. The Dresden State Orchestra under the direction of Rudolf Kempe. Seraphim S60283, $4.98.

Americans knew the late Rudolf Kempe mainly as a recording artist, though he had conducted New York's Metropolitan Opera briefly in the late 1950's. In Europe Kempe was generally regarded as one of the foremost living conductors. Those of his European recordings that were issued here tended to justify the high esteem the overseas audience had for him.

In the early years of this decade, Kempe and the Dresden State Orchestra—one of Europe's best—recorded all the orchestral works of Richard Strauss, a composer for whom he felt a particular affinity. The latest of those discs to be released in this country is the celebrated *Symphonic Poem* that

(continued)

opens the film *2001: A Space Odyssey*. It is absolutely stunning.

First, Kempe has been unusually successful in unifying the episodic elements of this sprawling score, so that the music unfolds seamlessly. Second, the Dresden State Orchestra's musicians respond to Kempe's direction with extraordinary precision, dynamism, and brilliance. Finally, the sound engineers have captured every note, from the quietest whisper to the wall-shattering roar of the climaxes, in spectacular fashion. What a joy that the organ, so important to the work's beginning, is perfectly in tune with the rest of the orchestra! The current catalogs list about eighteen recordings of this Nietzsche-inspired score, but none is finer, all-round, than this one. And at Seraphim's budget price, this is a real bargain.

Comment

Committed and convincing accounts of this score are also available from Haitink (Philips 6500624) and Solti (London CS6978)—both full-price. A budget-price recording to consider as an alternate to Kempe's is one by Reiner (RCA VICS1265), although for opulence of recorded sound, the Kempe disc surpasses the Reiner recording. ∎

May 1972

RICHARD STRAUSS: Death and Transfiguration, Opus 24; TCHAIKOVSKY: Francesca da Rimini, Opus 32. The New Philharmonia Orchestra conducted by Lorin Maazel. London SPC21067, $5.98.

This disc is in the Phase 4 London series, the special catalog in which unusual recording techniques are employed to produce sonic results of extraordinary vividness and dynamism, principally by deploying many microphones in positions very close to the various sections of the orchestra. At times the technique produces exaggeratedly microscopic sound that bears little relation to what one would normally hear at a "live" concert. In this record, however, the sound is brilliantly clear and detailed, with no unnatural spotlighting of individual sections or instruments. Both works are right up Maazel's alley, and they add to his already impressive list of successes in recording the music of both composers. In fact, the London Records catalog already has a fine Maazel-conducted version of *Death and Transfiguration* with the Vienna Philharmonic Orchestra (CS6415) recorded in the early sixties. The sweep and passion of this New Philharmonia performance propels it to a position near the top among recorded *Death and Transfigurations*.

The *Francesca da Rimini* performance joins Maazel's generally excellent recordings for London of the Tchaikovsky symphonies and the *Romeo and Juliet* and *Hamlet* fantasies. Again, it is the ardor and intensity of feeling that distinguish his performance. All in all, this is a very satisfying disc that should whet the appetites of Clevelanders in particular, for Maazel becomes the new music director of the Cleveland Orchestra in September.

Comment

Since September 1972, Maazel has led the Cleveland Orchestra with distinction and has made notable additions to the record catalog with that group. Chief among them are the recordings of Prokofiev's *Romeo and Juliet* ballet (London CSA2312), Gershwin's *Porgy and Bess* (London CSA13116) and Respighi's *Pines of Rome* and *Roman Festivals* (London CS7043). ■

September 1962

RICHARD STRAUSS: Don Juan; Death and Transfiguration. Eugene Ormandy and the Philadelphia Orchestra. Columbia MS6324, $5.98.

Two of Strauss' most popular symphonic poems, played by a great orchestra, conducted by a man who has made a specialty of them, aided by extremely vital and realistic sound. How can one go wrong? There are almost twenty available *Don Juan* recordings, and almost ten of *Death and Transfiguration*. Ormandy's new disc can rank with any of them.

November 1969

RICHARD STRAUSS: Don Juan; Till Eulenspiegel; Death and Transfiguration. The Vienna Philharmonic Orchestra conducted by Wilhelm Furtwängler. Seraphim 60094 (mono only), $2.98.

In the fifteen years since Furtwängler's death, many of his finest recorded performances have been reissued here, and this collection of the three most popular early symphonic poems by Richard Strauss is the latest such offering. *Don Juan* and *Till Eulenspiegel* were recorded in March 1954, a scant eight months before Furtwängler died; the *Death and Transfiguration* recording dates from 1950. Furtwängler was an immensely imposing figure on the podium, with a kind of demonic mysticism that often seemed to be its own justification, even when the conductor was being capricious and wayward with the music. Of the three pieces on this disc, the *Death and Transfiguration* benefits most from Furtwängler's flaming devotion; his insight is brilliantly transmitted to the orchestra, and we are given a most memorable account of a score that can seem endless and bombastic in the hands of a less inspired conductor.

The *Don Juan* and *Till Eulenspiegel* performances are less intense—the *Till*, in fact, is surprisingly tender and gentle—but they, too, are informed with a unique brand of musical and emotional sophistication. Except for some slight overloading in *Death and Transfiguration*, the sound transfers are superlative.

Comment

Several currently available single-disc stereo recordings of *Don Juan* and *Till Eulenspiegel* are outstanding. Bernstein's (Columbia MS6822) and Stokowski's (Everest 3023) are perhaps the most notable for their passion, splendid

(continued)

orchestral playing, and vivid sound reproduction. Surprisingly, Solti finds room for both works on one side of a disc and devotes the other side to an intense account of *Also Sprach Zarathustra* (London CS6978). ∎

September 1960

RICHARD STRAUSS: Don Quixote. The Berlin Philharmonic Orchestra conducted by Herbert von Karajan, with Mstislav Rostropovich, cello, and Ulrich Koch, viola. Angel S37057, $6.98.

Many consider *Don Quixote* to be Strauss' finest tone poem. Certainly it is (with the exception of *Till Eulenspiegel*) the one that stands up best on repeated hearings. It is, of course, program music, but the listener easily can forget the various adventures of the Don and Sancho Panza, and concentrate on the music as music. This performance easily meets the requirements of the score. Reiner, who has made the Chicago Symphony into a dazzling virtuoso ensemble, is an old Straussian who in recent years seems to have added a large degree of tenderness to his phenomenal technical ability. And Janigro plays the solo cello part with finesse, in a sensitive and understanding manner. He handles the closing section of the score especially well, and few listeners should fail to be touched. Add to this an extremely lifelike quality of sound—full and rich, with the solo instrument in excellent relation with the orchestra—and it adds up to the finest modern version.

August 1970

RICHARD STRAUSS: Don Quixote; Till Eulenspiegel. The Berlin Philharmonic Orchestra conducted by Rudolf Kempe, with Paul Tortelier, cello (in *Don Quixote*). Seraphim S60122, $2.98.

Kempe conducted Strauss and Wagner operas at the Metropolitan Opera in New York City in the early 1960s and is currently principal conductor of the Royal Philharmonic Orchestra in London. The two superb performances on this disc make one wonder why he has not enjoyed the big international career that surely should have been his.

 Don Quixote, subtitled "Fantastic Variations on a Theme of Knightly Character," is regarded by many as the finest of the Strauss symphonic poems. The theme, ten variations, and finale explore a wide range of the action of Cervantes' hero, and into the music Strauss poured much of his most inspired creativity. The solo cello speaks for Don Quixote, with Sancho Panza and Dulcinea impersonated, respectively, by solo viola and solo violin. It is a rich tapestry that Strauss weaves, and this sympathetic performance is truly memorable—a rich re-creation that sheds new light and shade on the music. Tortelier was the cellist in a marvelous Beecham recording of the music more than twenty years ago, and he repeats his glowing performance with Kempe.

 The *Till Eulenspiegel* performance, though not the revelation that the *Don*

Quixote is, is nevertheless fully satisfying. The Berlin Philharmonic plays marvelously in both pieces, and the recorded sound is as vivid and exciting as any in the current catalog.

September 1976

RICHARD STRAUSS: Don Quixote. The Berlin Philharmonic Orchestra conducted by Herbert von Karajan, with Mstislav Rostropovich, cello, and Ulrich Koch, viola. Angel S37057, $6.98.

Don Quixote is rated by many as the finest of Richard Strauss' symphonic poems. In translating Cervantes' novel into music, Strauss used the solo cello to personify the gallant knight, and the solo viola as the voice of the faithful squire who accompanies him, Sancho Panza.

The score begins with an Introduction, which hints at much of the main melodic material and states the themes of Don Quixote, Sancho Panza, and Dulcinea. Next come Ten Variations, each dealing with a different event in the Cervantes novel. The music ends with one of the composer's most inspired sections, the Finale (the final variation), which depicts the shattering of Don Quixote's illusions and his death.

Karajan is not a conductor whose work I normally admire. I find it hard to tolerate his generally narcissistic approach to music-making. But here—thanks perhaps to the presence of Rostropovich, the great humanist—Karajan eschews self-admiration and goes right to the heart of the musical matter. The result: an orchestral performance full of conviction, majesty, drama, and—rarest of all for Karajan—spontaneity.

What can one say of the playing of Rostropovich? His illumination of the music is a revelation—masterful, consuming, magical. The playing and sound reproduction are simply superb. The greatest conductors and orchestras have recorded *Don Quixote* again and again over the last half-century, but if the music has ever been better performed than on this recording, I am not aware of it.

Comment

To those for whom price is an important consideration, the Janigro-Reiner collaboration is an excellent choice. Another is a low-cost account by Fournier, with George Szell conducting (Odyssey Y32224). A fascinating alternative interpretation is the Munroe-Bernstein performance (Columbia M30067); it emphasizes the grotesque elements in the music to startling effect. ■

August 1971

RICHARD STRAUSS: Ein Heldenleben (Op. 40; A Hero's Life). The Concertgebouw Orchestra of Amsterdam conducted by Bernard Haitink. Philips 6500048, $5.98.

(continued)

When Richard Strauss composed the symphonic poem *Ein Heldenleben* in 1898, he was thirty-four years old. He dedicated the score to the Amsterdam Concertgebouw Orchestra and its conductor at the time, Willem Mengelberg. Mengelberg quickly took possession of it and became the preeminent interpreter of *Ein Heldenleben*; he recorded it twice, first with the New York Philharmonic and some years later with the Concertgebouw Orchestra. The latter recording, available in this country briefly on an early Capitol long-playing disc, was a marvel in its time, an exercise in sonics that seemed to establish new meaning for the term "high fidelity."

There have been exceptionally fine *Ein Heldenleben* recordings by other conductors since then, notably the performances by Beecham, Mehta, and Reiner (and a Toscanini performance from a 1941 broadcast available only through the Arturo Toscanini Society in Dumas, Texas). But the close association between *Ein Heldenleben* and the Amsterdam Concertgebouw Orchestra makes the present release particularly noteworthy.

Fortunately, Haitink's performance is worthy of standing alongside the best of all previous recordings of the score. He brings an exultation to the more grandiose passages and a lyrical tenderness to the contemplative ones, particularly the concluding "Hero's Departure From the World." He is helped by the splendid playing of the prominent violin solos by the orchestra's concertmaster, Herman Krebbers, and by the rich and vibrant sound reproduction.

Through it all, the members of the Concertgebouw Orchestra of Amsterdam play magnificently, and their performance is vividly recorded by the Dutch engineering team.

Comment

As conductors go, Haitink is still young. By now he has come to be recognized as one of today's master conductors. His music-making has a fierce and uncompromising integrity. We are fortunate that he is in our midst. ∎

August, 1978

RICHARD STRAUSS: Till Eulenspiegel's Merry Pranks; Don Juan; Salome: Dance of the Seven Veils; Der Rosenkavalier: First Waltz Sequence. The Cincinnati Symphony Orchestra under the direction of Thomas Schippers. Turnabout QTVS34666, $3.98.

The Cincinnati Symphony Orchestra recorded this disc in May 1976, shortly before illness forced Thomas Schippers, the Orchestra's music director, to cancel most of his commitments for the season. As heard here, the Cincinnati Symphony is a well balanced, well disciplined ensemble with some fine soloists. Given Schippers's extensive theatrical background, one would have expected performances of great urgency and drama. Instead, we have orderly, organized accounts of these works—hardly the no-holds-barred treatment to which I think this mercurial music responds best. And the so-called "First Waltz Sequence" from *Der Rosenkavalier*—devised in 1944 by

Strauss himself from his operatic masterpiece, according to the anonymous liner notes—is a shoddy mix of disparate elements from the opera that play hob with the continuity of the music. However, the orchestra plays well throughout, and the principal oboist deserves special praise for the lyrically beautiful solo playing in *Don Juan*. The recorded sound is uniformly clear and detailed.

Comment

The illness that forced Schippers to cancel most of his commitments turned out to be lung cancer; he subsequently succumbed to it. This disc commemorates the state of excellence to which Schippers had brought the Cincinnati Symphony during his tragically brief tenure as the orchestra's music director. ■

September 1968

STRAVINSKY: Firebird Suite; MUSSORGSKY: A Night on Bald Mountain; TCHAIKOVSKY: Marche Slave. The London Symphony Orchestra conducted by Leopold Stokowski. London 21026, $5.98. ●

One of the most extraordinary recordings of the pre-LP era was a performance of Stravinsky's *Firebird* suite by Leopold Stokowski and the Philadelphia Orchestra. After several subsequent recorded performances, none of which eclipsed memories of that old set of five 78-rpm sides, Stokowski is back again with his snarling impetuosity, his fiery vitality and brilliance, and his awesome orchestral discipline. Not all home systems will be able to cope with the extraordinary range of sound imprisoned in the record grooves, and the recording engineers have compounded the problem by cutting the record at such a high level that few phono cartridges are likely to track the innermost grooves without producing considerable distortion. But for those readers with the very finest playback equipment this *Firebird* recording, with its enormous power and wide stereo separation, will be a demonstration piece.

The two warhorses on the reverse side of the disc are similarly impressive, both in performance and in reproduction. But be warned: *A Night on Bald Mountain* is given the full Stokowski treatment—a complete reorchestration of what was already a demanding orchestration by Rimsky-Korsakov. The Stokowski version relies heavily on brass and percussion effects and on string harmonics high up in the stratosphere; they generate an electrical excitement. There are some orchestral retouches in the *Marche Slave*, too, along with unexpected changes of tempo and thematic emphasis. But the power of Stokowski's conviction overrides any disagreements in taste or judgment.

Comment

Stokowski's inimitable way with the *Firebird* music still exerts a spellbinding effect; his account is still far more powerful than any other recorded perform-

(continued)

ance. The same can be said of the two works on the overside if the listener can accept the conductor's "doctoring." The reproduction throughout is extraordinarily brilliant. ■

March 1966

STRAVINSKY: Orpheus; Apollo. Columbia Symphony Orchestra conducted by Igor Stravinsky. Columbia MS6646, $5.98.

Is there any other composer who has had the chance of putting his life's work on records? About everything of importance Stravinsky has composed—and much that is of relative unimportance—is endisced; and Stravinsky himself has either conducted the music or supervised the recording sessions. Here we have two ballet scores, both choreographed by Balanchine and in the repertoire of the New York City Ballet Company. Each is a major work. Of special interest is the recording of *Orpheus*, for it is the only one available. It fills a surprising gap, considering that *Orpheus* is almost the quintessence of the middle-period Stravinsky ballet scores (middle period being after *Le Sacre du printemps* and before the serial scores that have occupied the composer since the 1950s). Surely the serenade to the Furies is one of the most beautiful melodies that Stravinsky has ever written. *Apollo* is one of those Stravinsky scores with ever-present ostinatos, perky rhythmic shifts, highly individual harmonies, and economical orchestration. Presumably, the dry style of Conductor Stravinsky is exactly what Composer Stravinsky wants. Excellent recorded sound.

Comment

Both *Apollo* and *Orpheus* are among the best of Stravinsky's music for dance, so the disc seems certain to become a collector's item. This is the only currently available recording of *Orpheus*, which makes the disc doubly a "must." Incidentally, it is the Chicago Symphony Orchestra that Stravinsky conducts in the *Orpheus* recording on one of the two occasions that the orchestra has appeared on the Columbia label since the final years with Frederick Stock as its conductor. (Stock died in 1942.) The other instance is Robert Craft's recording of Schoenberg's orchestration of the Brahms *G minor Piano Quartet*. ■

March 1971

STRAVINSKY: Petrouchka (complete); Firebird Suite. The Boston Symphony Orchestra conducted by Seiji Ozawa. RCA LSC3167, $5.98. ▲ ●

These two colorful ballet scores by Stravinsky might seem to be tailor-made for the flamboyant and dynamic style of Seiji Ozawa, the new conductor of the San Francisco Symphony Orchestra. Unfortunately, the promise is only partially fulfilled, with the music from *The Firebird* having the better treat-

236

ment. In *Petrouchka*, Ozawa is not responsive enough to the fantasy and the grostesquerie. Ansermet (London 6009), Monteux (RCA LSC2376), and Stravinsky himself (Columbia MS6332) deal much more successfully than does Ozawa with that aspect of *Petrouchka*. In common with Stravinsky, Ozawa uses the composer's revised orchestration of 1947, a thinned-out version of the larger, more brilliant original orchestration.

For the *Suite* from *The Firebird*, Ozawa employs Stravinsky's standard 1919 reorchestration, the one now generally heard in concert halls and on recordings. Ozawa delivers a performance with all the notes in place, the cues cued, the louds loud, and the softs soft, but without much character. For that, we recommend that you turn to the inimitable Stokowski recording (London 21026), which is an electrifying rendition of interpretive imagination, orchestral virtuosity, and sonic splendor.

Perhaps the most impressive aspect of this new Ozawa disc is the superlative solo playing by the principals of the Boston Symphony Orchestra, especially Chester Schmitz, tuba, and Sherman Walt, bassoon, whose solo in the Berceuse is a model of tonal elegance, breath control, and artistic phrasing.

Comment

This disc was a harbinger of things to come, along with the RCA release of Orff's *Carmina Burana* with Ozawa and the Boston Symphony Orchestra LSC3161. In the fall of 1973, Ozawa became the music director of the Boston Symphony Orchestra, and since then their collaboration has become a regular one, both in the record catalogs and on the television screen. ∎

November 1966

STRAVINSKY: Pulcinella. Irene Jordan, soprano; George Shirley, tenor; Donald Gramm, bass; Columbia Symphony Orchestra conducted by Igor Stravinsky. Included in Columbia D3S761, 3 discs, $11.59.

Pulcinella, composed in 1920 for the Ballet Russe de Monte Carlo, is an early work. It is "after Pergolesi," just as the later *Baiser de la Fée* is "after Tchaikovsky." This means that Stravinsky went through a good deal of the early Italian composer's music, selected some that interested him, and proceeded to recompose it à la Stravinsky. Much of the lovely melody is Pergolesi's, but the rhythms, the orchestration, the entire approach are early Stravinsky neoclassicism. It is a perky score, full of humor and style, and probably a masterpiece.

In this performance the three soloists are excellent, and the composer-conductor presumably offers a definitive interpretation.

The recorded sound is first-class. Ignore the box in the liner notes that says the recording was made in 1953. Columbia reprinted the liner notes from a previous Stravinsky recording, including by mistake the date of that version.

(continued)

Comment

That 1953 recording of the complete *Pulcinella* music that Stravinsky made was with the Cleveland Orchestra, and it offered a more pungent orchestral performance. But the soloists in the later recording are far more secure in their roles. In any case, the Cleveland disc—recorded in monophonic sound only— is no longer available and the present one will satisfy most listeners' needs. The *Pulcinella* performance, incidentally, takes up only one disc of this three-disc set. The other two discs include composer-conducted performances of Stravinsky's *Apollo*, *Orpheus*, and *Le Baiser de la Fée*. ∎

July 1962

STRAVINSKY: Le Sacre du printemps (The Rite of Spring). Columbia Symphony Orchestra conducted by Igor Stravinsky. Columbia MS6319, $5.98.

About two years ago, Columbia brought out an elaborately packaged two-disc album in its KS series. That album, since discontinued, contained Stravinsky conducting *Le Sacre* and *Petrouchka*. Now the good news is that *Le Sacre* is available separately, at standard record prices (so is *Petrouchka*, on MS6332). It could well be that *Le Sacre* is the most important individual score of the century, and after sixty years it has held its strength. It still is barbaric, colorful, a tour de force of rhythm and orchestration. At this stage there is no point recommending the music, but a few words can be said about this particular recording. Stravinsky always has felt that few conductors went about *Le Sacre* correctly, and he was determined to leave his own definitive version. How definitive it really is can, of course, be argued. There will be those who say that Stravinsky as a conductor leaves much to be desired; that his beat is stiff, and that he lacks control. But there will be just as many to point out that a composer should know how his music should sound, and that so great a creator as Stravinsky can bring things to it that nobody else can. One cannot deny that Stravinsky's performance of his score is often quite different from all others. He emphasizes inner strands more than any conductor who has recorded the work. He seems obsessed by the search for clarity. And thus details of the orchestration are heard as if for the first time. For this kind of instrumental definition alone, the disc is worth having. The recorded sound, too, is exciting. The stereo has great color and vitality.

July 1966

STRAVINSKY: Le Sacre du printemps (The Rite of Spring); Four Études for Orchestra. Orchestre National de la Radio-Télévision Française conducted by Pierre Boulez. Nonesuch 71093, $2.98.

Definitely a Best Buy. Pierre Boulez is the famous French avant-garde composer who in recent years has been concentrating on the baton, confining himself almost exclusively to the interpretation of contemporary music. He is considered one of the most remarkable conducting talents to have appeared for many years, and this disc of the great Stravinsky score testifies to the validity of his new fame. He takes the music at a rather fast tempo, but with extraordinary detail, brio, and authority. What comes out is a performance of unusual tensile strength. Nothing ever sounds knotted; all is lean, pulsating, with a formidable rhythmic drive. One listens to the familiar work as to a new piece of music. Boulez fills out the disc with Stravinsky's four *Études*, little chips from the master's workshop, deft and amusing.

The recorded sound in *Le Sacre du printemps* is a little bleak, but clear and well defined. There is a brighter sound to the four *Études*; they probably were recorded later.

August 1970

STRAVINSKY: Le Sacre du printemps (The Rite of Spring). The Cleveland Orchestra conducted by Pierre Boulez. Columbia MS7293, $5.98. ●

This is the second time in the last half dozen years that Boulez has recorded this notable twentieth-century score. The earlier recording, with the French Orchestre National RTF (Nonesuch 71093), catapulted Boulez into the international conducting spotlight. This new version, with the Cleveland Orchestra (which Boulez serves as principal guest conductor), has the same strengths and weaknesses as the earlier performance. Again, the conductor clarifies the textures remarkably, so that the listener can easily separate the many diverse and complicated horizontal lines. On the other hand, the concentration on clarity and balance is accomplished, to some extent, at the expense of the inherent drama and passion, so that the music is surprisingly impersonal.

The orchestra responds beautifully to the conductor's direction, and the whole is engraved in vivid stereo sound. But Columbia's own earlier recording by Bernstein and the New York Philharmonic (MS6010) continues to be the preferred performance by virtue of its greater dynamism and emotional impact.

Comment

As does Stravinsky's own recording of the *Sacre* (Columbia M31830), the Boulez-Cleveland Orchestra account downplays some of the drama brought to this score by many other conductors, including Bernstein (Columbia M31520), Abbado (Deutsche Grammophon 2530635), Mehta (Columbia XM34557), Ozawa (RCA LSC3026), and Solti (London CS6885). ■

March 1963

TCHAIKOVSKY: Concerto No. 1 in B flat minor for Piano and Orchestra. Sviatoslav Richter and Vienna Symphony Orchestra conducted by Herbert von Karajan. Deutsche Grammophon 138822, $6.98. ▲ ●

(continued)

Richter has recorded the Tchaikovsky B flat minor several times in the past, but always with orchestras behind the Iron Curtain. His notions about the concerto always have been unorthodox, and this new version is no exception. It is, indeed, so unorthodox that it may prove unsettling to many listeners. Richter and Karajan feature constant change of tempo and a prevailing slowness (the first movement is the slowest ever recorded). This slowness extends to the rising octaves ending the first movement. Where every living pianist licks his lips and waits for that great moment, Richter solemnly and turgidly mounts the scale. The effect is unusual, but it cannot have been what Tchaikovsky intended. Richter, of course, can break speed records when he wants to, and the prestissimo section of the slow movement is as fleet and feathery as one could desire. But on the whole, this disc of the popular concerto is too unorthodox, and has too many flabby moments, to be recommended. Nor is the recorded sound all it might be. Pianissimo sections in the stereo disc are out of relation to fortissimo passages, and when the volume is raised, so that the quiet sections can be heard without strain, the fortes tend to blast you from your seat. For better versions of the B flat minor try Cliburn (RCA LSC2252) or, for a blistering but low-fidelity performance, Vladimir Horowitz (RCA Victrola VIC1554), mono only.

July 1976

TCHAIKOVSKY: Piano Concerto No. 1 in B Flat minor. Lazar Berman, piano, with the Berlin Philharmonic Orchestra conducted by Herbert von Karajan. Deutsche Grammophon 2530677, $7.98. ●

TCHAIKOVSKY: The Nutcracker: Suite No. 1; GRIEG: Peer Gynt: Suite. The Boston Pops Orchestra conducted by Arthur Fiedler. London SPC21142, $6.98.

TCHAIKOVSKY: Francesca da Rimini; Hamlet. The Utah Symphony Orchestra conducted by Maurice Abravanel. Turnabout QTVS34601, $3.98.

Tchaikovsky has long been, and probably always will be, the most popular composer. These three recordings offer some of his best-known and best-loved scores, which are among the most-played of all orchestral works.

The Deutsche Grammophon disc gives us the legendary Soviet pianist, Lazar Berman, in his first recording with an orchestra. Berman's reputation had led us to expect a fire-breathing virtuoso for whom supreme musical fulfillment was to play faster than anyone else could—or cared to. But his American debut this season laid that myth to rest. True, Berman has prodigiously deft fingers, but they produce much more than mere speed.

His playing is richly representative of a Romantic tradition that sometimes finds its most natural expression in tempos that are somewhat slow, as his performance of the Tchaikovsky Concerto shows. That is a very different approach to this classic of classics and essentially resembles Herbert von Karajan's other recordings of the score (with Richter on Deutsche Grammophon and with Weissenberg on Angel). Whether Berman would play the music another way with another conductor remains to be seen. Still, listeners hoping to be overwhelmed physically may find this performance disappointing. One can't escape an overall sense of stodginess, despite splendid playing from all and equally splendid sound reproduction. Many other versions of Tchaikovsky's *First Piano Concerto* give me greater pleasure, including those recorded by Gilels, Cliburn, Janis, Joselson, and Rubinstein.

The Fiedler/Boston Pops disc of *The Nutcracker* and *Peer Gynt* suites is notable, first of all, for its label. After 40 years of recording, mainly with RCA but lately with Polydor and Deutsche Grammophon, Fiedler and the Boston Pops now make their pressings for the Phase 4 wing of London Records. Result: what may well be the best Boston Pops sound ever recorded. The wizards of English Decca, London Records's parent company, provide sound reproduction that is a model of clarity, warmth, and resonance.

Abravanel's linking of the familiar *Francesca da Rimini* with the relatively unfamiliar *Hamlet* is one of the best bargains in the current catalog. The orchestra plays both scores extraordinarily well—and *Hamlet* comes in for an especially impassioned, white-hot performance. The stereo sound is first-rate. (The disc is quadraphonic, but compatible with stereo systems.) Finally, let it be proclaimed that in his 30-odd years with the Utah Symphony, Maurice Abravanel has fashioned an orchestra that is, incontestably, a pride of the nation.

Comment

Karajan's perverse attitude toward the Tchaikovsky *B flat minor Piano Concerto* has now disfigured yet another recorded performance; it makes his international fame a rueful commentary on contemporary values. Two young pianistic titans, however, have provided superlative recorded performances of this ubiquitous concerto: Tedd Joselson, with Eugene Ormandy and the Philadelphia Orchestra (RCA ARL10751); and Horacio Gutierrez, with André Previn and the London Symphony Orchestra (Angel S37177). ■

June 1966

TCHAIKOVSKY: Concerti No. 2 in G for Piano and No. 3 in E flat for Piano. Gary Graffman and Philadelphia Orchestra conducted by Eugene Ormandy. Columbia MS6755, $5.98.

There must be some two dozen recorded versions of Tchaikovsky's *Piano Concerto No. 1 in B flat minor.* Before this disc came out there was only one of *No. 2 in G,* and that an old one. There is none of *No. 3* at all (years back there was a recording by Mewton-Wood, long since gone). Graffman is thus doing a real service. Neither concerto deserves its neglect. *No. 2* is a large-scale, exciting work, full of fireworks and simon-pure Tchaikovsky melodies. *No. 3* is in one movement, and it too has moments of great interest.

Graffman goes about his playing with an immense technique, clarity, and complete integrity. He is one of the best of the American pianists. And Ormandy backs him beautifully. The recorded sound is very good.

(continued)

Comment

The Graffman-Ormandy recording of Tchaikovsky's Second Piano Concerto gives us a rather bizarre text: Tchaikovsky's original in the end movements, with the slow movement as abridged by Alexander Siloti, a Tchaikovsky pupil. Despite this, the performance can be recommended because pianist, conductor and orchestra are as one in their response to the music's moods and shades. An uncut, "un-Silotied" performance of the score is available from the pianist Sylvia Kersenbaum, with the late Jean Martinon conducting the Orchestre National of France (Connoisseur Society 2076). Graffman and Ormandy are more persuasive and committed in their interpretation. ■

June 1975

TCHAIKOVSKY: Violin Concerto in D; SAINT-SAËNS: Introduction and Rondo Capriccioso. Eugene Fodor, violin, with the New Philharmonia Orchestra under Erich Leinsdorf. RCA ARL10781, $6.98. ▲ ●

Fodor is the 24-year-old American violinist who last year shared top honors with two Soviet violinists at Moscow's famed Tchaikovsky Competition. Mindful that first prize in a Tchaikovsky Competition nearly two decades ago launched Van Cliburn's international career, a veritable army went to work promoting Fodor. Results to date: much publicity, centered mainly on the artist's "good looks"; a performance at the White House last fall; and an impressive schedule of engagements for this season and next. Judged by this disc, however, the young violinist's celebrity may be short-lived.

Both the Tchaikovsky *Concerto* and the short Saint-Saëns work are vehicles for a blazing display of technique. Fodor's way with both is scaled-down, understated, temperamentally pallid. He seems to be fighting an inclination to play sharp.

When Pinchas Zukerman and Kyung-Wha Chung shared first prize in the Leventritt Competition some years ago, both were younger than Fodor is today, and both were masters ready for great international careers. But whatever the qualities that earned him his high place in Moscow, Fodor sounds on this recording like a student who has a long way to go.

Comment

Unfortunately, the words above have the ring of prophecy. In the years since his victory at Moscow's Tchaikovsky Competition, Fodor has shown little artistic growth. He continues to play a considerable number of engagements each season, but his future does not appear to be bright. ■

March 1971

TCHAIKOVSKY: Eugen Onegin (complete). The Bolshoi Theater Orchestra and Chorus conducted by Mstislav Rostropovich, with Yuri Mazurok,

baritone; Galina Vishnevskaya, soprano; Vladimir Atlantov, tenor. Melodiya/
Angel 4115, 3 discs, $17.98.

Tchaikovsky's flawed but compelling operatic treatment of Pushkin's epic
poem "Eugen Onegin," has been in and out of the repertoire of New York's
Metropolitan Opera Company in recent seasons. The work, however, has
not been consistently performed outside the Soviet Union. That is strange,
because it contains some of Tchaikovsky's most inspired melodic invention,
the Letter Scene being one of the most moving solos in operatic literature.
Admittedly, the casting of the heroine, Tatiana, constitutes a problem. She
must undergo during the course of the opera a complete vocal and character
change. In the beginning she is a bright-voiced young romantic whose love
for Onegin is spurned; by the end of the opera, she has become a hardened
sophisticate who, in her turn, rejects Onegin.

This performance, recorded in Paris last year by Moscow's Bolshoi Opera
Company, is unlikely to be bettered in the foreseeable future, though Vishnevskaya is now past her prime in the role of Tatiana. One longs for more
voluptuousness and passion, especially in the last act. The real hero of the
performance is Rostropovich, the extraordinary cellist and pianist who here
makes his recording debut as a conductor. He gives us passion and assurance
in plenty, plus the special spontaneity that enlivens his instrumental playing. His rapport with the score is rare among today's conductors, so that one
looks forward to more of his conducting.

The other principal singers do well with their roles, despite an overall lack
of tonal beauty, and the recorded sound is equal to the best currently being
produced in commercial recording studios anywhere.

Comment

The only other currently available recording of this flawed masterpiece is a
performance conducted by Sir Georg Solti (London CSA13112), with Teresa
Kubiak, Stuart Burrows, and Bernd Weikl in the principal roles. It is rather more
contained than the performance conducted by Rostropovich, and Kubiak is
definitely the vocal superior of Vishnevskaya. But the intensity and passion of
Rostropovich, even in excess, is hard to resist.   ■

September 1967

**TCHAIKOVSKY: Four Suites for Orchestra (Op. 43, 53, 55, 61
Mozartiana).** New Philharmonia Orchestra conducted by Antal Dorati. Mercury 77008, 3 discs, $17.94.

In a way, these are equivalent to the better known Tchaikovsky symphonies,
being full-scale works for orchestra. The music is melodious, attractive, and
brilliantly scored. Yet the suites are seldom heard. The first two will probably
come as complete novelties to most listeners. The "Theme and Variations"
from *No. 3* has been choreographed by Balanchine in the ballet of that name.

(continued)

Suite No. 4, the weakest, includes an orchestration of several pieces by Mozart, hence its name: *Mozartiana.*

Some marvelous music is contained in this album; and, it should be noted, some marvelous ballet music, even though none of the suites was conceived as a ballet. In theme, mood, texture, and rhythm, a good deal of the music recalls *Sleeping Beauty* and *Swan Lake.* Thus this album is recommended not only as a change from the last three Tchaikovsky symphonies, which are played to death, but as an enchanting musical experience in itself.

The performances are excellent, and so is the sound. Mercury has been most generous in its grooving, getting a great deal of music on each side. Despite the wealth of music, there is no apparent inner-groove distortion. The stereo features strong separation—violins at the left, horns at the right and so on. But the total effect is natural, and the results never sound gimmicked.

Comment

Dorati's performance of all four suites—he has no other recorded competition for the first two—is masterly, bringing out the essentially balletic nature of the music to splendid effect. The orchestra plays superlatively for him, and the reproduction is still first-rate. The three-disc set has been renumbered; it is now Mercury 77008. ∎

September 1976

TCHAIKOVSKY: Francesca da Rimini; Serenade in C for String Orchestra. The London Symphony Orchestra conducted by Leopold Stokowski. Philips 6500921, $7.98.

The Stokowski "miracle" continues! This recording, made when the venerable maestro was 92, has the flaming abandon of impetuous youth. That quality is particularly evident in *Francesca da Rimini,* a symphonic fantasy inspired by the Fifth Canto of Dante's "Inferno." Stokowski fairly revels in the opportunities for color and drama afforded by Tchaikovsky's musical account of the tragic love of Francesca and Paolo.

In somewhat characteristic fashion, Stokowski sometimes chooses to "improve" Tchaikovsky's scoring, especially in the emphasis he allows the tamtam. Stokowski has made other recordings of this work in his long career but never with more conviction than he shows on this particular disc.

The players of the London Symphony Orchestra give their all as Stokowski weaves a rich tapestry of glorious sound in the *Serenade for Strings.* Admittedly, there are some quirks here and there, including an interpretation of the Waltz that might reasonably be regarded as overinflected. But they are the quirks of genius; Stokowski makes them work, and the music comes alive in a very special way. The sound reproduction is in the best tradition of the Philips engineers, which means it is very good indeed.

Comment
Unlike Stokowski's London Philharmonic recording for Philips (6500766) of Tchaikovsky's *Nutcracker Suite* and *Capriccio Italien*, this disc does give us Stokowski at his best. ∎

May 1976

TCHAIKOVSKY: The Nutcracker: Suite No. 1; Capriccio Italien; Eugen Onegin: Waltz and Polonaise. The London Philharmonic Orchestra conducted by Leopold Stokowski. Philips 6500766, $7.98. ▲ ●

Tchaikovsky's music has tended to bring out the best, and the worst, in Leopold Stokowski over a recording career that spans nearly 60 years. The past decade has given us his latest thoughts on the composer's last three symphonies, recorded under various labels: the *Fourth* (Vanguard VSD10095), a fascinating horror in which he pushes and pulls the music around mercilessly; the *Fifth* (London SPC21017), in which the Maestro lavishly, and with perhaps the perversity of genius, personalizes the score, even to the point of partial reorchestration; and also the *Sixth* (RCA ARL 10426), which combines elements of willfulness with elements of undeniable persuasiveness. The latest sample of Tchaikovsky *à la* Stokowski is another wildly varied mix.

Some very strange things happen in the *Suite* from *The Nutcracker*. Again, the scoring includes some apparent touch-ups. An impossibly fast tempo makes a shambles of the music in at least one section, the *March*. The *Capriccio Italien* lacks much of the swagger one might expect from Stokowski; it gets a somewhat straitlaced, deadpan performance. But there are some extremely felicitous touches here and there. Several of the *Characteristic Dances* in *The Nutcracker* have character and a heady glow. The two popular orchestral excerpts from the opera *Eugen Onegin* fare nicely, particularly the *Polonaise*. The orchestra's playing and sound reproduction are unexceptionable.

Comment
Although not a good example of Stokowski's magic near the end of his life, this disc still has some remarkable moments. ∎

March 1971

TCHAIKOVSKY: Overture 1812; Romeo and Juliet Overture-Fantasy. The Los Angeles Philharmonic conducted by Zubin Mehta. London 6670, $5.98. ●

Tchaikovsky's *Festival Overture 1812* was written in 1880, to be performed in a Moscow public square with cannon, cathedral bells, and brass band, in addi-
(continued)

tion to a huge orchestra. That scoring, impractical at best in a concert hall, has come within feasible range in the age of electronic recording. A landmark recording with cannon was made back in the mid-1950s by Antal Dorati and the Minneapolis Symphony Orchestra under the Mercury label, and other companies have since followed suit. This London record adds bells and carillon, but the jacket material gives particular emphasis to the cannon. The front lists "Original Civil War cannon" right under Zubin Mehta and the Los Angeles Philharmonic Orchestra, and an inside credit line reads, "Original Civil War Cannon fired under the supervision of Atlas Fireworks Company (Bernard W. Wells) by the cannon's owner, Charles Marsh." There are also three good-sized pictures, one showing a cannon on display and two showing a cannon being fired by a man in Bermuda shorts.

The emphasis on the cannon pretty much characterizes Mehta's response to the score. Although bombast is dominant in the *1812*, there are other passages, tender and contemplative, for which the conductor has not seen fit to change the mood. This listener prefers the cannonless recording by Reiner (RCA VISC1025). If you want a recording that does include extramusical elements, we suggest that you listen to the one by Buketoff (RCA LSC3051), who is more disciplined and stylish than Mehta.

Unfortunately, the *Romeo and Juliet* performance also suffers from an approach that puts excitement ahead of a penetrating and perceptive musical response. The reproduction is loud on this disc.

Comment

Another superior performance of *1812*, complete with bells, (electronic) cannon, and chorus, is the RCA release by Eugene Ormandy and the Philadelphia Orchestra (LSC3204). The recorded sound is a considerable improvement over that of the earlier Ormandy-Philadelphia recording (Columbia M30447), despite its sound "refurbishing." And the Fiedler-Boston Pops recording (Deutsche Grammophon 2584003) earns high marks both musically and technically. There are any number of outstanding recorded performances of *Romeo and Juliet*; among them, surely, are those conducted by Abbado (Deutsche Grammophon 2530137), Munch (RCA AGL11331), and Rodzinski (Seraphim S60074). ∎

March 1966

TCHAIKOVSKY: Symphony No. 2 in C minor (Little Russian). Vienna Philharmonic Orchestra under Lorin Maazel. London 6427, $5.98.

In effect, this pleasant symphony is little more than a bundle of folk melodies. But though Tchaikovsky had not yet found his style, even these rather second-hand materials are shaped in a highly personal manner, and the orchestration is characteristically rich and brilliant. Most listeners should like this score, taking it for what it is. It has been recorded several times in the past, but this is the best version—the fullest-sounding, the most spirited, the best-controlled. There is something very Toscanini-like about Maazel's conducting. Rich, vital recorded sound. The climax at the end of side two achieves terrific volume without the least suggestion of distortion.

November 1972

TCHAIKOVSKY: Symphony No. 2 in C minor (Little Russian).
The New York Philharmonic Orchestra conducted by Leonard Bernstein. Columbia M31195, $5.98.

This release is the next to last in a series by Bernstein and the New York Philharmonic of all the symphonies of Tchaikovsky. The *Second*, reviewed here, had been sitting in Columbia's files for about four years prior to issue, and the *Third* ("*Polish*")—yet to be released—was recorded five years ago.

One would have expected Bernstein to be an ideal conductor of the Tchaikovsky symphonies; the surging drama of much of the music seems so like his own emotional makeup. But he has been largely disappointing as a Tchaikovsky conductor. Too often his responses have been hysterical, so that the already feverish music was pushed beyond tolerable limits. Nothing really outlandish happens in this performance of the "*Little Russian*" *Symphony*, but there are parts that teeter on the brink: the climax of the first movement's development section, for instance, and the frenzied approach to the scherzo movement. Too, there are spots of rhythmic unsteadiness that almost get out of control.

There are other, far more persuasive accounts of this score now available, including those by Dorati (included in a six-disc Mercury set of all the Tchaikovsky symphonies—SR69121), Maazel (London CS6427), and Markevitch (Philips 835390).

Comment

Both Maazel and Bernstein are among the conductors to have recorded all six of the Tchaikovsky symphonies—and each performance can be had either as a single disc or in an album that groups the symphonies. This writer has no hesitation in preferring Maazel's treatment of the "*Little Russian*" *Symphony* to Bernstein's—for reasons that should be clear from reading the above. But Bernstein and the Philharmonic are to be preferred in some of the other recordings—most particularly, perhaps, in the *Fourth Symphony* (Columbia XM33886) for its vibrant reproduction and impassioned performance. Another worthy recording of the "*Little Russian*" *Symphony* is a performance by Gennady Rozhdestvensky, the leading contemporary Soviet conductor (Melodiya/Angel SR40262). ∎

July 1969

TCHAIKOVSKY: Symphony No. 5 in E minor; MUSSORGSKY: A Night on Bald Mountain.
The Chicago Symphony Orchestra conducted by Seiji Ozawa. RCA LSC3071, $5.98. ▲

(continued)

Ozawa's recording has a fine sound reproduction, and the Chicago Symphony is unusually responsive to the conductor, although Ozawa has no moments of special interest to rival those of some other conductors of this work. Space is found on this disc to include a fiery performance of Mussorgsky's *A Night on Bald Mountain*, in the orchestration by Rimsky-Korsakov.

This disc rates high among the many recordings of Tchaikovsky's *Fifth*. But this department recommends that you at least listen to the version conducted by Stokowski (London 21017). He introduces wholesale changes in orchestration and some highly personal innovations in dynamics and voice balancing. Whatever your personal taste, the result is exciting. And it is well matched by the vivid sound recorded by London's Phase 4 process.

January 1973

TCHAIKOVSKY: Symphony No. 5 in E minor. The Cleveland Orchestra conducted by George Szell. Odyssey Y30670, $2.98. ●

Among the 20 or so available recordings of this favorite symphony, there are several outstanding performances. The best, perhaps, are the lucid and vibrant accounts conducted by Mehta (London CS6606), Ormandy (Columbia MS6109) and Ozawa (RCA LSC 3071), and the idiosyncratic but arrestingly alive performance under the direction of Stokowski (London SPC21017). All of those, however, are on labels that list from $4.98 to $5.98. In the budget-price category, this Szell-Cleveland recording is unquestionably the leader.

A product of recording sessions held about a dozen years ago, this performance was first released on Columbia's Epic label. Its reissue on Odyssey restores to circulation a performance that abundantly displays all the hallmarks of the Szell-Cleveland collaboration. Szell has scrubbed the score clean of the melodrama and bathos, accumulated over generations, that too many other conductors have slavishly incorporated. Instead, he delivers a lithe and lean reading characterized principally by energy and uncomplicated emotion. The result is bracing. The orchestra plays superbly, with particularly outstanding work from the principal horn, bassoon and oboe players. And the reproduction, from the early stereo age, is still serviceable enough to reveal the special qualities of the performance. Having it to savor once again—and at such a bargain price—is a pleasure.

Comment

Ozawa has since rerecorded Tchaikovsky's *Fifth Symphony* with the Boston Symphony Orchestra (Deutsche Grammophon 2530888) in a reading similar to the earlier one with the Chicago Symphony. If anything, the earlier performance has greater spontaneity. Also worthy of consideration are the performances conducted by Abbado (Deutsche Grammophon 2530198), Haitink (Philips 6500922), and Mehta (London CS6606). All three of them have great drive and all are splendidly played, with brilliant sound reproduction.

Horenstein's recording of this evergreen symphony with London's New Philharmonia Orchestra (Quintessence 7002) is another first-rate recorded performance in the bargain-price category. Where Szell is generally objective in his view of the score, Horenstein imbues it with passion and conveys a personal statement. Either approach brings its own rewards. ■

May 1969

TCHAIKOVSKY: Symphony No. 6 in B minor (Pathétique). The Philadelphia Orchestra under Eugene Ormandy. RCA LSC3058, $5.98. ▲ ●

Eugene Ormandy's first recording with the Philadelphia Orchestra—made in 1936—was of Tchaikovsky's *Pathétique Symphony*. And, "perhaps for sentimental reasons," he chose the *Pathétique* last May as the first of six recordings made to mark the return of conductor and orchestra to RCA after a quarter of a century with Columbia. With this pressing the Philadelphia Orchestra also returned to its home recording auditorium, The Academy of Music, which Columbia had vetoed for poor acoustics. RCA claims to have overcome the problem with an electronic device that increases reverberation and makes for a warmer, richer sound.

On the evidence of this disc, the results are variable at best. The listener seems to be standing in the conductor's shoes, so that individual solo instruments come through larger than life. There is, however, reasonably good balance between the several sections of the orchestra. There are also unusually wide stereo separation and a very solid low-frequency foundation. That kind of sound results from using a number of microphones. When the orchestra is in full voice, the sound sometimes teeters on the brink of distortion (as in some passages in the first movement) and sometimes goes over the brink into total disintegration (as in some stretches in the third movement). The result is reminiscent of the early RCA Dynagroove discs made half a dozen years ago.

The performance itself is typical Philadelphia—imperturbable and rock-steady, with an assured brilliance. And Ormandy brings his familiar clear-headed and objective view to his conducting of the *Pathétique*—a symphony that, in the hands of some conductors, has wallowed in its own excesses. Still, this record is not the best example of Ormandy's way with the score. For that reason, and because of the technical shortcomings, the Ormandy-Philadelphia recording made by Columbia (MS7169) in the early 1960s is preferred.

June 1975

TCHAIKOVSKY: Symphony No. 6 in B minor (Pathétique). The London Symphony Orchestra conducted by Leopold Stokowski. RCA ARL10426, $6.98. ▲ ●

Though ties between André Previn and the London Symphony Orchestra have grown increasingly close in recent years, the orchestra's intense activity in the concert, touring, and recording fields makes collaboration with guest
(continued)

conductors a necessity. Leopold Stokowski has been a frequent guest of late. Indeed, the maestro celebrated his 90th birthday in a memorable series of concerts with the London Symphony in April 1972. (That event was superbly recorded in concert on two discs as London SPC21090/1.) With the release of the *"Pathétique,"* Stokowski caps his most recent "reading" of the composer's last three symphonies.

The conductor's undertaking, begun over a decade ago and pursued with three different orchestras under as many record labels, started with a recording of the *Fifth Symphony* (London SPC21017) that though highly personal, displayed great vitality and conviction. Stokowski's "new" version of Tchaikovsky's *Fourth Symphony* (Vanguard VCS10095), which dates back about five years, was close to travesty—quixotic phrasing, exaggerated dynamic contrasts, and tempi pulled hither and yon.

Stokowski's latest recording of the *Sixth Symphony* is not so bad as his handling of the *Fourth*, but it's bad. Again the musical line is sometimes twisted and pulled like taffy. True, one can listen with morbid fascination, trying to guess at what excesses may lie ahead—but surely that is no substitute for music that should be presented with dignity and persuasiveness. Stokowski and the London Symphony Orchestra have made outstanding recordings together in recent years. This isn't one of them.

October 1975

TCHAIKOVSKY: Symphony No. 6 in B minor (Pathétique). L'Orchestre de Paris conducted by Seiji Ozawa. Philips 6500850, $7.98 ●

This performance has none of the deficiencies we deplored in RCA's recent release (ARL10426) under Stokowski's baton. Nor does it challenge the best recordings already available of this work. The main trouble with Ozawa's performance is rhythmic slackness. Though crisp, clearly articulated pulses are essential to this symphony, especially in the two inner movements, Ozawa fails to provide that rhythmic snap. Aside from that, the Orchestre de Paris continues to impress as a virtuoso ensemble. And the Philips engineers have provided full-bodied, resonant sound.

Some other currently available versions of the *"Pathétique"* that we rate higher than Ozawa's are Abbado's (Deutsche Grammophon 2530350), Haitink's (Philips 6500081), Ormandy's (Columbia M31833—not his more recent RCA recording, LSC3058), and Reiner's (RCA LSC3296). The best buy of all is Giulini's penetrating performance (Seraphim S60031). Splendidly played by London's Philharmonia Orchestra and beautifully recorded by the engineers, it is in the Seraphim budget line at $3.98.

March 1977

TCHAIKOVSKY: Symphony No. 6 in B minor (Pathétique). The London Symphony Orchestra under the direction of Jascha Horenstein. Vanguard Cardinal VCS10114, $3.98.

The career of Jascha Horenstein has been strange indeed. At his death in

1973, one month short of his 75th birthday, Horenstein was widely admired in Europe and by a small coterie in this country as one of the greatest conductors of our time. Yet in the 40's, when he was a refugee from Hitler's Germany and living in New York, Horenstein had been able to get only occasional assignments as a conductor—and usually with an indifferent collection of musicians at that. One can only speculate on how different American musical life might have been if Horenstein had been chosen in the late 40's as a successor to the New York Philharmonic's Rodzinski, the Boston Symphony's Koussevitzky, or the Chicago Symphony's Defauw. Horenstein was fairly active as a recording conductor in his last decade, however. His performances of Mahler's *First*, *Third*, and *Sixth Symphonies* (Nonesuch 71240, 73023, and 73029, respectively) are far and away the preferred renditions of those scores.

The present recording of Tchaikovsky's *"Pathétique"* derives from brief association with Britain's huge Electric and Musical Industries (EMI), an association that also yielded a fine recording of Mahler's *Fourth Symphony* (currently available on Monitor S2141). The *"Pathétique"* performance may disappoint some in its underplaying of the work's high drama; better that, however, than the emotional bath for which some conductors find this score an excuse. Jacket notes indicate that the relatively brief pause between the march and concluding movement reflects Horenstein's feeling that "the forced elation of the third movement should be very quickly followed by the resigned depressed mood of the fourth." (One wonders how Horenstein handled that pause in a concert performance, since the explosive conclusion of the march invariably evokes thunderous applause.)

Comment

The safest recommendations for the *"Pathétique" Symphony* may be two budget-price recordings: Giulini's (Seraphim S60031) and the Horenstein reviewed above. Both conductors bring lucidity and proportion to their performance, and the reproduced sound in both cases is quite good. In the full-price category, my first recommendation would be Haitink's recording (Philips 6500081). The performance is finely proportioned, lucidity predominates, and the sound reproduction is extraordinarily brilliant. ∎

June 1964

TIPPETT: A Child of Our Time. Elsie Morison (soprano); Pamela Bowden (contralto); Richard Lewis (tenor); Richard Standen (bass). Royal Liverpool Philharmonic Orchestra and Choir conducted by John Pritchard. Argo ZDA19/20, 2 discs, $11.90.

Michael Tippett is a British composer, born in 1905, who is hardly known in this country. His most famous work is the oratorio *A Child of Our Time*. It was first performed in 1944 and reflects the antiwar feeling of the composer (who was a conscientious objector). Tippett wrote his own text, which is based, roughly, on the story of the Jewish youth who shot von Rath in Paris in 1938
(continued)

and thereby hastened the Nazi pogroms. Tippett's musical style is traditional though unmistakably contemporary. He has gone to baroque traditions and used them in a twentieth-century manner. The most interesting, and certainly the most publicized, thing about *A Child of Our Time* is its use of undisguised Negro spirituals, inserted into the oratorio the way Bach inserted chorales into his passion music. Tippett handles these spirituals with a good deal of musical tact, avoiding sentimentality or vulgarity. *A Child of Our Time* is a powerful work, full of personality and strong feeling. This recording was released in England in 1958, but has just been made available here. It may not come up to the best recordings made today, but it is perfectly serviceable. The recorded sound is not bad, though there is some tape hiss and some surface noise. The performance is excellent. *A Child of Our Time* occupies three of the four sides; on side four are the "Ritual Dances" from Tippett's *Midsummer Marriage*, an opera produced in 1955. These are attractive excerpts, well scored, rhythmically ingenious. Tippett would appear to be a composer worth looking into.

June 1970

TIPPETT: Symphony No. 2; The Weeping Babe for Chorus and Soprano Solo; Sonata for Four Horns. The London Symphony Orchestra conducted by Colin Davis (in the *Symphony*); the John Alldis Choir and April Cantelo, soprano (in *The Weeping Babe*); the Barry Tuckwell Horn Quartet (in the *Sonata*). Argo ZRG535, $5.95.

Sir Michael Tippett is best known for his operas and for his 1944 oratorio, *A Child of Our Time*. His *Second Symphony* was composed in the years 1956 to 1957. Tippett writes in the aural language of the 1940s, that of Stravinsky and Hindemith. The first and last movements of the score are characterized by a drive strongly reminiscent of Stravinsky's *Symphony in Three Movements*; the two middle movements tend to bog down aimlessly and fail to sustain the listener's interest. While certainly not a major creation of the mid-twentieth century, this symphony is a representative work by a steady craftsman whose output is known insufficiently in this country. It receives a splendid performance and recording at the hands of Davis and the engineers.

The other two brief works, essentially fillers, are also well performed and recorded.

Comment

Just as Sir Thomas Beecham was for Delius a few generations ago, Colin Davis has become for Tippett the most articulate, committed, and compelling interpreter of his music. Davis's recent recording of *A Child of Our Time* (Philips 6500985) shows far more personal involvement and depth of feeling than does Pritchard's account. And Davis fits the entire work on a single disc; the Pritchard representation takes three sides. The symphony is intrinsically less interesting than the oratorio, but it, too, is given a first-rate recorded performance. ∎

January 1961

VARÈSE: Ionisation; Density 21.5; Intégrales; Octandre; Hyperprism; Poème électronique. Ensemble conducted by Robert Craft. Columbia MS6146, $5.98.

By now Varèse is an authentic Old Master, unconventional as his music is. During the 1920s he was already anticipating the experiments of the avant-garde composers of the 1950s. Most of his works up to the *Poème électronique* were for percussion orchestra (he is not a prolific composer, and the major portion of his life's work is on this disc), and featured experimentation with timbres and rhythms. Melody, in the accepted sense, is not present in any of these works. The *Poème électronique* is something of a departure for Varèse. It is an example of tape-recorder music, lasts exactly 480 seconds, and was composed in collaboration with Le Corbusier, the architect, for an exhibition at the Brussels World's Fair of 1958. It is fascinating, with its surrealistic use of altered voice effects on tape. As for the recorded sound, percussion records nearly always can make a fifty-dollar "hi-fi" system sound like the last word, and this one is no exception. Heard on wide-range equipment the stereo version is thrilling, with its sharp directionality and pinpointed timbres.

January 1963

VARÈSE: Arcana; Déserts; Offrandes. Donna Precht, soprano; Columbia Symphony Orchestra conducted by Robert Craft. Columbia MG31078, $5.98.

The jacket of this disc says "A Sound Spectacular," and a sound spectacular it is. Varèse composes for percussion orchestras, tape recorders, and other media that are ideal for stereo. The three works on this disc date from 1922 (*Offrandes*), 1927 (*Arcana*), and 1954 (*Déserts*, which is a score for orchestra and tape). Varèse is one of the authentic avant-gardists and a composer who, perhaps more than any other of the century, has investigated the potential of sound *qua* sound. Even the early *Offrandes*, with soprano solo, sounds more revolutionary than much of the music being composed today. An interesting and important disc; and what stereo sound!

Comment

These two discs present clear, well-prepared performances of most of the major works of Edgard Varèse (1883-1965). *Arcana*, *Ionisation*, and *Amériques*—all large-scale orchestral scores—are given strong interpretive profiles in the performances conducted by Boulez (Columbia M34552), and *Offrandes*, *Intégrales*, *Octandre*, and *Ecuatorial* fare very well indeed on a budget-price Nonesuch disc (71269) by Arthur Weisberg and the Contemporary Chamber Players. ∎

November 1973

VARÈSE: Arcana; Intégrales; Ionisation. The Los Angeles Philharmonic Orchestra conducted by Zubin Mehta. London CS6752, $5.98.

Paris-born Edgard Varèse settled in the United States in 1915, at the age of 32, and from then until his death in 1965 was a towering figure in the musical avant-garde. Except for that indomitable innovator, Leopold Stokowski, who was conducting Varèse in Philadelphia as far back as the 1920's, our leading conductors and orchestras largely ignored the composer's large-scale works until his very last years. Still, Varèse was a strong compositional influence for nearly four decades before his death, and he has become an even more pervasive musical presence since then.

Varèse was principally interested in instrumental timbres and colors, and almost all his music explores the uses of sonorities. Interestingly, many of his instrumental combinations anticipate the sounds of electronic music though he himself did not employ electronic means until very late in his career. The three works included on this disc are vintage Varèse: He composed *Intégrales* in 1924, *Arcana* in 1927 and *Ionisation* in 1931. *Intégrales* is scored for winds and greatly augmented percussion, *Arcana* for a very large and full symphony orchestra, and *Ionisation* for percussion alone.

All three works are rhythmically intricate, and they all rise to shattering climaxes, with superimposed layers of sound. *Ionisation* may be the most completely realized of the three, but *Arcana* and *Intégrales* are also formidable creations. There have been previous recordings of all three works, but these new performances under Mehta's dynamic leadership surpass them all. Mehta's performances are outstandingly lucid, and they demonstrate an intuitive response to the shifting rhythmic patterns. The Los Angeles Philharmonic continues its impressive series of recordings with one of its best efforts yet, and the London engineers have captured Varèse's vivid, multitextured sound.

Comment

Splendid as the Mehta-Los Angeles Philharmonic disc is, the recording conducted by Boulez and the New York Philharmonic (M34552) is even more impressive, especially for linear clarity and spectacular sound. Boulez's disc includes both *Arcana* and *Ionisation*. ∎

June 1973

VAUGHAN WILLIAMS: Fantasia on a Theme by Thomas Tallis; Fantasia on Greensleeves; The Lark Ascending; Five Variants of "Dives and Lazarus." The Academy of St. Martin-in-the-Fields conducted by Neville Marriner. Argo ZRG696, $5.95.

The four works on this disc surely rank among the most beautiful music ever created. That they are all the products of the twentieth century is a clear indication that not all composers of our time are concerned solely with ugliness and brutality. Vaughan Williams, one of the great humanists among modern composers, directed his attention, instead, toward lofty and noble aspirations. The result was an uplifting body of music, creditably represented by the four works on this disc. Each is graced with a gentle serenity and repose. And each is given a supremely perceptive performance by Marriner and his musicians. British engineers have captured it all in glowing sound.

Comment

Nothing more need be added to the above—except to urge everyone to acquire this superb record. ∎

August 1978

VAUGHAN WILLIAMS: Fantasia on a Theme by Thomas Tallis; PURCELL-STOKOWSKI: Dido and Aeneas: When I Am Laid in Earth; DVOŘÁK: Serenade in E for String Orchestra. Strings of the Royal Philharmonic Orchestra under the direction of Leopold Stokowski. Desmar DSM1011, $8.98. ●

Leopold Stokowski was in his 90's when he made these recordings. They bubble over with youthful intensity. It is remarkable that Stokowski had apparently never conducted the Dvořák *Serenade* before. His performance of it here is free from the mannerisms that marked much of his work when he was in his 60's and 70's, but it is nevertheless full of surprises.

For one thing, Stokowski takes the Moderato marking of the opening movement quite literally, but his very moderate tempo gives the strings their head and produces voluptuous sound. For another, he is rather brisk with the waltz movement that follows, and avoids the caressing phrases that mark such performances as Barenboim's (Angel S37045) and Kubelik's (London STS15037). And the editing leaves very little air space between the separate movements of the *Serenade*, doubtless at Stokowski's direction, so the music has a headlong quality that may not suit everyone's taste.

There is pure magic in Stokowski's performance of the Vaughan Williams *Fantasia*, surely one of the most sensuous of all compositions. The musical tensions never flag, and the inexorable logic of the music as it unfolds sweeps this listener off his feet. Stokowski's own arrangement for strings of Dido's Lament, from Purcell's *Dido and Aeneas*, is effective and affecting. The strings of London's Royal Philharmonic Orchestra play with extraordinary strength and precision throughout. And the recorded sound is a model of clarity and richness.

Comment

The mastering and pressing of this disc are meticulous. Desmar's executives fussed for the better part of a year before they finally approved the blend and

(continued)

balance. The effort was well worth it: The sound inscribed in these grooves is positively sumptuous. ∎

September 1970

VAUGHAN WILLIAMS: Five Tudor Portraits. Elizabeth Bainbridge, contralto, and John Carol Case, baritone, with the Bach Choir and New Philharmonia Orchestra conducted by David Willcocks. Angel S36685, $5.98.

The recording industry's renewed interest in the music of Ralph Vaughan Williams finds further expression in this first stereo release of one of the composer's most characteristic scores. *Five Tudor Portraits* is a choral suite, a setting of poems by the English Poet Laureate, John Skilton (1460-1529). The music covers a wide emotional range, from gay and roaring abandon to quiet and pensive reflection. Through it all, the composer's easygoing warmth lights up Skilton's imagery with wit and verve. It is difficult to understand why *Five Tudor Portraits* should be so little known; perhaps this fine new recording will help change that situation.

Willcocks, a conductor little known outside England, has been in the vanguard of the Vaughan Williams revival with a number of splendid recordings, but the present disc is the best so far. His sweep and drive inspire a vibrant performance from the assembled participants. The engineering, too, is wide-ranging and vivid.

Comment
The vocal soloists deserve special mention. Each is among England's finest contemporary singers. They are still little known on the international scene, but recordings such as this one are bound to spread their fame. Mark their names: They will be heard increasingly as time goes on. ∎

November 1971

VAUGHAN WILLIAMS: Job, A Masque for Dancing. The London Symphony Orchestra conducted by Sir Adrian Boult. Angel S36773, $5.98.

As has been noted here before, music lovers will owe a substantial debt to Angel Records for that company's project of recording all the Vaughan Williams symphonies under the direction of the composer's most devoted and authoritative interpreter, Sir Adrian Boult. In adddition to the symphonies, Boult and Angel have been recording a large number of Vaughan Williams' other orchestral works. This release of the composer's great ballet score on the subject of Job is the latest in the sequence.

The music dates from the late 1920s. It was first performed as a concert suite in 1930 and as a ballet in London a year later. In the forty years since, there have been occasional productions of the ballet in Britain, but the music has earned for itself an independent identity as a vibrant concert score. Into the eight scenes and the Epilogue of *Job*, Vaughan Williams poured some of his most profound music. It has an elegiac quality that leaves the listener spiritually and emotionally fulfilled.

Sir Adrian has recorded *Job* twice before in the past quarter of a century, but the present performance—aided by outstanding sound reproduction—is the best and most perceptive of the three. This recording will doubtless acquaint many new listeners with this sublime music.

Comment

We are fortunate to have Sir Adrian's matchless interpretation of Vaughan Williams' *Job* reproduced with such vivid sound. The London Symphony Orchestra players are inspired throughout by the conductor's conviction and dedication. This is a disc to treasure; it supersedes Sir Adrian's earlier recording of the score with the London Philharmonic Orchestra, now back in the catalog in electronic stereo (Everest 3019). ∎

June 1971

VAUGHAN WILLIAMS: A Sea Symphony (Symphony No. 1). The London Symphony Orchestra and Chorus conducted by André Previn, with Heather Harper, soprano, and John Shirley-Quirk, baritone. RCA LSC3170, $5.98.

This is the third release in RCA's recorded cycle of the Vaughan Williams symphonies with André Previn and the London Symphony Orchestra. Four of the composer's nine symphonies are now available in this series; *No. 7*, the *Antartica*, is on RCA LSC3066, and *Nos. 6* and *8* are on RCA LSC3114. This performance of *A Sea Symphony* is the most successful in the series so far. The sea has exerted a particular inspiration for English artists for centuries, so it is not surprising that Vaughan Williams should have used the sea poetry of Walt Whitman—poems from "Sea-Drift," "Passage to India," and "Song of the Exposition."

A work for orchestra and chorus with two vocal soloists, *A Sea Symphony* requires a good deal of time and money to perform. Repeated hearings—made possible only through recording—show the work to be absolutely seminal in the composer's creativity.

Here one finds all the hallmarks of the Vaughan Williams style: the harmonies derived from medieval church music, the emphasis on the dark colors of the orchestral palette (with strings and woodwinds often in their low registers), and the gentle sensitivity to word meanings and phrasings. The musical settings of Whitman's words linger in the memory.

Sir Adrian Boult, that most authoritative and dedicated of Vaughan Williams conductors, has recorded *A Sea Symphony* twice during the past two decades, the most recent of his two recordings (Angel S3739; 2 discs) being a
(continued)

particularly glowing reproduction of an inspired performance. That this new Previn recording can be compared favorably with Boult's is impressive in itself. Previn quite obviously feels a close affinity for the Vaughan Williams symphonies, and he coaxes from his assembled forces playing and singing of great understanding; indeed, his two soloists are even more imbued with the atmosphere of this score than are Boult's. And in one important respect, the new RCA recording offers a decided advantage over Boult's: The sixty-five-minute score fits on a single disc, whereas Boult's performance requires three record sides (the fourth being devoted to a suite from Vaughan Williams' *Incidental Music* for the Aristophanes play, *The Wasps*). So Previn's recording costs only half as much as Boult's.

Comment

André Previn, Hollywood's former "wunderkind," has assuredly become one of the world's leading conductors. And his activities in this country as music director of the Pittsburgh Symphony Orchestra are making him as popular a figure in the concert hall, on tour, and on television as he was in Europe during the decade or so when he was principal conductor of the London Symphony Orchestra. ∎

February 1971

VAUGHAN WILLIAMS: Serenade to Music; Symphony No. 5 in D.
Sixteen solo singers (in the *Serenade*), with the London Philharmonic Orchestra conducted by Sir Adrian Boult. Angel S36698, $5.98.

The third of Vaughan Williams' nine symphonies bears the official subtitle "Pastoral," but the word could be applied with equal validity to either work on this disc. The *Serenade to Music*, set to words from Act V of Shakespeare's *The Merchant of Venice*, was composed in 1938 for the golden jubilee of Sir Henry Wood, the guiding spirit behind London's Promenade Concerts; however, this treasure of musical grace and civility has transcended the momentary occasion that inspired it.

Vaughan Williams wrote with sixteen particular solo singers in mind, and Sir Henry Wood himself recorded the *Serenade* with those singers in a superb English set of two 78-rpm discs. There have been other recordings of the score over the years, but not until now has one approached that pioneer version. Sir Adrian Boult, long Vaughan Williams' most perceptive interpreter, delivers a beautiful and affecting performance. All the solo singers share Sir Adrian's inspired mood; the orchestra plays superbly, with particular sensitivity to the soft passages.

Vaughan Williams produced his great *Fifth Symphony* five years later, while German bombers nightly pounded much of London and other British cities into rubble. One might have expected the music to reflect the terror of the times, but instead it is seraphic, almost idyllic—not unlike the *Serenade* in its gentle grace and reflective grandeur. Only two conductors have recorded the *Fifth*—Sir John Barbirolli and Sir Adrian Boult, each twice. Even more than

258

Sir Adrian's earlier recording (once available as London LL975), this new version reveals the music's essential serenity. This listener also prefers this disc to either of Sir John's performances and gives it an unqualified recommendation.

Comment

Even with the later RCA release of the Previn-London Symphony recording of this seraphic symphony—and a highly successful performance it is—Boult's offering remains unique in its breadth and sensitivity to the music's spiritual qualities. And Boult's companionpiece (the *Serenade to Music*) is more substantial than Previn's (the overture from the composer's *Incidental Music* for Aristophanes' play *The Wasps*). ■

May 1963

VAUGHAN WILLIAMS: Symphony No. 5 in D major. Philharmonia Orchestra conducted by Sir John Barbirolli. Angel S35952, $5.98.

Vaughan Williams is a composer with a great reputation, but his music is seldom played outside of England. More's the pity. This symphony is one of the most beautiful that the twentieth century has to offer. It is a flowing, gentle work, imbued with the spirit of English folk music. Unlike the fiercely dissonant *Fourth Symphony*, it contains almost no jagged sounds. The *Fourth*, of 1935, has been construed as the composer's revolt against war. But the *Fifth*, composed in 1943 during the war, echoes none of that terrible period in England. Perhaps Vaughan Williams was trying to comfort his compatriots, trying to write music that would make them forget their time and place. Vaughan Williams was seventy-one years old at the time (he lived to the age of eighty-five), and through the entire *Fifth Symphony* breathes an autumnal calm and serenity. The performance of this disc is superb. Sir John had a close association with the composer and is a specialist in his music. The recording is excellent, too. Highly recommended.

Comment

Barbirolli may bring a shade more serenity to parts of the score—particularly in the third movement—but Boult's performance (see preceding review) has the benefit of pellucid sound and splendid playing. ■

September 1968

VAUGHAN WILLIAMS: Symphony No. 6 in E minor; The Lark Ascending. New Philharmonia Orchestra conducted by Sir Adrian Boult, with
(continued)

Hugh Bean, violin (in *The Lark Ascending*). Angel S36469, $5.98. ●

Sir Adrian Boult conducted the world premiere performance of Vaughan Williams' *Sixth Symphony* in 1948, and this is his third recording of the score. The first three movements of the symphony seem to be one long cry of anguish; an early commentator dubbed the work the "War Symphony," and certainly the years of crisis that surrounded its composition left their imprint upon the score. Alienation often succeeds violence, and Vaughan Williams gives that idea musical expression in the Finale. Directing that the music must never rise above a whisper, he surrounds the hearer with drifting wisps of themes that eerily suggest disengagement from reality.

The first three movements could stand a bit more of the verve that Sir Adrian brought to his very first recording of the score nearly twenty years ago. The last movement is more satisfying, with finely shaded, balanced sound throughout.

By contrast, *The Lark Ascending* is a gentle romance for violin and orchestra in Vaughan Williams' most direct and engaging manner, played affectionately by Hugh Bean, the New Philharmonia's concertmaster.

August 1970

VAUGHAN WILLIAMS: Symphonies No. 6 in E Minor and No. 8 in D minor. The London Symphony Orchestra conducted by André Previn. RCA LSC3114, $5.98.

Previn is currently recording all nine Vaughan Williams symphonies with the London Symphony Orchestra; this disc is the second in the series to be released domestically. As he demonstrated in his earlier recording of the *Antartica Symphony (No. 7)*, Previn has a genuine affinity for the Vaughan Williams style and mood. In both the *Sixth* and *Eighth Symphonies*, he delivers persuasive and sensitive accounts of the music's shifting character.

Both scores are products of the composer's late years: The *Sixth* was produced when he was seventy-five, the *Eighth* eight years later. Both incorporate the unique power that would make one expect Vaughan Williams to be far more popular than he is in the standard orchestral repertoire; he is unquestionably the most underrated symphonist of the twentieth century. Perhaps the Previn series of symphony recordings will give the music a needed boost.

The *Sixth Symphony*, composed right after World War II, is extremely powerful. Its four movements are played with no pauses in between and thus form one continuous mosaic. The first three movements, each in its own way, are full of violence and menace. But the last movement is an Epilogue of strange and hushed mystery that somehow suggests swirling mists and vapors. A postatomic holocaust perhaps, in which Earth is a lifeless sphere revolving aimlessly? Let each listener decide.

The Eighth Symphony, by contrast, is not so profound. It is an amiable work with much exotic sound—bell-like Middle Eastern timbres, and two middle movements scored successively for winds alone and strings alone.

Previn's performance of the *Sixth* is perhaps not quite so authoritative as Sir Adrian Boult's recent recording (Angel S36469); Previn's *Eighth* is thoroughly engaging. The London Symphony is perfection, and its efforts are recorded superlatively: rich, full and well-balanced.

Comment

The complete cycle of all the Vaughan Williams symphonies conducted by both Boult and Previn are recording landmarks. Boult's rendering of the *Eighth Symphony* (Angel S36625) is marginally more atmospheric and responsive to the shifting moods of the score than Previn's. But Previn has the advantage in the choice of selections, with both the *Sixth* and *Eighth* together on the same disc. Boult's *Eighth Symphony* companion piece is somewhat less substantial—the *Concerto for Two Pianos and Orchestra*, played by Vronsky and Babin. ∎

March 1959

VAUGHAN WILLIAMS: Symphony No. 9 in E minor. London Philharmonic Orchestra conducted by Sir Adrian Boult. Everest 3006, $4.98.

Many consider Ralph Vaughan Williams to be the greatest of twentieth-century symphonists. The *Ninth* is his last work, and he was scheduled to participate in this recording session. But, as Sir Adrian says in a brief, spoken preface to the recording, death took place seven hours before. In the *Ninth*, Vaughan Williams exploits a folk-music idiom and completely avoids the complexities and dissonances of some of his previous symphonies. The writing is mellow and songful, and while it may ramble a bit, especially in the last movement, the symphony has an authority and sheer mastery that none but a great composer could achieve. Everest, the company that made this record, is new in the field. Apparently it is going to feature a type of very close-up recording technique. This disc is heavily cut, too, and will provide a rugged test for any playback equipment. On high-quality components, the stereo sound is exceptionally brilliant and sonorous. But unless a pickup tracks perfectly and has a smooth response, there is going to be "shatter" and distortion (as there was with several pickups used to play this disc). Try the beginning of side two, with its explosion of percussion and brass instruments. The stereo version is lifelike and colorful. But unless your equipment is first-class, there will be trouble.

Comment

This was the first recording of Vaughan Williams' *Ninth Symphony*, released, if memory serves, even before the score had a live performance in this country. In the intervening years, Boult has rerecorded the symphony (Angel S36742) in a smoother sounding performance and recording, but one that does not have quite the bite of this 1958 Everest account. On the other hand, the Angel disc has room to include the composer's *Fantasia (quazi variazione) on the "Old*
(continued)

261

104th" Psalm Tune. All things considered, the newer recording is probably the preferred one. ∎

September 1966

VERDI: Don Carlos. Carlo Bergonzi, tenor (Don Carlos); Renata Tebaldi, soprano (Elizabeth); Nicolai Ghiaurov, bass (Philip II); Dietrich Fischer-Dieskau, baritone (Rodrigo); Grace Bumbry, mezzo-soprano (Eboli); Martti Talvela, bass (Inquisitor). Chorus and Orchestra of Royal Opera House, Covent Garden, conducted by Georg Solti. London 1432, 4 disc, $23.92.

Verdi's great opera is given here with an all-star cast. Unfortunately some of the stars are not in best voice. Tebaldi works hard and her conception is rudimentary. Bumbry has temperament, but produces a spread, often shrill sound. Fischer-Dieskau's voice sounds dry, and one misses an Italianate quality. The best singing is contributed by Bergonzi, a smooth tenor with a lovely lyric quality; and by Ghiaurov, who is most impressive when not singing too loud. Talvela sounds like a fine bass. On the whole this album is a disappointment, despite the fine conducting of Solti and the realistic recorded sound. This version of the opera is the four-act revision and not the one used by the Metropolitan Opera.

Comment

The only other available stereo recording—Angel S3774, with Giulini conducting an all-star cast including Caballé, Verrett, Domingo, Raimondi, and Milnes—is on the whole better sung, if less stirringly dramatic in its realization of this tempestuous music. You pay your money and you take your choice. ∎

March 1959

VERDI: Falstaff. Tito Gobbi, baritone (Falstaff); Rolando Panerai, baritone (Ford); Luigi Alva, tenor (Fenton); Elisabeth Schwarzkopf, soprano (Mistress Ford); Anna Moffo, soprano (Nannetta); Nan Merriman, mezzo-soprano (Mistress Page); Fedora Barbieri, mezzo-soprano (Mistress Quickly). Philharmonia Orchestra and Chorus conducted by Herbert von Karajan. Angel S3552, 3 discs, $17.94.

Falstaff is Verdi's last opera. He composed it when he was almost eighty years old, and it is a miracle: an eternally witty, bubbling work, subtle and melodious, with idea following idea. No more concentrated opera has been composed, and that is one of the reasons why *Falstaff* never has achieved great popularity. For despite its great wealth of melody, its material flashes by before listeners can get their teeth into it. Thus, it demands many listenings—which is exactly what records can provide. *Falstaff*, when one is familiar with the opera, stands right next to Mozart's *Marriage of Figaro* and *Cosi fan tutte* as the greatest of comic operas. Angel provides the only stereophonic recording of the work (it was issued monophonically about two years ago), and in this album Herbert von Karajan leads a most interesting performance. Many *aficionados* of Italian opera do not especially like it, claiming it to be too restricted metrically and lacking in heart. But Karajan exercises perfect control over his forces, has a brilliant group of singers to work with, and generates plenty of excitement. Most listeners will want to know how he stacks up against RCA's Toscanini. The great Italian conductor, of course, achieved a style and a sense of tradition that were unique. Toscanini, though, had nowhere near a comparable group of singers. Gobbi, in the Angel set, comes right through the vinyl in his vivid performance, making Valdengo sound tame. Moffo and Alva are much more convincing as the lovers than their RCA equivalents. And so on. Well-heeled collectors should by all means own both sets. Those who must make a choice should find the Angel set preferable. As for the Angel stereo, it is a little disappointing. The stereo illusion is present, as witness the concluding fugue, with voices coming from all directions. But the sound itself, throughout the album, is rather tight and constricted without the color and resonance that the finest recordings can give. It is listenable, certainly, but seldom thrilling. Surfaces are fairly quiet. The old Toscanini album, it should be mentioned, still stands up quite well as a recording.

May 1967

VERDI: Falstaff. Dietrich Fischer-Dieskau, baritone (Falstaff); Regina Resnik, mezzo-soprano (Dame Quickly); Ilva Ligabue, soprano (Mrs. Ford); Rolando Panerai, baritone (Mr. Ford); Graziella Sciutti, soprano (Nannetta); Juan Oncina, tenor (Fenton). Vienna Philharmonic Orchestra and State Opera Chorus conducted by Leonard Bernstein. Columbia D3S750, 3 discs, $17.94.

This is probably Verdi's greatest opera. Only *Otello* can challenge it. Verdi wrote it at the age of seventy-nine, but it is young, ardent, and anything but the product of an old man. It is also the fastest-moving opera ever composed. There are very few set arias, and those there are, with the exception of Ford's monologue and Falstaff's "Honor" monologue, whiz by. The musical substance is sheer gold and there is not a weak note in the entire opera. It cannot be assimilated at one hearing. It is too much of a piece, and the listener coming to it for the first time will have to listen together with the libretto until all the thematic interrelationships become clear. The orchestra also plays a much more important part than in any other Verdi opera. It comments on the action: It laughs, chuckles, pokes fun. *Falstaff* is unique in the history of opera.

Bernstein created a sensation when he conducted it at the Metropolitan Opera a few seasons back. He made an equally big impression at the Vienna Staatsoper, and this recording is a facsimile of his performances there, with the same cast and orchestra. The cast is strong all the way through. Some critics have wondered if Fischer-Dieskau's voice has the "fatness" for Falstaff. But its good size, its virility, and the intelligent way it is used put his interpretation on a plane that only Tito Gobbi has equaled. There is no need

(continued)

to go down the list. All the singers are good, and the orchestra is one of the best in the world. And Bernstein dominates everything. A theater man himself, he has real affinity for the fast-moving *Falstaff*, conducting with color, knowledge, and wonderful spirit. Only the Toscanini recording can rival it.

Columbia has given Bernstein brilliant recorded sound, marred only by a few pre-echoes (as in the big chords on the first quarter of side four). Surfaces are quiet. The closing fugue, *"Tutto nel mondo è burla,"* has the voices spread in a wide canvas in the stereo.

Comment

The sets conducted by Karajan and Bernstein continue to dominate the stereo field where *Falstaff* is concerned. The monophonic, three-disc Toscanini recording (RCA LM6111) may be difficult to find but is worth the search. It remains a supremely invigorating account of this masterly score. ■

May 1960

VERDI: Macbeth. Leonard Warren, baritone (Macbeth); Leonie Rysanek, soprano (Lady Macbeth); Jerome Hines, bass (Banquo); Carlo Bergonzi, tenor (Macduff). Metropolitan Opera Orchestra and Chorus conducted by Erich Leinsdorf. RCA VICS6121, 3 discs, $8.94.

Early Verdi is very much the rage these days. When *Macbeth* was revived at the Metropolitan Opera, with the same leading singers heard in these discs, it was greeted with much seriousness, and the Sleepwalking Scene especially created something of a furor. There is no doubt that *Macbeth* is a lusty and exciting opera, full of the vitality of the young Verdi. But don't expect much subtlety. Anyway, for those who want to look into this interesting work, here is the Metropolitan performance. And a brilliant performance it is. The late Leonard Warren seldom sounded better: resonant, rich-voiced, commanding. Rysanek was made for her role of Lady Macbeth. She has passion and intensity; is a superior musician; and, above all, is a singing actress. The other singers are capable, the orchestral direction is in the experienced hands of Leinsdorf (no flaming temperament, but exact and thorough), and even the chorus rises to the occasion. As for the recorded sound, it is superb—up to a point. RCA has gone in for pronounced separation. Thus, in the first Macbeth–Banquo duet, the voices come from different locations. When Lady Macbeth makes her entrance, reading the letter, she is heard only in the left speaker. Then she passes across stage to the right speaker just before Macbeth's entrance. And so on. The recording supplies tremendous volume without shattering. All of which is fine. But, alas, there is considerable inner-groove distortion. Were it not for this (check the ending of sides one, five, and six), the album would be ideal.

Comment

Despite the excellence of a number of later releases (Abbado conducting La

Scala artists including Verrett, Domingo, Cappuccilli, and Ghiaurov on Deutsche Grammophon 2709062, for example, or Muti conducting a London team with Cossotto, Carreras, Milnes, and Raimondi on Angel SX3833), this pioneering RCA set is still a treasure, principally for an extraordinary portrayal of the title role by the great American baritone Leonard Warren. ■

January 1967

VERDI: Nabucco. Tito Gobbi, baritone (Nabucco); Elena Suliotis, soprano (Abigaille); Carlo Cava, bass (Zaccaria); Bruno Prevedi, tenor (Ismaele); Dora Carral, soprano (Fenena). Vienna Opera Orchestra and Chorus conducted by Lamberto Gardelli. London 1382, 3 discs, $17.37.

Nabucco, Verdi's first great success, was an unknown quantity in this country until the Metropolitan Opera revived it in 1960. It turned out to be a wonderful work: immature, but full of ideas, passion, and sweep. Stylistically it looks back to the bel-canto school (the writing for solo voices is full of Donizettian flourishes) and also ahead to *Rigoletto* and the other operas in which Verdi broke free of his predecessors.

Up to now, *Nabucco* has been represented on records only by an old, inadequate Everest/Cetra performance. Now a modern version arrives, brilliantly recorded, with the spatial advantages of the stereo process. It is well sung and played, too. Gobbi's voice may be a little rough, but few singers around have his authority and knowledge of style. Prevedi is one of the smoothest tenors anywhere (although *Nabucco* unfortunately gives the tenor very little to do). Elena Suliotis, the Greek soprano who sings Abigaille, is a newcomer. She is interesting. She has a voice of large size and range, though she still has a great deal to learn about the technique of singing. For one thing, she has at least two breaks in her register. But she has temperament, and she brings a great deal of excitement to her interpretation. The other singers are competent, and Gardelli conducts with plenty of force. This is definitely an album for anybody interested in Italian opera.

Comment

Philips Records, which has performed an invaluable service in recording many of the early Verdi operas, has a new release of *Nabucco* on the way. Meantime, this trailblazing set from London Records—apart from Suliotis—is more than adequate both in performance and sound reproduction. ■

May 1965

VERDI: Requiem Mass. Elisabeth Schwarzkopf, soprano; Christa Ludwig, mezzo-soprano; Nicolai Gedda, tenor; Nicolai Ghiaurov, bass. Philharmonia Orchestra and Chorus conducted by Carlo Maria Giulini. Angel S3649, 2 discs, $11.96.

(continued)

VERDI: Requiem Mass. Lucine Amara, soprano; Maureen Forrester, contralto; Richard Tucker, tenor; George London, bass-baritone. Westminster Choir and Philadelphia Orchestra conducted by Eugene Ormandy. Columbia M2S707, 2 discs, $11.98.

It is very hard to choose between these two versions of the Verdi choral masterpiece. For every strength in the Giulini-conducted version, an equivalent strength can be cited in the Ormandy. If Giulini is a little more dynamically subtle, Ormandy achieves more of the work's grandeur and drama. If the Angel vocal quartet has the great Bulgarian bass, Ghiaurov, the Columbia has Tucker in exceptionally brilliant voice. The point is that both albums are exceedingly fine.

Even the recorded sound in both is above average, though the Angel does have more surface noise and tape hiss. Both recordings use a good deal of stereo separation. In the Columbia recording, the soloists are a bit more forward; listeners hear them as though they were on the podium. In the Angel album the soloists sound more as they would from a seat in the auditorium.

March 1971

VERDI: Requiem Mass. The London Symphony Orchestra and Chorus conducted by Leonard Bernstein, with Martina Arroyo, soprano; Josephine Veasey, mezzo-soprano; Placido Domingo, tenor; and Ruggero Raimondi, bass. Columbia M230060, 2 discs, $11.98.

VERDI: Requiem Mass. The New Philharmonia Orchestra and Chorus conducted by Sir John Barbirolli, with Montserrat Caballé, soprano; Fiorenza Cossotto, mezzo-soprano; Jon Vickers, tenor; and Ruggero Raimondi, bass. Angel 3757, 2 discs, $11.98.

Giuseppe Verdi's setting of the Roman Catholic requiem mass has been called the "most operatic" work by this supreme composer of operas. His *Requiem* spans the extremes of emotion, from exaltation to despair, from pious devotion to an almost pagan abandon, from frenzied rage to calm reflection. A single release of the score with distinguished conductor, orchestra and chorus, together with four superlative soloists, automatically becomes a special event. The simultaneous release of two such presentations should constitute an embarrassment of riches. In this case, however, it does not—primarily because the technology of both reproductions leaves something to be desired. Bernstein's recorded sound is frequently out of balance, and there is more than a hint of overmodulation in the heavily scored passages. Barbirolli's, on the other hand, often suffers from a kind of sonic undernourishment that neutralizes some of the biggest moments.

As it happens, the quality of recorded sound aptly characterizes the two conductors' contrasting views of the music. Bernstein is electrifying in the emotional passages; for example, under him the apocalyptic "Dies Irae" rises to a frightening intensity. Barbirolli is less compelling at such moments, but more so in the compassion with which he invests the more reflective parts of the music. Both orchestras play superbly. Bernstein's chorus is more spontaneous, Barbirolli's perhaps a bit smoother.

Each team of solo singers has its own strengths and weaknesses. Caballé, Barbirolli's soprano, outpoints Bernstein's Arroyo in her effortless ease and her greater feeling for the music. But Bernstein's tenor, Domingo, is much better than Barbirolli's Vickers; Domingo produces a rich, even sound throughout his entire range, while Vickers is sometimes forced to strain unpleasantly. Both mezzo-sopranos are excellent, while Raimondi—who sings bass in both recordings—adjusts easily to the contrasting demands of the two conductors.

Bernstein's recording is undoubtedly the more arresting of the two. But Angel's recording of about half a dozen years ago by Giulini (S3649; 2 discs) is still the most consistently successful stereo performance that is available.

Comment

The Ormandy performance has moved to Columbia's low-price Odyssey label (Y235230). Other distinguished conductors who have contributed recordings of the Verdi *Requiem* are Karajan (Deutsche Grammophon 2707065), Leinsdorf (RCA LSC7040), and, on two occasions, Solti (London CSA1294 and RCA ARL22476). Yet, Giulini's basically humane treatment of the music may be the most consistently satisfying of all. ■

February 1964

VERDI: La Traviata. Joan Sutherland, soprano (Violetta); Carlo Bergonzi, tenor (Alfredo Germont); Robert Merrill, baritone (Giorgio Germont); Maggio Musicale Fiorentino conducted by John Pritchard. London 1366, 3 discs, $17.94. ●

The role of Violetta seems to be beyond the capabilities of living sopranos; we have not had a great Violetta since Lucrezia Bori. Verdi asks much: a coloratura approach in the first act, a lyric approach later, and in spots almost a dramatic one. One had hoped that Sutherland would take complete command of the role, but in this album there are some disappointments. Most of these are histrionic rather than vocal. Sutherland's voice is as beautiful as ever, but she does little to convince the listener that Violetta is a flesh-and-blood character. Sutherland's diction is sloppy; her enunciation is so lax that often she gives the impression she is singing a vocalise. She is even developing questionable vocal habits, one of which is her tendency to slide from note to note. On the credit side are her soaring upper register, the brilliance of the coloratura work in the first act's *"Sempre libera,"* and the haunting color she can bring to a long, flowing line. The others in the cast are very good. Merrill is firm-voiced, clear and resonant; and Bergonzi sings one of the best Alfredos ever recorded. He has as good a high C as any tenor around (listen to the end of side two). Pritchard conducts in a lively manner.
(continued)

267

The engineers have inserted some unintentionally humorous effects in the gambling scene. Coins ring like carillons, and cards and knuckles slam down as though the cards were sandbags and the knuckles were rock. There is excellent recorded sound.

January 1970

VERDI: La Traviata. Pilar Lorengar, soprano (Violetta); Giacomo Aragall, tenor (Alfredo); Dietrich Fischer-Dieskau, baritone (Germont); and other soloists, with the Berlin German Opera conducted by Lorin Maazel. London 1279, 2 discs. $11.96. ●

The idea of recording this very Italian opera in Berlin may strike some listeners as peculiar. But the explanation seems simple enough: The stage production of *Traviata* by this company was successful enough to warrant recording. According to the libretto booklet included with the record, the recording company had available "three brilliant soloists—a chorus that 'acted' with their voices—and orchestra and cast absolutely at one with its conductor in matters of tempo, dynamics, phrasing and expression." London Records' notes go on to express the hope that the experiment of recording this kind of seasoned performance has worked out well.

It has worked out very well. Throughout this recording is a feeling of live theater. Although none of the principals is ideal in his role, all three breathe life and vitality into their characterizations, and together they create a genuine ensemble interaction. What Pilar Lorengar lacks in easy vocal production and voluptuous sound, she makes up for in warmth and compassion. Aragall, a tenor who sang several times at New York's Metropolitan Opera last season, gives a finely shaded interpretation of a shallow, one-dimensional figure. And Fischer-Dieskau, without hamming up the unsympathetic role of the elder Germont, transforms him from a cardboard facsimile of a protective father into a believable and even rather admirable aristocratic gentleman.

But the real hero is Maazel, the conductor. Often, in the past, he has been guilty of ice-cold, if meticulous, performances; here he is all fire and passion, matching the drama and heartbreak of Verdi's score. Despite the extremely fast tempi in some places, one reaches the end deeply moved.

London's engineers use stereo and stage effects most judiciously, achieving superb sound. Here, in short, is one of the most successful of recent operatic recordings.

Comment

Of the many recordings of *La Traviata* currently available, the performance conducted by Carlos Kleiber (Deutsche Grammophon 2707103), with Ileana Cotrubas, Placido Domingo, and Sherrill Milnes—all at the top of their form—stands out as an emotional and dramatic experience, surpassing even the exceedingly fine Maazel effort. ∎

VILLA-LOBOS: Forest of the Amazon. Bidú Sayão, soprano; The Symphony of the Air and chorus conducted by Heitor Villa-Lobos. United Artists 5506, $5.98.

Very few movie scores are worth the celluloid they are printed on. But here is one that can be taken seriously. Villa-Lobos wrote it for the film version of *Green Mansions*, and it is an exotic, typically imaginative piece of writing. A few sections, true, are conventional, with the chorus wailing in the background (though even here the writing is miles above the routine Hollywood effort). But there also are strokes of genius. And when Bidú Sayão, who used to be one of the Metropolitan Opera's most admired sopranos, starts singing (toward the end of side one and well into side two) the music is beautiful. Villa-Lobos has adapted Brazilian folk tunes for her, and the melodies are haunting. United Artists has provided a massive quality of sound in the stereo version. As in many orchestral discs these days, a slight treble reduction is needed to bring the strings into line; otherwise they will sound edgy. But even at best, the loud sections sound fuzzy. Otherwise the sound is good.

Comment

This disc has considerable documentary interest: Villa-Lobos died shortly after the recording was made in 1959. In recent years his music has suffered something of an eclipse. This is a pity, for he was a true primitive in music, who composed gorgeously exotic and colorful scores no matter what medium he worked in. *Forest of the Amazon* is voluptuous, sensual, and typical of Villa-Lobos at his most seductive. ∎

VIVALDI: Concertos for Two, Three and Four Violins with Orchestra. Pinchas Zukerman, Kenneth Sillito, José-Luis Garcia and John Tunnell, violins, with the English Chamber Orchestra conducted by Pinchas Zukerman. Columbia M32230, $5.98. ●

Not all of Vivaldi's many concertos for diverse solo instruments are of high quality. But Zukerman has chosen wisely, and the four works here recorded sustain interest throughout. The best, perhaps, is the *A minor Concerto for Two Violins*. At one time there was a famous monophonic recording of this concerto on the Columbia label with David Oistrakh and Isaac Stern as soloists. Here, Zukerman and Sillito yield nothing to their more celebrated colleagues in virtuosity, and their playing is even more stylish.

Not only does Zukerman play in all four works contained on the disc, but he also conducts them all as well, securing from the members of the English Chamber Orchestra performances of crisp and rhythmic vitality. And the recorded sound is immaculately clear.

(continued)

Comment

This program has become rather a specialty with Zukerman, the violinist and conductor, with orchestras around the world. These recorded performances have a spontaneous vitality and enthusiasm that are irresistible. ■

August 1978

VIVALDI: The Four Seasons. Simon Standage, violin, with the English Concert under the direction of Trevor Pinnock. CRD Records Limited 1025, $7.98.

I once described *The Four Seasons* as the *Scheherazade* of the Baroque period—Vivaldi's imagery and vivid tone painting have made it the best-known creation of the Italian music of that era. Since performances and recordings of the work abound, any new effort should have something special going for it, as this one does.

The English Concert, a group of players formed in 1973, performs the music of the seventeenth and eighteenth centuries on period instruments or on good modern copies of them. By virtue of its impact in London music circles, the group recently earned the title of "baroque ensemble of the Victoria and Albert Museum."

Simon Standage, the solo violinist, plays an instrument with a smaller, sweeter tone than reigning virtuosos have accustomed us to, but without scaling down his performance. On the contrary, his manner, which his colleagues share, is vigorous, extroverted, and quite winning overall. The recorded sound is a model of clarity. Though more than two dozen recordings of this work are available, the English Concert's is one of the best.

Comment

Other commendable recordings of this work include the budget-price versions of the Italian Chamber Orchestra (RCA VICS1469) and the Toulouse Chamber Orchestra (Seraphim S60144) and the full-price versions by Itzhak Perlman (Angel S37053) and Pinchas Zukerman (Columbia M31798). In each of the latter two performances, the solo violinist doubles as conductor. ■

March 1973

WAGNER: American Centennial March; Huldigungsmarsch; Kaisermarsch; Overtures to Die Feen and Das Liebesverbot. The London Symphony Orchestra conducted by Marek Janowski. Angel S36879, $5.98.

The three marches and two overtures contained here are among the most obscure of all Wagner's orchestral works. *Die Feen* and *Das Liebesverbot* were his first two operas, finished in 1834 and 1836. The overtures give only slight indication of the dramatic titan to come, but they are nevertheless finely wrought examples of early 19th-century Romanticism. The overture to *Die Feen* has the elfin charm of Weber, while that to *Das Liebesverbot* has Offenbach's rollicking exuberance.

The three marches are products of Wagner's later life—and they are all potboilers, with few if any redeeming qualities. The most outlandish of the three is the *American Centennial March*, composed on commission for the 100th anniversary of the American Revolution, held in Philadelphia in 1876. For his shoddy collection of bombast and clichés Wagner received the then-princely sum of $5000; he himself is supposed to have said that the best thing about the march was the money. Let us hope that the forthcoming bicentennial of American Independence will not let loose a revival of this awful march.

Comment

Happily, we were spared a revival of Wagner's dreadful *American Centennial March* during the Bicentennial celebrations. Trying as the three marches on this disc may be, there is still a morbid fascination in having them available for repeated listening. And the two overtures, although stylistically immature, are nevertheless rewarding in their own right.   ■

September 1959

WAGNER: Das Rheingold. Kirsten Flagstad, soprano (Fricka); George London, bass-baritone (Wotan); Set Svanholm, tenor (Loge); Gustav Neidlinger, bass-baritone (Alberich); Kurt Böhme, bass (Fafner); Paul Kuen, tenor (Mime); Eberhard Wächter, baritone (Donner). Vienna Philharmonic Orchestra conducted by Georg Solti. London 1309, 3 discs, $17.94. ●

Though some years ago a pirated, and not very good, *Rheingold* made the rounds, it can be said with some truth that the current *Rheingold* from London is the first recorded version in history from a major company. It is a marvelous job. There are a few weaknesses, however. George London, with all his musical intelligence, is not in the great tradition of Wagner singers, and he sometimes forces his voice into an unpleasant wobble. Otherwise the cast is excellent. Flagstad, here singing a mezzo role, remains incredibly rich-voiced and secure; the giants and dwarfs are entirely convincing; and in Eberhard Wächter, who sings the role of Donner, London has come up with a potentially great singer. The stereo recording is extremely exciting. At the very beginning one gets a spatial illusion with the three Rhine maidens: Woglinde heard as if from the upper right; Wellgunde at the left; Flosshilde now in the middle, now at the side. Later, as Wotan and Loge descend into Nibelheim, the tinkling of anvils (purists may object because this sound is heard close up and is much louder than is ever heard in the opera house) supplies the atmosphere. And one of the sensational moments comes near the end, where Donner's hammer falling on the rock caps the climax of one

(continued)

of the most exciting sequences ever captured on records. The opera itself is the least-played of Wagner's *Ring* cycle, but that does not necessarily mean it is inferior. Many listeners will find themselves returning to it with admiration and respect. It is a supreme score, and this recording does it justice.

September 1963

WAGNER: Siegfried. Wolfgang Windgassen, tenor (Siegfried); Birgit Nilsson, soprano (Brünnhilde); Hans Hotter, baritone (The Wanderer); Gerhard Stolze, tenor (Mime); Gustav Neidlinger, bass (Alberich); Kurt Böhme, bass (Fafner); Marga Höffgen, contralto (Erda); Joan Sutherland, soprano (Forest Bird). The Vienna Philharmonic Orchestra conducted by Georg Solti. London 1508, 5 discs, $29.90. ●

Music lovers have had to wait a long while for this album—since the invention of the phonograph. For this is the first time that Wagner's *Siegfried* has ever been commercially recorded. London Records has previously given us a stereo *Das Rheingold*, and not long ago RCA came out with a *Die Walküre*. The only complete *Götterdämmerung*, though, was released by London in prestereo days. But now those who feel inclined have access to all four operas of the *Ring des Nibelungen*. As far as the new and welcome *Siegfried* goes, it is idle to bewail the fact that there are not as many great Wagner singers as there used to be. We have to make do with what we have; and if Windgassen cannot summon the trumpetlike tones of a Melchior, he nevertheless is the finest and most experienced. Heldentenor currently in action. And Nilsson, of course, is the greatest living Brünnhilde. Perhaps a richer-voiced singer than Hotter might have been found for the role of The Wanderer, but no singer can surpass Hotter in style, feeling, and dignity. The other singers are excellent, and Solti does a brilliant job with the orchestra. Especially impressive is his subtle and unfaltering rhythm. Thus, this long-awaited recording turns out to be a most impressive one. It has received good sound, too. The stereo is handled very "operatically": it conveys a feeling of movement. Thus, for instance, during the "Forging Song" (side three), Mime can be heard to dart anxiously around Siegfried, now right, now left. The stereo is full of this kind of detail, and it is all legitimate.

January 1966

WAGNER: Götterdämmerung. Birgit Nilsson, soprano (Brünnhilde); Wolfgang Windgassen, tenor (Siegfried); Gustav Niedlinger, bass (Alberich); Gottlob Frick, bass (Hagen); Claire Watson, soprano (Gutrune); Dietrich Fischer-Dieskau, baritone (Gunther). Vienna Philharmonic Orchestra and State Opera Chorus under Georg Solti. London 1604, 6 discs, $35.88. ●

A great opera, a great performance, a great recording. Everything comes together in these six discs, an uncut version of the final opera of Wagner's *Ring des Nibelungen* cycle, and the first in stereo. The cast is the best available today, and, with one exception, it can rival any of the outstanding Wagner casts of the 1930s. The exception is Wolfgang Windgassen, who is as good as anybody around, but who nevertheless lacks the trumpetlike brilliance of a Melchior. Nilsson is in fine voice and sings the "Immolation" scene incandescently. And special honors go to Frick for a powerful black-voiced Hagen. The hero of the album, though, might well be Solti, whose conducting is flexible, rhythmically pliable, shattering (emotionally, not sonically) in the climaxes, and full of personality and character. As for the recorded sound, it illustrates John Culshaw's philosophy of opera on discs. Culshaw, the recording director, believes that records should take advantage of magnetic tape, even if their doing so leads to effects not achievable in the opera house. Thus, in the confrontation scene with Brünnhilde on the rock, he has actually changed (electronically) Windgassen's voice, making it sound like Fischer-Dieskau's. Alberich's voice fades away in an eerie manner after he leaves the sleeping Hagen. And the strange noises heard about a third of the way in on side seven, which sound as if they come from the foghorn of an ocean liner, are made by steerhorns, scored by Wagner but not used in modern times (trombones are substituted). The recorded sound has exceptional life, presence, and color. One instance of well-used stereo occurs at the end of side four, where the voices of the Rhine Maidens dart from speaker to speaker. Too bad that some surface noise mars the recording (the end of the aforementioned side four, for example). Otherwise, this is a spectacular set, one that will be the standard for many years to come.

March 1967

WAGNER: Die Walküre. Birgit Nilsson, soprano (Brünnhilde); Régine Crespin, soprano (Sieglinde); James King, tenor (Siegmund); Gottlob Frick, bass (Hunding); Hans Hotter, baritone (Wotan); Christa Ludwig, mezzo-soprano (Fricka). Vienna Philharmonic Orchestra conducted by Georg Solti. London 1509, 5 discs, $29.90. ●

It was in 1959 that London Records started its monumental cycle of the four operas that form Wagner's *Ring des Nilbelungen*. That year came *Das Rheingold*. It was followed by *Siegfried*, then *Götterdämmerung*. Now we have *Die Walküre* (the second opera of the tetralogy). From the beginning, the aim was to bring together the finest available casts, to present the long operas uncut, to bring to bear the most modern recording techniques. In short, this was to be a *Ring* cycle for the ages. And that is how it has turned out. The new *Walküre* is typical. No finer group of singers could have been brought together; and if anybody complains that James King is no Melchior, or that Hans Hotter is no Friedrich Schorr, the fact remains that nobody today is apt to equal King and Hotter in their respective roles. Nilsson, of course, can hold her own with any Wagnerian soprano of the century. Ludwig is an appropriately hard-voiced, shrewish Fricka, Crespin is an appealing Sieglinde (some hard, driven notes in the upper register notwithstanding), and Frick is the biggest-sounding, blackest-voiced Hunding in action today. In Georg Solti the album has a Wagner conductor of force, imagination, and color. He ranks with the great ones—with Furtwängler, Walter, or any of the other giants. As in the previous albums of the cycle, the recording director is
(continued)

John Culshaw, who believes in taking full advantage of the medium of contemporary tape recording. Some critics have been complaining that he uses too many gimmicks. To most listeners, however, the stereo effects used throughout the four operas add to the illusion of a stage presentation. In *Die Walküre*, Siegmund makes his entrance from outside Hunding's house. Why shouldn't his voice get stronger as he approaches? When Wotan summons Loge, it is with a tremendous, authoritative rap of steel against steel; and why not? Wotan is a god. The recorded sound has exceptional depth and presence. This album of *Die Walküre*, like its predecessors in the *Ring* cycle, is a triumph, and the complete cycle should provide a lifetime of listening pleasure.

Comment

The supremacy of Solti's *Ring* cycle has only been confirmed by DG's later release of its own *Ring* cycle with Karajan conducting. Karajan's *Ring* is, for the most part, fussy and self-conscious when compared with the titanic power and overwhelming passion of Solti's. And the London recording engineers have far outshone their German colleagues in imagination and breadth of sound reproduction. There is no question about it; Solti's (and John Culshaw's) *Ring* is one of the great achievements in the history of recording art.

There are interesting things in the only other available stereo release of the *Ring* operas—the Böhm-conducted performances deriving from Bayreuth Festival productions in 1966 and 1967 (Philips 6747037, sixteen discs)—but the Solti fire and drama remain unsurpassed. Notable for its lofty and mystical insights is the monophonic recording based on performances for the Italian radio conducted by Wilhelm Furtwängler (Seraphim 6100, nineteen discs). Although the frequency and dynamic range of the sound are greatly restricted, the overall conception may sweep aside other considerations. The recording of 1950 Furtwängler performances at La Scala, to be found on various labels, suffers from sound reproduction that is almost unbearably primitive. ■

November 1977

STOKOWSKI CONDUCTS WAGNER. Rienzi: Overture; Die Walküre: Magic Fire Music; Die Meistersinger: Prelude to Act III, Dance of the Apprentices, and Entrance of the Mastersingers; Tristan and Isolde: Prelude and Love-Death. The Royal Philharmonic Orchestra conducted by Leopold Stokowski. RCA ARL10498, $7.98. ▲ ●

This release has been held up for a couple of years at least, and Stokowski's last recordings were made for Columbia. This RCA recording is uneven and even infuriating in one instance, of which more later. But at its best the disc features playing of awesome power and beauty, as with the Magic Fire Music from *Die Walküre*, which builds to a climax of shattering intensity. That Stokowski in his 90's was able to get such power and brilliance from the Royal Philharmonic Orchestra—especially from the brass section—borders on the unbelievable. And what commitment there is in the playing! One can imagine the musicians in the orchestra on the edges of their seats, mesmerized by the wizard on the rostrum before them. RCA's engineers have captured the dynamism of the Fire Music in sound that fairly leaps from the record grooves.

The disc starts with an account of the Overture to Wagner's early opera, *Rienzi*, which is much less convincing. The tempo comes in for a good deal of pulling around, and the orchestral ensemble is itself less riveting than in the excerpt from *Die Walküre*.

The familiar orchestral Suite from Act III of *Die Meistersinger* goes along well, with decent playing, good sound, and no surprises. So, too, until the very end, does the music from *Tristan and Isolde*, a sensuous, erotic score tailor-made for Stokowski's temperament; but then Stokowski replaced the last chord Wagner wrote with a spineless, diaphanous string chord that completely changes the character of the music. When this disc is good, it's very, very good, and when it is bad, it's horrid.

Comment

But that Magic Fire Music must be heard to be belived!　　　　■

May 1962

WAGNER: Tannhäuser. Hans Hopf, tenor (Tannhäuser); Marianne Schech, soprano (Venus); Elisabeth Grümmer, soprano (Elisabeth); Gottlob Frick, bass (Landgrave); Dietrich Fischer-Dieskau, baritone (Wolfram); Lisa Otto, soprano (Shepherd); Fritz Wunderlich, tenor (Walther); Gerhard Unger, tenor (Heinrich), and others with Chorus and Orchestra of the German State Opera, Berlin, conducted by Franz Konwitschny. Angel S3620, 4 discs, $23.92.

The redeeming feature of this recording is the way in which Franz Konwitschny conducts his human materials toward a generally satisfying performance. He reveals the sacred and profane aspects of Wagner's music with transparency and great feeling; soloists, chorus, and orchestra are always responsive to his will. Elisabeth Grümmer is a warm, moving, radiant Elisabeth. Her voice is secure, her feeling for word values always expresses the required emotion. Fischer-Dieskau as Wolfram adapts all the sensitivity and vocal beauty of his Lieder singing to opera; a more touching, noble characterization of Wolfram is difficult to imagine. Gottlob Frick and Lisa Otto are both first-rate. Unfortunately, Hans Hopf in the title role exhibits one of the two notable weaknesses in this performance. His voice sounds worn and lackluster; it is frequently pushed to the point of unpleasantness. Neither in the first-act duet with Venus nor in "The Contest of Song," and only briefly toward the end of the "Rome Narrative," does he sound convincing. Hopf simply cannot, as does Fischer-Dieskau, make his voice convey different emotional situations. The other drawback is Marianne Schech as Venus. The soprano is slightly wobbly in the middle register, although she is capable of some stunning high tones. Both she and Hopf are rather pedes-
(continued)

trian in the near-eroticism of the first-act pages. Minor roles, save for Lisa Otto's shepherd, are handled competently, no more. This is far from an ideal overall performance of *Tannhäuser*, although it is still the best available on discs to date.

Comment

Of the several complete *Tannhäuser* recordings issued after this set, London's Solti-conducted album (1438), full of power and passion, undoubtedly sweeps the field. ∎

September 1970

WAGNER: Tannhäuser: Overture and Venusberg Music; STRAUSS: Der Rosenkavalier: Suite. London Symphony Orchestra conducted by Erich Leinsdorf. London 21037, $5.98.

In this, his first recording since stepping down as music director of the Boston Symphony Orchestra, Leinsdorf is considerably more animated and vital than he was during his final seasons in Boston. There is a most attractive freedom about these performances, including a degree of spontaneity in his London players that was notably absent from his Boston music-making. Though there is no indication of the fact anywhere, either on the label or the record jacket, a female chorus makes the called-for interpolations in the *Tannhäuser Venusberg Music*. The reproduction is vivid, in the somewhat exaggerated manner of London's Phase 4 series. But no matter—this music can take it.

Comment

Nearly every other available recording of the *Overture and Venusberg Music* from *Tannhäuser* presents it in combination with other Wagner material. This disc, then, has a special claim on the attention of those in search of a more varied musical program. ∎

March 1977

WALDTEUFEL: Assorted Waltzes, Polkas and Galops. The Monte Carlo Opera Orchestra under the direction of Willi Boskovsky. Angel S37208, $6.98.

Charles Emil Waldteufel has been called "the Johann Strauss of Paris." The comparison is appropriate, for Waldteufel, who was born in Strasbourg in 1837 and died in Paris in 1915, captured the flavor and the feeling of the 19th-century French Imperial Court just as Strauss captured that of the Austrian Court. In this respect, Waldteufel even outdid Offenbach. This disc includes such familiar works as the three *Waltzes* ("España," "Estudiantina," and "The Skaters"), along with such comparatively unknown compositions as the three *Polkas* ("Minuit," "Bella Bocca," and "L'Esprit français").

Willi Boskovsky does as honorably by Waldteufel here as he has by Strauss—of whom he is surely the reigning champion. These performances have a lilt and lift that are quite irresistible, and they are beautifully enshrined in a vibrant recording. The Monte Carlo Opera Orchestra may not be one of today's virtuoso ensembles, but it rises splendidly to the occasion, showing fine spirit and great enthusiasm. This disc is, all in all, a real delight.

Comment

Strangely, there is only one other currently available collection of Waldteufel works (London CS6899). The music is uniformly bright and invigorating. And just in case you think the only Waldteufel waltz you know is "The Skaters," wait until you hear the "Estudiantina." (You will recognize it immediately as the music that was appropriated for a familiar beer commercial on radio and television.) ∎

June 1973

WALTON: Belshazzar's Feast; Improvisations on an Impromptu of Benjamin Britten. John Shirley-Quirk, baritone, with the London Symphony Orchestra and Chorus conducted by André Previn. Angel S36861, $5.98.

Combined on this disc are Sir William Walton's most recent large-scale orchestral work, *Improvisations*, and his still enormously exciting oratorio of 40 years earlier, *Belshazzar's Feast*. The *Improvisations*, dating from 1970, are a series of variations from the slow movement of Britten's piano concerto. *Belshazzar's Feast* deals with the Biblical stories of the Jewish exile in Babylonia, the handwriting on the wall that foretells the defeat of Belshazzar, the King of Babylon, and the final rejoicing of the liberated Israelites.

Starting softly and mysteriously, the *Improvisations* introduce contrasting episodes that reveal Walton's compositional craft, undiminished by age and illness. It may not be one of the masterpieces of our age, but it is a totally professional score that will continue to pay pleasure on repeated listening.

Belshazzar's Feast, on the other hand, *is* a landmark work. In it, the young Walton reinforced the strong claims to international celebrity he had established some years earlier with his music for the Sitwell entertainment, *Façade*. *Belshazzar's Feast* remains an exhilarating and dynamic score, full of extraordinary instrumental and vocal color. The present recording derives from concert presentations given in London last year in celebration of Walton's seventieth birthday. The drama of the occasion has been preserved in the vitality of both the performance and the recording. Listeners with long memories will be disappointed in the bland characterization of baritone John Shirley-Quirk, if they compare it with Dennis Noble's ringing performance in a composer-conducted recording of the score dating from the early 1940's. But otherwise, all the elements come together to produce a memorable ac-
(continued)

count of one of the glories of twentieth-century music.

Comment

In the early days of stereo, Walton made another recording of *Belshazzar's Feast* (Angel S35681) with the Philharmonia Orchestra and Chorus; it has more of the fiery intensity inherent in the music than Previn summons in his otherwise excellent account. But Previn's performance is preferable to the more recent recording conducted by Solti (London OSA26525), which is surprisingly bland. ∎

June 1961

WALTON: Concerto for Violin and Orchestra; LALO: Symphonie espagnole for Violin and Orchestra. Zino Francescatti and the Philadelphia Orchestra conducted by Eugene Ormandy (in the Walton); New York Philharmonic conducted by Dimitri Mitropoulos (in the Lalo). Columbia MS6201, $5.98.

This disc contains the only available recording of the Walton *Violin Concerto*. Sir William Walton is a contemporary British composer who writes in a conservative, Romantic tradition. His *Violin Concerto* is tuneful, glittering, and long-phrased—a virtuoso's delight. Francescatti is exactly the kind of virtuoso to approach it. He has all the technique in the world, a rich tone, and a good deal of musical elegance. He also does a brilliant job with the familiar Lalo work. As customary, he omits the Intermezzo movement. This is a clear and well-defined recording, with honors going to its greater color and smoothness.

September 1974

WALTON: Violin Concerto; STRAVINSKY: Violin Concerto in D. Kyung-Wha Chung, violin, with the London Symphony Orchestra conducted by André Previn. London CS6819, $5.98.

These two violin concertos frame the decade of the 1930s: Stravinsky's was composed in 1931, Walton's in 1939. It would be hard to imagine two more dissimilar scores. Walton's is rich and glowing, in his most Romantic vein; Stravinsky's belongs to his neoclassic period and is more rigid in structure and expression. Both works are among the finest musical products of the 20th century, and both are firmly entrenched in the literature for violin and orchestra.

The extraordinary Korean-born violinist, Kyung-Wha Chung, plays the two scores superbly. The lyrical graces of the Walton concerto soar magnificently in her performance, and she expresses the disciplined severities of the Stravinsky with equal sensitivity. Both concertos have been recorded many times, but these new performances rank with the very best—

particularly since Previn and the London Symphony Orchestra provide impeccable support.

WALTON: Concerto for Viola and Orchestra; HINDEMITH: Der Schwanendreher for Viola and Small Orchestra. Paul Doktor, viola, with the London Philharmonic Orchestra conducted by Edward Downes. Odyssey 32160368, $2.98.

The viola, that larger, deeper-voiced cousin of the violin, has nearly always been an instrumental stepchild. Almost every viola player begins his musical life as a violinist, switching to the viola usually because of ensemble requirements at school or in chamber music. The result has been a dearth of literature for solo viola. Thus, many composers in recent years have made a conscious effort to add to the viola repertoire, and the two works on this disc are among the most successful contemporary scores for viola.

The Walton concerto is now forty years old, but it was a milestone in the composer's career, signaling as it did his inclination toward the Romantic idiom. The work has been recorded several times before, but never in this edition as revised by Walton in 1961. The principal change is the addition of a prominent harp part, which adds to the rhapsodic and improvisational quality of the music.

Hindemith's score makes use of several early German folk songs, including the one in the last movement that gives the work its overall title. This, too, is a first-rate work for viola, exploiting its unique color and timbre to maximum effect.

One does think of performances more dynamic than Doktor's—performances such as those recorded by William Primrose nearly twenty years ago. But in their neat and smaller-scaled framework, Doktor's performances are perfectly acceptable. Orchestral support and sound reproduction are both fine.

Comment

A second recording of the 1961 revision of the Viola Concerto is now available (Angel S36719), and it has the advantage of being conducted by Walton himself. The soloist is Yehudi Menuhin; although he is what amounts to a "Sunday violist"—the violin, of course, being his principal instrument—he nevertheless gives the music a far stronger profile than does Doktor. The other side of that recording is a Menuhin performance of Walton's Violin Concerto—with the composer conducting. The combination of these two artistic personalities produces a virile and elegant account of the score—one a mite more interesting than the Francescatti-Ormandy collaboration. Neither in concert nor in recording is it any longer customary to omit the Intermezzo movement from the Lalo Symphonie espagnole. Among performances that present the entire five-movement score, the Perlman-Previn collaboration (RCA AGL11329) is a fine mixture of virtuoso fireworks and poetic sensitivity. The Francescatti disc now carries Columbia's low-price Odyssey label (Y33229).

Kyung-Wha Chung is still a selective performer where recorded efforts are
(continued)

concerned. She generally restricts her recordings to music with which she has lived and matured—music she feels ready to commit to a "permanent" recording. The result is that almost all of her recorded performances offer a very special kind of musical pleasure. This disc is certainly one of her best, imbued with experience yet full of spontaneity and passion. ∎

September 1972

WALTON: Façade—An Entertainment. The London Sinfonietta conducted by Sir William Walton, with Peggy Ashcroft and Paul Scofield, speakers. Argo ZRG649, $5.98.

In 1923 *Façade*, a stage entertainment of poems by Edith Sitwell set to music by the 19-year-old British composer William Walton received its world premiere in London. The work became an instant sensation. Between then and 1942, Sitwell and Walton added some new pieces and subtracted others; the final version consists of an opening Fanfare followed by 21 Sitwell poems set to Walton's music. The poems themselves are musical conceptions, with definite rhythmic patterns and melodic rises and falls. Walton's music extends their imagery and color, so that the result is an extraordinary unity of words and music. Dame Edith herself once described the *Façade* poems in these words: "My experiments in *Façade* are in the nature of an enquiry into the effect on rhythm, and on speech, of the use of rhymes, assonances and dissonances, placed outwardly and inwardly (at different places in the line) and in most elaborate patterns."

This new recording of Sir William Walton's most popular score was made as part of the 1972 celebration of his 70th birthday. There has been particular interest in the Argo version since it is the first time that Walton himself has recorded *Façade*. Alas, it is a disappointment. The Angel release conducted by Neville Marriner is much better than the composer's own. Marriner conducts a spikier, more incisive performance, and Marriner's musicians are more uninhibited than those conducted by Walton. More important is the superiority in the delivery of the poems. Ashcroft and Scofield may be more renowned than Fielding and Flanders, but the latter much better communicate the kaleidoscopic nature of the poems, from their mercurial patter to their languorous sensuality. Too, the assignment of the poems to the male and female voices is more convincing in the Angel release than in the Argo. In sum, the Angel disc far outclasses the Walton version in every department.

Any readers who have not yet heard this classic 20th-century creation are due for a very special treat.

Comment

Wouldn't you know it? With the perversity that may be peculiar to the record industry, the far superior Marriner-Fielding-Flanders recording of *Façade* has been withdrawn from circulation! Columbia has a disc of *Façade* (M33980) played by an instrumental ensemble conducted by Arthur Fiedler, but Tony

Randall gives a less satisfactory reading of the Sitwell poems. ■

September 1973

WIENIAWSKI: Violin Concertos No. 1, in F sharp minor, and No. 2, in D minor. Itzhak Perlman, violin, with the London Philharmonic Orchestra conducted by Seiji Ozawa. Angel S36903, $5.98.

Wieniawski's *Second Violin Concerto* is a staple of the literature for violin and orchestra. The entire work soars on a very high level of inspiration, with a profusion of inventive musical ideas and materials, particularly in the Romance middle movement, which is one of the most graceful and lyrical works ever written for the violin. The *First Concerto*, on the other hand, is a comparative stranger to the concert hall. This is a pity, for though it is less distinguished than the *Second Concerto*, it is still a beautiful vehicle for the solo instrument; its last movement, particularly, is vivacious and contagious, requiring all manner of virtuoso fireworks of the soloist.

Perlman is particularly well equipped to supply all the necessary feats of technique and gymnastics. And he has the temperament to go with this Romantic music. Ozawa completes this most welcome issue by providing a perfect orchestral framework, with marvelously alert playing by the London Philharmonic.

Comment

Surprisingly, this is still the only release that includes both Wieniawski concertos. The excellence of the Perlman disc may intimidate other violinists and record companies. If so, the intimidation is justifiable. ■

September 1969

WOLPE: Chamber Piece No. 1; ROCHBERG: Serenata d'estate; SHIFRIN: Satires of Circumstance. The Contemporary Chamber Ensemble conducted by Arthur Weisberg, with Jan DeGaetani, mezzo-soprano (in the Shifrin). Nonesuch 71220, $2.98.

This is one of three Nonesuch releases recorded under a grant from the Martha Baird Rockefeller Fund for Music, Inc. All three discs offer performances by the Contemporary Chamber Ensemble, a superb group formed by bassoonist Arthur Weisberg expressly to perform the most difficult contemporary ensemble music. Since 1965, under grant from the Rockefeller Foundation, the group has been in residence at Rutgers University in New Brunswick, N.J.

The three works included here are pretty tough going, especially the Wolpe and the Shifrin. Both were composed in 1964, and both are excellent examples of the compositional techniques of the 1960s: Sounds and sound patterns are used as ends unto themselves, form is practically nonexistent,

(continued)

horizontal lines include leaps of wide intervals, and silences can be just as important as sounds. In the hands of untalented composers, those techniques can result in chaos. But repeated listenings to the Wolpe and Shifrin works disclose sustained and highly emotional moods. Full of restlessness, urgency, and panic, the pieces are upsetting—precisely, one is convinced, the effect the composers sought.

The Rochberg work, a product of an earlier time (1955), is less complicated, even though its vocabulary derives from the twelve-tone system of Schoenberg. The music has a definite ebb and flow and is structured along fairly traditional lines.

All three performances are expert. In the Shifrin settings of Thomas Hardy poems, Jan DeGaetani negotiates her extremely difficult music smoothly. However, one could wish for clearer enunciation, especially since Nonesuch has not given the texts in the liner notes. The sound throughout is extremely clear and evenly balanced.

Comment

The three composers represented here are among the most important of their contemporaries. Each has also been active as a teacher of composition, Wolpe (until his death in 1972) privately, Rochberg at the University of Pennsylvania, and Shifrin at Brandeis University. Thus, their influence on new generations of composers has been great. These are among their finest works, and they repay repeated listening. ∎

COLLECTIONS

THE ART OF JUSSI BJOERLING. Songs and Oratorio and Opera Arias recorded between 1930 and 1952. Jussi Bjoerling, tenor, with miscellaneous piano and orchestral accompaniment. Seraphim 60168, $2.98.

Until his death in 1960, at the age of forty-nine, Jussi Bjoerling was one of the world's greatest singing talents, possessing both a superbly lyrical tenor voice and rare musical intelligence. He made his Metropolitan Opera debut in 1938, spent the war years in Sweden, then returned to America's premiere opera house. Those who remember such radio programs as *The Voice of Firestone* and *The Telephone Hour* may recall that Bjoerling was as much at ease with songs, ballads, and oratorio arias as he was with opera itself.

The selections on this disc contain some of Bjoerling's most memorable performances, recorded over a period of twenty-two years. They all predate stereo recording, of course, but their reissue should be of prime interest to lovers of great singing. It's certainly justification enough for us to waive our rule of reviewing only stereo releases.

Included on the disc are such classic Bjoerling performances as Beethoven's *Adelaid*, Strauss' *Cäcilie* and *Morgen*, the Berceuse from Godard's *Jocelyn*, the Cuius Animam from Rossini's *Stabat Mater*, and Ingemisco from Verdi's *Requiem*. To them—and to the other songs and arias—Bjoerling brings his supreme vocal and musical gifts so that each is a gem of recreative art. The transfers from the original recordings (78 rpm for the most part) have been excellently accomplished, and a brochure containing the words to all the songs is included with the disc. Here, in short, is a treasurable release.

Comment

Other souvenirs of Bjoerling's art are to be found on the following monophonic discs: *Bjoerling in Opera* (RCA LM2269), *Bjoerling in Concert* (RCA LM2784), *Bjoerling Sings at Carnegie Hall* (RCA LM2003), and *The Art of Jussi Bjoerling, Volume 2* (Seraphim 60219). ∎

THE ART OF THE PRIMA DONNA: Joan Sutherland, soprano, with Orchestra and Chorus of the Royal Opera House, Covent Garden, conducted by Francesco Molinari-Pradelli. London 1214, 2 discs, $11.96. ●

Chances are that you have been hearing wonderful things about this album; and everything that you have been hearing is true. Sutherland here makes most sopranos sound like amateurs. She has an extraordinary vocal tech-
(continued)

nique, and—even more unusual—a large-size voice to go with it. Most coloratura sopranos are small-voiced, but Sutherland has enough strength to encompass roles like Norma (dramatic soprano) as well as Gilda (coloratura) and Violetta (lyric). The somewhat gimmicky idea behind this release was to have Sutherland sing arias associated with great coloraturas of the past. There is nothing gimmicky, however, in the magnificent manner she sweeps through things like Handel's *"Let the Bright Seraphim"* (*Samson*), Bellini's *"Casta Diva"* (*Norma*), Rossini's *"Bel Raggio"* (*Semiramide*), the Jewel Song from *Faust*, the Bell Song from *Lakmé*, *"Caro Nome"* from *Rigoletto*, and others. In all, she sings seventeen arias. Her work is a sheer technical lexicon: expertly turned trills, arpeggios, running scales, clear registers (up to E above C without apparent strain), and legato phrasing. But all is not only technical derring-do. Sutherland sings this elaborate material with taste and refinement, subordinating bravura to musical values. This remarkable album is one of the most thrilling of the decade, and a real throwback to the so-called Golden Age. It also is good to report that she has received clear and undistorted recorded sound.

Comment

This two-disc album, recorded in 1960, came early in Joan Sutherland's international career. It is still a most impressive document of her strengths and continues to be a rich and rewarding listening experience. ■

May 1962

MARIA CALLAS SINGS GREAT ARIAS FROM FRENCH OPERAS with Orchestre de la RTF conducted by Georges Prêtre. Angel S35882, $5.98. ▲ ●

In a musically satisfying program of material not hitherto associated with her, Maria Callas proves she still is one of the supreme operatic interpreters of our time. Few singers of today could equal her in executing so varied an assemblage of great arias, from the classic, dramatic lines of Gluck's *Orpheus* or *Alceste* to the seductiveness of *Carmen*; from the contralto tones of *Delilah* to the coloratura prettiness of Titania in Thomas' *Mignon* or of Juliet in Gounod's opera. Vocal flaws there are, and the Callas top notes can still attack the ears unmercifully. The coloratura arias are models of interpretation but not of voice control. The Gluck, Bizet, and Saint-Saëns arias come off best. Splendid accompaniment enhances this recorded exhibition of style, musical understanding, and artistic insight. The stereo gives a spacious sound.

Comment

This recording, one of the last Callas made, is of great documentary importance as one of her best—particularly because she performs a repertoire outside the one considered to be her specialty. ■

May 1963

CANTOS DE ESPAÑA. Victoria de los Angeles, soprano, and Paris Conservatoire Orchestra conducted by Rafael Frühbeck de Burgos. Angel S35937, $5.98.

In her last few releases, De los Angeles has been busy with Spanish material. The contents of the present disc are as follows: Falla, two arias from *La Vida Bréve;* Granados, two *Canciones Amatorias;* Rodrigo, four *Madrigales Amatorios;* Espla, five *Canciones Playeras Españolas;* Montsalvatge, five *Canciones Negras.* All of the music is attractive, and the Montsalvatge unusually so. What comes to mind on hearing the *Canciones Negras* are the Canteloube arrangements of Auvergne songs. There is much the same sophistication, much the same evocative orchestration (though the music itself is, in both cases, of course, entirely different). Nobody alive sings this kind of material better than De los Angeles. The disc is a jewel.

Comment

There was a time during the 1960s and 1970s when De los Angeles had, for practical purposes, retired from the stage. In recent years she has again become active as a singer and recording artist. This disc, from a particularly rich period in her artistic life, is still a gem. ∎

July 1977

DANSE INFERNALE. Music by Mussorgsky, Saint-Saëns, Khachaturian, Dukas, Stravinsky, and Ginastera. The Boston Pops Orchestra under the direction of Arthur Fiedler. Deutsche Grammophon 2584004, $7.98.

This disc groups six examples of brilliant music that deal with exciting and sometimes diabolical doings. All six enjoy the ultimate in performance and recording virtuosity, which are worthy of a "demonstration" record. The album's title refers to the Infernal Dance from Stravinsky's *Firebird* ballet, played and recorded so excitingly that one longs to hear Fiedler and his musicians perform the complete score.

Other material includes Mussorgsky's *Night on Bald Mountain*, Saint-Saëns's *Danse Macabre*, the Sabre Dance from Khachaturian's *Gayne* ballet, Dukas's *The Sorcerer's Apprentice*, and the Final Dance ("Malambo") from Ginastera's *Estancia* ballet.

This release points up a paradox. Arthur Fiedler and the Boston Pops Orchestra are probably responsible for more record sales than any other artists in the field of classical music, and their televised concerts on the Public Broadcasting Service have earned them nationwide popularity. Strangely, however, no record company has Fiedler and the Boston Pops under contract at this time.

(continued)

285

Comment

Technically, this disc is still one of the finest renderings of the playing of the Boston Pops Orchestra. ■

May 1969

GUITAR MUSIC IN THE CLASSIC STYLE. Works by Bach, Weiss, and Tansman. Christopher Parkening, guitar. Angel S36019/20, $5.98. ▲ ●

This California guitarist is only twenty years old, yet he has been concertizing on the West Coast for about half a dozen years—and to extraordinary acclaim. This disc, which marks his recording debut, demonstrates the reasons for his concert hall success. A pupil of Segovia, Parkening has—like the master—developed an individual musical stamp. And the young man seems to have solved all problems of technique. Here, in short, is an artist with an interesting musical approach and the technical means to convey his insights uninhibitedly.

The high point of the album is Parkening's performance of the Segovia transcription of the Chaconne from Bach's *Solo Violin Partita No. 2*. To this great score Parkening brings fine analysis and disciplined intensity. He conveys the distinguishing character of each of the twenty-nine variations, at the same time maintaining the sense of the broad overall structure. The shorter works receive similarly impressive performances and the recorded sound could serve as a model for guitar reproduction. Remember the name Christopher Parkening; this observer believes that you will be hearing it with increasing frequency.

Comment

New recordings from Parkening have been few and far between. Since he is highly critical of his own efforts, one can be sure that any recording bearing his name will have special virtues. This collection remains particularly recommendable. ■

January 1966

AN HISTORIC RETURN: HOROWITZ AT CARNEGIE HALL. BACH-BUSONI: Toccata in C; SCHUMANN: Fantasy in C; SCRIABIN: Sonata No. 9; Poème; CHOPIN: Mazurka in C sharp minor; Étude in F; Ballade in G minor; DEBUSSY: Doll's Serenade; SCRIABIN: Étude in C sharp minor; MOSZKOWSKI: Étude in A flat; SCHUMANN: Träumerei. Vladimir Horowitz, piano. Columbia M2S728, 2 discs, $11.96.

As just about everybody knows, this album was recorded right from the stage of Carnegie Hall on the occasion of the return of Vladimir Horowitz, after a twelve-year absence from the scene. The date was May 9, 1965. The hall was crowded, emotion ran high, and Horowitz amply demonstrated once again the extraordinary hold he has over the public. He also demonstrated that his virtuosity is as unlimited as ever, his fingers are as strong, his sonorities just as powerful, and his color resources absolutely fantastic. Much has been written about "the new Horowitz," the idea apparently being that his long retirement has added depth and maturity to his playing. But several hearings of this album leave one wondering whether there is really anything new. The *G minor Ballade* comes out in a nervous-sounding, almost spasmodic manner and the Bach-Busoni is full of Horowitz's old tricks. In each the playing itself is wonderful and exciting, but, then, it always was. All music lovers will want this recital, both for the brilliance of the playing and for the sentiment of the occasion. Considering the conditions under which it was made, the recorded sound is excellent.

January 1969

HOROWITZ ON TELEVISION. CHOPIN: Ballade in G minor; Nocturne in F minor; Polonaise in F sharp minor; SCARLATTI: Sonatas in E major and G major; SCHUMANN: Arabeske; Träumerei; SCRIABIN: Étude in D sharp minor; HOROWITZ: Variations on a Theme from Bizet's Carmen. Vladimir Horowitz, piano. Columbia MS7106, $5.98. ▲ ●

This recording is taken from the concert taped by Horowitz last February in New York's Carnegie Hall for showing on the CBS television network. The literature is for the most part contemplative and poetic, as if Horowitz deliberately chose to deemphasize his vaunted reputation as a thunderer of the keyboard. He is at the very top of his form throughout the program; the presence of the television cameras seems in no way to have intruded upon the serenity of his playing, and the presence of an audience apparently served as a stimulus to the freedom and spontaneity of the occasion.

Several of the pieces in the concert have been recorded by Horowitz previously. The Schumann *Arabeske* and the Scriabin *Étude*, in fact, are included on the disc that served as the pianist's Columbia Records debut half a dozen years ago. Good as those performances were, the newer ones are even better. The Schumann is a good example: Here is surely the quintessence of effortless art. Horowitz plays it simply and lovingly so that the whole takes on an improvisational quality that is totally disarming. An indication of the contrasting natures of the older and newer performances may be had from a comparison of their running times. The 1962 recording runs 5 minutes, 31 seconds, the 1968 version runs 7 minutes, 7 seconds—a clear indication that with the passage of time the Horowitz interpretation has gained in breadth and serenity.

In the two works that *are* stunning display pieces—the Scriabin *Étude* and the pianist's own *Variations* on material from Bizet's *Carmen*—the inimitable Horowitz razzle-dazzle is as awesome as ever. Throughout the disc the sound captured by the engineers is unusually faithful to the Horowitz sound in the concert hall.

(continued)

Comment

Both these collections offer the spontaneity of live concert conditions. There is no question that the presence of an audience serves to stimulate the pianist. These performances offer the supreme artistry of one of the greatest masters of the keyboard. ∎

May 1972

HOROWITZ PLAYS CHOPIN. Polonaise Fantaisie, Opus 61; Mazurka in A minor, Opus 17, No. 4; Waltz in A minor, Opus 34, No. 2; Étude in G flat (Black Key); Introduction and Rondo, Opus 16; Polonaise in A flat major, Opus 53. Vladimir Horowitz, piano. Columbia M30643, $5.98.

Horowitz has been playing Chopin for public consumption and delectation for nearly half a century now. Chances are, however, that he has never played better than in this new release. All but the *Polonaise Fantaisie* were studio-recorded in Spring 1971; the *Polonaise Fantaisie* comes from a Carnegie Hall recital in April 1966. To everything, Horowitz brings his uniquely vibrant sound and his extraordinarily searching intelligence. The virtuosic *A flat major Polonaise* blazes with temperament and passion; the *Polonaise Fantaisie* and the *Introduction and Rondo* have their full measure of architectural and panoramic sweep. Perhaps most memorable of all is his performance of the *A minor Mazurka*, a quiet, introspective work that reaches new heights of pensive intensity in this performance.

Fine recorded sound prevails throughout, though one could wish that somehow Columbia might have edited out the overly enthusiastic admirer in Carnegie Hall who interrupts the final note of the *Polonaise Fantaisie* before it has finished.

Comment

Now that Horowitz seems to be increasing the number of his public performances, we may be getting an accelerated flow of new recordings by him for RCA Records. It is doubtful, however, that any new Horowitz recordings will eclipse the extraordinary qualities of virtuosity and musicianship evident in the performances on this disc. ∎

January 1969

JOURNEY THROUGH OPERA. PONCHIELLI: La Gioconda: Cielo e mar; MOZART: Don Giovanni: Il mio tesoro; Dalla sua pace; DONIZETTI: L'Elisir d'Amore: Una furtiva lagrima; PUCCINI: Manon Lescaut: Donna non vidi mai; FLOTOW: Martha: M'appari; MEYERBEER: L'Africana: O Paradiso; BOITO: Mefistofele: Dai campi, dai prati; VERDI: Aida: Celeste Aida; La Forza del Destino: O tu che in seno agli angeli; GLUCK: Paris and Helen: O del mio

dolce ardor. Jan Peerce, tenor, with Vienna Festival Orchestra conducted by Julius Rudel. Vanguard Cardinal C10036, $3.98.

Jan Peerce is simply amazing. In his middle sixties, an age when most tenors have long since abandoned their singing careers for positions as teachers or coaches or administrators, he goes right along singing in opera and concert in undiminished vocal splendor. To be sure, there is now a more resonant chest quality in the lower register and he can no longer ascend to the higher reaches of the scale without betraying some signs of pressure. But the sheer excitement of the voice, matched with his impeccable musical phrasing and absolutely secure intonation make Peerce performances unique even today. Not everything on this disc is handled with equal success. The two Mozart arias, for example, are sung more stylishly and smoothly by other tenors. But everything is endowed with a vitality and dramatic thrust that make the performances vibrant and dynamic experiences. The orchestral performances are all very convincing, and the sound is vivid and full of life.

Comment

"Toscanini's favorite tenor," as Peerce came to be known for his many appearances under the Maestro's direction, is in fine fettle on this disc. The longevity of his career testifies to his extraordinary discipline and intelligence—to say nothing of his unique vocal gifts.　　　　　　　　　　　　　　　　　　■

March 1959

THE PLAY OF DANIEL. New York Pro Musica conducted by Noah Greenberg. Decca 79402, $5.98. ▲

About seven hundred years ago, students at the Cathedral of Beauvais got together to produce a play for the Christmas season. They settled on the biblical subject of Daniel, provided dialogue in Latin, and set the result to music. Not until recently was the manuscript exhumed and restudied, to the great amazement of scholars. *The Play of Daniel* is an early link between sacred music and the opera. But it is not a dusty library piece. It has a lusty sort of humor, extraordinary vitality, and considerable imagination. The New York Pro Musica, among the world's outstanding specialists in early music, has not attempted to present *Daniel* in a souped-up modern setting. Instead the group uses ancient instruments (rebec, portative organ, bell carillon, recorders, bagpipes, and others), adheres to the original text, and brings to the music all the resources of contemporary scholarship. The singers and musicians present the score with utmost clarity and delicacy; and the sound of the old instruments is enchanting. To fill the cup to brimming, Decca has provided beautiful recorded sound. The surfaces are noiseless—really noiseless. Quite a bit of separation provides a legitimate antiphonal effect. The singers do not dominate the ensemble in the recording. They have been placed to blend with the instruments. For clear, natural-sounding recording, this disc is a model of its kind.

(continued)

Comment

The New York Pro Musica came into being thanks to the extraordinary vision and musical brilliance of Noah Greenberg. Although his life was tragically short—he died of a heart attack in his mid-forties—Greenberg left a legacy of musical scholarship and performing excellence that will enrich the world for years to come. This disc is one of the most eloquent testimonials to his greatness. It now is available on the MCA label (MCA2504). ∎

January 1968

RUSSIAN SONGS. Jennie Tourel, mezzo-soprano, accompanied by Allen Rogers, piano, and Gary Karr, double-bass. Odyssey 32160070, $2.98.

Very little of the Russian song literature is available on LP, and this welcome disc fills a need. Tourel has selected songs by Glinka, Mussorgsky, Balakirev, Rimsky-Korsakov, Borodin, Rachmaninoff, Cui, Tchaikovsky, and Stravinsky. The chances are that only one of the songs—Tchaikovsky's "None But the Lonely Heart"—will be familiar to most listeners. The other songs are interesting, some even beautiful, so the disc may introduce many listeners to a rewarding genre. Tourel sings in Russian. One can't pretend that her voice is the instrument it used to be. But there is no diminution in her style and artistry; she makes an absorbing experience of each song. Her sometimes shaky production is more satisfying than most other singers' best work. The recorded sound is first-rate.

Comment

This is a particularly attractive disc at Odyssey's budget price. A fitting memorial to the art of this great singer, this recording is recommended to all who are interested in unusual vocal literature. ∎

February 1971

SALUTE TO PERCY GRAINGER. Peter Pears, tenor; John Shirley-Quirk, baritone; Viola Tunnard, piano; with the Ambrosian Singers and the English Chamber Orchestra conducted by Benjamin Britten. London 6632. $5.98.

Percy Grainger, the Australian-born pianist and composer, died in 1961 when he was almost eighty. His true importance in twentieth-century music has been largely overshadowed by his worldwide fame as the composer of the charming but innocuous *Country Gardens*.

This record displays Grainger's talent in arranging British folk music, which he has given real artistic distinction. In his settings for voice and small chamber orchestra, he used the cantatas and passions of Bach as an example and made small masterpieces out of less-than-distinguished raw material.

The sound approaches perfection, and Britten is the principal hero amid a galaxy of stunning performers, revealing as he does a glorious rapport with Grainger's intention. All told, this is a standout of the 1970 recording season.

Comment

And it remains a standout to this day. The quality of joy that pervades these performances is rare, and to be cherished. ∎

November 1973

SOPRANO ARIAS FROM ITALIAN OPERA. DONIZETTI: Anna Bolena (Piangete voi . . . Al dolce guidami castel natio); BELLINI: I Puritani (Qui la voce sua soave . . . Vien, diletto); VERDI: Aida (Qui Radames verrà . . . Oh patria mia); BOITO: Mefistofele (L'altra notte in fondo al mare); PUCCINI: La Boheme (Si, mi chiamano Mimi; Donde lieta usci); Suor Angelica (Senza mamma, o bimbo, tu sei morto); Manon Lescaut (In quelle trine morbide); Turandot (Signore ascolta); MASCAGNI: Lodoletta (Ah! il suo nome . . . Flammen perdonami). Maria Chiara, soprano, with the Vienna Volksoper Orchestra conducted by Nello Santi. London OS26262, $5.98.

Earlier, we expressed our disappointment in the debut recording of Katia Ricciarelli, a young Italian soprano being thrust upon the international music scene. We are happy to report that the case is quite different with Maria Chiara, yet another new and young Italian opera soprano who is being presented to the public. Unlike Ricciarelli, Chiara is ready for such exposure; indeed, she gives the exciting promise here of becoming an important opera singer. Her voice is beautiful—pure, well focused, warm. And she seems to have had excellent training, so that she produces luscious sounds that are rich and accurate through all registers. There is a certain sameness that characterizes all her performances here, but Chiara will doubtless increase her dramatic variety as she matures. In the meantime, her recording debut is most auspicious, and one looks forward to her future development. The orchestral accompaniments and sound engineering are entirely satisfactory.

Comment

Since these words were written, Maria Chiara has indeed gone on to great success in the opera houses of Europe. But her much-anticipated Metropolitan Opera debut during the 1977-78 season was considerably less than spectacular. One can surmise that she was off her form in New York—but time alone will tell. Meantime, interestingly, Katia Ricciarelli has developed into a mature and sensitive vocal artist with much to offer both as a lyric and dramatic soprano. ∎

September 1972

VIOLIN ROMANCES. Works for Violin and Orchestra by Beethoven, Berlioz, Tchaikovsky, Wieniawski and Svendsen. Arthur
(continued)

Grumiaux, violin, with the New Philharmonia Orchestra conducted by Edo de Waart. Philips 6580047, $6.98.

This release, in the Universo series issued by Philips Records, brings together seven short works from the 19th-century repertoire for violin and orchestra—all of them played with taste and finesse by one of today's most cultured artists, the Belgian violinist, Arthur Grumiaux. To the expected list of Beethoven's two *Romances* and the *Reverie and Caprice* by Berlioz are added such unanticipated delights as *Legend* by Wieniawski and *Romance* by the Norwegian composer Johan Svendsen. The latter work, especially, is a joy—wistful, delicate and beautifully written to exploit the lyrical quality of the violin.

Grumiaux is at the top of his form, the orchestra under the direction of the young Dutch conductor (and former assistant conductor of the New York Philharmonic) Edo de Waart is sensitive and polished, and the sound provided by the engineers is appropriately intimate. This disc provides gentle but lasting pleasure.

Comment

Edo de Waart went on to become first the principal guest conductor and then, succeeding Seiji Ozawa, the music director of the San Francisco Symphony Orchestra. He is clearly an uncommonly gifted conductor. As for Grumiaux, nothing more need be said: He is quite simply one of the best of the violinists around. ∎

July 1962

WALTZES FROM OLD VIENNA. Alexander Schneider, Paul Wolfe, and Felix Galimir, violins; Walter Trampler, viola; Julius Levine, double bass. Odyssey 32160300, $2.98.

This disc is a novelty. It contains Johann Strauss, Jr., Josef Strauss, and Joseph Lanner, and is played by only five strings, much as the music is played to this very day in Viennese cafés and kellers. This makes chamber music out of the waltzes. To hear *"Wiener Blut"* under such circumstances takes some reorientation, but the effect is delicious.

Comment

One generally hears this music played nowadays by the full and imposing resources of a symphony orchestra. This disc affords us a much more intimate listening experience, with the expert performances we might expect from this quintet of distinguished musicians. The repertory is among the most gracious waltz music of Emperor Franz Josef's Vienna. ∎

A BASIC DISCOGRAPHY
OF CLASSICAL MUSIC

CHAMBER MUSIC

BARTÓK: *Quartets (complete).* Juilliard Quartet. Columbia D3S717, 3 discs.

BEETHOVEN: *Grosse Fugue* (with BEETHOVEN: *Quartet No. 16*). Yale Quartet. Vanguard 10097.

Quartet No. 14. Quartetto Italiano. Philips 802915.

Quartets (Op. 18). Guarneri Quartet. RCA VCS6195, 3 discs.

Septet. Vienna Octet Members. London STS15361.

Violin Sonata No. 9 in A (Kreutzer) (with BEETHOVEN: *Sonata No. 5 in F*). Szeryng, Rubinstein. RCA LSC2377.

Trio for Piano in B flat No. 6, Op. 97 (Archduke). Stern, Rose, Istomin. Columbia MS6819.

BLOCH: *Quintet for Piano and Strings.* Glazer and Fine Arts Quartet. Concert Disc 252.

BORODIN: *Quartet No. 2* (with DVOŘÁK: *String Quartet No. 12*). Quartetto Italiano. Philips 802814.

BRAHMS: *Quartets (complete)* (with SCHUMANN: *Quintet.* Serkin and the Budapest Quartet). Budapest Quartet. Columbia M2S734, 2 discs.

Quartets for Piano and Strings (complete). Brown, Schneider, Trampler, Parnas. Vanguard 71221/2, 2 discs.

Quintet in B flat minor for Clarinet and Strings. Stoltzman and Cleveland Quartet. RCA ARL11993.

Sonatas for Violin and Piano (complete). Suk, Katchen. London 6549.

Trio in E flat for Horn, Violin, and Piano (with SCHUBERT: *Songs*). Bloom, Tree, Rudolf Serkin. Columbia MS6243.

DEBUSSY: *Quartet* (with RAVEL: *String Quartet*). Quartetto Italiano. Philips 835361.

DVOŘÁK: *Quintet in A major.* Peter Serkin, Schneider, etc. Vanguard S288.

Trio in E minor, Op. 90 (Dumky) (with SMETANA: *Trio in G minor*). Yuval Trio. DG2530594.

FRANCK: *Sonata in A for Violin and Piano* (with BRAHMS: *Horn Trio in E flat*). Perlman, Ashkenazy. London 6628.

MENDELSSOHN: *Octet* (with MENDELSSOHN: *Variations and Scherzo*). Cleveland and Tokyo Quartets. RCA ARL12532.

Trio No. 1 in D minor (with BEETHOVEN: *Trio No. 3*). Stern, Rose, Istomin. Columbia MS7083.

MOZART: *Quartets Nos. 14-19.* Guarneri Quartet. RCA CRL31998, 3 discs.

Quintets K. 515, 516. Primrose and Griller Quartet. Vanguard HM29.

Quintet in A major for Clarinet and Strings (with MOZART: *Quartet for Oboe and Strings*). De Peyer and Amadeus Quartet. DG2530720.

(continued)

SCHUBERT: *Octet*. Berlin Philharmonic Octet. DG139102.

Quartet No. 13 (with SCHUBERT: *Quartet No. 9*). Amadeus Quartet. DG139194.

Quartet No. 14 (Death and the Maiden) (with SCHUBERT: *Quartet No. 12*). Melos Quartet. DG2530533.

Quintet in A (Trout). Peter Serkin, Schneider, etc. Vanguard 71145.

Quintet in C. Guarneri Quartet and Leonard Rose. RCA ARL11154. ▲ ●

Trio No. 1 (piano) in B flat. Stern, Rose, Istomin. Columbia MS6716.

SMETANA: *Quartet No. 1* (with DVOŘÁK: *Quartet No. 14*). Guarneri Quartet. RCA LSC2887.

CHORAL

BACH: *Cantatas Nos. 4, 140*. Prohaska. Vanguard HM20.

Mass in B minor. Richter. DG ARC2710001, 3 discs.

St. Matthew Passion. Münchinger. London 1431, 4 discs.

BEETHOVEN: *Missa Solemnis*. Bernstein. Columbia M2S619, 2 discs.

BERLIOZ: *The Damnation of Faust*. Davis. Philips 6703042, 3 discs.

L'Enfance du Christ. Munch. RCA VICS6006, 2 discs.

Requiem. Davis. Philips 6700019, 2 discs. ●

BERNSTEIN: *Chichester Psalms* (with BERNSTEIN: *Facsimile*). Bernstein. Columbia MS6792.

BLOCH: *Sacred Service*. Abravanel. Angel S37305.

BRAHMS: *German Requiem*. Klemperer. Angel S3624, 2 discs.

BRITTEN: *War Requiem*. Britten. London 1255, 2 discs. ●

DVOŘÁK: *Requiem*. Kertesz. London 1281, 2 discs.

Stabat Mater. Kubelik. DG2707099, 2 discs.

ELGAR: *The Dream of Gerontius*. Britten. London 1293, 2 discs.

FAURÉ: *Requiem*. Cluytens. Angel S35974.

HANDEL: *Israel in Egypt*. Mackerras. DG ARC2708020, 2 discs.

Messiah. Mackerras. Angel S3705, 3 discs.

HAYDN: *The Creation*. Bernstein. Columbia M2S773, 2 discs.

Mass No. 9 in D minor, Missa Solemnis (Nelson Mass). Willcocks. Argo 5325.

HONEGGER: *Roi David*. Abravanel. Vanguard 2117/8, 2 discs.

MOZART: *Requiem*. Davis. Philips 802862. ▲ ●

ORFF: *Carmina Burana*. Ozawa. RCA LSC3161. ▲

PALESTRINA: *Missa Papae Marcelli* (with VICTORIA: *Motets*). Wagner Chorale. Angel S36022.

PERGOLESI: *Stabat Mater*. Gracis. DG ARC2533114. ●

POULENC: *Gloria* (with POULENC: *Piano Concerto*). Frémaux. Angel S37246.

Stabat Mater (with POULENC: *Motets*). Prêtre. Angel S36121.

PROKOFIEV: *Alexander Nevsky*. Previn. Angel S36843. ●

RAVEL: *Daphnis et Chloé*. Boulez. Columbia M33523.

STRAVINSKY: *Oedipus Rex*. Bernstein. Columbia M33999.

Symphony of Psalms (with STRAVINSKY: *Symphony in C*). Stravinsky. Columbia MS6548.

VERDI: *Requiem*. Giulini. Angel S3649, 2 discs.

VIVALDI: *Gloria* (with PERGOLESI: *Magnificat*). Willcocks. Argo ZRG505.

WALTON: *Belshazzar's Feast*. Walton. Angel S35681.

CONCERTO

BACH: *Harpsichord Concerti Nos. 1 and 2*. Malcolm. London 6392.

Concerti for 2, 3, and 4 Harpsichords. Heiller. Bach Guild 70659, 2 discs.

Concerti for Violin Nos. 1 and 2 (with BACH: *2-Violins Concerto*). Melkus. DG ARC2533075.

Concerto for Violin and Oboe (with BACH: *Violin Concerti in D minor and A minor*). Perlman and Black. Angel S37076.

BARBER: *Concerto for Piano and Orchestra* (with SCHUMAN: *Song of Orpheus*). Browning. Columbia MS6638.

Concerto for Violin and Orchestra (with HINDEMITH: *Violin Concerto*). Stern. Columbia MS6713.

BARTÓK: *Concerto No. 3 for Piano* (with BARTÓK: *Piano Concerto No. 1*). Barenboim. Angel S36605.

Concerto for Violin and Orchestra (1938). Perlman. Angel S37014.

BEETHOVEN: *Concerto No. 5 for Piano and Orchestra (Emperor)*. Rudolf Serkin. Columbia MS6366.

Concerto for Violin. Suk. Vanguard S353.

BRAHMS: *Concerto for Violin and Cello*. Oistrakh and Rostropovitch. Angel S36032. ▲ ●

Concerto for Piano No. 1. Curzon. London 6329.

Concerto for Piano No. 2. Fleisher. Odyssey Y32222. ●

Concerto in D for Violin. Perlman. Angel S37286. ●

(continued)

BRUCH: *Concerto No. 1 for Violin* (with **MOZART:** *Violin Concerto No. 4*). Heifetz. RCA LSC2652. ▲

CHOPIN: *Concerto No. 1 for Piano*. Rubinstein. RCA LSC2575. ▲ ●

Concerto No. 2 for Piano (with **BACH:** *Harpsichord Concerto No. 1*). Ashkenazy. London 6440. ●

DVOŘÁK: *Concerto for Cello* (with **SAINT-SAËNS:** *Concerto for Cello No. 1*). Rostropovitch. Angel S37457.

GRIEG: *Concerto for Piano* (with **GRIEG:** *Piano Encores*). Rubinstein. RCA LSC2566. ▲

MENDELSSOHN: *Concerti Nos. 1 and 2 for Piano*. Rudolf Serkin. Columbia MS6128.

Concerto for Violin (with **BRUCH:** *Violin Concerto*). Perlman. Angel S36963. ▲ ●

MOZART: *Concerto No. 15 for Piano* (with **MOZART:** *Concerto No. 14 for Piano*). P. Serkin. RCA ARL11492. ▲ ●

Concerto No. 20 for Piano. Barenboim. Angel S36430.

Concerto No. 4 for Violin (with **BRUCH:** *Violin Concerto No. 1*). Heifetz. RCA LSC2652. ▲

Concerto No. 5 for Violin (with **MOZART:** *Violin Concerto No. 4*). Zukerman. Columbia M30055.

PROKOFIEV: *Concerto No. 3 for Piano* (with **PROKOFIEV:** *Piano Concerto No. 1 and Piano Sonata No. 3*). Graffman. Columbia MS6925.

Concerti Nos. 1 and 2 for Violin. Milanova. Monitor S90101. ●

RACHMANINOFF: *Concerto No. 2 for Piano* (with **RACHMANINOFF:** *Rhapsody on a Theme by Paganini*). Wild. Quintessence 7006.

Concerto No. 3 for Piano. Horowitz. RCA CRL12633. ▲ ●

SAINT-SAËNS: *Concerto No. 1 for Cello and Orchestra* (with **FAURÉ:** *Elégie* and **LALO:** *Cello Concerto*). Schiff. DG2530793.

Concerti Nos. 2 and 4 for Piano. Entremont. Columbia MS6778.

SCHUMANN: *Concerto for· Piano* (with **SCHUMANN:** *Introduction and Allegro*). Rudolf Serkin. Columbia MS6688.

Concerto for Cello (with **BLOCH:** *Schelomo*). Rose. Columbia MS6253.

SIBELIUS: *Concerto for Violin* (with **PROKOFIEV:** *Concerto No. 2 for Violin*). Heifetz. RCA LSC4010.

TCHAIKOVSKY: *Concerto No. 1 for Piano*. Cliburn. RCA LSC2252. ▲ ●

Concerto for Violin (with **MENDELSSOHN:** *Concerto for Violin*). Heifetz. RCA LSC3304. ▲ ●

VIVALDI: *Concerti for Violin. The Four Seasons*. Perlman. Angel S37053. ▲ ●

KEYBOARD

BACH: *Goldberg Variations.* Leonhardt (harpsichord). Vanguard S175. Gould (piano). Columbia MS7096.

Partitas for Harpsichord. Gould (piano). Columbia M2S693, 2 discs.

Well-Tempered Clavier (complete). Gould (piano). Columbia D3S733, D3M31525, 6 discs.

BEETHOVEN: *Sonatas Nos. 8 (Pathétique), 14 (Moonlight), and 23 (Appassionata) for Piano.* Rubinstein. RCA LSC4001. ▲

Sonatas Nos. 21 (Waldstein) and 31. Brendel. Philips 6500762. ●

Sonatas Nos. 31 and 32 for Piano. Ashkenazy. London CS6843.

BRAHMS: *Piano Recital* (with **BRAHMS:** *Piano Sonata No. 3*). Rubinstein. RCA LSC2459.

CHOPIN: *Ballades.* Rubinstein. RCA LSC2370.

Études. Pollini. DG2530291. ▲ ●

Impromptus (with **CHOPIN:** *Andante and Polonaises*). Rubinstein. RCA LSC7037, 2 discs.

Mazurkas. Rubinstein. RCA LSC6177, 3 discs.

Nocturnes. Rubinstein. RCA LSC7059, 2 discs. ▲ ●

Scherzos. Rubinstein. RCA LSC2368. ▲

Sonatas 2 and 3. Rubinstein. RCA LSC3194.

Waltzes. Rubinstein. RCA LSC2726. ▲ ●

GRIEG: *Lyric Pieces.* Gilels. DG2530476. ●

LISZT: *Hungarian Rhapsodies Nos. 2, 3, 8, 13, 15, 17.* Brendel. Vanguard C10035.

Mephisto-Waltz (with **LISZT:** *Piano Music*). Wild. Vanguard C10041.

Sonata in B minor (with **SCHUBERT:** *Wanderer Fantasie*). Rubinstein. RCA LSC2871.

MENDELSSOHN: *Variations sérieuses* (with **GRIEG:** *Sonata*). De Larrocha. London 6676.

MOZART: *Sonata No. 8 for Piano* (with **MOZART:** *Piano Pieces*). Brendel. Vanguard C10043.

MUSSORGSKY: *Pictures at an Exhibition.* Richter. Odyssey Y32223. ●

PROKOFIEV: *Sonatas Nos. 2 and 8 for Piano.* Joselson. RCA ARL11570.

SCHUBERT: *Sonata in A for Piano* (with **SCHUBERT:** *Wanderer Fantasie*). Richter. Angel S36150.

SCHUMANN: *Carnaval; Fantasiestücke.* Rubinstein. RCA LSC2669.

Fantasia in C (with **SCHUMANN:** *Sonata, Op. 11*). Pollini. DG2530379.

(continued)

Symphonic Études (with SCHUMANN: *Papillons*). Perahia. Columbia M34539.
●
VILLA-LOBOS: *Piano Music.* Freire. Telefunken 641299.

OPERA

BEETHOVEN: *Fidelio.* Ludwig, etc. Angel S3625, 3 discs.
BELLINI: *Norma.* Callas, etc. Angel S3615, 3 discs.
BERG: *Wozzeck.* Lear, etc. DG2707023, 2 discs.
BIZET: *Carmen.* Horne, etc. DG2709043, 3 discs. ●
BRITTEN: *Peter Grimes.* Pears, etc. London 1305, 3 discs.
DONIZETTI: *Lucia di Lammermoor.* Sutherland, etc. London 13103, 3 discs. ●
GOUNOD: *Faust.* Gedda, etc. Angel S3622, 4 discs.
HUMPERDINCK: *Hansel and Gretel.* Donath, etc. RCA ARL20637, 2 discs.
LEONCAVALLO: *Pagliacci* (with MASCAGNI: *Cavalleria Rusticana*). Del Monaco,
    etc. London 1330, 3 discs.
MOZART: *Così fan tutte.* Schwarzkopf, etc. Angel S3631, 4 discs.
   Don Giovanni. Taddei, etc. Angel S3605, 4 discs.
   The Magic Flute. Fischer-Dieskau, etc. London 1397, 3 discs.
   The Marriage of Figaro. Siepi, etc. London 1402, 4 discs.
MUSSORGSKY: *Boris Godounov.* Christoff, etc. Angel S3633, 4 discs.
OFFENBACH: *The Tales of Hoffmann.* Gedda, etc. Angel S3667, 3 discs.
PUCCINI: *La Bohème.* Freni. London 1299, 2 discs. ●
   Gianni Schicchi. Gobbi. Columbia M34534.
   Madama Butterfly. Scotto, etc. Angel S3702, 3 discs.
   Tosca. Price, etc. RCA ARL20105, 2 discs.
   Turandot. Sutherland, etc. London 13108, 3 discs. ●
PURCELL: *Dido and Aeneas.* Baker, etc. Oiseau-Lyre 60047.
ROSSINI: *The Barber of Seville.* Milnes, etc. Angel SX3761, 3 discs. ●
STRAUSS, J.: *Die Fledermaus.* Rothenberger, etc. Angel S3790, 2 discs. ●
STRAUSS, R.: *Elektra.* Nilsson, etc. London 1269, 2 discs.
   Der Rosenkavalier. Crespin, etc. London 1435, 4 discs. ●
   Salome. Nilsson, etc. London 1218, 2 discs.
VERDI: *Falstaff.* Fischer-Dieskau, etc. Columbia D3S750, 3 discs.
   Otello. Vickers, etc. Angel SX3809, 3 discs.
   Rigoletto. Fischer-Dieskau, etc. DG2709014, 3 discs. ●

La Traviata. Cotrubas, etc. DG2707103. ●
Il Trovatore. Price, etc. RCA LSC6194, 3 discs.
WAGNER: *Götterdämmerung.* Nilsson, etc. London 1604, 6 discs.
Lohengrin. Thomas, etc. Angel S3641, 5 discs.
Die Meistersinger. Fischer-Dieskau, etc. DG2713011, 5 discs. ●
Das Rheingold. London, etc. London 1309, 3 discs. ●
Siegfried. Windgassen, etc. London 1508, 5 discs. ●
Tristan und Isolde. Nilsson, etc. DG2713001, 5 discs. ●
Die Walküre. Nilsson, etc. London 1509, 5 discs. ●

ORCHESTRAL

BACH: *Brandenburg Concerti.* Leppard. Philips 6747166, 2 discs. ●
Suites for Orchestra. Harnoncourt. Telefunken 2635046, 2 discs. ●
BARTÓK: *Concerto for Orchestra.* Bernstein. Columbia MS6140.
Music for Strings, Percussion and Celesta (with STRAVINSKY: *Firebird Suite*). Boulez. Columbia MS7206.
BERLIOZ: *Harold in Italy.* Barenboim. Columbia M34541. ●
BOULEZ: *Le Marteau sans maître.* Boulez. Columbia M32160.
BRAHMS: *Variations on a Theme by Haydn; Academic Festival Overture; Tragic Overture.* Szell. Columbia MS6965.
BRITTEN: *Young Persons' Guide to the Orchestra* (with MUSSORGSKY: *Pictures at an Exhibition*). Ozawa. RCA LSC2977. ▲
COPLAND: *Appalachian Spring; Fanfare for the Common Man; A Lincoln Portrait.* Copland. Columbia M30649.
Billy the Kid; Rodeo. Bernstein. Columbia MS6175.
CORELLI: *Concerti Grossi (Op. 6).* Marriner. Argo ZRG773/5, 3 discs.
DEBUSSY: *Images pour Orchestre.* Martinon. Angel S37066. ●
La Mer (with DEBUSSY: *Nocturnes*). Monteux. Quintessence 7027.
DELIUS: *Brigg Fair; On Hearing the First Cuckoo in Spring,* etc. Beecham. Seraphim S60134.
DUKAS: *The Sorcerer's Apprentice* (with D'INDY: *Symphony on a French Mountain Air* and RAVEL: *Ma Mère l'Oye*). Munch. RCA VICS1060. ▲
DVOŘÁK: *Othello Overture; Amid Nature; Carnival Overture* (with DVOŘÁK: *Scherzo*). Kertesz. London 6574.
Serenade for Strings, Op. 22. Kubelik. London STS15037.
ENESCO: *Roumanian Rhapsody No. 1* (with LISZT: *Hungarian Rhapsody No. 2,* etc.). Stokowski. RCA LSC2471.

(continued)

FALLA: *Nights in the Gardens of Spain* (with RODRIGO: *Guitar Concerto*). Argenta. London 6046.

FRANCK: *Symphonic Variations* (with LISZT: *Totentanz*). Watts. Columbia M33072. ▲ ●

GERSHWIN: *An American in Paris; Rhapsody in Blue*. Bernstein. Columbia MS6091.

GRIEG: *Peer Gynt Suite No. 1* (with BIZET: *L'Arlésienne Suite*). Szell. Columbia MS6877.

HANDEL: *Concerti Grossi (Op. 6)*. Marriner, London 2309, 3 discs.

Royal Fireworks Music (with HANDEL: *Concerto No. 2 for Two Wind Choirs*). Mackerras. Angel S37404. ●

Water Music. Leppard. Philips 6500047. ▲

HINDEMITH: *Mathis der Maler; Symphonic Metamorphosis of Themes by Weber*. Ormandy. Columbia MS6562.

IVES: *Three Places in New England; Browning Overture; Washington's Birthday*.Ormandy, Stokowski, Bernstein. Columbia MS7015.

MENDELSSOHN: *A Midsummer Night's Dream: incidental music* (with SCHUBERT: *Rosamunde: incidental music*). Szell. Columbia MS7002.

MOZART: *Serenade in G, Eine kleine Nachtmusik* (with MOZART: *German Dances and Serenade No. 6*). Davis. Seraphim S60057.

MUSSORGSKY: *Pictures at an Exhibition* (Orchestration by Ravel) (with PRO-KOFIEV: *Classical Symphony*). Giulini. DG2530783. ●

OFFENBACH: *Gaîté Parisienne* (Ballet score arranged by Rosenthal). Munch. London 21011.

PROKOFIEV: *Lieutenant Kijé Suite* (with KODÁLY: *Háry János Suite*). Szell. Columbia MS7408.

Peter and the Wolf (with SAINT-SAËNS: *Carnival of the Animals*). Lillie. London 6187.

RAVEL: *Boléro; Pavanne; Alborada del gracioso; Daphnis et Chloé, Suite No. 2*. Martinon. Quintessence 7017.

RESPIGHI: *The Pines of Rome; The Fountains of Rome*. Munch. London 21024. ●

RIMSKY-KORSAKOV: *Capriccio espagnol* (with *miscellaneous Russian Orchestral works*). Rozhdestvensky. Angel S36889. ●

Scheherazade. Beecham. Angel S35505. ▲ ●

RUGGLES: *The Sun-Treader* (with IVES: *Three Places in New England*). Thomas. DG2530048.

SIBELIUS: *Finlandia; Tapiola; Valse triste; Swan of Tuonela*. Karajan. Angel S37408. ●

SMETANA: *The Moldau* (with SMETANA: *Bartered Bride Overture*; ENESCO: *Rouma-*

nian Rhapsody No. 1; and LISZT: *Hungarian Rhapsody No. 2).* Stokowski. RCA LSC2471.

STRAUSS, R.: *Don Juan; Salome: Dance of the 7 Veils; Till Eulenspiegel.* Bernstein. Columbia MS6822.

Don Quixote. Karajan. Angel S37057. ●

Ein Heldenleben. Beecham. Seraphim S60041.

STRAVINSKY: *The Firebird (complete); Petrouchka; Le Sacre du printemps.* Stravinsky. Columbia D3S705, 3 discs.

TCHAIKOVSKY: *Nutcracker Suites Nos. 1 and 2.* Previn. Angel S36990. ▲ ●

Romeo and Juliet (with SCRIABIN: *Poem of Ecstasy).* Abbado. DG2530137.

Serenade for Strings (with ARENSKY: *Variations on a Theme by Tchaikovsky).* Barbirolli. Angel S36269.

Sleeping Beauty Suite; Swan Lake Suite. Stokowski. London 21008. ●

VAUGHAN WILLIAMS: *Fantasia on a Theme by Tallis* (with VAUGHAN WILLIAMS: *Fantasia on "Greensleeves"* and ELGAR: *Introduction and Allegro* and *Serenade in E minor).* Barbirolli. Angel S36101.

WAGNER: *Miscellaneous orchestral works.* Horenstein. Quintessence 7047.

SYMPHONY

BEETHOVEN: *Symphony No. 3 (Eroica).* Barbirolli. Angel S36461. ▲ ●

Symphony No. 5. Kleiber. DG2530516. ▲ ●

Symphony No. 7. Kleiber. DG2530706. ●

Symphony No. 9. Schmidt-Isserstedt. London 1159.

BERLIOZ: *Symphonie fantastique.* Davis. Philips 6500774. ▲ ● Munch. RCA LSC2608.

BOYCE: *Eight Symphonies.* Janigro. Vanguard HM23.

BRAHMS: *Symphonies Nos. 1-4.* Szell. Columbia D3S758, 3 discs.

BRUCKNER: *Symphony No. 7* (with WAGNER: *Siegfried Idyll).* Karajan. DG2707102. ●

DVOŘÁK: *Symphony No. 7.* Mehta. London 6607.

Symphony No. 8. (with DVOŘÁK: *Slavonic Dances).* Szell. Angel S36043. ●

Symphony No. 9. Horenstein. Quintessence 7001.

FRANCK: *Symphony in D minor.* Monteux. RCA LSC2514.

HAYDN: *Symphonies Nos. 82-87.* Bernstein. Columbia D3S769, 3 discs.

Symphonies Nos. 93-104. Jones. Nonesuch 73019, 6 discs. ●

IVES: *Symphony No. 2* (with IVES: *"Fourth of July").* Bernstein. Columbia MS6889.

(continued)

Symphony No. 4. Stokowski. Columbia MS6775.

MAHLER: *Das Lied von der Erde.* Bernstein. London 26005.

Symphony No. 1. Horenstein. Nonesuch 71240. ●

Symphony No. 4. Szell. Columbia MS6833.

Symphony No. 9. Giulini. DG2707097, 2 discs. Walter. Odyssey Y230308, 2 discs.

MENDELSSOHN: *Symphonies Nos. 4 and 5.* Leppard. RCA ARL12632. ▲ ●

MOZART: *Symphonies Nos. 32, 35, and 38 (Prague).* Barenboim. Angel S36512.

Symphonies Nos. 36 (Linz) and 39. Walter. Columbia MS6493.

Symphonies Nos. 40 and 41 (Jupiter). Klemperer. Angel S36183.

NIELSEN: *Symphony No. 3.* Bernstein. Columbia MS6769.

Symphony No. 5. Bernstein. Columbia MS6414.

PROKOFIEV: *Symphony No. 5.* Bernstein. Columbia MS7005.

SCHUBERT: *Symphonies Nos. 5 and 8 (Unfinished).* Walter. Columbia MS6218.

Symphony No. 9 (The Great). Szell. Angel S36044. ▲ ●

SCHUMANN: *Symphonies Nos. 1 (Spring) and 4.* Mehta. London 7039. ●

SHOSTAKOVICH: *Symphony No. 5.* M. Shostakovich. Melodiya/Angel S40163.

SIBELIUS: *Symphony No. 1* (with **SIBELIUS:** *Finlandia*). Davis. Philips 9500140. ●

Symphony No. 2. Szell. Philips 6570084. ●

Symphony No. 5; En Saga. Karajan. Angel S37490. ●

STRAVINSKY: *Symphony of Psalms; Symphony in C.* Stravinsky. Columbia MS6548.

TCHAIKOVSKY: *Symphony No. 4.* Abbado. DG2530651.

Symphony No. 5 Haitink. Philips 6500922. ● Stokowski. London 21017.

Symphony No. 6 (Pathétique). Giulini. Seraphim S60031.

VAUGHAN WILLIAMS: *Symphony No. 2 (London).* Boult. Angel S36838. ●

Symphony No. 5 (with **VAUGHAN WILLIAMS:** *Serenade to Music*). Boult. Angel S36698.

VOCAL

BACH: *Arias.* Baker. Angel S37229.

BARBER: *Hermit Songs; Knoxville: Summer of 1915.* Price. Steber. Odyssey 32160230.

BEETHOVEN: *Fifteen Songs.* Fischer-Dieskau. DG139197.

BRAHMS: *Songs.* Valente. Desmar 1010G. ●

Liebeslieder Waltzes, Op. 52 and 65. Morison, etc. Seraphim S60033.

CANTELOUBE: *Songs of the Auvergne*. De los Angeles. Angel S36897.

FALLA: *Seven Popular Spanish Songs* (with *Songs* by GRANADOS, etc.) De los Angeles. Angel S37425.

GESUALDO: *Madrigals and Motets*. Stevens. Nonesuch 71277.

GRIEG: *Songs*. Flagstad. London 33222.

MAHLER: *Kindertotenlieder; Songs of a Wayfarer*. Prey. Philips 6500100.

MOZART: *Arias*. M. Price. RCA AGL11532.

POULENC: *Songs* (and other *Songs* by DUPARC, RAVEL, and SATIE). Norman. Philips 9500356.

RAVEL: *Chansons madécasses* (and other *Songs* by RAVEL, CHAUSSON, and DELAGE). Baker. Oiseau-Lyre S298.

Shéhérazade (with FALLA: *El Amor Brujo*. Horne. Columbia M35102. ●

SCHUBERT: *Die schöne Müllerin*. Fischer-Dieskau. DG2530544.

Songs. Fischer-Dieskau. Angel S36341/2, 2 discs.

Die Winterreise. Fischer-Dieskau. DG2707028, 2 discs.

SCHUMANN: *Dichterliebe; Liederkreis*. Fischer-Dieskau. DG139109.

Songs. Fischer-Dieskau. DG2530543.

STRAUSS, R.: *Four Last Songs* (with five other STRAUSS songs). Schwarzkopf. Angel S36347.

WOLF: *Italienisches Liederbuch*. Schwarzkopf, Fischer-Dieskau. Angel S3703, 2 discs (with SCHUMANN: *Songs*). Prey. London 26115.

INDEX

This book is compiled alphabetically by the composer of the main composition on a recording or in an album. Other composers who share the recording or album appear in the index of composers, below.

The page numbers in **boldface** indicate references to recordings under review.

COMPOSERS

(continued)

CONDUCTORS

(continued)

ORCHESTRAS AND GROUPS

(continued)

Index of Orchestras and Groups

(continued)

PERFORMERS

(continued)

Index of Performers

(continued)

Index of Performers

ABOUT THE AUTHOR

Author and critic, and music consultant to CONSUMER REPORTS since 1968, Martin Bookspan is well known to lovers of classical music as the host and commentator for the New York Philharmonic radio broadcasts and for the "Live from Lincoln Center" telecasts. He is also a member of the permanent panel of critics of classical recordings on the nationally syndicated radio series, "First Hearing."

For the past ten years, Bookspan has been coordinator of symphonic and concert activities for the American Society of Composers, Authors and Publishers (ASCAP). He is the author of *101 Masterpieces of Music and Their Composers,* coauthor of *Zubin: The Zubin Mehta Story,* and contributing author to *The New York Times Guide to Recorded Music.* He has also written numerous magazine and newspaper articles and reviews on classical music and recordings.

PAPERBOUNDS FROM
CONSUMER REPORTS BOOKS